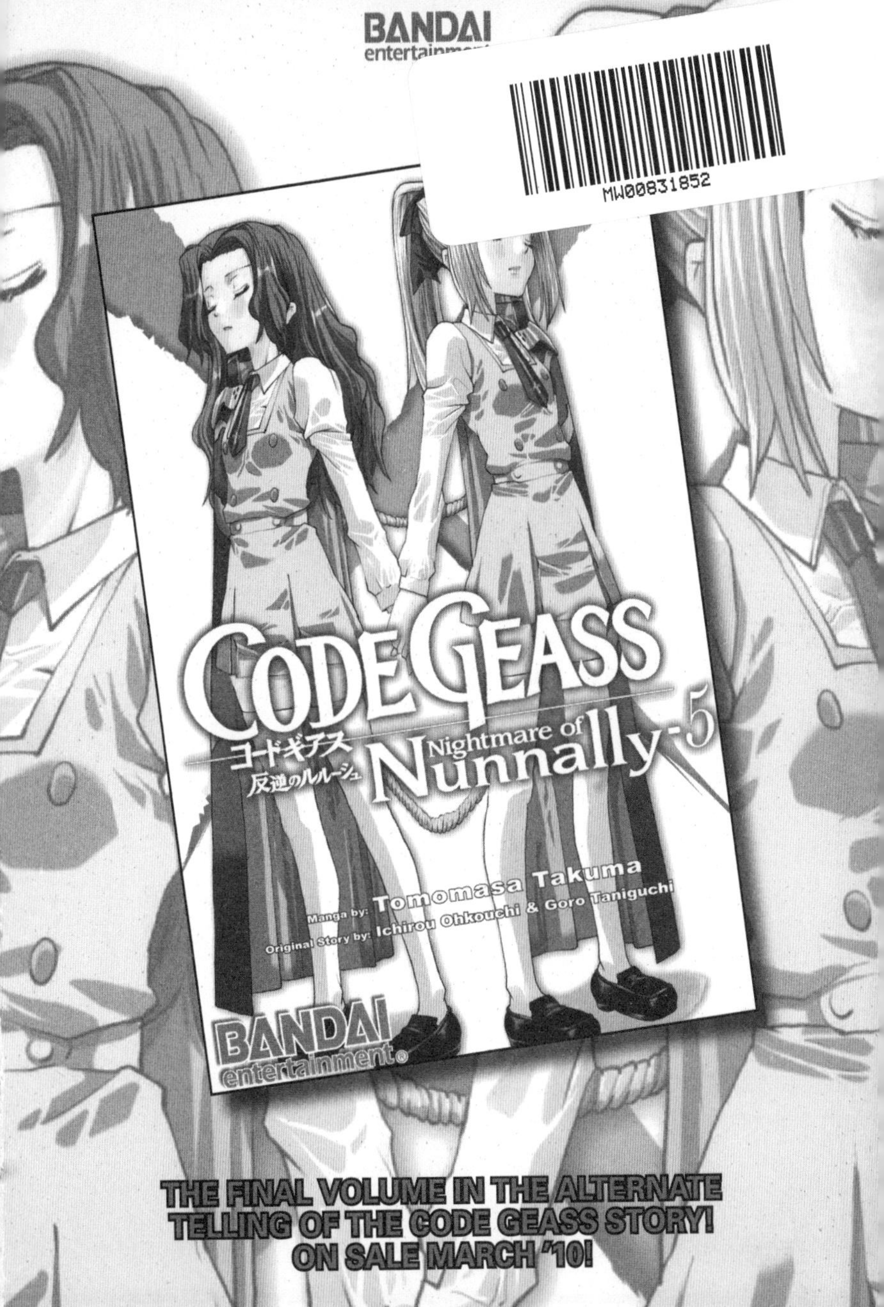
BANDAI
entertainment
CODE GEASS
コードギアス
反逆のルルーシュ
Nightmare of Nunnally-5
Manga by: Tomomasa Takuma
Original Story by: Ichirou Ohkouchi & Goro Taniguchi
BANDAI
entertainment®
THE FINAL VOLUME IN THE ALTERNATE
TELLING OF THE CODE GEASS STORY!
ON SALE MARCH '10!

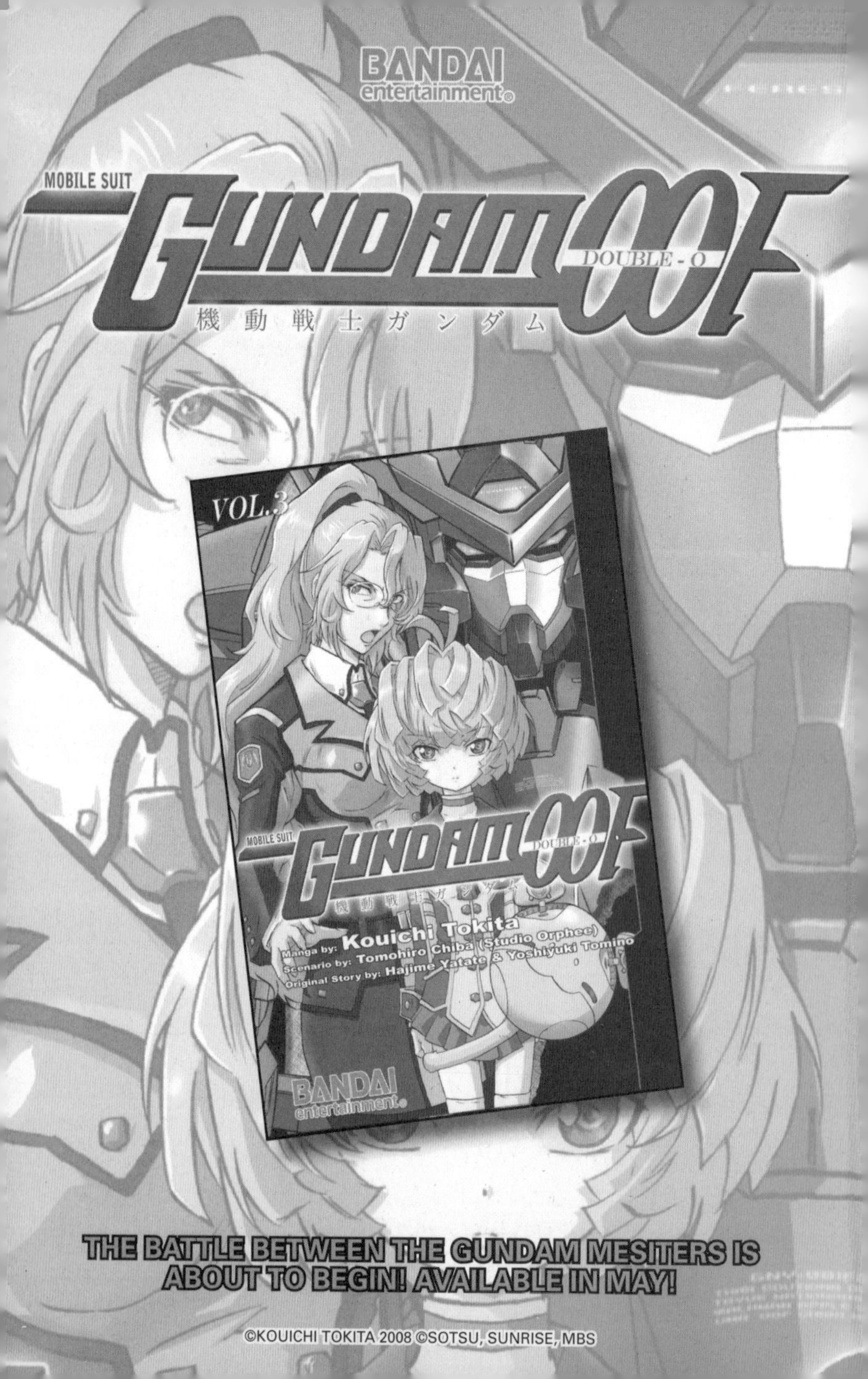
BANDAI entertainment
MOBILE SUIT GUNDAM 00F DOUBLE-O
機動戦士ガンダム
VOL.3
MOBILE SUIT GUNDAM 00F DOUBLE-O
Manga by: Kouichi Tokita
Scenario by: Tomohiro Chiba (Studio Orphee)
Original Story by: Hajime Yatate & Yoshiyuki Tomino
BANDAI entertainment
THE BATTLE BETWEEN THE GUNDAM MESITERS IS ABOUT TO BEGIN! AVAILABLE IN MAY!

THE MANGA ADAPTATION OF THE HIT
ANIME CONTINUES!
ON SALE NOW!

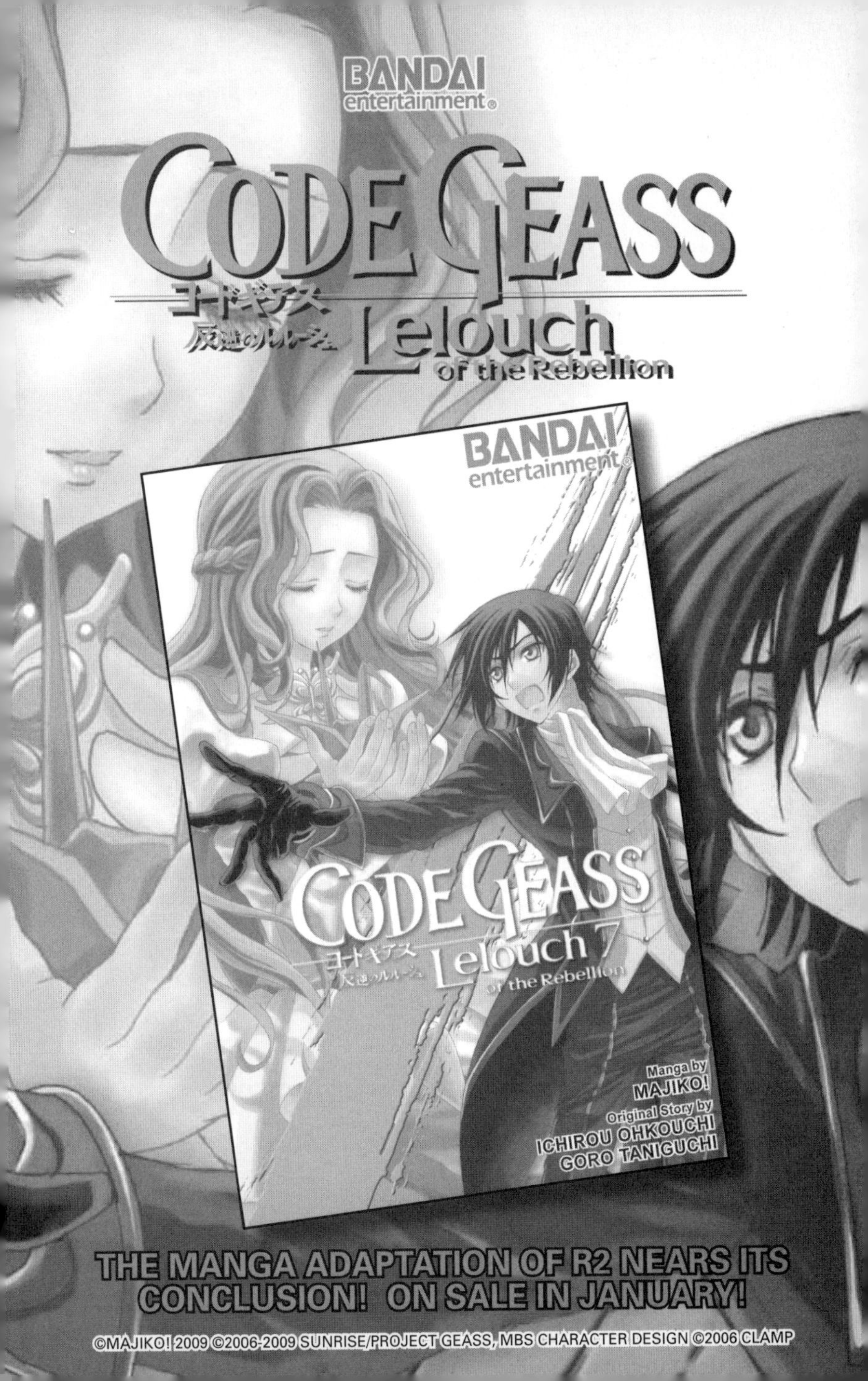
BANDAI entertainment®
CODE GEASS
コードギアス 反逆のルルーシュ
Lelouch of the Rebellion
BANDAI entertainment®
CODE GEASS
コードギアス 反逆のルルーシュ
Lelouch 7 of the Rebellion
Manga by MAJIKO!
Original Story by ICHIROU OHKOUCHI GORO TANIGUCHI
THE MANGA ADAPTATION OF R2 NEARS ITS CONCLUSION! ON SALE IN JANUARY!
©MAJIKO! 2009 ©2006-2009 SUNRISE/PROJECT GEASS, MBS CHARACTER DESIGN ©2006 CLAMP

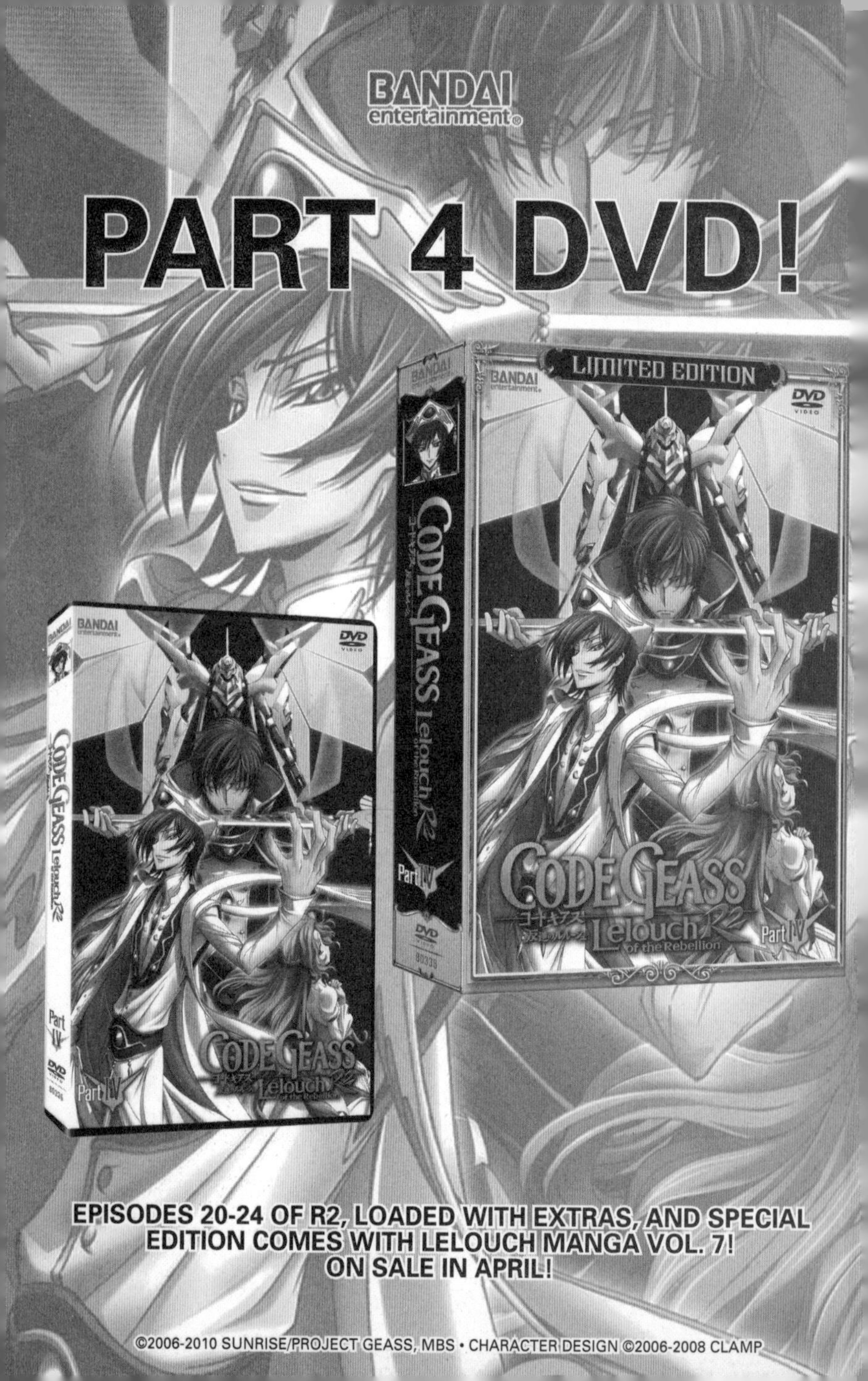
BANDAI entertainment®
PART 4 DVD!
LIMITED EDITION
BANDAI entertainment
DVD VIDEO
CODE GEASS Lelouch of the Rebellion R2
Part IV
EPISODES 20-24 OF R2, LOADED WITH EXTRAS, AND SPECIAL EDITION COMES WITH LELOUCH MANGA VOL. 7!
ON SALE IN APRIL!
©2006-2010 SUNRISE/PROJECT GEASS, MBS • CHARACTER DESIGN ©2006-2008 CLAMP

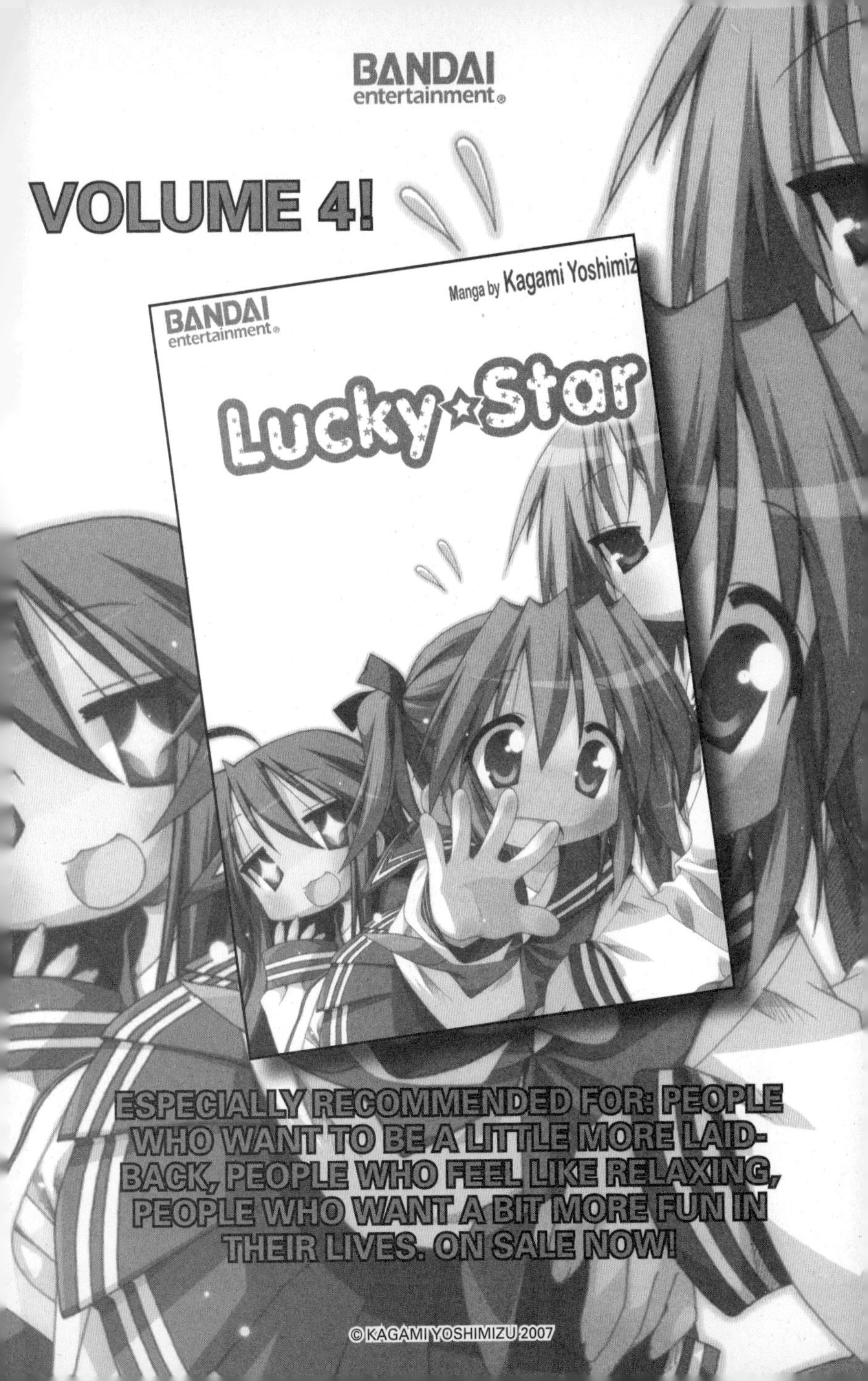
BANDAI
entertainment
VOLUME 4!
Manga by Kagami Yoshimiz
BANDAI
entertainment
Lucky☆Star
ESPECIALLY RECOMMENDED FOR: PEOPLE WHO WANT TO BE A LITTLE MORE LAID-BACK, PEOPLE WHO FEEL LIKE RELAXING, PEOPLE WHO WANT A BIT MORE FUN IN THEIR LIVES. ON SALE NOW!
© KAGAMI YOSHIMIZU 2007

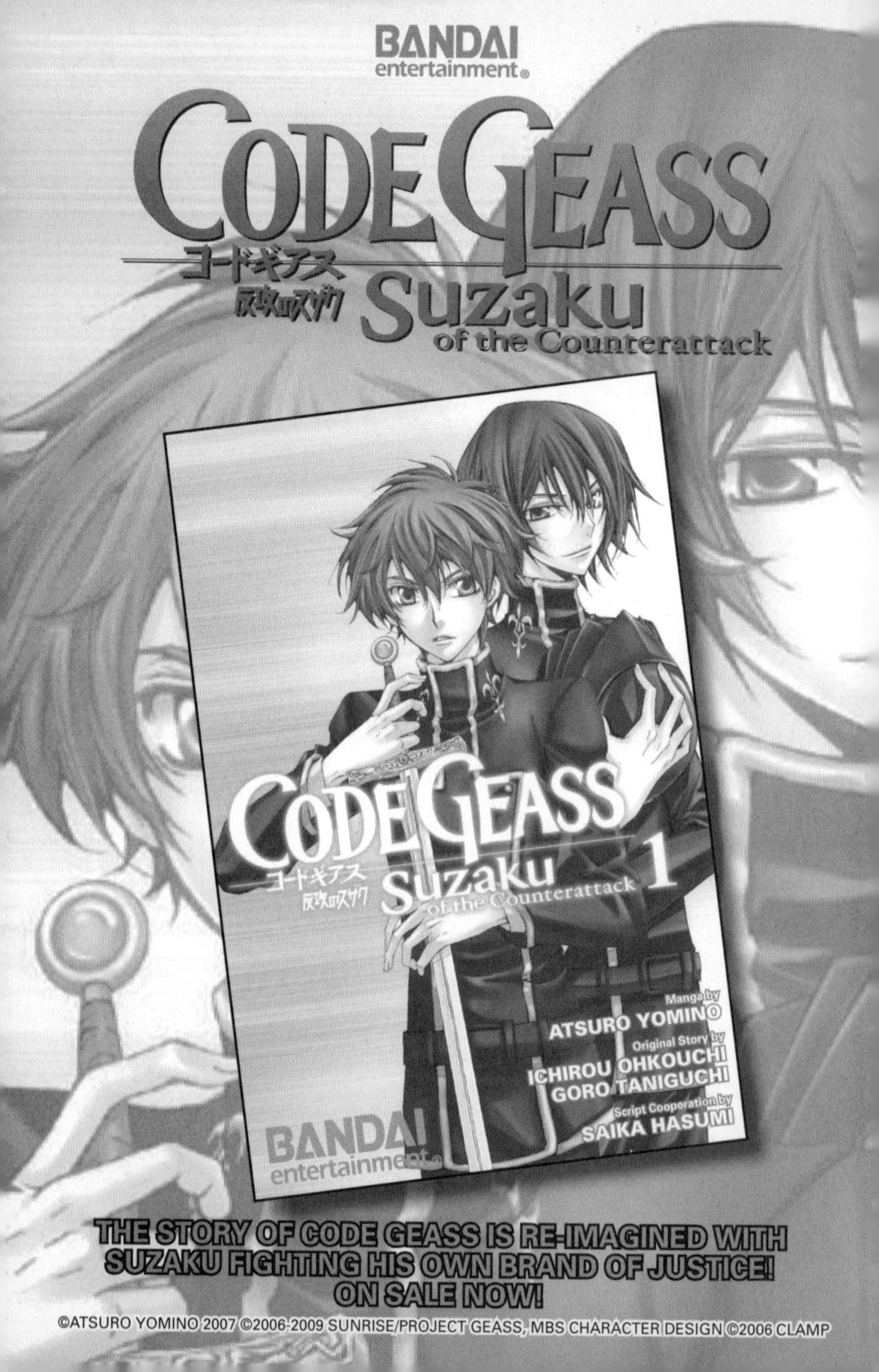

BANDAI entertainment®
CODE GEASS
コードギアス
反攻のスザク
Suzaku
of the Counterattack
CODE GEASS
コードギアス
反攻のスザク
Suzaku 1
of the Counterattack
Manga by
ATSURO YOMINO
Original Story by
ICHIROU OHKOUCHI
GORO TANIGUCHI
Script Cooperation by
SAIKA HASUMI
BANDAI entertainment®
THE STORY OF CODE GEASS IS RE-IMAGINED WITH
SUZAKU FIGHTING HIS OWN BRAND OF JUSTICE!
ON SALE NOW!
©ATSURO YOMINO 2007 ©2006-2009 SUNRISE/PROJECT GEASS, MBS CHARACTER DESIGN ©2006 CLAMP

VOLUME 2

MANGA BY KOUZOH OHMORI
ORIGINAL STORY BY HAJIME YATATE & YOSHIYUKI TOMINO

ENGLISH PRODUCTION CREDITS

TRANSLATION & ADAPTATION BY HISASHI KOTOBUKI
PRODUCTION BY JOSE MACASOCOL, JR.
EDITED BY ROBERT PLACE NAPTON
PUBLISHED BY KEN IYADOMI

©Kouzoh OHMORI 2009
©SOTSU, SUNRISE, MBS

ORIGINALLY PUBLISHED IN JAPAN IN 2009 BY KADOKAWA SHOTEN
PUBLISHING CO.,LTD., TOKYO.

ENGLISH TRANSLATION PUBLISHED BY BANDAI ENTERTAINMENT INC.,
UNDER THE LICENSE OF SUNRISE, INC.

ISBN-13: 978-1-60496-237-6

FIRST BANDAI PRINTING:
MAY 2010

10, 9, 8, 7, 6, 5, 4, 3, 2, 1

PRINTED IN THE USA

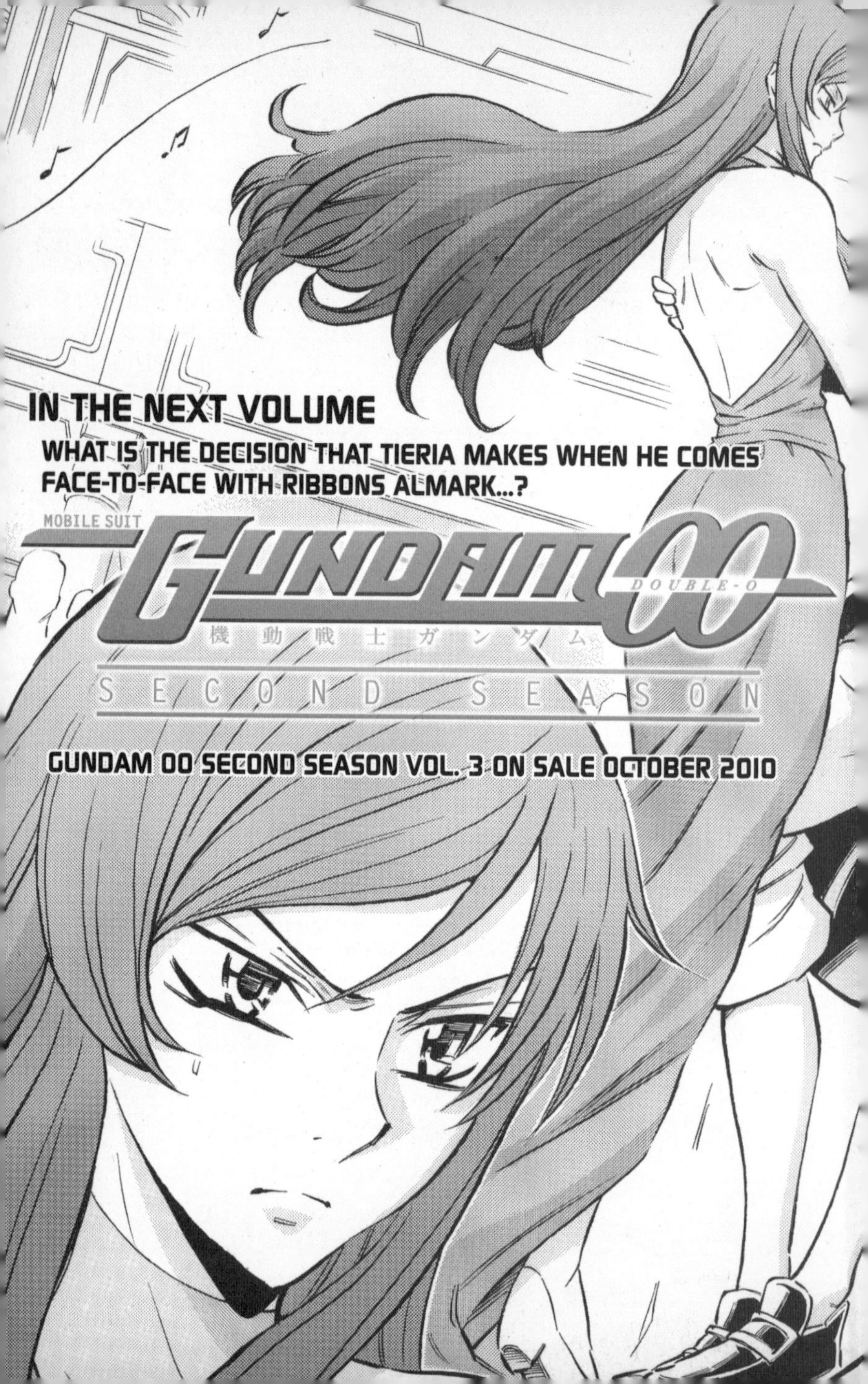
IN THE NEXT VOLUME
WHAT IS THE DECISION THAT TIERIA MAKES WHEN HE COMES FACE-TO-FACE WITH RIBBONS ALMARK...?
MOBILE SUIT
GUNDAM 00
DOUBLE-O
機動戦士ガンダム
SECOND SEASON
GUNDAM 00 SECOND SEASON VOL. 3 ON SALE OCTOBER 2010

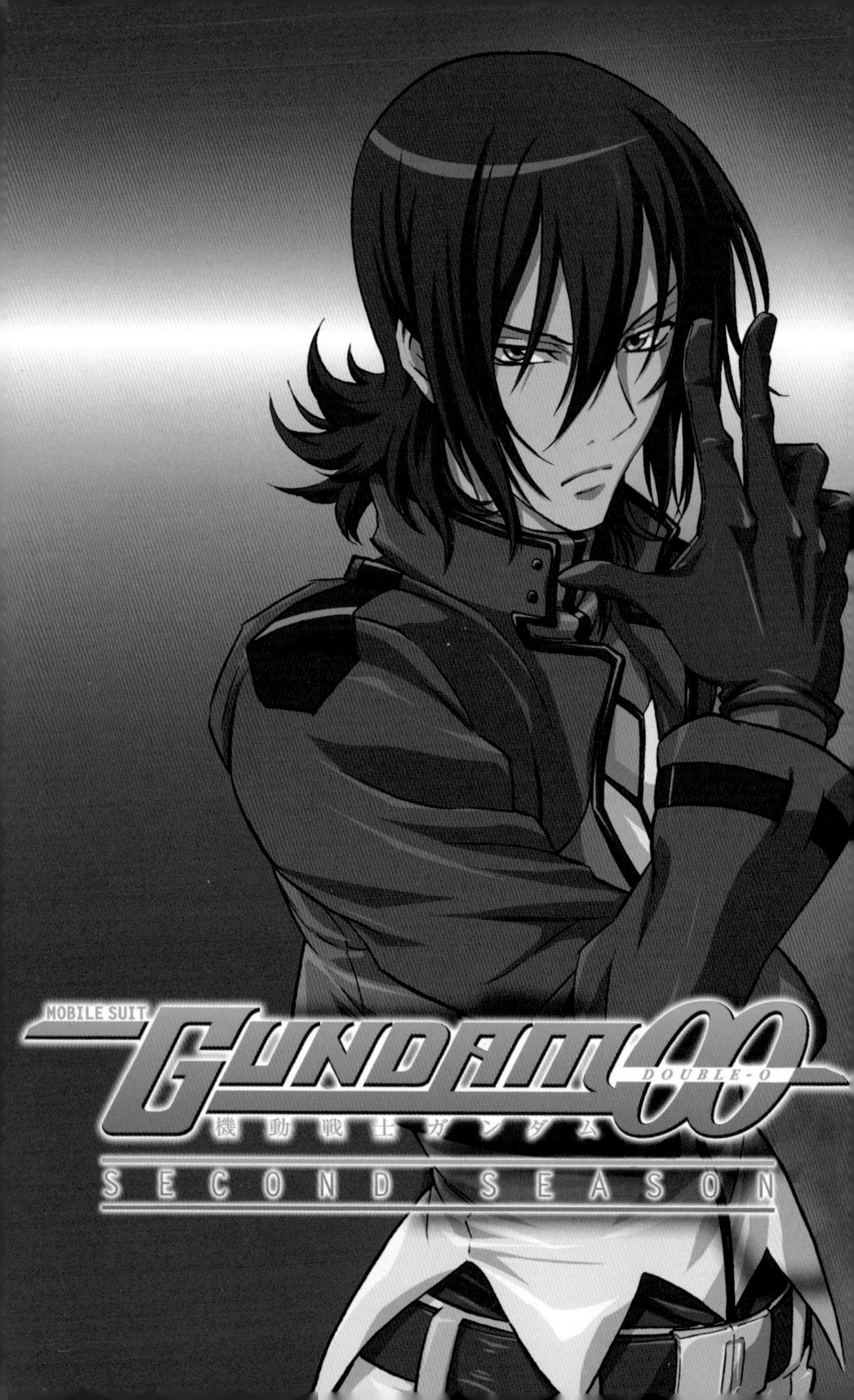
MOBILE SUIT
GUNDAM 00
DOUBLE-O
機動戦士ガンダム
SECOND SEASON

Kadokawa Comics A KCA146-9 MOBILE SUIT GUNDAM 00 2nd.season VOL.02

Drawing : Kouzoh Ohmori Story : Hajime Yatate, Yoshiyuki Tomino

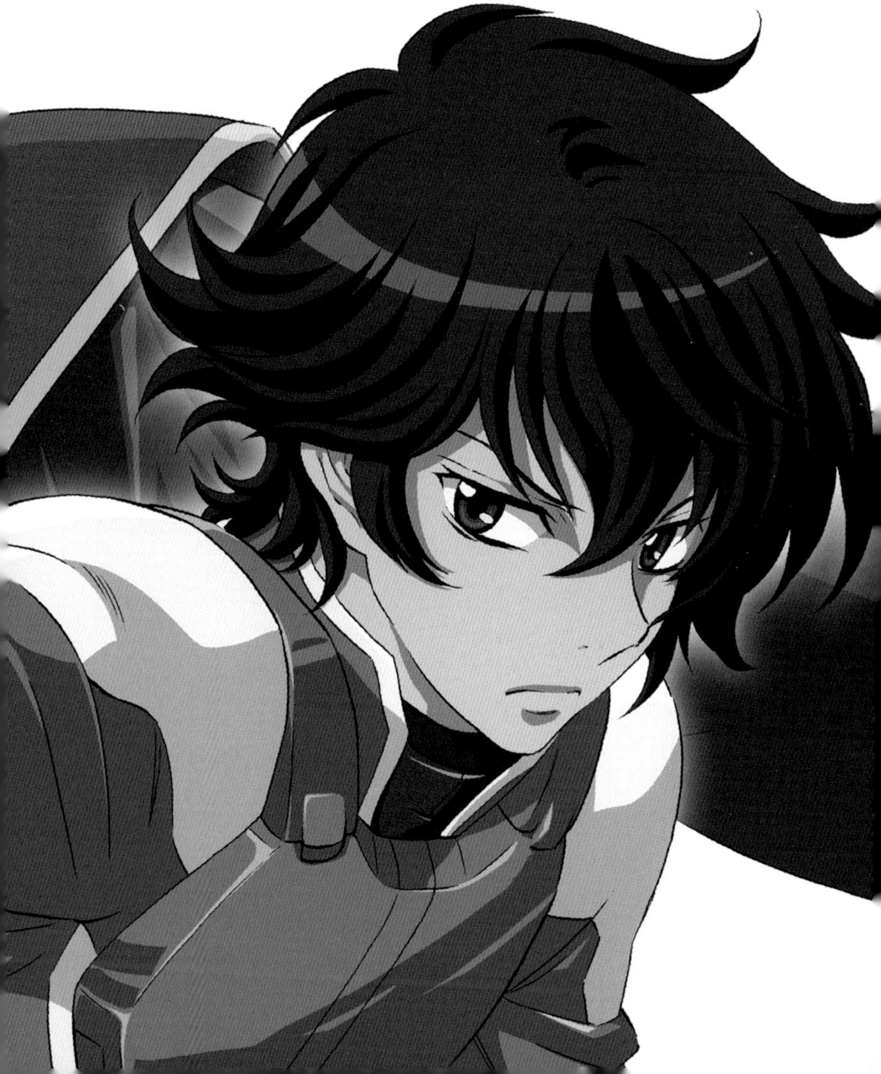

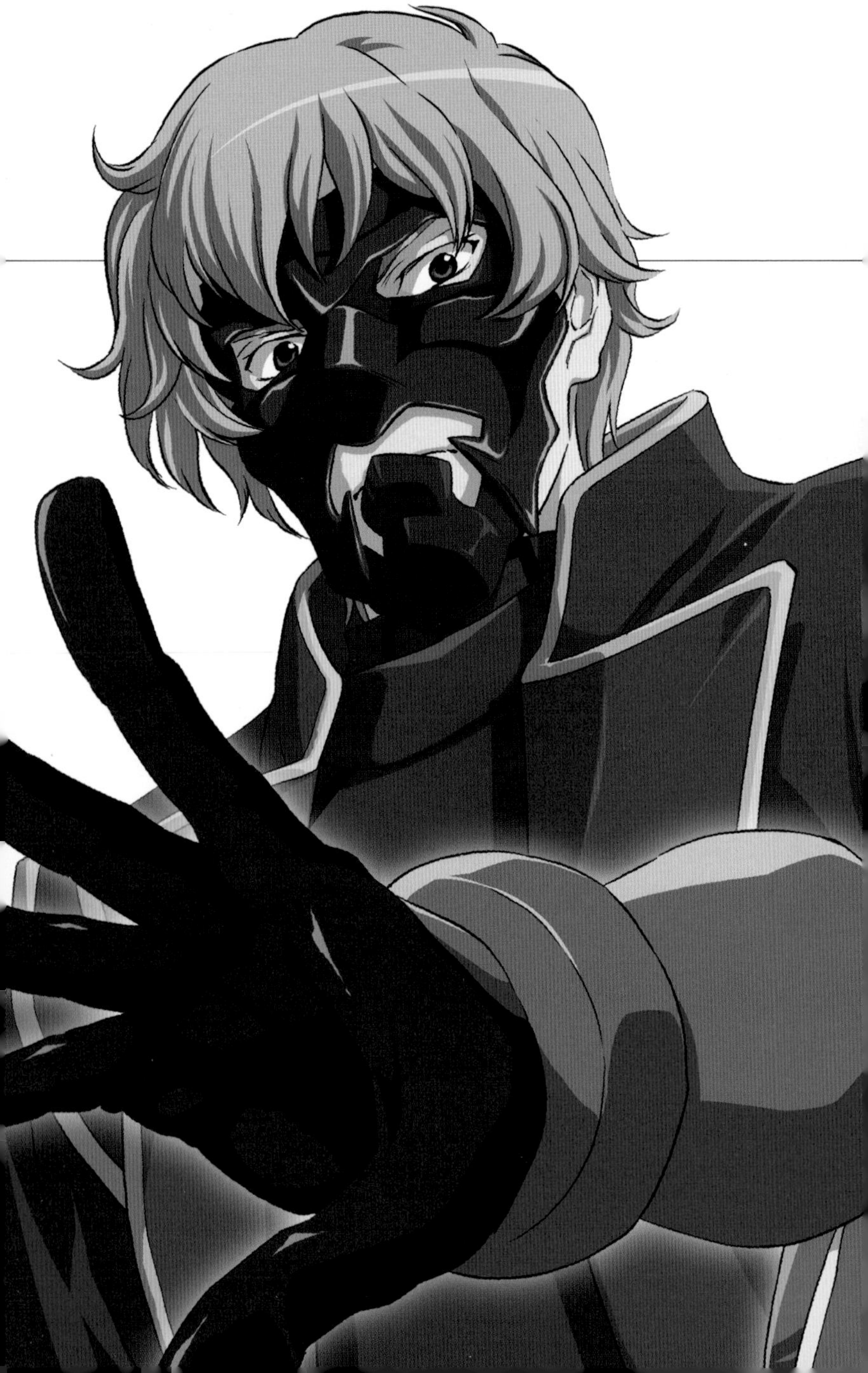

機動戦士 ガンダム 00
MOBILE SUIT GUNDAM
2nd.season 2

Kadokawa Comics A KCA146-9
MOBILE SUIT GUNDAM 00
2nd.season VOL.02

CONTENTS

Chapter 4: A Reason to Fight 009

Chapter 5: Scars 054

Chapter 6: Reunion and Separation 124

Drawing : Kouzoh Ohmori
Story : Hajime Yatate, Yoshiyuki Tomino

MOBILE SUIT GUNDAM 00

PREVIOUS STORY

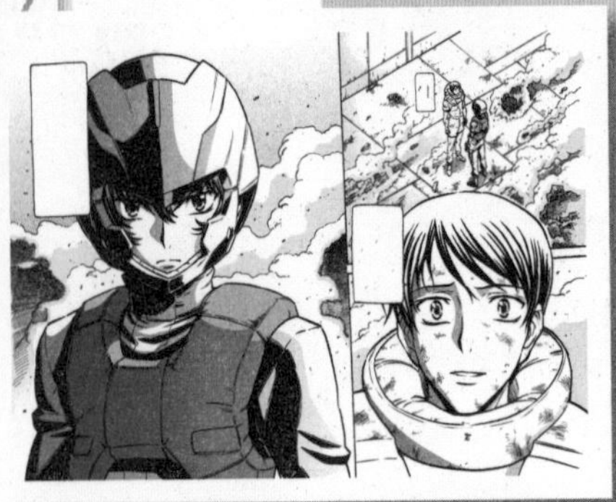

The Story Thus Far...

2312 AD. Under the new name of The Earth Sphere Federation, the world is unified. Battles around the globe were supposed to end and peace was expected to prosper. However, against the countries and people still resisting unification, an autonomous peacekeeping force known as the A-LAWS was formed to quell such anti-federation sentiments.

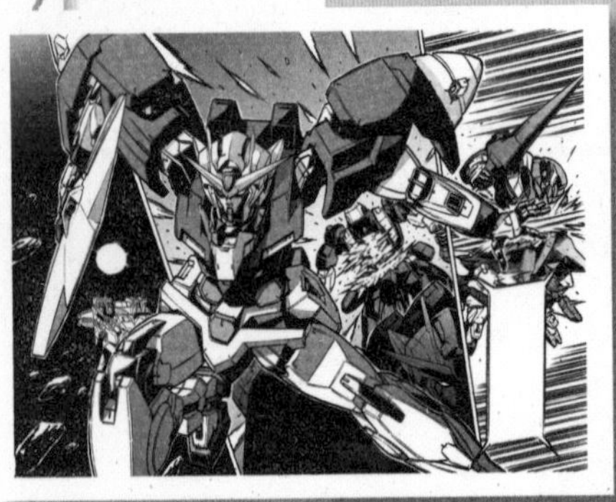

Mistaken as a member of the Anti-Federation group, Katharon, Saji Crossroad had found himself at the wrong place at the wrong time and is captured by the A-LAWS. However, before Saji could be taken in, he is rescued by the pilot of the Gundam Exia, Setsuna F. Seiei.

Having bided their time for the right moment, Celestial Being once again commences their operations...

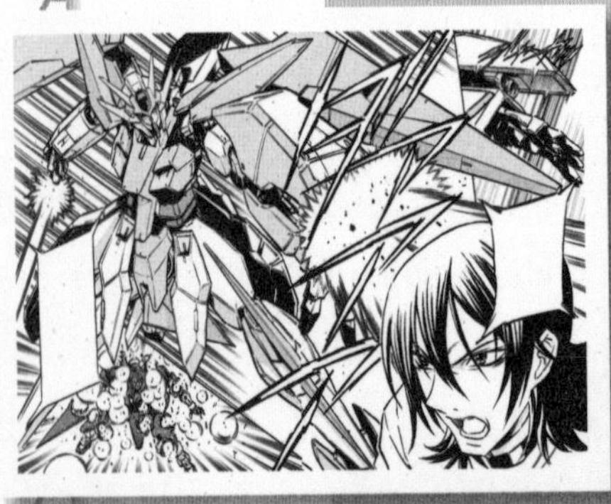

The twin brother of the deceased Lockon Stratos (Neil Dylandy), Lyle Dylandy takes on his brother's code name and joins Celestial Being. Aboard their new flagship, Ptolemaios 2, they plunge into the atmosphere to perform a daring rescue of Allelujah Haptism from a Federation Detention facility. Now armed with four new Gundams; Double-Oh, Cherudim, Arios and Seravee, the four Gundam Meisters are once again reunited to fight for the future they believe in...

MOBILE SUIT GUNDAM 00 2nd.season Character

SETSUNA F. SEIEI

CELESTIAL BEING

OF ALL THE GUNDAM MEISTERS, HE HOLDS THE GREATEST ATTACHMENT TO HIS GUNDAM AND DESIRE TO END ALL CONFLICT. FOR THE LAST FOUR YEARS HE HAS TRAVELED THE GLOBE OBSERVING FROM THE SHADOWS. IN HIS YOUTH, HE WAS A REBEL SOLDIER. HIS REAL NAME IS SORAN IBRAHIM.

SAJI CROSSROAD

CELESTIAL BEING

FULFILLING HIS PROMISE TO LOUISE, SAJI BECAME A SPACE ENGINEER AND WORKED AT A COLONY CONSTRUCTION SITE. MISTAKEN AS A MEMBER OF KATHARON, SAJI IS TAKEN INTO CUSTODY BY THE A-LAWS BUT IS RESCUED BY SETSUNA.

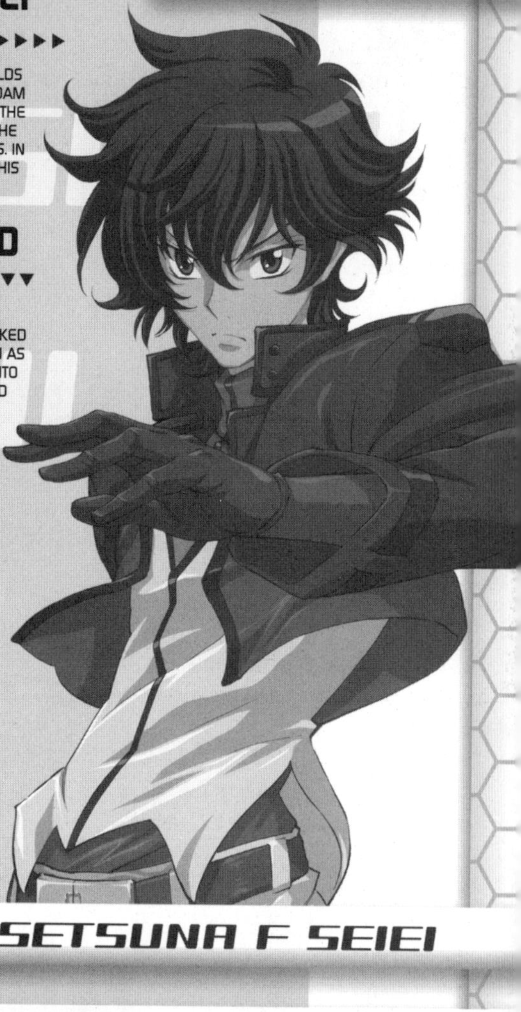
SETSUNA F SEIEI

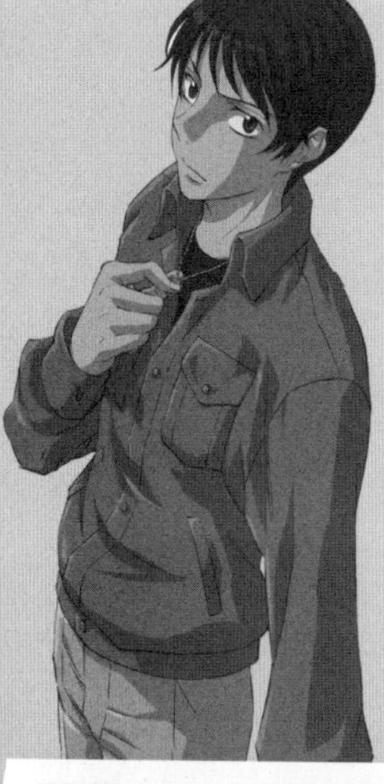
SAJI CROSSROAD

LOCKON STRATOS
CELESTIAL BEING ▶▶▶▶▶▶▶▶▶▶

TAKING OVER THE CODENAME USED BY HIS DECEASED TWIN BROTHER NEIL, LYLE DYLANDY PILOTS THE NEW CHERUDIM GUNDAM. LYLE IS ALSO A MEMBER OF KATHARON.

ALLELUJAH HAPTISM
CELESTIAL BEING ◀◀◀◀◀◀◀◀◀

RESCUED BY HIS COMRADES FROM WHERE HE HAD BEEN IMPRISONED FOR FOUR YEARS, ALLELUJAH RETURNS TO CELESTIAL BEING. IN THE DAYS OF HIS YOUTH HE WAS KNOWN AS SUBJECT E-57 BEING EXPERIMENTED UPON AT THE HUMAN REFORM LEAGUE'S EXPERIMENTAL SUPER SOLDIER FACILITY.

LOCKON STRATO

ALLELUJAH HAPTISM

TIERIA ERDE
CELESTIAL BEING ▼▼▼▼▼▼

TIERIA WAS INJURED IN THE FINAL BATTLE FOUR YEARS AGO. SINCE THEN HE HAS BEEN WORKING TO REBUILD CELESTIAL BEING. HE IS NOW SEARCHING FOR HIS OWN REASONS FOR FIGHTING.

SUMERAGI LEE NORIEGA
CELESTIAL BEING ▶▶▶▶▶▶

TACTICAL FORECASTER. AFTER THE COLLAPSE OF CELESTIAL BEING FOUR YEARS EARLIER, SHE HAD LOST FAITH IN THE WORLD AND HAS SPENT THE TIME DRINKING AT HER OLD COLLEGE FRIEND, BILLY'S PLACE. HOWEVER, SETSUNA FINDS HER AND PULLS HER BACK INTO THE FOLD.

SUMERAGI LEE NORIEGA

MARINA ISMAIL
AZADISTAN ◀◀◀◀◀◀◀◀◀

FIRST PRINCESS OF THE AZADISTAN ROYAL FAMILY. SHE IS A PACIFIST WHO ABHORS BATTLE. BECAUSE OF HER ACQUAINTANCE WITH SETSUNA, SHE HAS BEEN DETAINED BY THE A-LAWS FOR THE PAST FOUR YEARS. SHE IS RESCUED AT THE SAME TIME AS ALLELUJAH FROM THE FEDERATION DETENTION FACILITY.

MARINA ISMAIL

TIERIA ERD

ALI AL-SAACHEZ

▶▶▶▶▶▶▶▶▶▶▶▶▶▶▶▶▶▶▶

HE WAS A MERCENARY FOR A PRIVATE
MILITARY COMPANY BUT WAS SEVERELY
INJURED IN THE BATTLE FOUR YEARS
EARLIER. TREATED BACK TO HEALTH
BY THE FEDERATION, HE NOW
WORKS FOR RIBBONS.

ALI AL-SAACHEZ

SOMA PERIES

SOMA PERIES

A-LAWS ▲▲▲▲▲▲▲▲▲▲

SHE WAS THE FIRST OF THE "SUPER SOLDIERS" DEVELOPED BY
THE HUMAN REFORM LEAGUE. SHE SPENT HER CHILDHOOD
WITH ALLELUJAH AT THE SUPER SOLDIER RESEARCH FACILITY,
BUT SEEMS TO HAVE LOST HER MEMORIES OF THAT TIME.

MOBILE SUIT GUNDAM 00
2nd.season Character

Mr.BUSHIDO

MR. BUSIDO

A-LAWS ▲▲▲▲

A MYSTERIOUS MASKED PILOT WITH A
SPECIAL LICENSE TO OPERATE ON HIS
OWN ACCORD. HE PILOTS AN ESPECIALLY
TUNED AHEAD NAMED "SAKIGAKE."
HE IS LEFT-HANDED AND IS A VIRGO.

RIBBONS ALMARK

RIBBONS ALMARK

INNOVATOR ▲▲▲▲▲▲▲▲▲▲

LEADER OF THE INNOVATORS. HE USED
CELESTIAL BEING'S OBSERVER, ALEJANDRO
CORNER, TO WARP AEOLIA SCHENBERG'S
PLAN FOR HIS OWN.

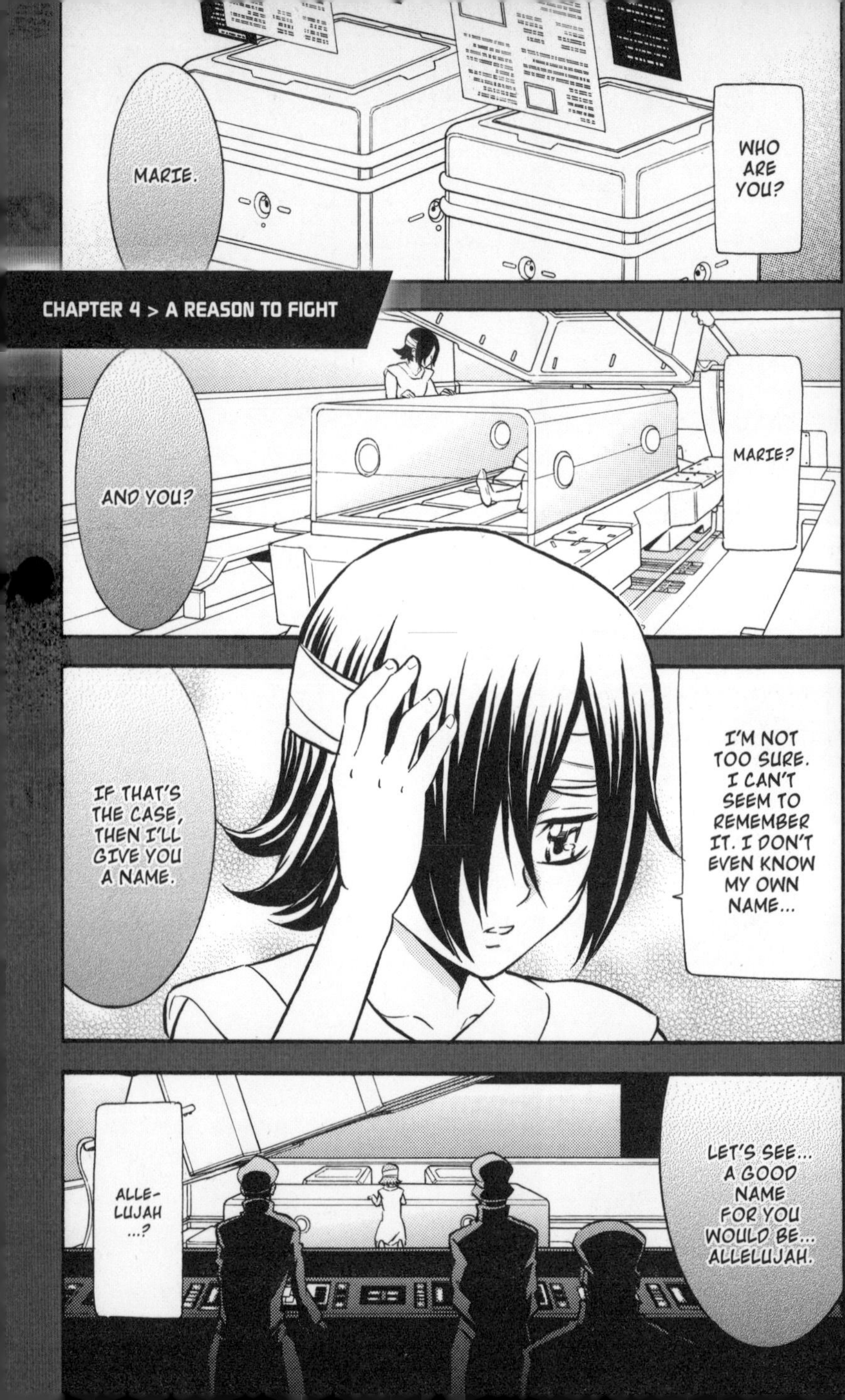
WHO ARE YOU?
MARIE.
CHAPTER 4 > A REASON TO FIGHT
MARIE?
AND YOU?
I'M NOT TOO SURE. I CAN'T SEEM TO REMEMBER IT. I DON'T EVEN KNOW MY OWN NAME...
IF THAT'S THE CASE, THEN I'LL GIVE YOU A NAME.
LET'S SEE... A GOOD NAME FOR YOU WOULD BE... ALLELUJAH.
ALLE-LUJAH ...?

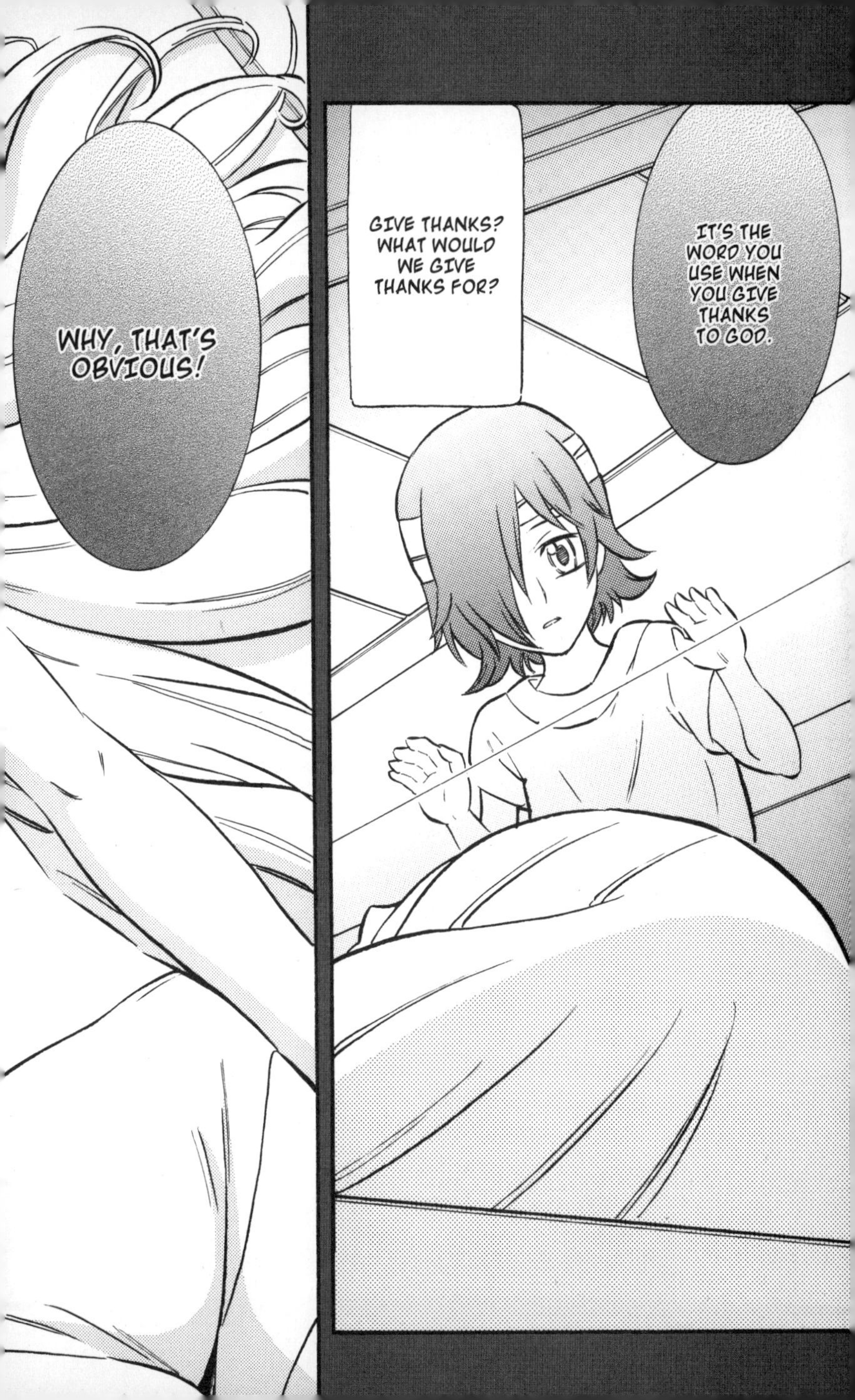
IT'S THE WORD YOU USE WHEN YOU GIVE THANKS TO GOD.
GIVE THANKS? WHAT WOULD WE GIVE THANKS FOR?
WHY, THAT'S OBVIOUS!

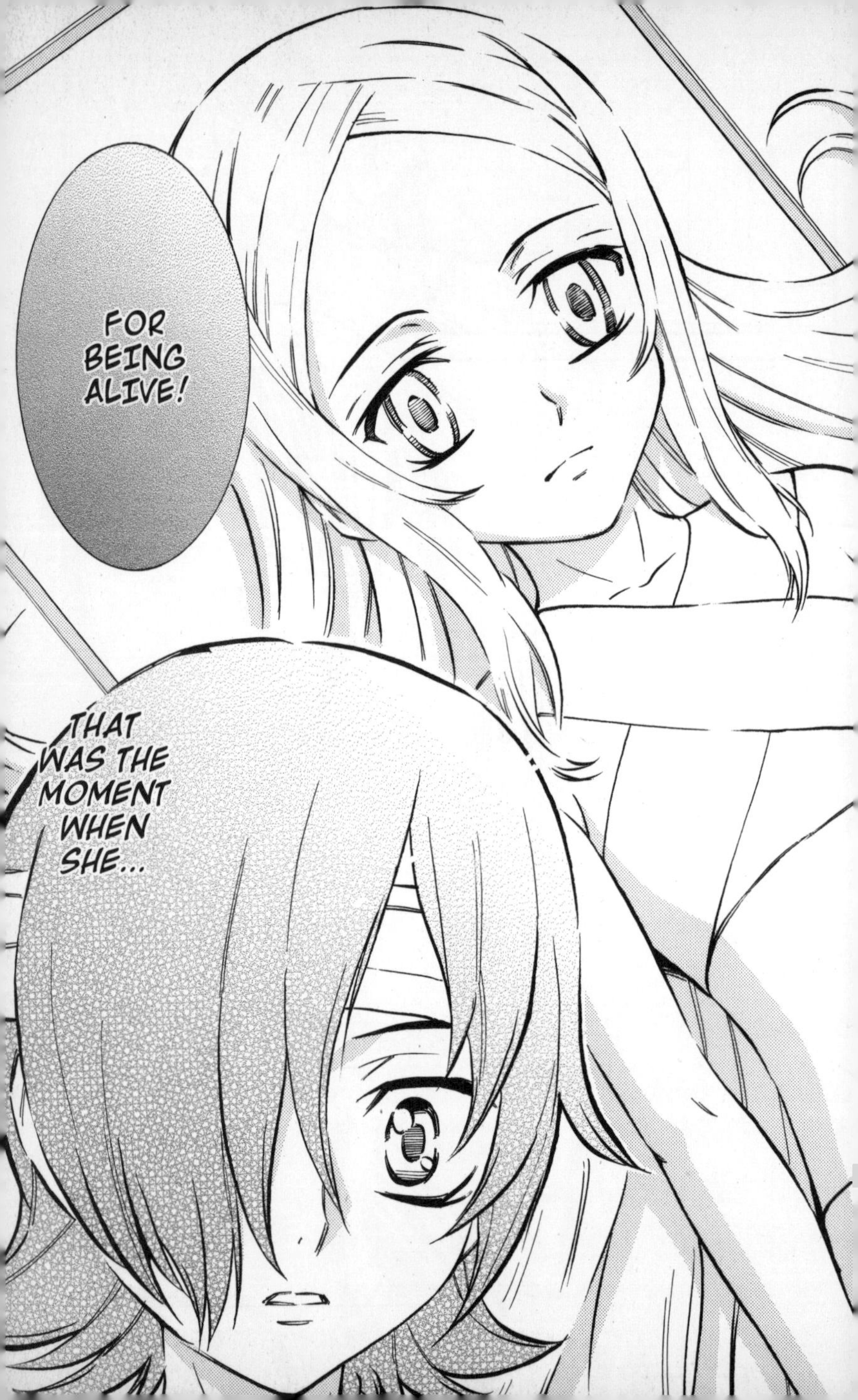
FOR BEING ALIVE!
THAT WAS THE MOMENT WHEN SHE...

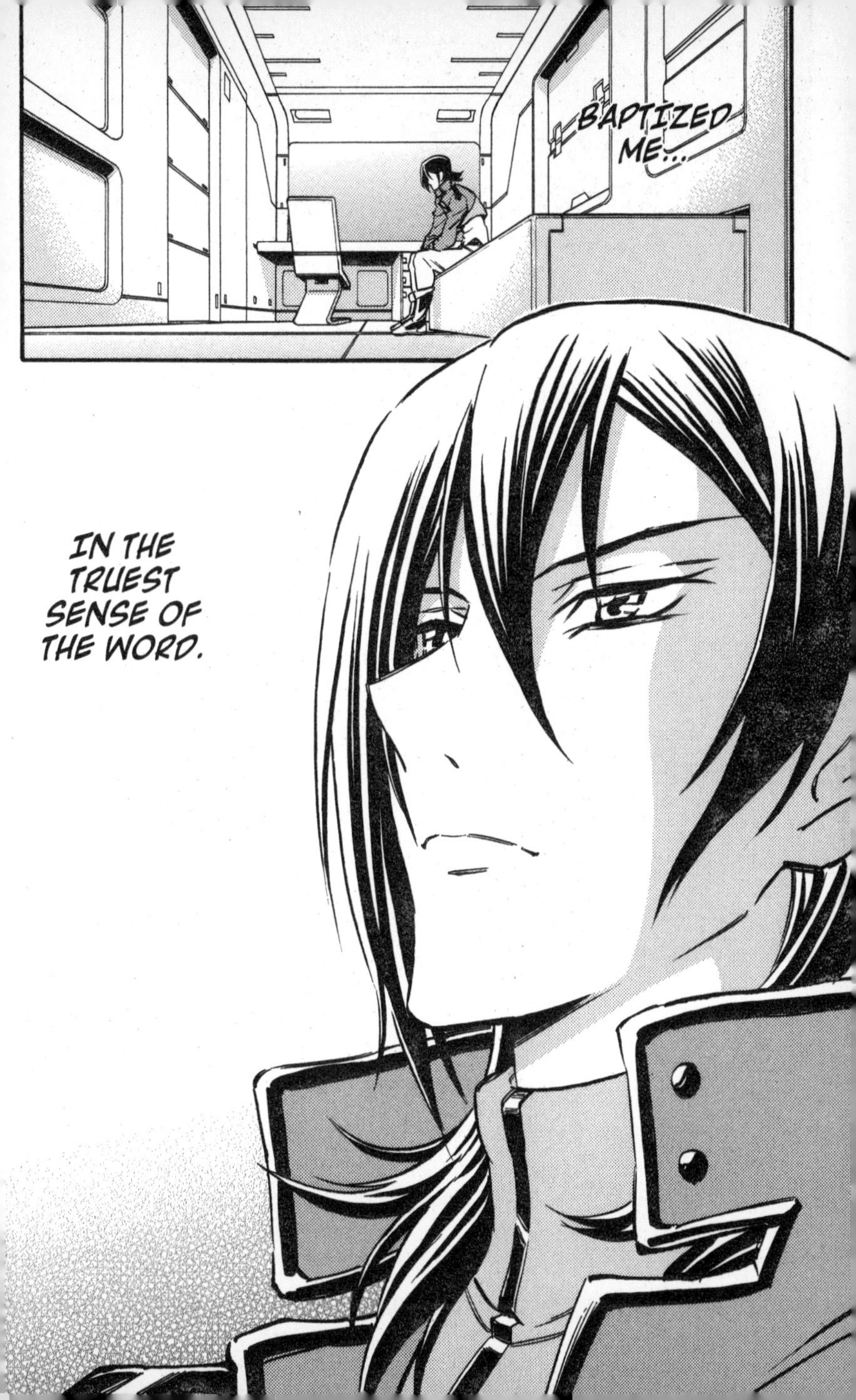
BAPTIZED ME...
IN THE TRUEST SENSE OF THE WORD.

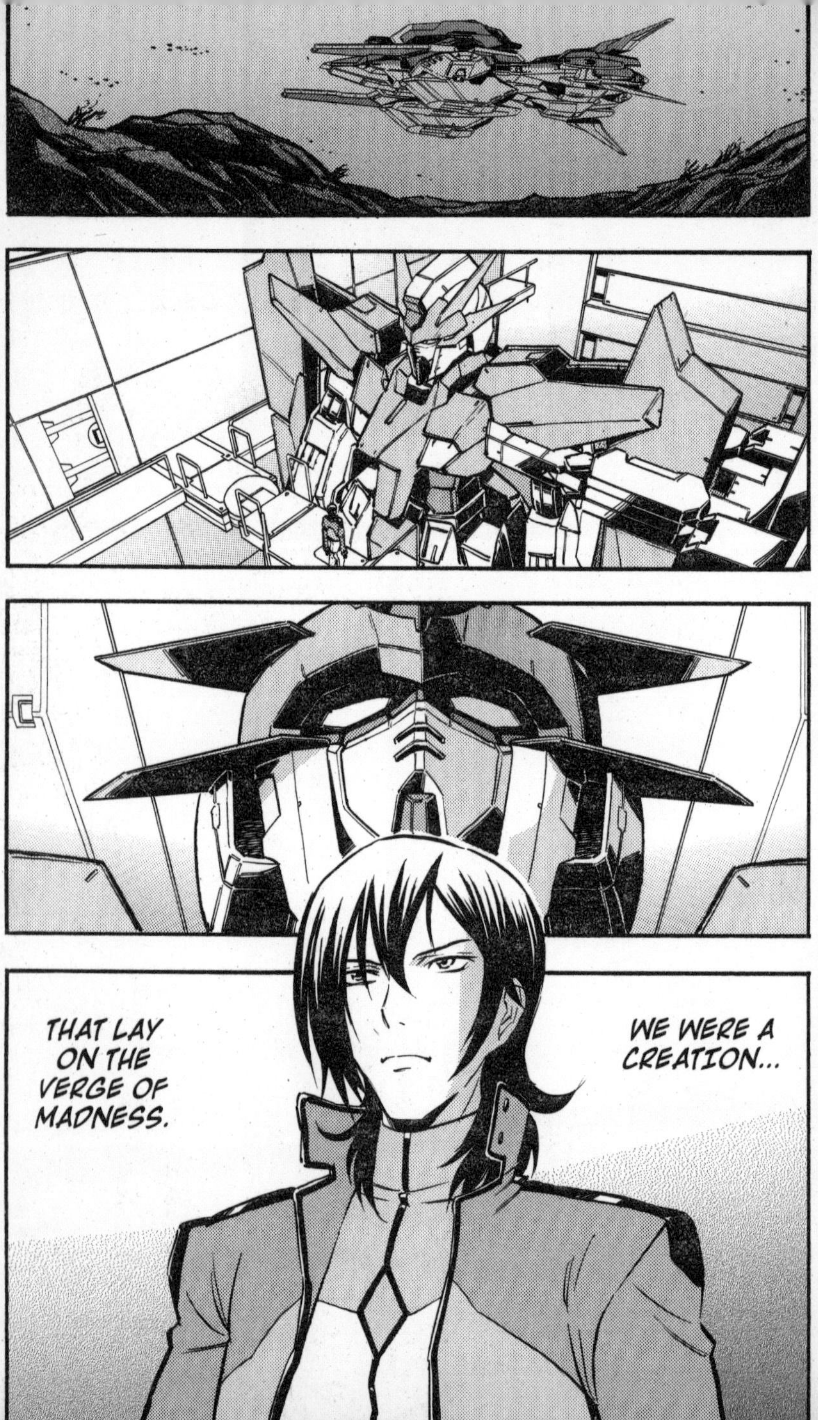
WE WERE A CREATION...
THAT LAY ON THE VERGE OF MADNESS.

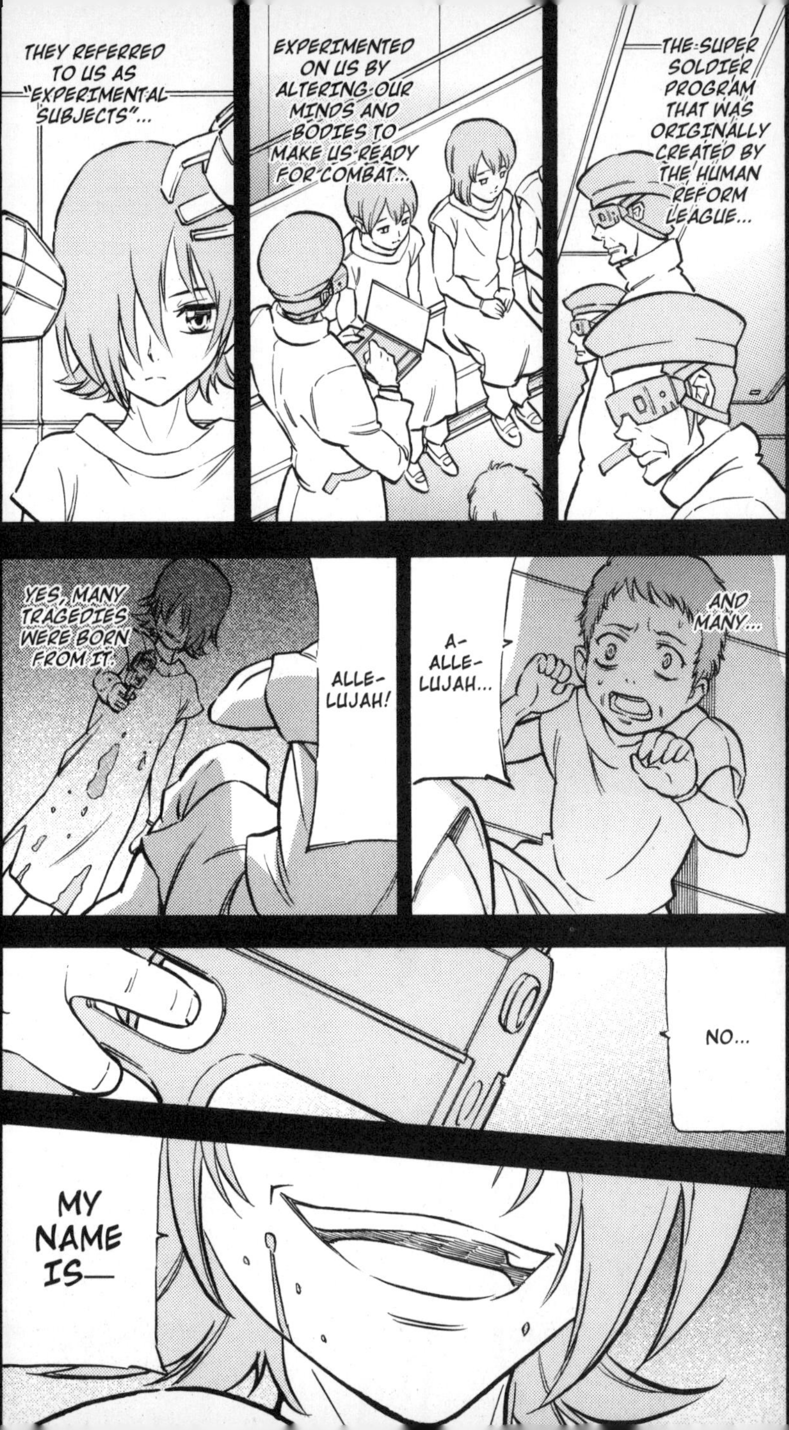
THE SUPER SOLDIER PROGRAM THAT WAS ORIGINALLY CREATED BY THE HUMAN REFORM LEAGUE...
EXPERIMENTED ON US BY ALTERING OUR MINDS AND BODIES TO MAKE US READY FOR COMBAT...
THEY REFERRED TO US AS "EXPERIMENTAL SUBJECTS"...
AND MANY...
A- ALLE-LUJAH...
ALLE-LUJAH!
YES, MANY TRAGEDIES WERE BORN FROM IT.
NO...
MY NAME IS—

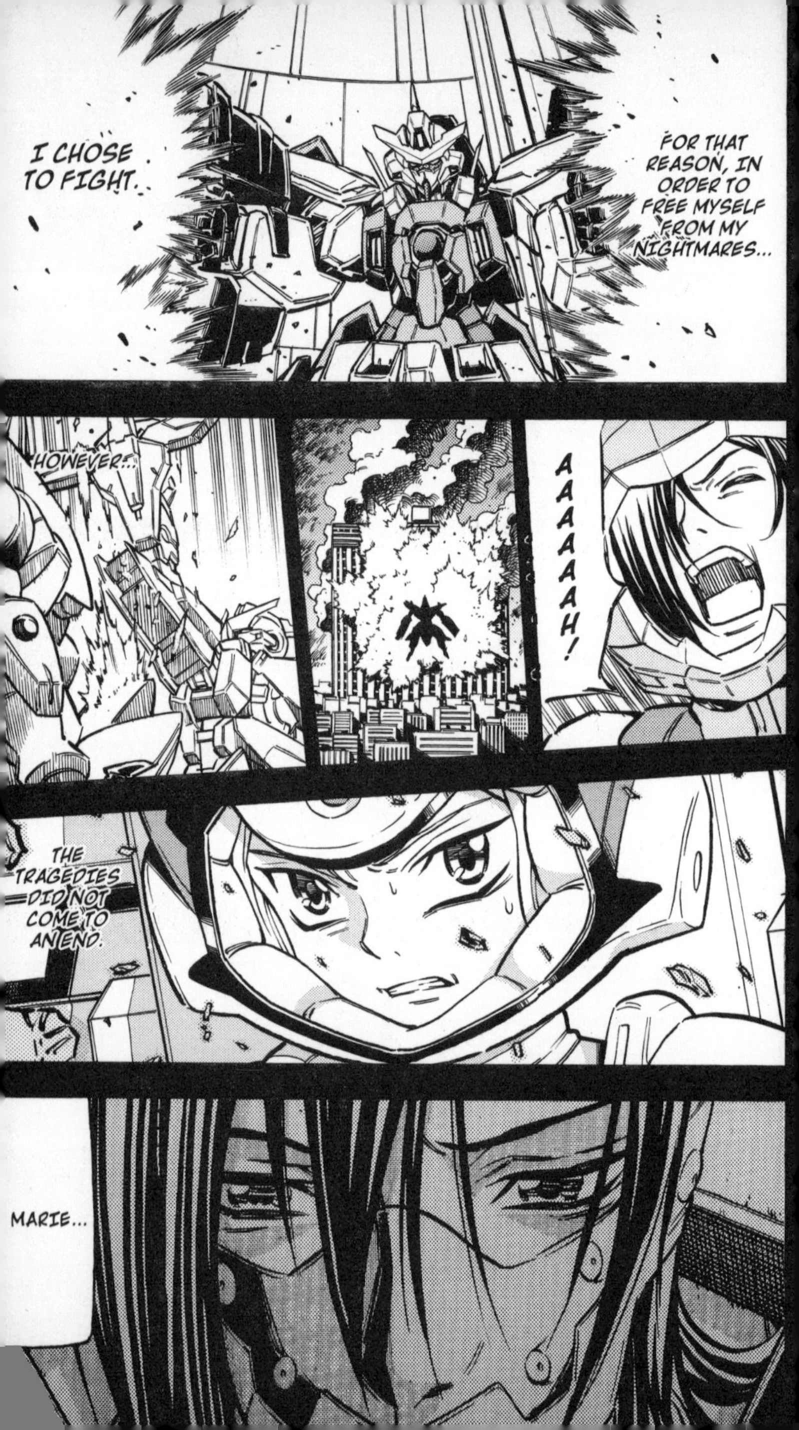
FOR THAT REASON, IN ORDER TO FREE MYSELF FROM MY NIGHTMARES...
I CHOSE TO FIGHT.
AAAAAAH!
HOWEVER...
THE TRAGEDIES DID NOT COME TO AN END.
MARIE...

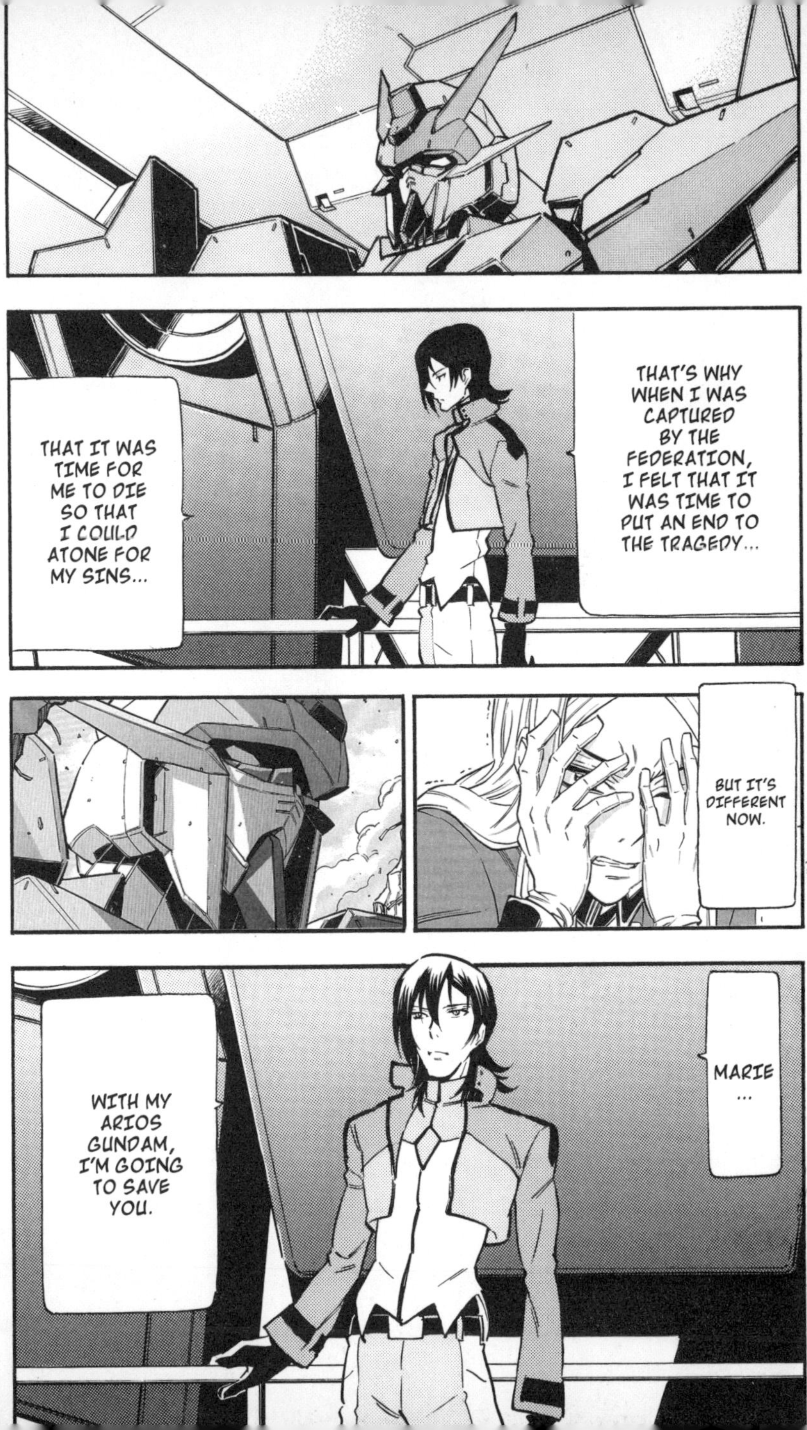
THAT'S WHY WHEN I WAS CAPTURED BY THE FEDERATION, I FELT THAT IT WAS TIME TO PUT AN END TO THE TRAGEDY...
THAT IT WAS TIME FOR ME TO DIE SO THAT I COULD ATONE FOR MY SINS...
BUT IT'S DIFFERENT NOW.
MARIE...
WITH MY ARIOS GUNDAM, I'M GOING TO SAVE YOU.

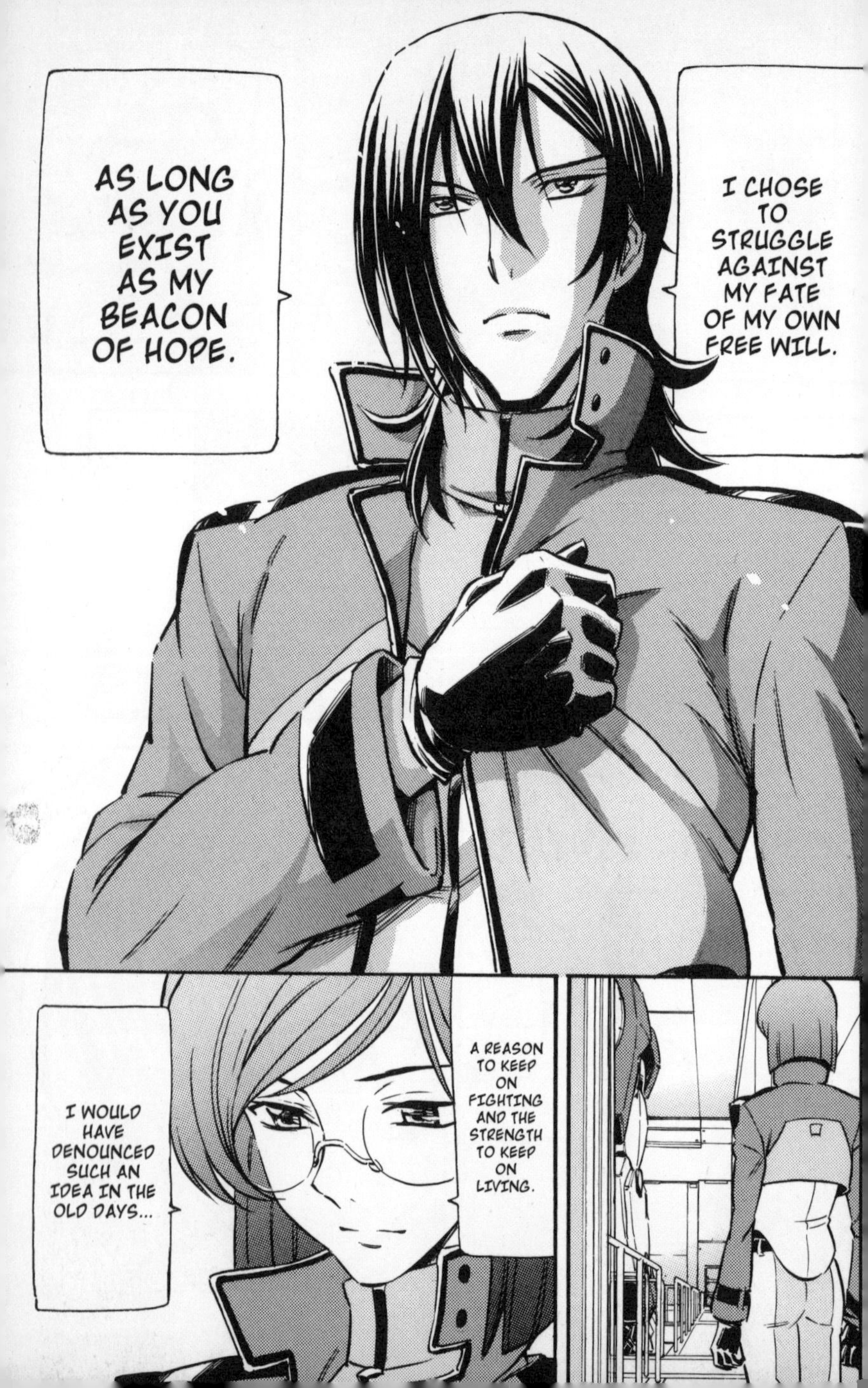
I CHOSE TO STRUGGLE AGAINST MY FATE OF MY OWN FREE WILL.
AS LONG AS YOU EXIST AS MY BEACON OF HOPE.
A REASON TO KEEP ON FIGHTING AND THE STRENGTH TO KEEP ON LIVING.
I WOULD HAVE DENOUNCED SUCH AN IDEA IN THE OLD DAYS...

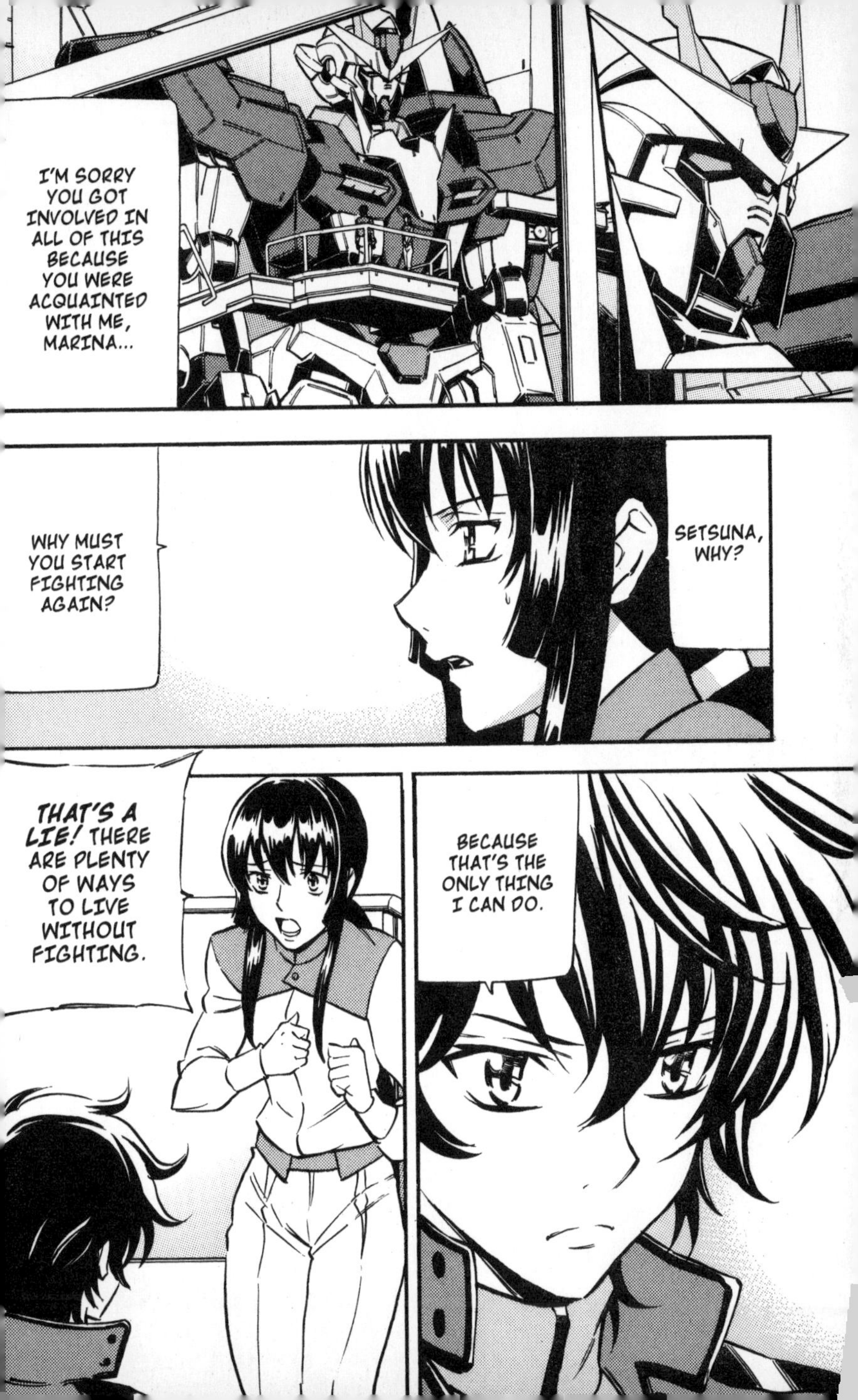
I'M SORRY YOU GOT INVOLVED IN ALL OF THIS BECAUSE YOU WERE ACQUAINTED WITH ME, MARINA...
SETSUNA, WHY?
WHY MUST YOU START FIGHTING AGAIN?
BECAUSE THAT'S THE ONLY THING I CAN DO.
THAT'S A LIE! THERE ARE PLENTY OF WAYS TO LIVE WITHOUT FIGHTING.

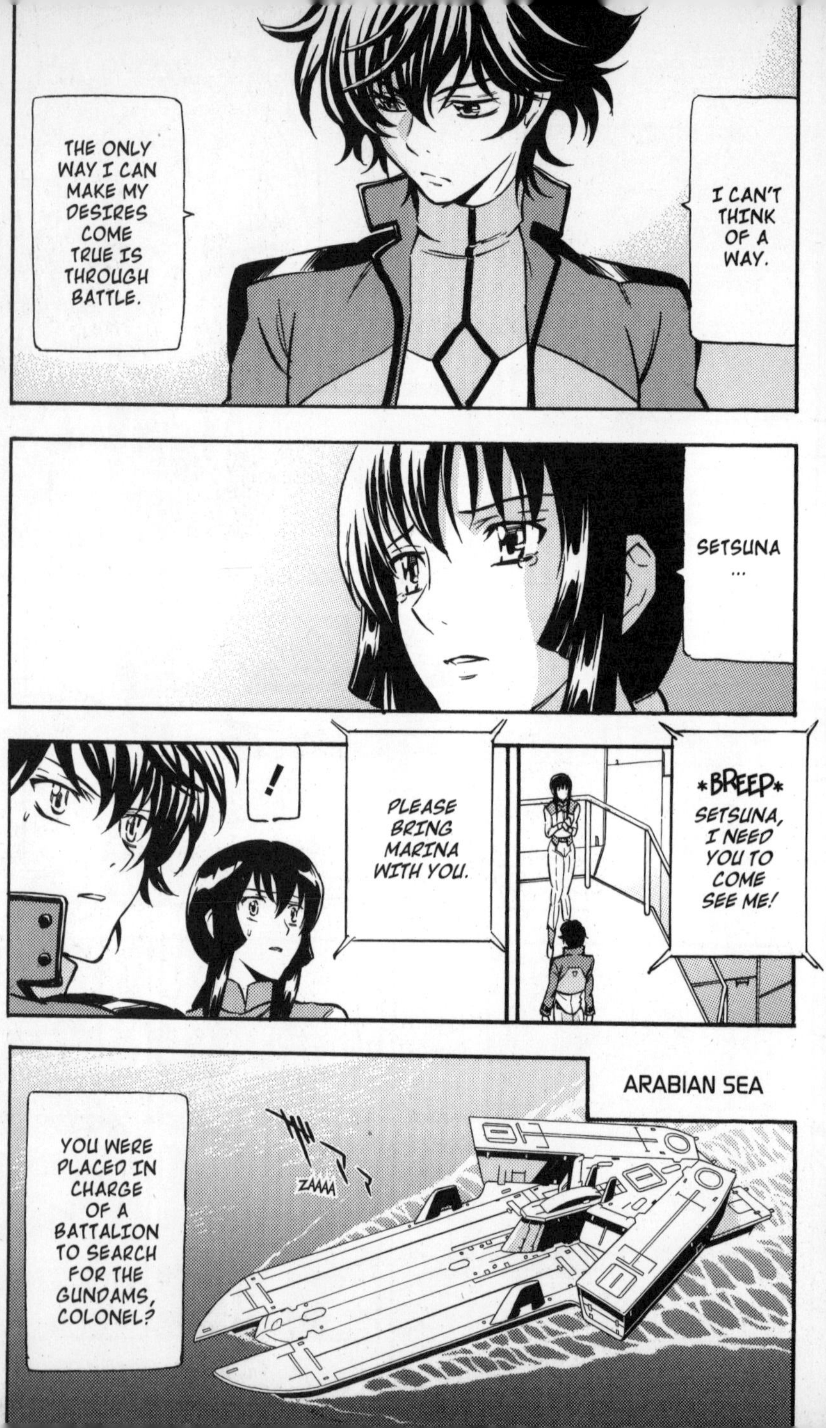

I CAN'T THINK OF A WAY.
THE ONLY WAY I CAN MAKE MY DESIRES COME TRUE IS THROUGH BATTLE.
SETSUNA ...
BREEP SETSUNA, I NEED YOU TO COME SEE ME!
PLEASE BRING MARINA WITH YOU.
!
ARABIAN SEA
ZAAAA
YOU WERE PLACED IN CHARGE OF A BATTALION TO SEARCH FOR THE GUNDAMS, COLONEL?

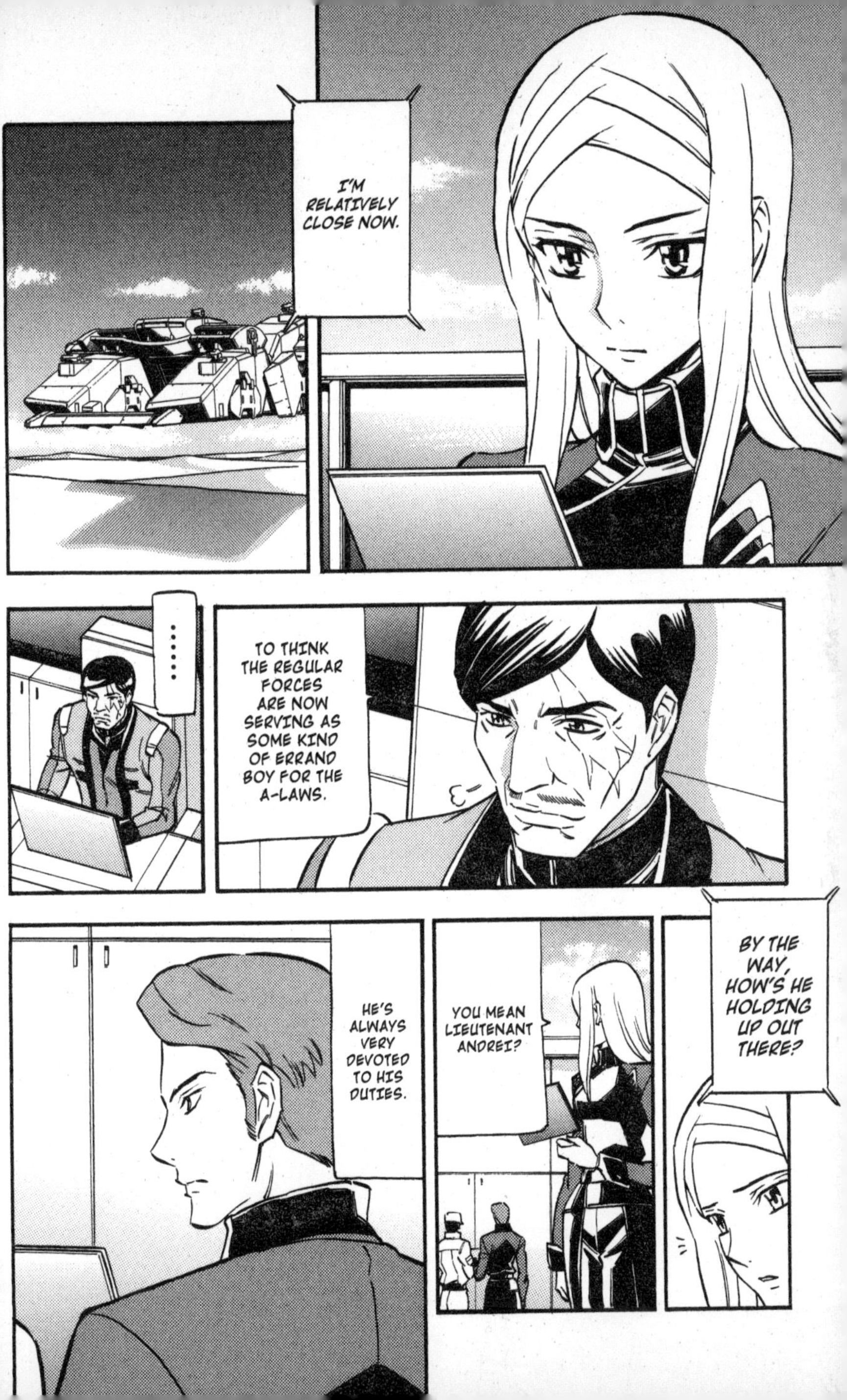
I'M RELATIVELY CLOSE NOW.
TO THINK THE REGULAR FORCES ARE NOW SERVING AS SOME KIND OF ERRAND BOY FOR THE A-LAWS.
......
BY THE WAY, HOW'S HE HOLDING UP OUT THERE?
YOU MEAN LIEUTENANT ANDREI?
HE'S ALWAYS VERY DEVOTED TO HIS DUTIES.

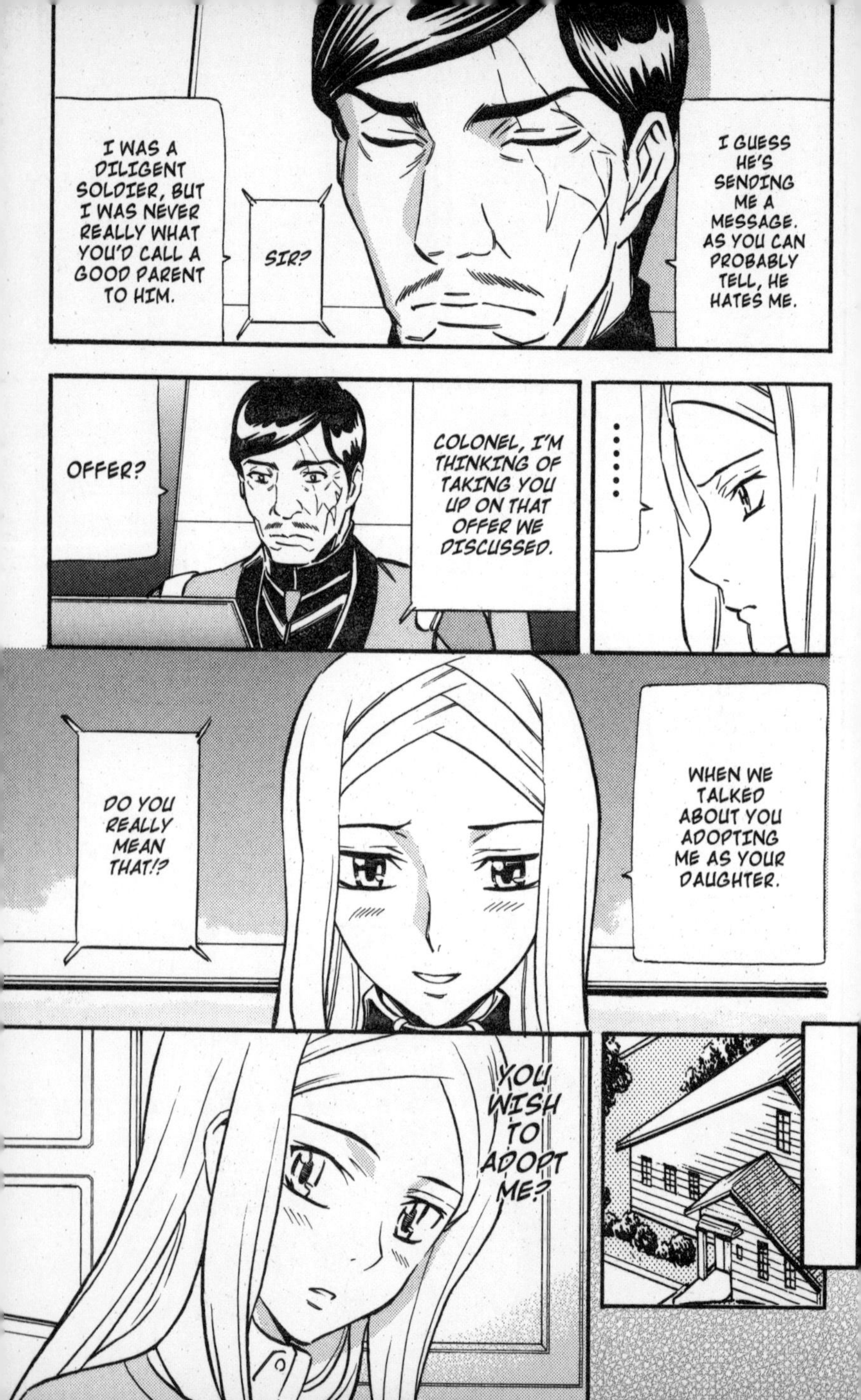
I GUESS HE'S SENDING ME A MESSAGE. AS YOU CAN PROBABLY TELL, HE HATES ME.
SIR?
I WAS A DILIGENT SOLDIER, BUT I WAS NEVER REALLY WHAT YOU'D CALL A GOOD PARENT TO HIM.
......
COLONEL, I'M THINKING OF TAKING YOU UP ON THAT OFFER WE DISCUSSED.
OFFER?
WHEN WE TALKED ABOUT YOU ADOPTING ME AS YOUR DAUGHTER.
DO YOU REALLY MEAN THAT!?
YOU WISH TO ADOPT ME?

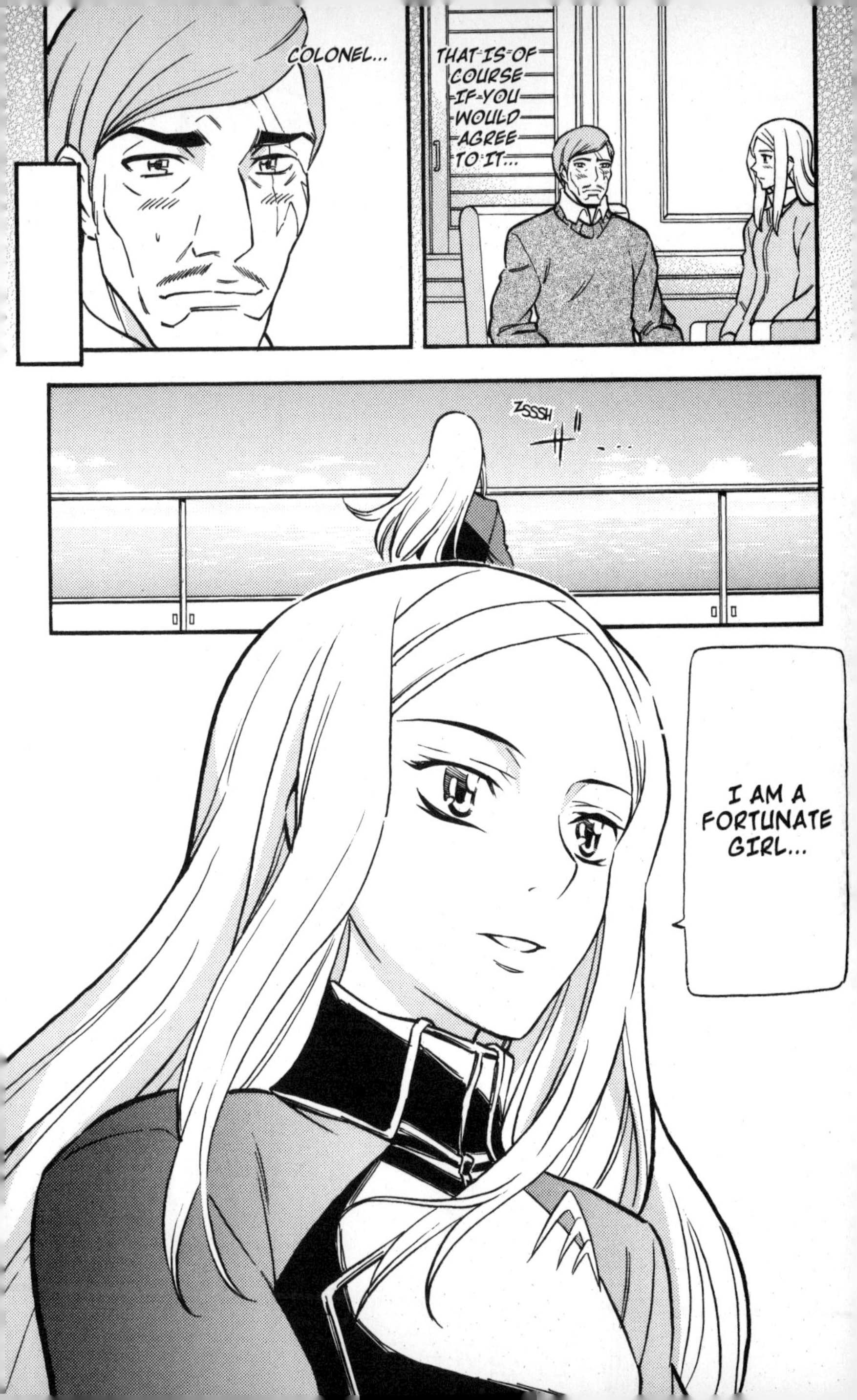
THAT IS OF COURSE IF YOU WOULD AGREE TO IT...
COLONEL...
ZSSSH
I AM A FORTUNATE GIRL...

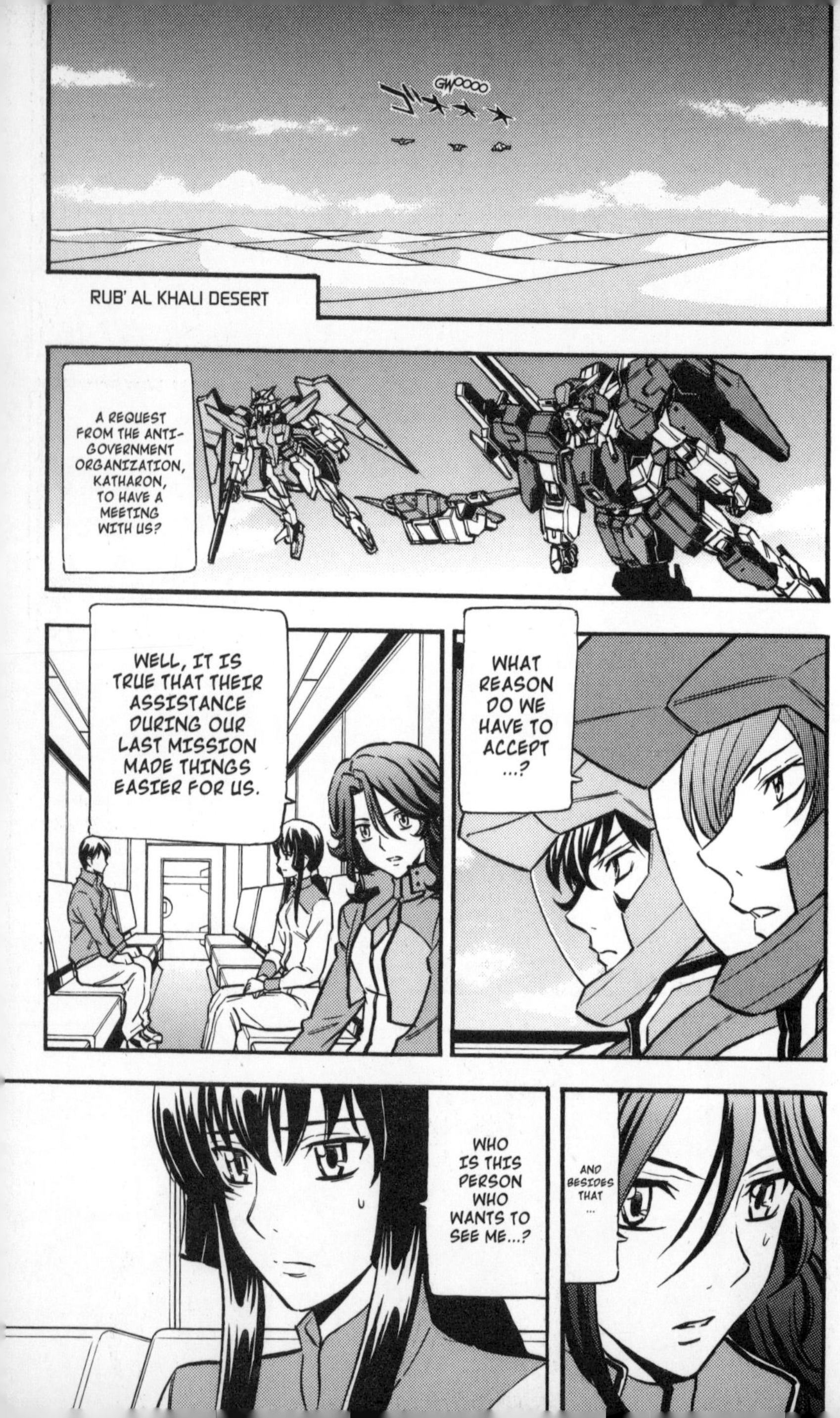
GWOOOO
RUB' AL KHALI DESERT
A REQUEST FROM THE ANTI-GOVERNMENT ORGANIZATION, KATHARON, TO HAVE A MEETING WITH US?
WHAT REASON DO WE HAVE TO ACCEPT ...?
WELL, IT IS TRUE THAT THEIR ASSISTANCE DURING OUR LAST MISSION MADE THINGS EASIER FOR US.
AND BESIDES THAT ...
WHO IS THIS PERSON WHO WANTS TO SEE ME...?

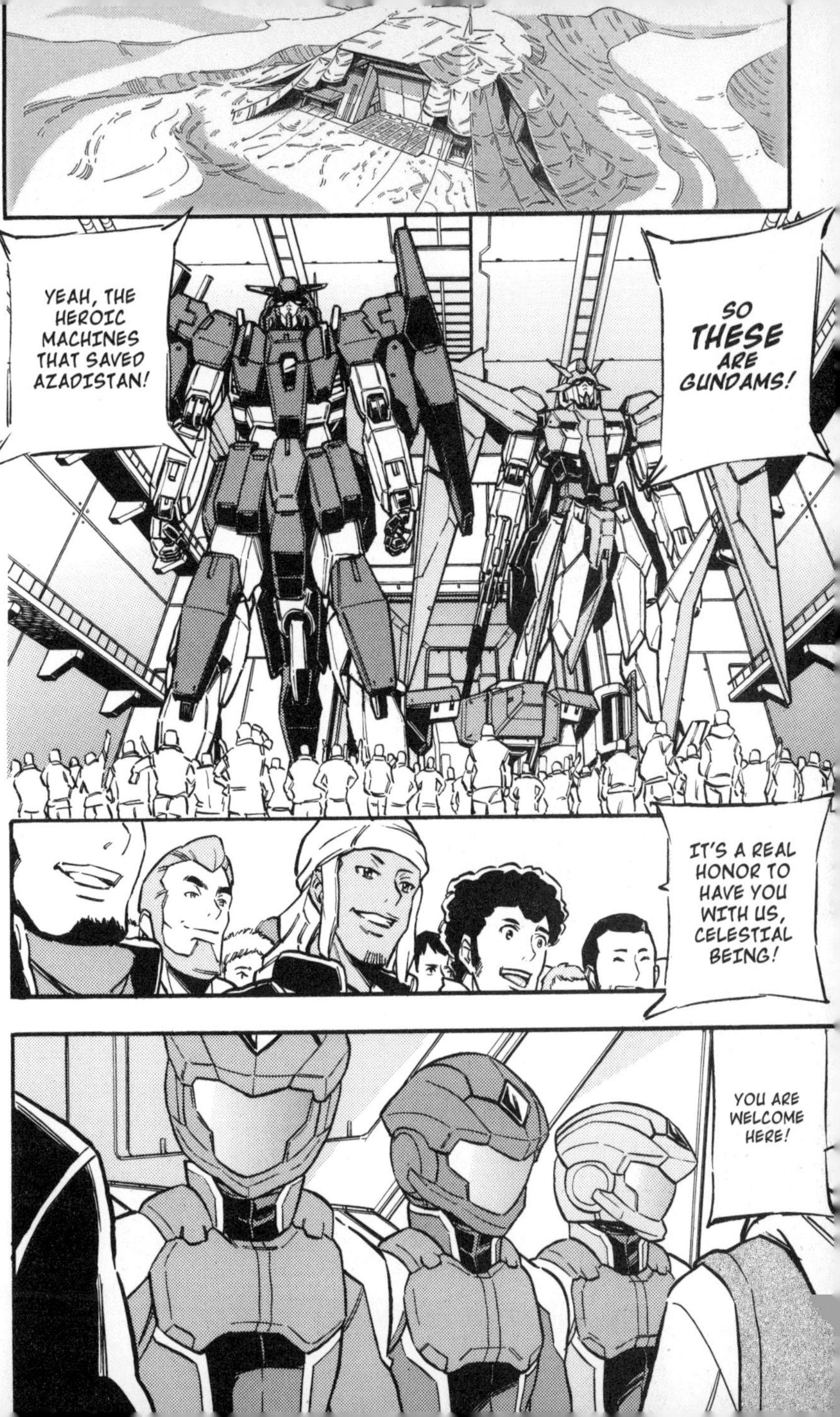
SO THESE ARE GUNDAMS!
YEAH, THE HEROIC MACHINES THAT SAVED AZADISTAN!
IT'S A REAL HONOR TO HAVE YOU WITH US, CELESTIAL BEING!
YOU ARE WELCOME HERE!

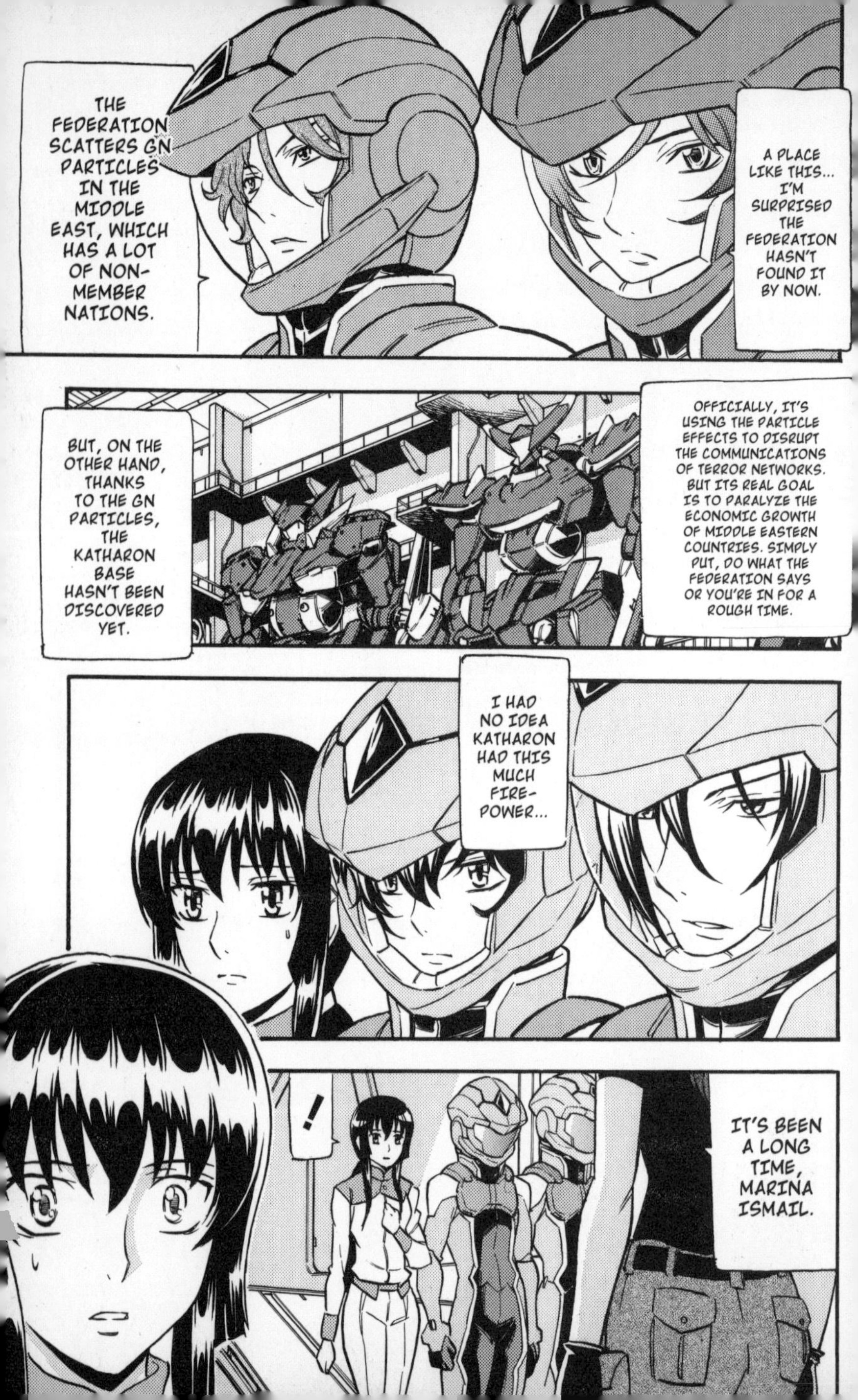
A PLACE LIKE THIS... I'M SURPRISED THE FEDERATION HASN'T FOUND IT BY NOW.
THE FEDERATION SCATTERS GN PARTICLES IN THE MIDDLE EAST, WHICH HAS A LOT OF NON-MEMBER NATIONS.
OFFICIALLY, IT'S USING THE PARTICLE EFFECTS TO DISRUPT THE COMMUNICATIONS OF TERROR NETWORKS. BUT ITS REAL GOAL IS TO PARALYZE THE ECONOMIC GROWTH OF MIDDLE EASTERN COUNTRIES. SIMPLY PUT, DO WHAT THE FEDERATION SAYS OR YOU'RE IN FOR A ROUGH TIME.
BUT, ON THE OTHER HAND, THANKS TO THE GN PARTICLES, THE KATHARON BASE HASN'T BEEN DISCOVERED YET.
I HAD NO IDEA KATHARON HAD THIS MUCH FIRE-POWER...
IT'S BEEN A LONG TIME, MARINA ISMAIL.
!

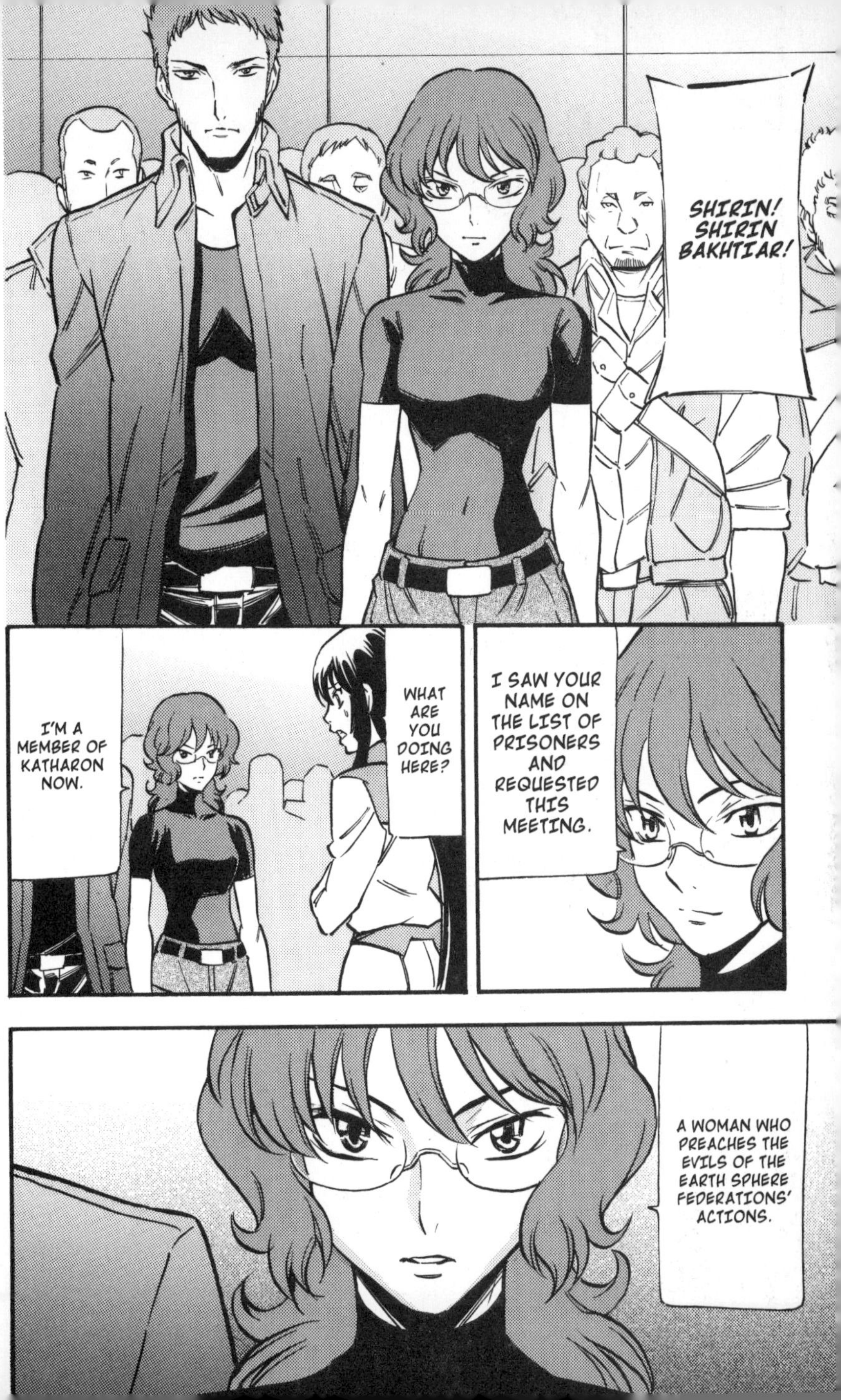
SHIRIN! SHIRIN BAKHTIAR!
I SAW YOUR NAME ON THE LIST OF PRISONERS AND REQUESTED THIS MEETING.
WHAT ARE YOU DOING HERE?
I'M A MEMBER OF KATHARON NOW.
A WOMAN WHO PREACHES THE EVILS OF THE EARTH SPHERE FEDERATIONS' ACTIONS.

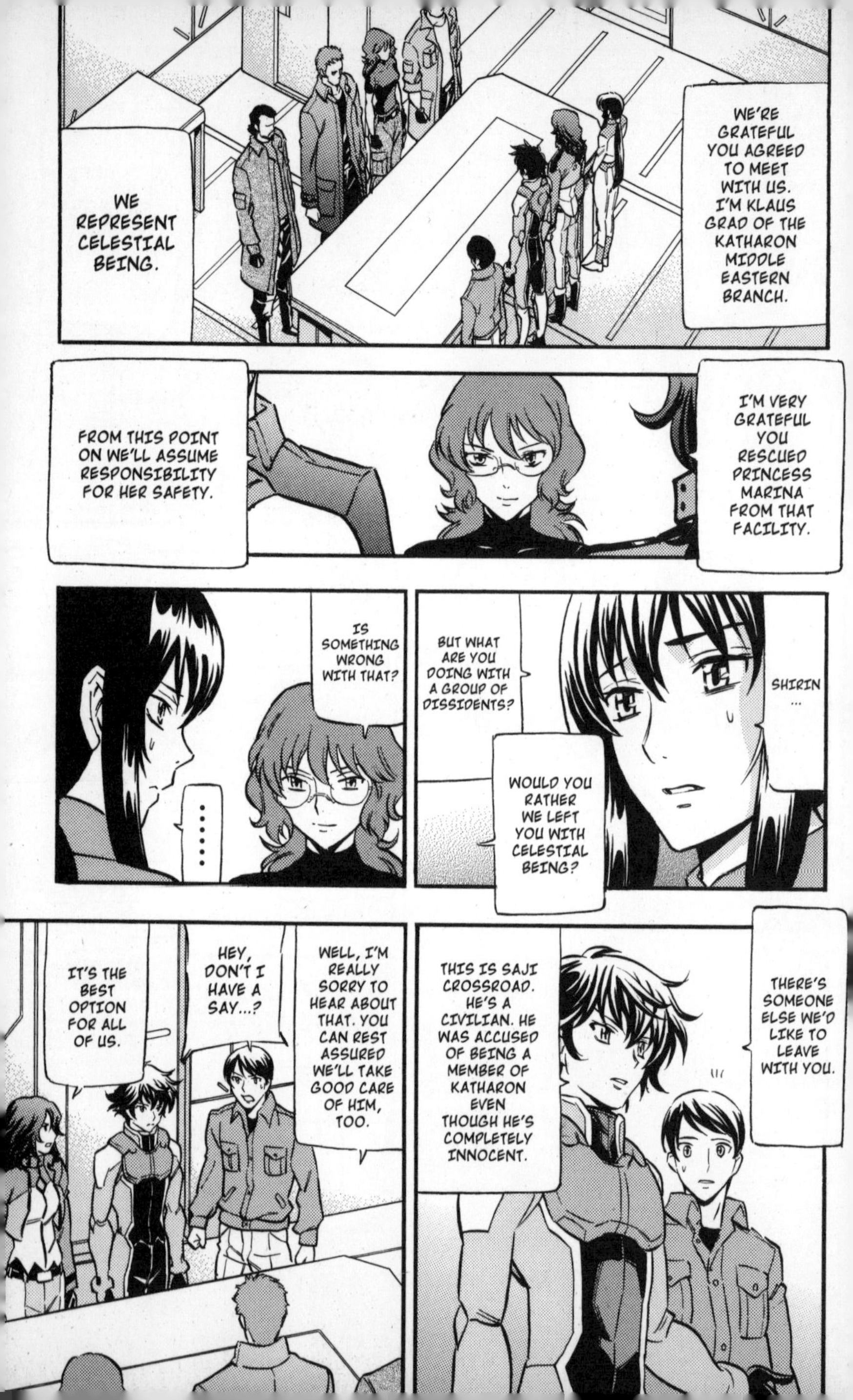
WE'RE GRATEFUL YOU AGREED TO MEET WITH US. I'M KLAUS GRAD OF THE KATHARON MIDDLE EASTERN BRANCH.
WE REPRESENT CELESTIAL BEING.
I'M VERY GRATEFUL YOU RESCUED PRINCESS MARINA FROM THAT FACILITY.
FROM THIS POINT ON WE'LL ASSUME RESPONSIBILITY FOR HER SAFETY.
SHIRIN ...
BUT WHAT ARE YOU DOING WITH A GROUP OF DISSIDENTS?
WOULD YOU RATHER WE LEFT YOU WITH CELESTIAL BEING?
IS SOMETHING WRONG WITH THAT?
......
THERE'S SOMEONE ELSE WE'D LIKE TO LEAVE WITH YOU.
THIS IS SAJI CROSSROAD. HE'S A CIVILIAN. HE WAS ACCUSED OF BEING A MEMBER OF KATHARON EVEN THOUGH HE'S COMPLETELY INNOCENT.
WELL, I'M REALLY SORRY TO HEAR ABOUT THAT. YOU CAN REST ASSURED WE'LL TAKE GOOD CARE OF HIM, TOO.
HEY, DON'T I HAVE A SAY...?
IT'S THE BEST OPTION FOR ALL OF US.

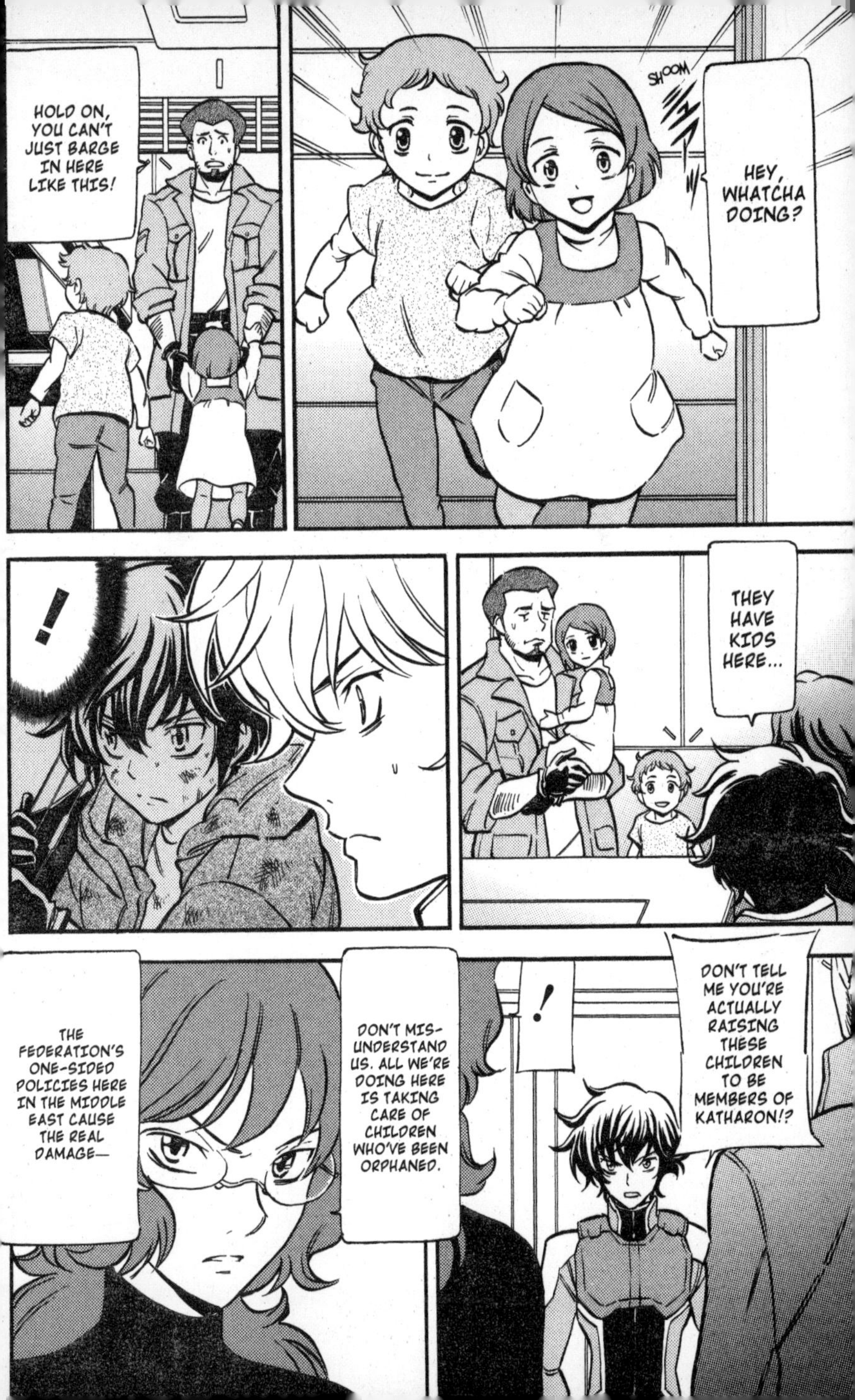
SHOOM
HEY, WHATCHA DOING?
HOLD ON, YOU CAN'T JUST BARGE IN HERE LIKE THIS!
THEY HAVE KIDS HERE...
!
DON'T TELL ME YOU'RE ACTUALLY RAISING THESE CHILDREN TO BE MEMBERS OF KATHARON!?
!
DON'T MIS-UNDERSTAND US. ALL WE'RE DOING HERE IS TAKING CARE OF CHILDREN WHO'VE BEEN ORPHANED.
THE FEDERATION'S ONE-SIDED POLICIES HERE IN THE MIDDLE EAST CAUSE THE REAL DAMAGE—

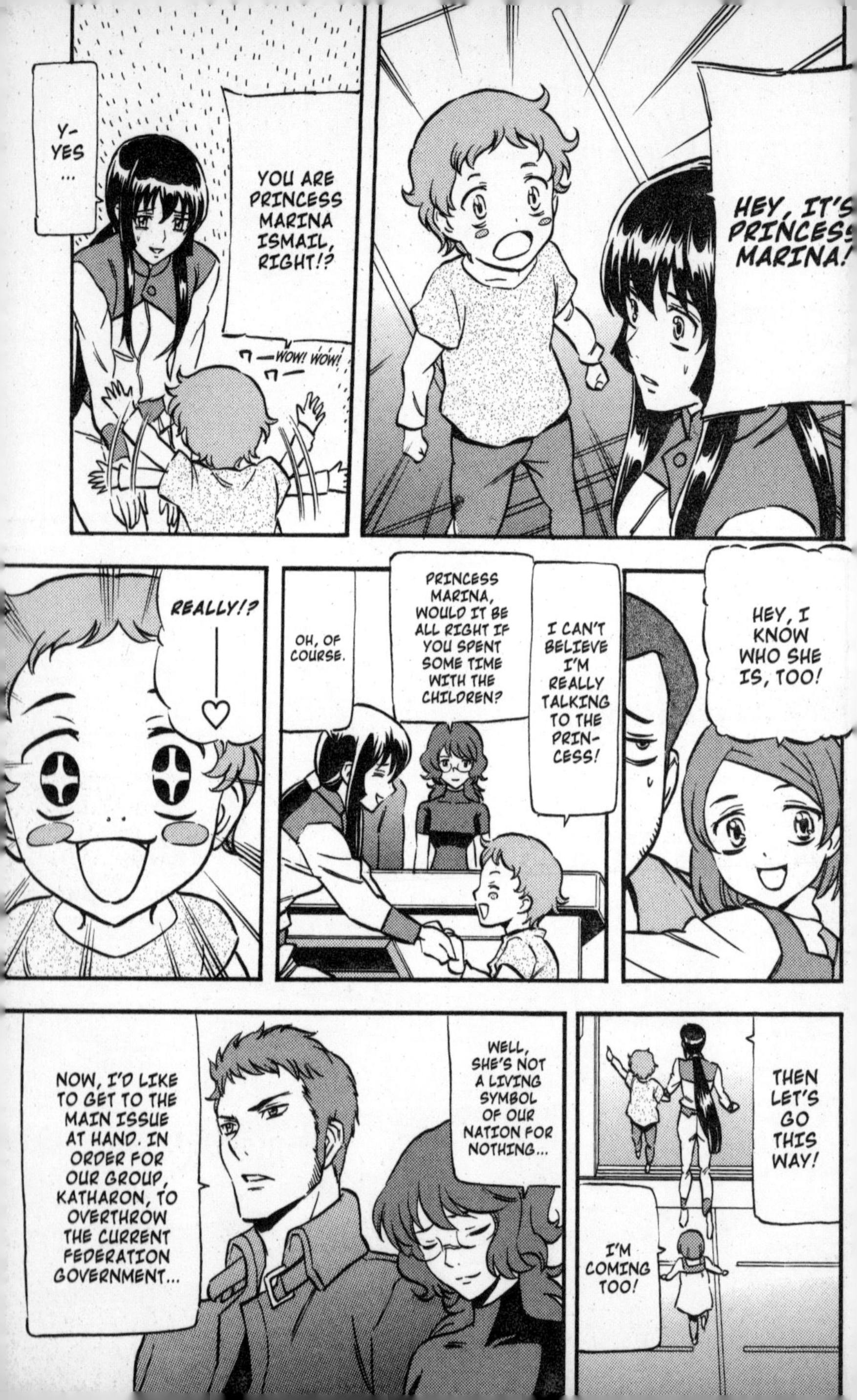
HEY, IT'S PRINCESS MARINA!
YOU ARE PRINCESS MARINA ISMAIL, RIGHT!?
Y-YES...
WOW! WOW!
HEY, I KNOW WHO SHE IS, TOO!
I CAN'T BELIEVE I'M REALLY TALKING TO THE PRIN-CESS!
PRINCESS MARINA, WOULD IT BE ALL RIGHT IF YOU SPENT SOME TIME WITH THE CHILDREN?
OH, OF COURSE.
REALLY!? ♡
THEN LET'S GO THIS WAY!
I'M COMING TOO!
WELL, SHE'S NOT A LIVING SYMBOL OF OUR NATION FOR NOTHING...
NOW, I'D LIKE TO GET TO THE MAIN ISSUE AT HAND. IN ORDER FOR OUR GROUP, KATHARON, TO OVERTHROW THE CURRENT FEDERATION GOVERNMENT...

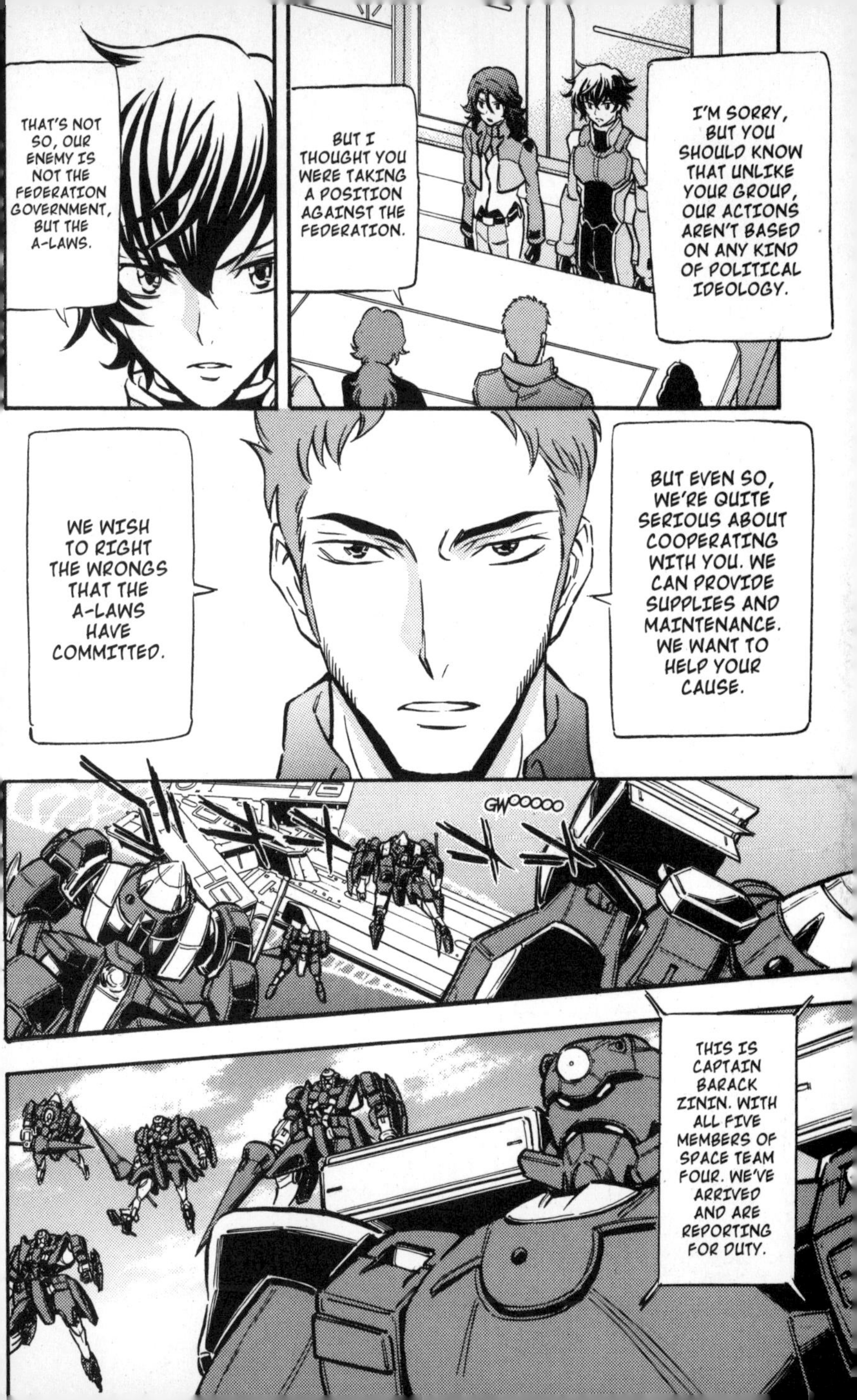

I'M SORRY, BUT YOU SHOULD KNOW THAT UNLIKE YOUR GROUP, OUR ACTIONS AREN'T BASED ON ANY KIND OF POLITICAL IDEOLOGY.
BUT I THOUGHT YOU WERE TAKING A POSITION AGAINST THE FEDERATION.
THAT'S NOT SO, OUR ENEMY IS NOT THE FEDERATION GOVERNMENT, BUT THE A-LAWS.
BUT EVEN SO, WE'RE QUITE SERIOUS ABOUT COOPERATING WITH YOU. WE CAN PROVIDE SUPPLIES AND MAINTENANCE. WE WANT TO HELP YOUR CAUSE.
WE WISH TO RIGHT THE WRONGS THAT THE A-LAWS HAVE COMMITTED.
GWOOOOO
THIS IS CAPTAIN BARACK ZININ. WITH ALL FIVE MEMBERS OF SPACE TEAM FOUR. WE'VE ARRIVED AND ARE REPORTING FOR DUTY.

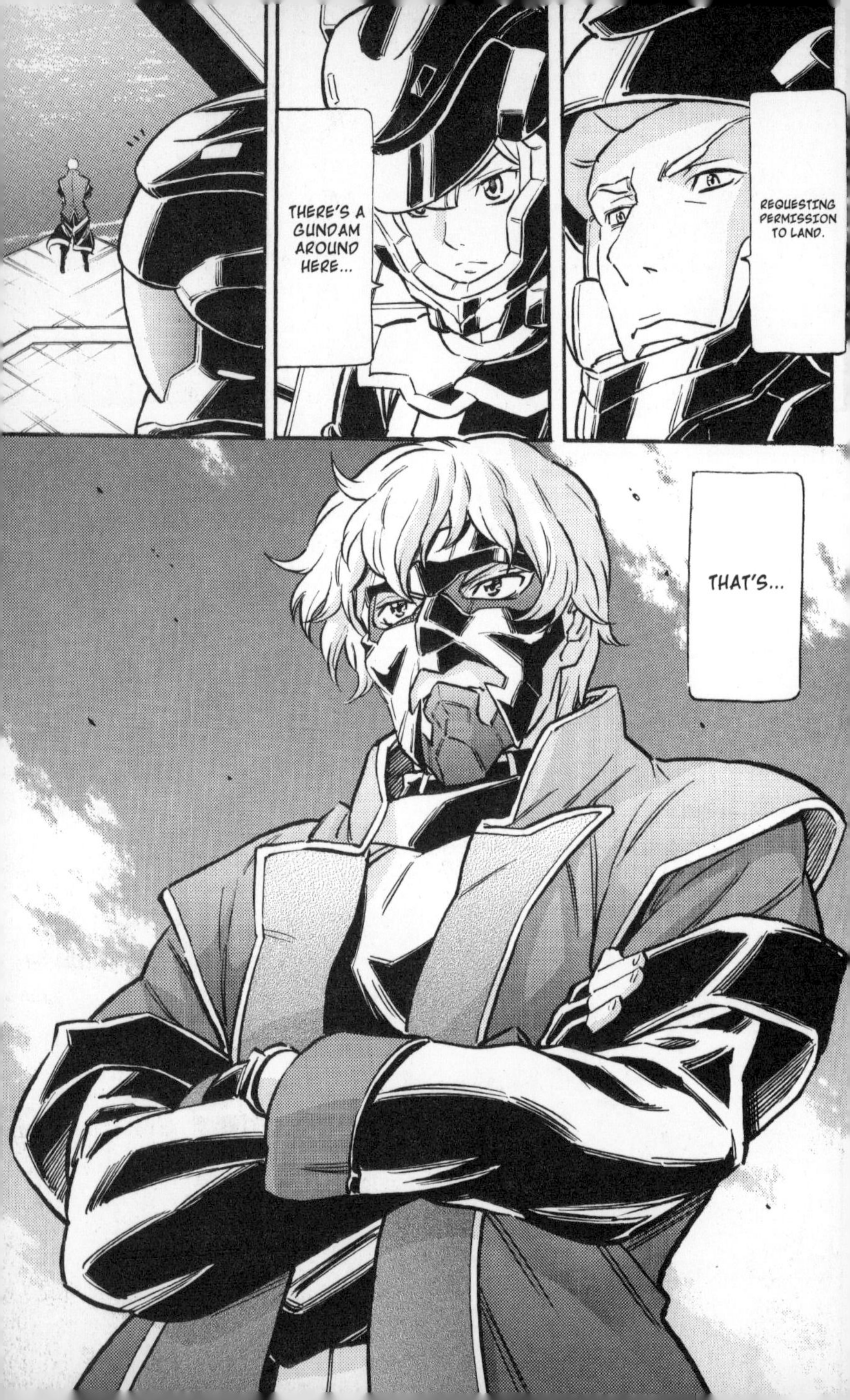
REQUESTING PERMISSION TO LAND.
THERE'S A GUNDAM AROUND HERE...
THAT'S...

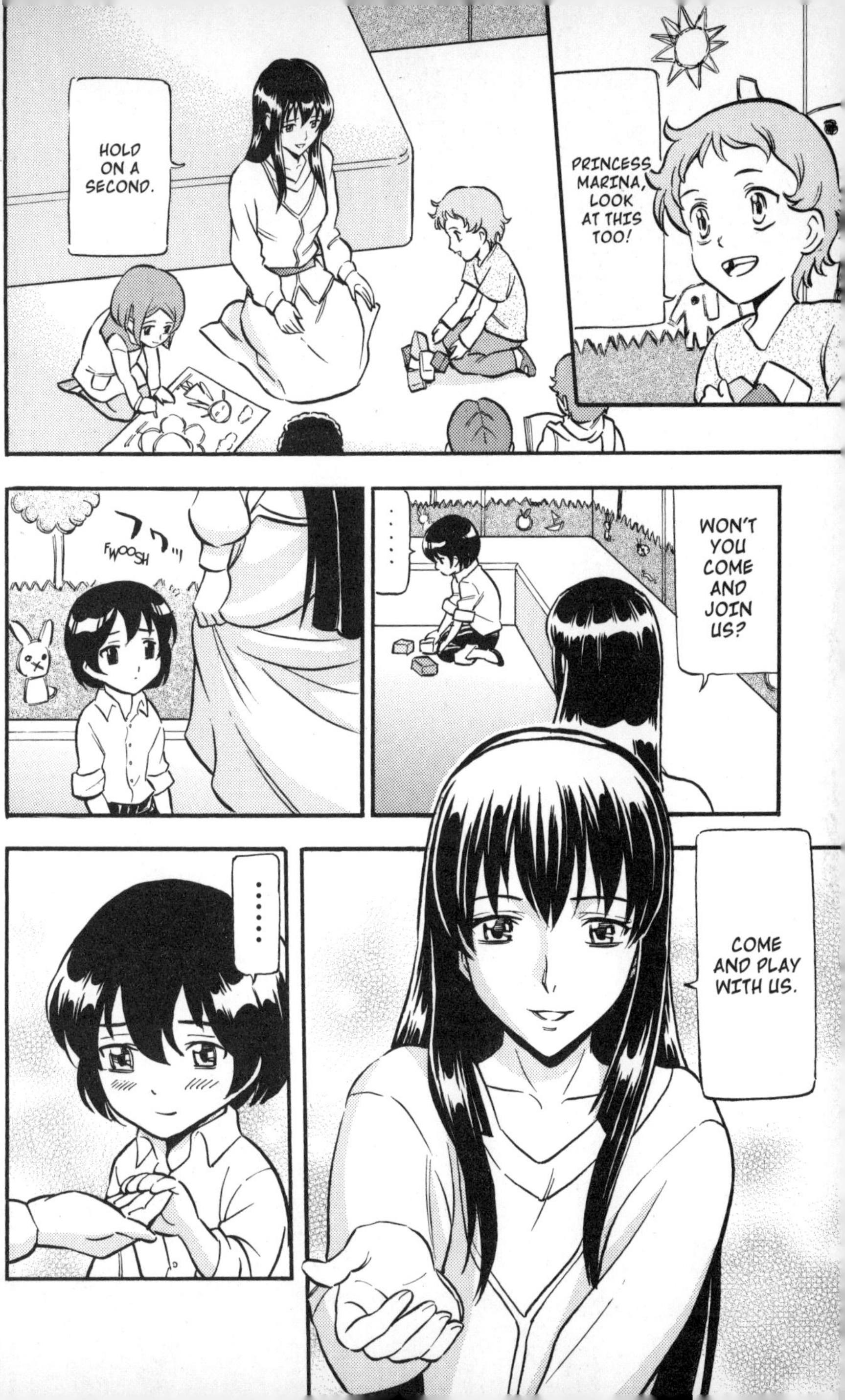
PRINCESS MARINA, LOOK AT THIS TOO!
HOLD ON A SECOND.
WON'T YOU COME AND JOIN US?
.....
FWOOSH
COME AND PLAY WITH US.
......

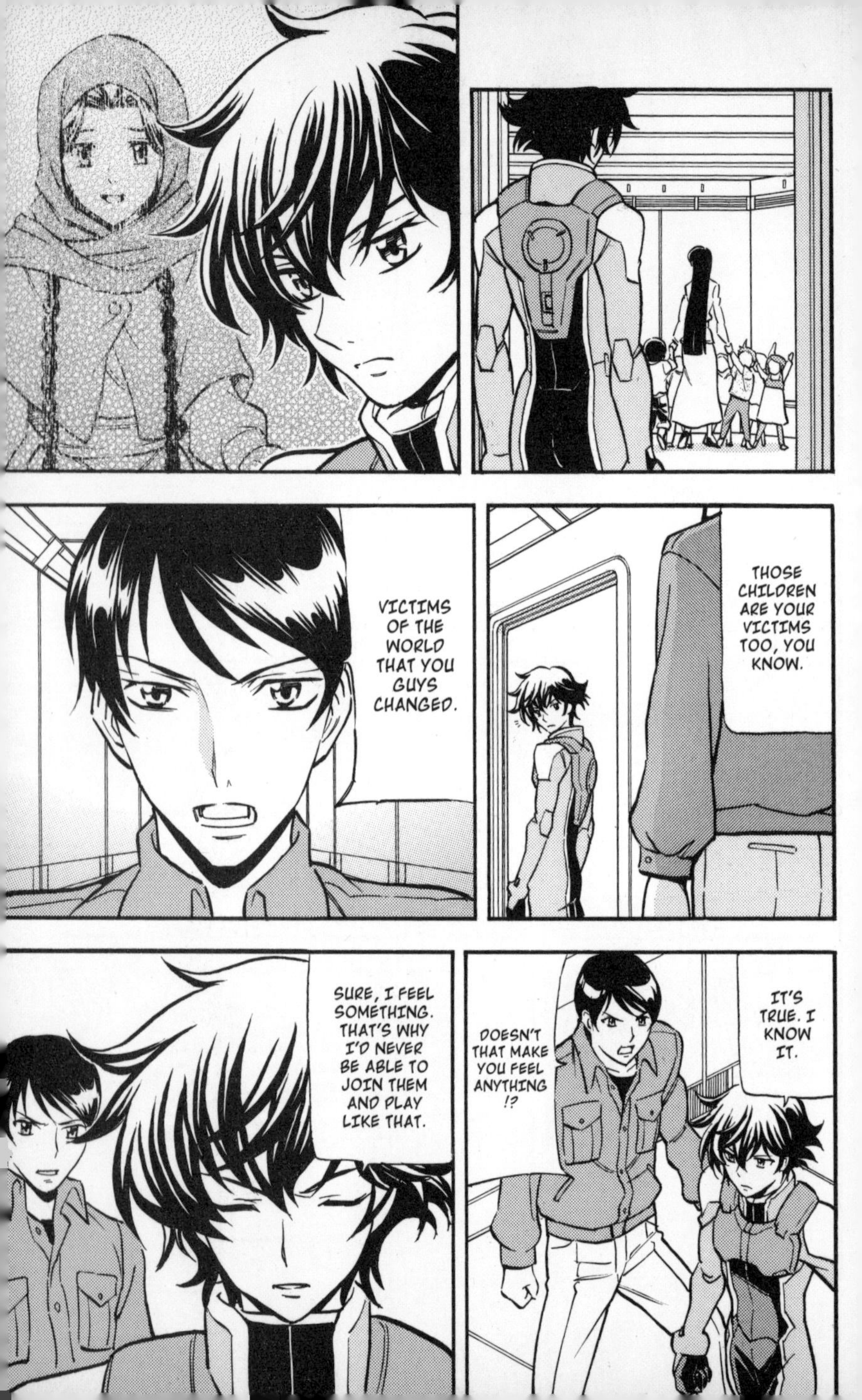
THOSE CHILDREN ARE YOUR VICTIMS TOO, YOU KNOW.
VICTIMS OF THE WORLD THAT YOU GUYS CHANGED.
IT'S TRUE. I KNOW IT.
DOESN'T THAT MAKE YOU FEEL ANYTHING!?
SURE, I FEEL SOMETHING. THAT'S WHY I'D NEVER BE ABLE TO JOIN THEM AND PLAY LIKE THAT.

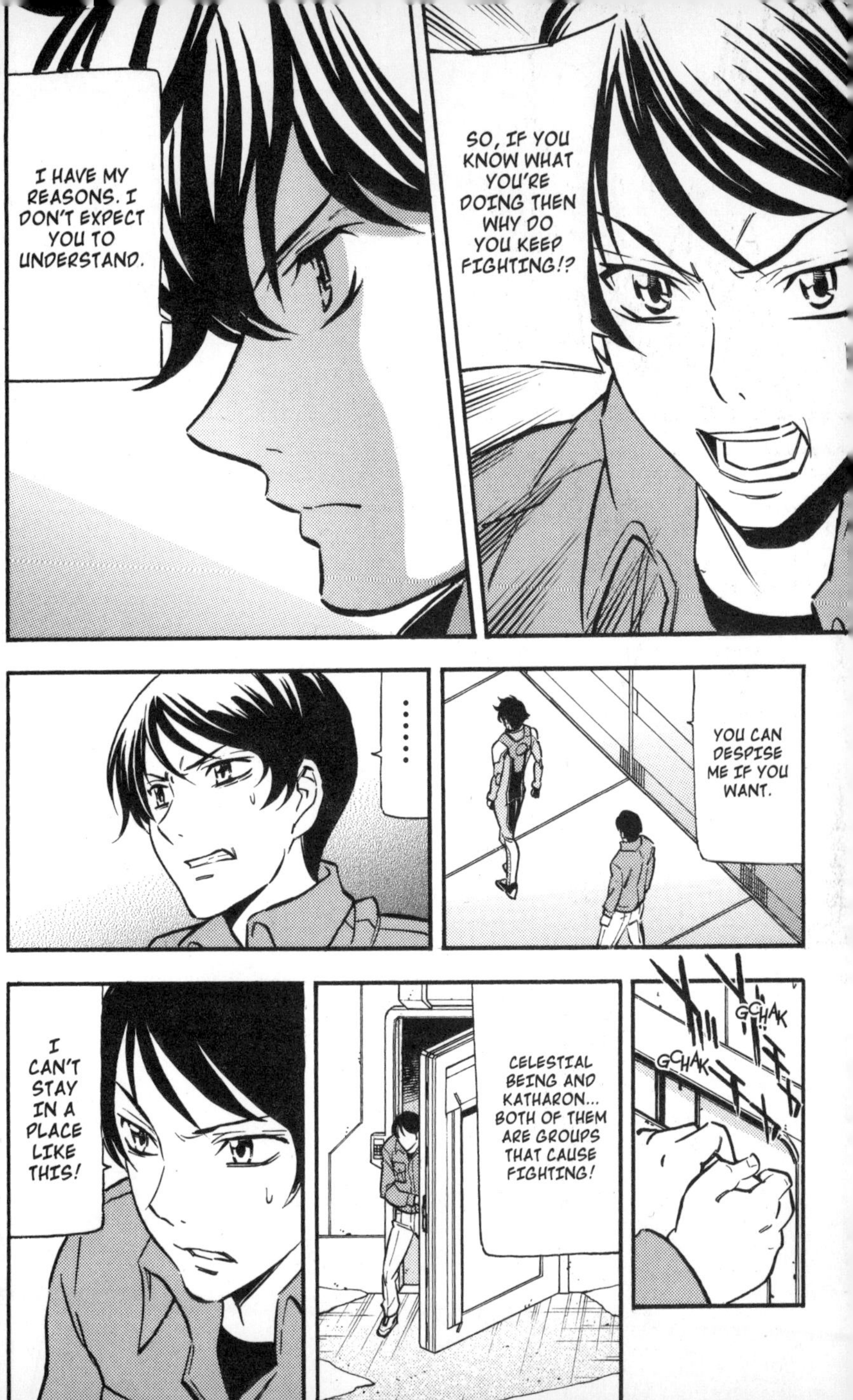
SO, IF YOU KNOW WHAT YOU'RE DOING THEN WHY DO YOU KEEP FIGHTING!?
I HAVE MY REASONS. I DON'T EXPECT YOU TO UNDERSTAND.
YOU CAN DESPISE ME IF YOU WANT.
......
GCHAK
GCHAK
CELESTIAL BEING AND KATHARON... BOTH OF THEM ARE GROUPS THAT CAUSE FIGHTING!
I CAN'T STAY IN A PLACE LIKE THIS!

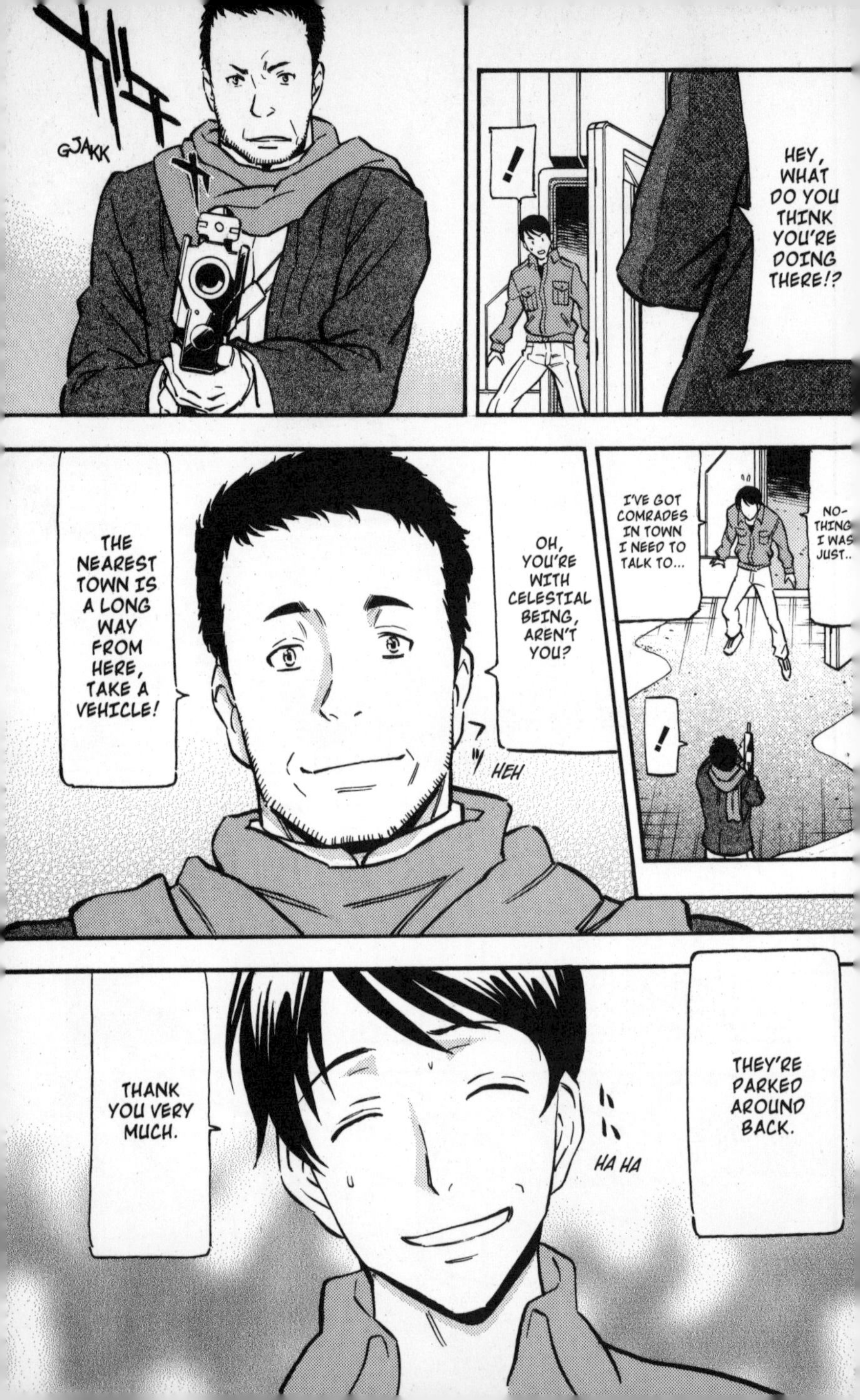
!
HEY, WHAT DO YOU THINK YOU'RE DOING THERE!?
GJAKK
NO-THING I WAS JUST..
I'VE GOT COMRADES IN TOWN I NEED TO TALK TO...
!
OH, YOU'RE WITH CELESTIAL BEING, AREN'T YOU?
HEH
THE NEAREST TOWN IS A LONG WAY FROM HERE, TAKE A VEHICLE!
THEY'RE PARKED AROUND BACK.
HA HA
THANK YOU VERY MUCH.

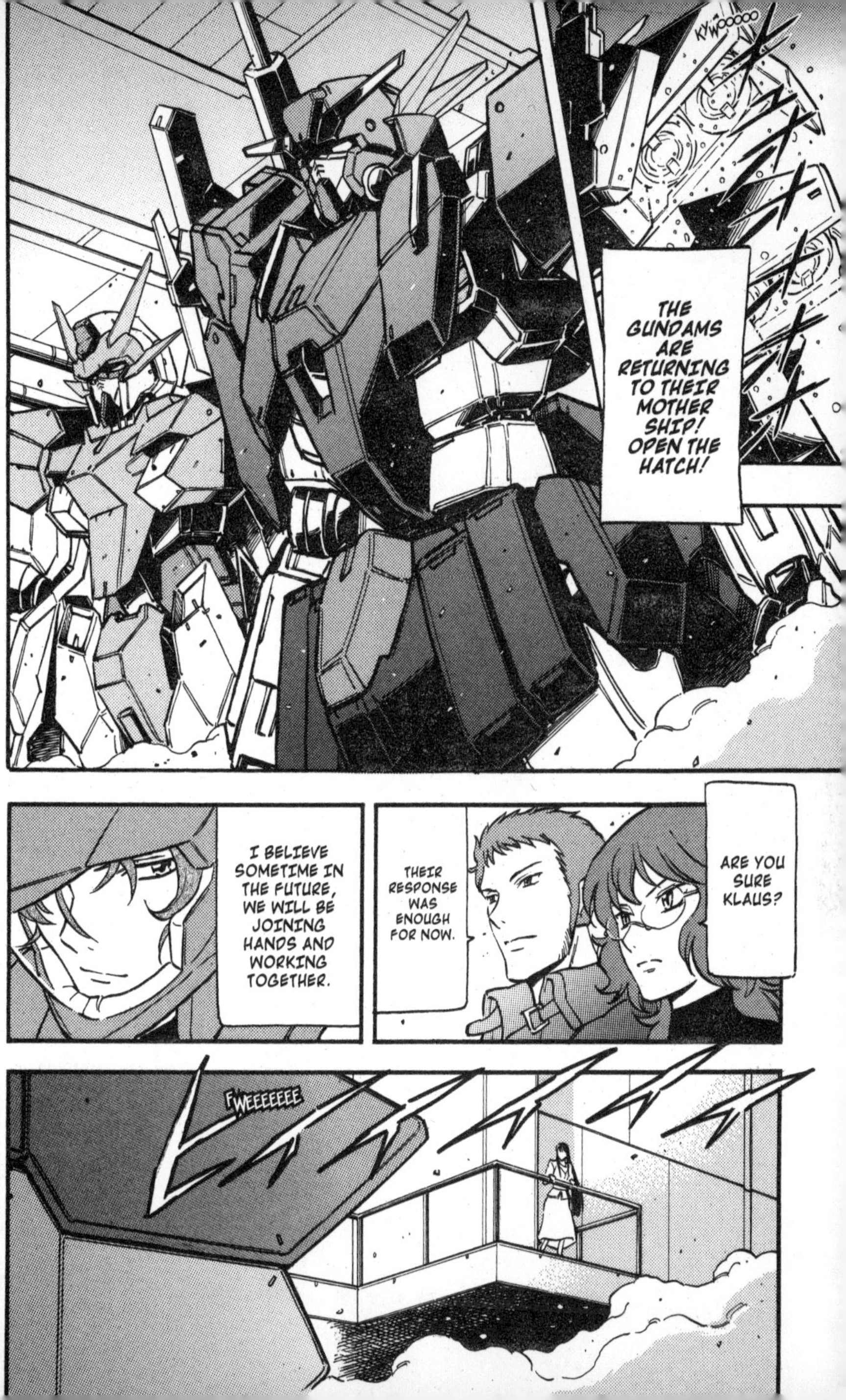
KYWOOOOO
THE GUNDAMS ARE RETURNING TO THEIR MOTHER SHIP! OPEN THE HATCH!
ARE YOU SURE KLAUS?
THEIR RESPONSE WAS ENOUGH FOR NOW.
I BELIEVE SOMETIME IN THE FUTURE, WE WILL BE JOINING HANDS AND WORKING TOGETHER.
FWEEEEEEE

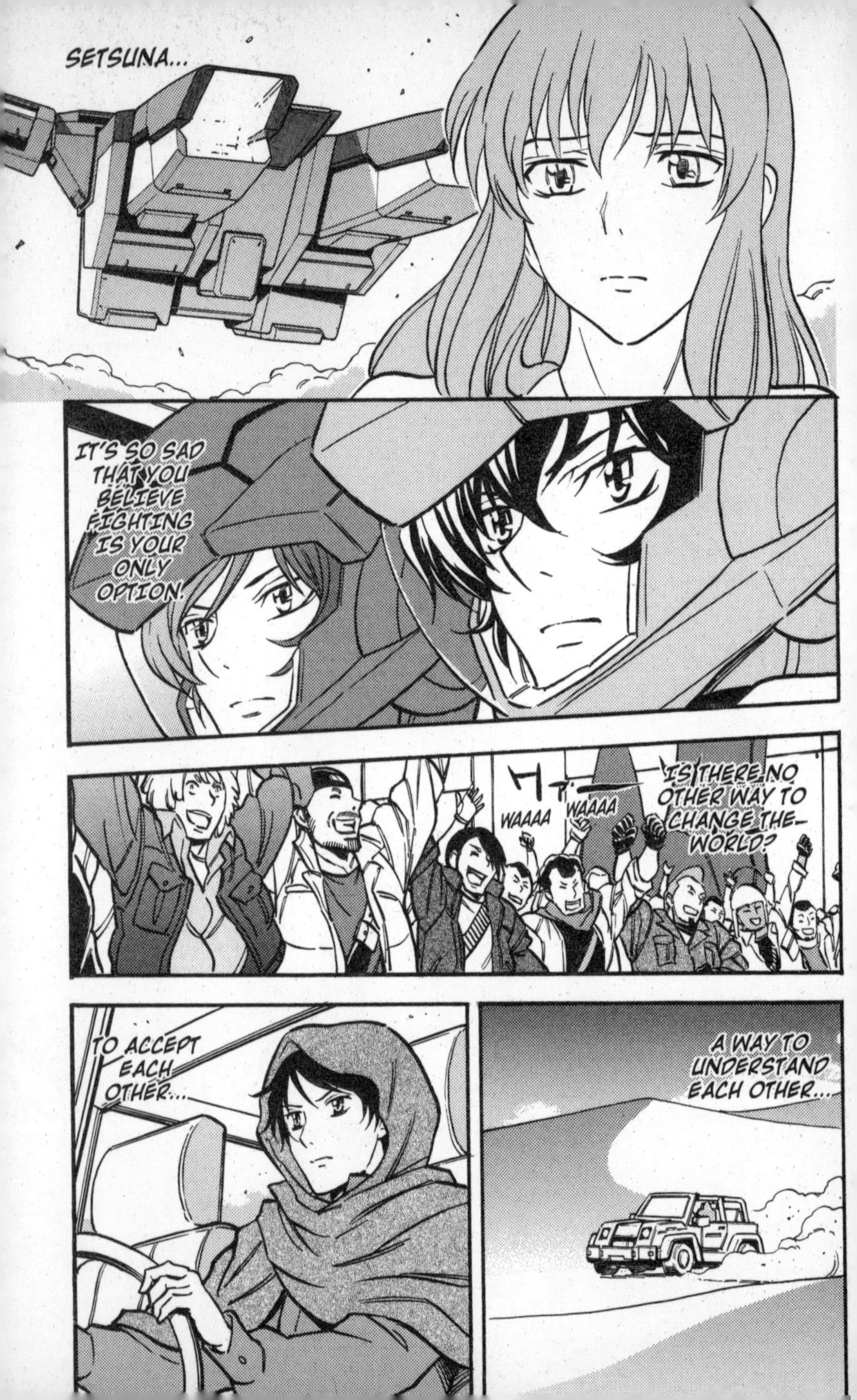
SETSUNA...
IT'S SO SAD THAT YOU BELIEVE FIGHTING IS YOUR ONLY OPTION.
IS THERE NO OTHER WAY TO CHANGE THE WORLD?
WAAAA
WAAAA
A WAY TO UNDERSTAND EACH OTHER...
TO ACCEPT EACH OTHER...

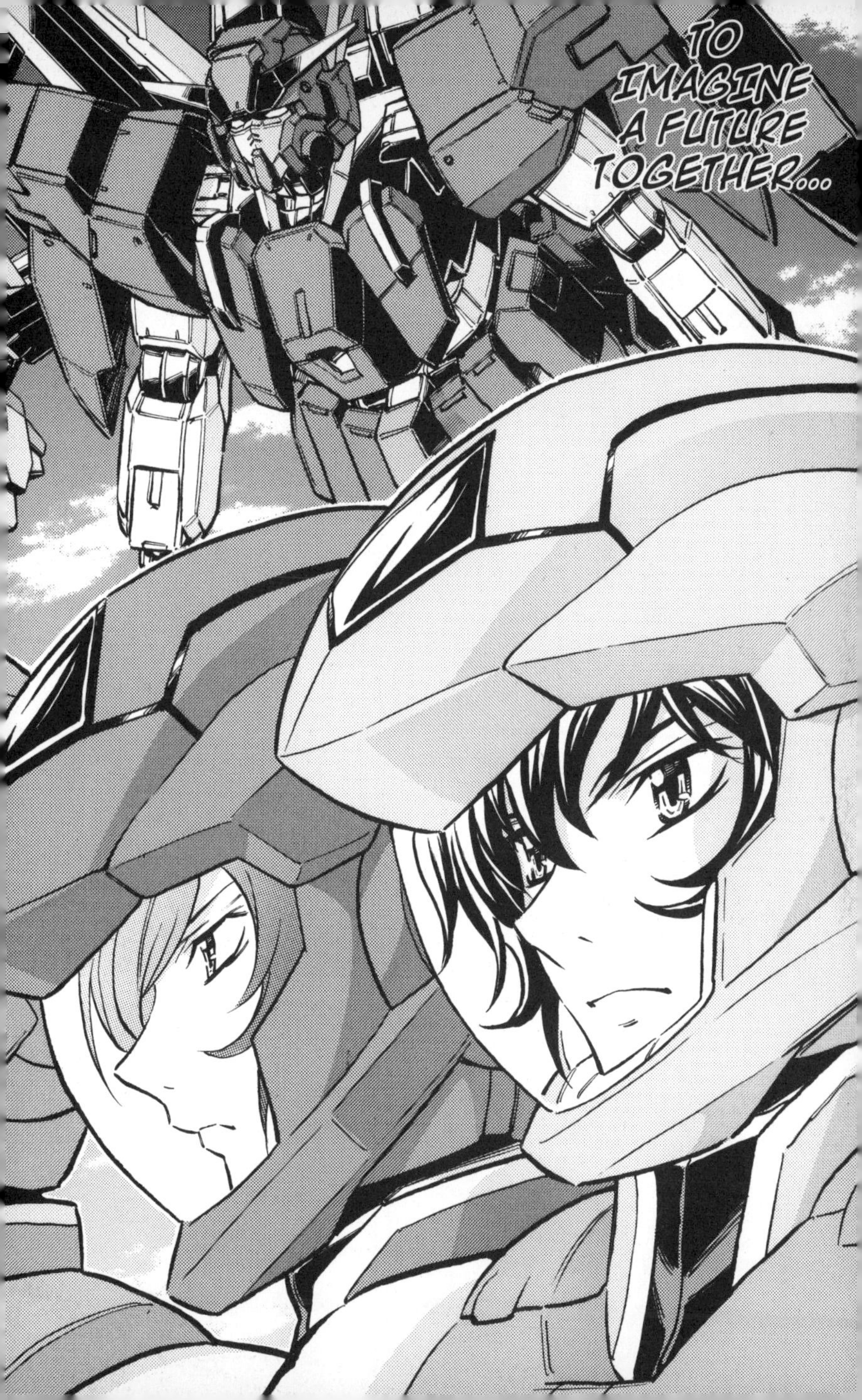
TO IMAGINE A FUTURE TOGETHER...

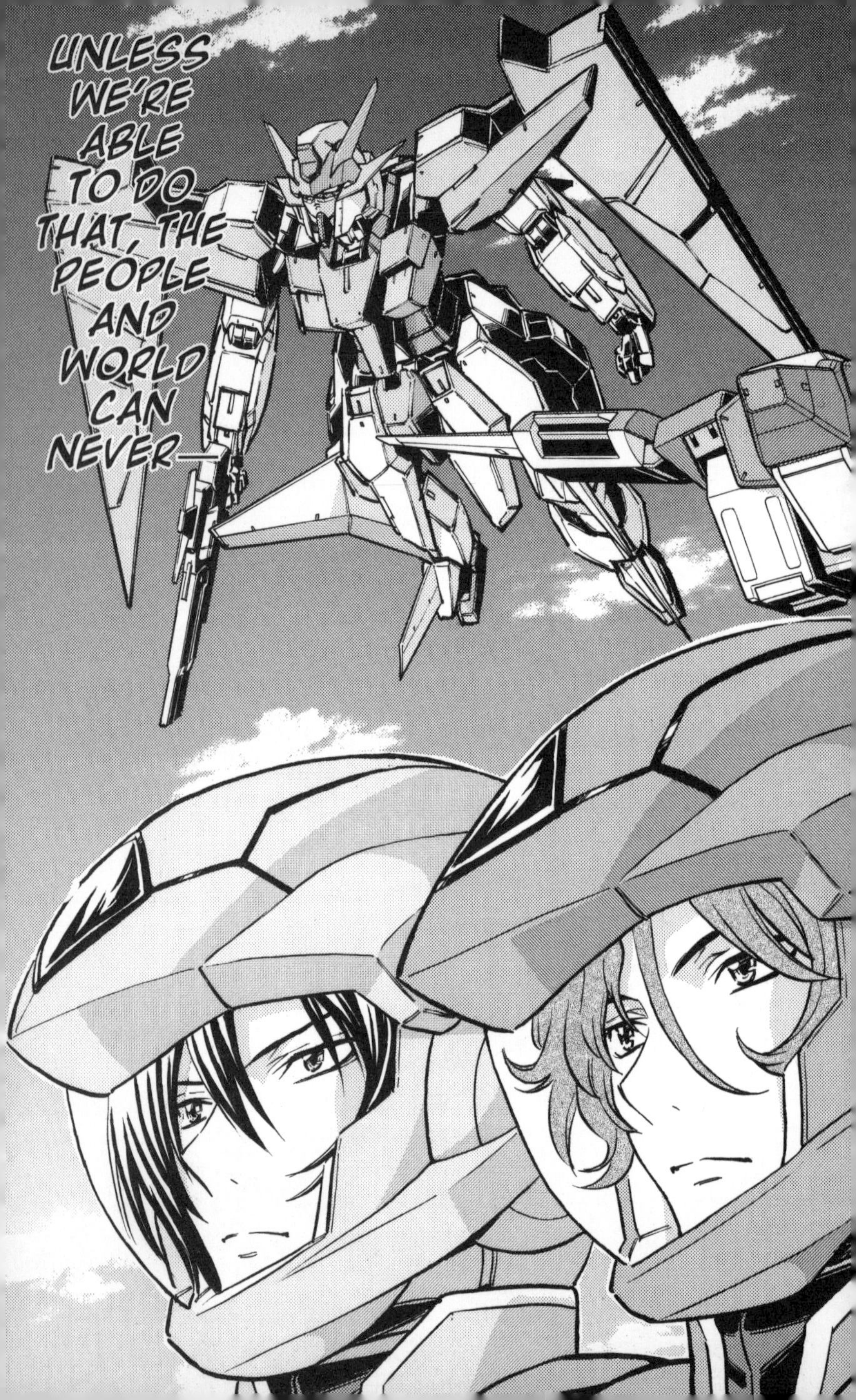
UNLESS WE'RE ABLE TO DO THAT, THE PEOPLE AND WORLD CAN NEVER—

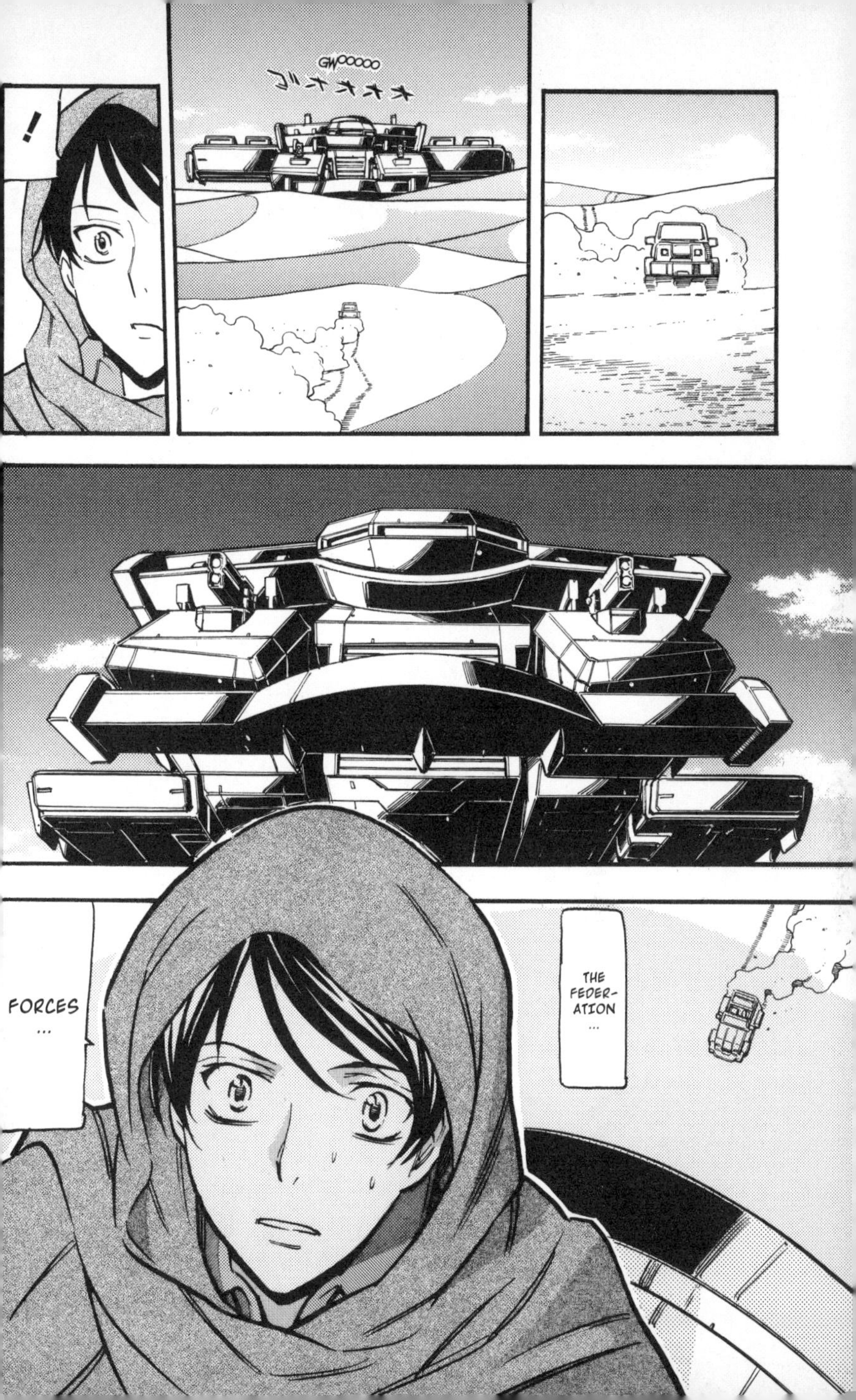
GWOOOOO
ゴーオオオオ
!
THE FEDER-
ATION
...
FORCES
...

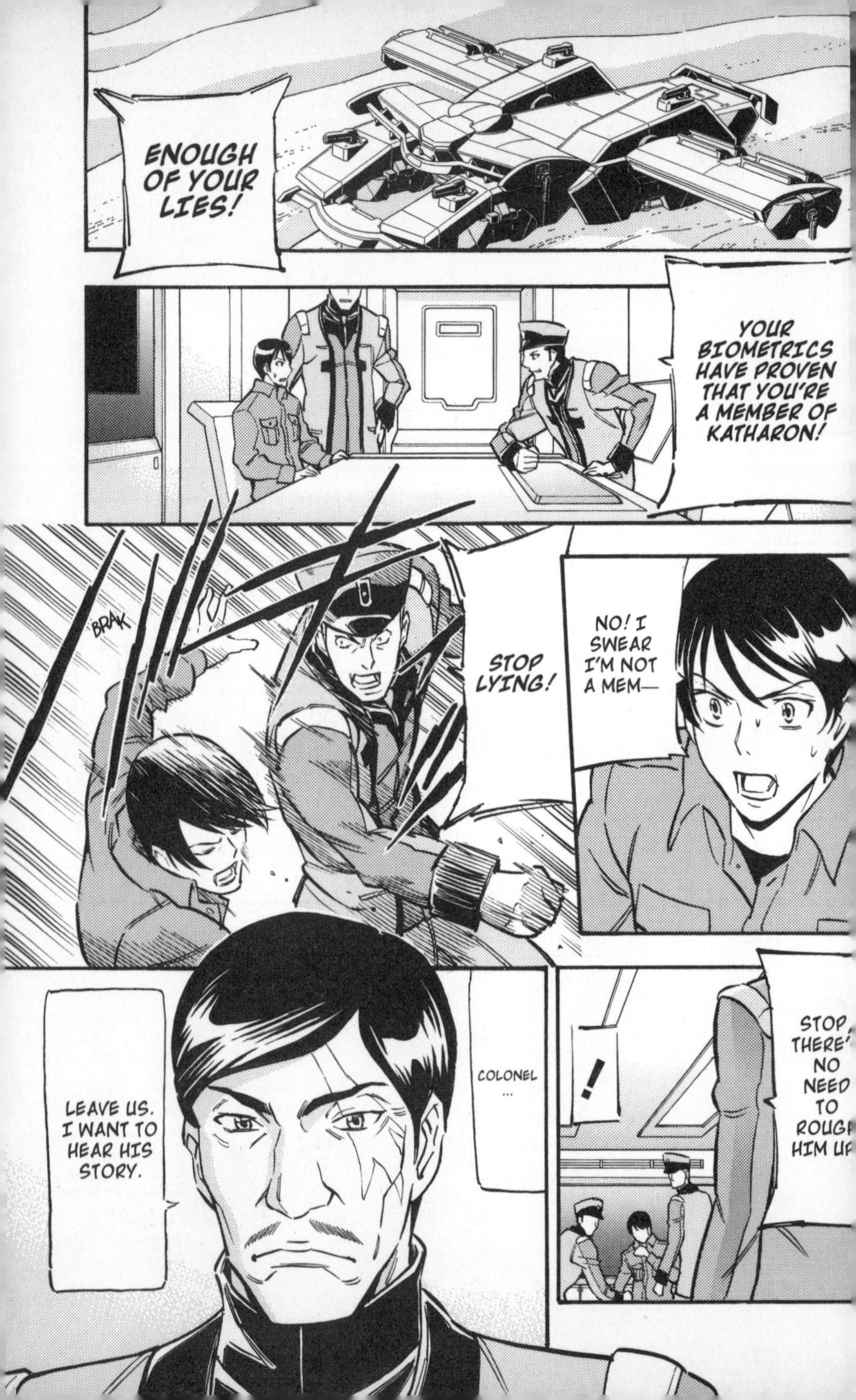
ENOUGH OF YOUR LIES!
YOUR BIOMETRICS HAVE PROVEN THAT YOU'RE A MEMBER OF KATHARON!
NO! I SWEAR I'M NOT A MEM—
STOP LYING!
BRAK
STOP, THERE' NO NEED TO ROUG HIM U
!
COLONEL ...
LEAVE US. I WANT TO HEAR HIS STORY.

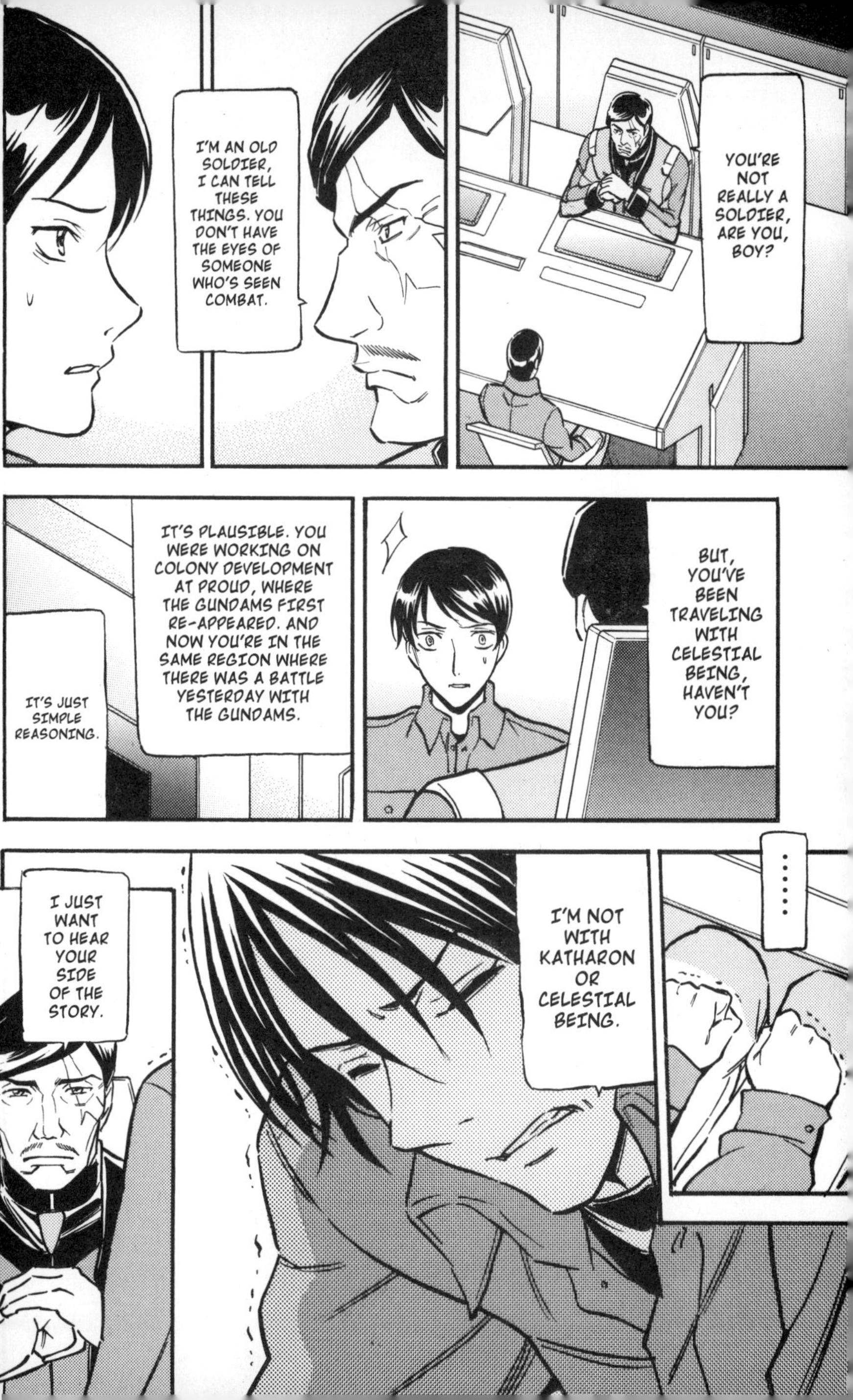
YOU'RE NOT REALLY A SOLDIER, ARE YOU, BOY?
I'M AN OLD SOLDIER, I CAN TELL THESE THINGS. YOU DON'T HAVE THE EYES OF SOMEONE WHO'S SEEN COMBAT.
BUT, YOU'VE BEEN TRAVELING WITH CELESTIAL BEING, HAVEN'T YOU?
IT'S PLAUSIBLE. YOU WERE WORKING ON COLONY DEVELOPMENT AT PROUD, WHERE THE GUNDAMS FIRST RE-APPEARED. AND NOW YOU'RE IN THE SAME REGION WHERE THERE WAS A BATTLE YESTERDAY WITH THE GUNDAMS.
IT'S JUST SIMPLE REASONING.
......
I'M NOT WITH KATHARON OR CELESTIAL BEING.
I JUST WANT TO HEAR YOUR SIDE OF THE STORY.

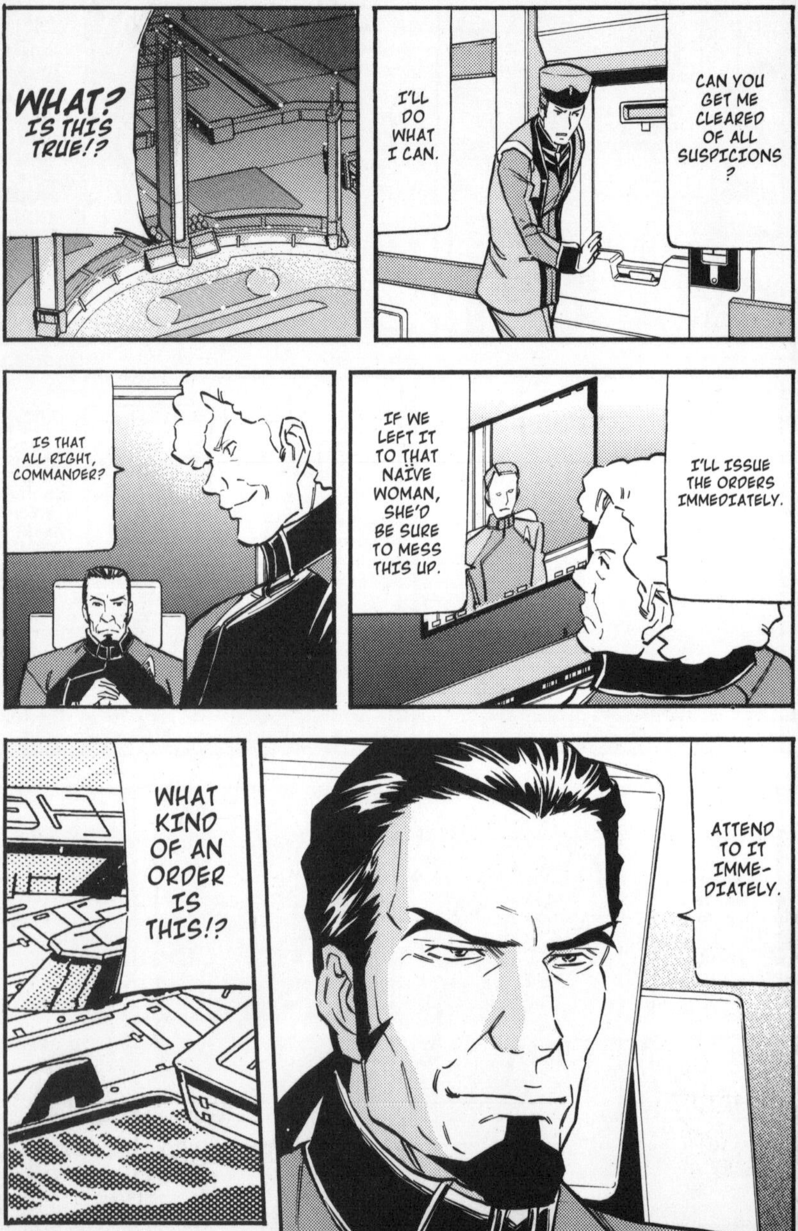
CAN YOU GET ME CLEARED OF ALL SUSPICIONS?
I'LL DO WHAT I CAN.
WHAT? IS THIS TRUE!?
I'LL ISSUE THE ORDERS IMMEDIATELY.
IF WE LEFT IT TO THAT NAÏVE WOMAN, SHE'D BE SURE TO MESS THIS UP.
IS THAT ALL RIGHT, COMMANDER?
ATTEND TO IT IMME-DIATELY.
WHAT KIND OF AN ORDER IS THIS!?

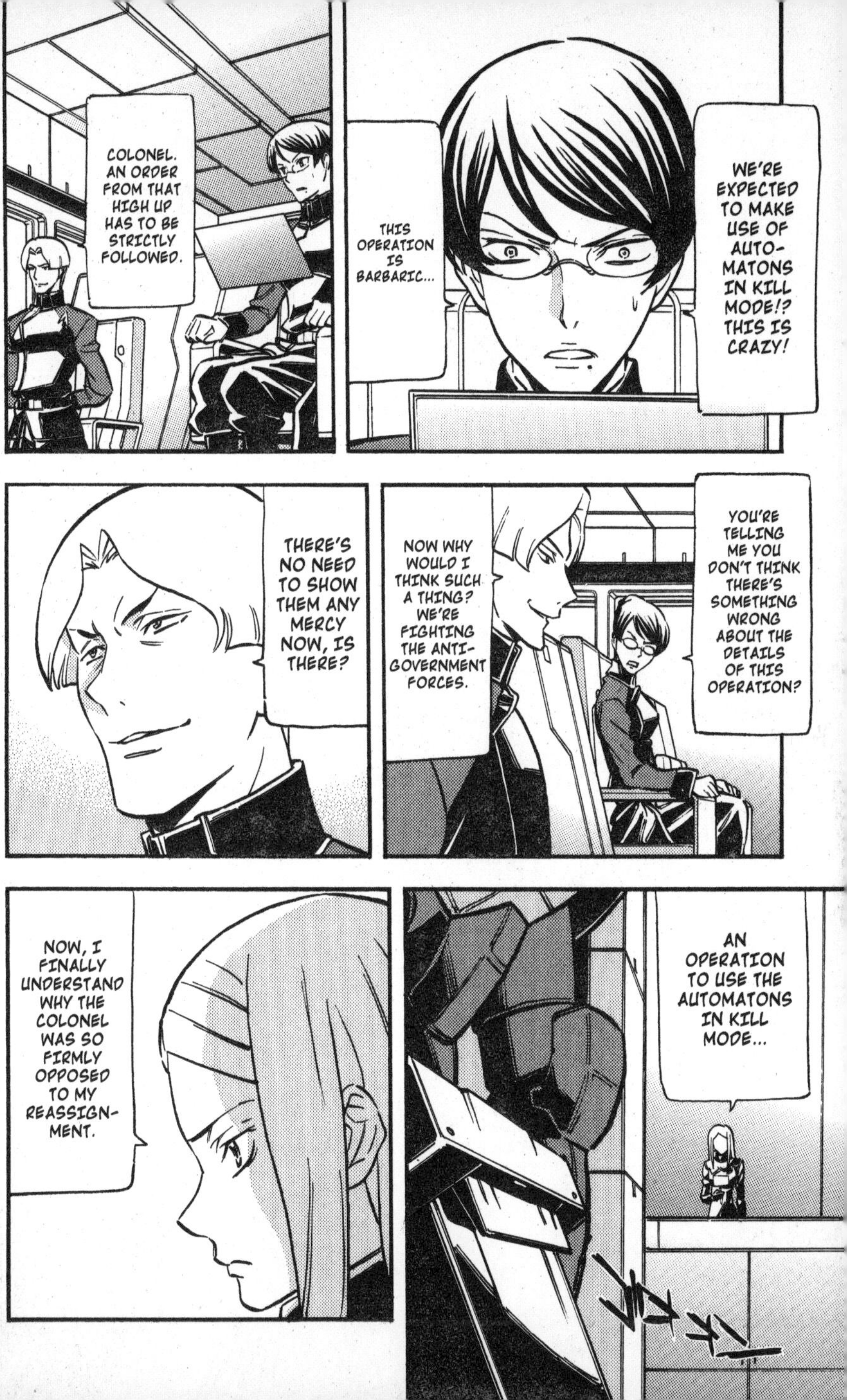
WE'RE EXPECTED TO MAKE USE OF AUTO-MATONS IN KILL MODE!? THIS IS CRAZY!
THIS OPERATION IS BARBARIC...
COLONEL. AN ORDER FROM THAT HIGH UP HAS TO BE STRICTLY FOLLOWED.
YOU'RE TELLING ME YOU DON'T THINK THERE'S SOMETHING WRONG ABOUT THE DETAILS OF THIS OPERATION?
NOW WHY WOULD I THINK SUCH A THING? WE'RE FIGHTING THE ANTI-GOVERNMENT FORCES.
THERE'S NO NEED TO SHOW THEM ANY MERCY NOW, IS THERE?
AN OPERATION TO USE THE AUTOMATONS IN KILL MODE...
NOW, I FINALLY UNDERSTAND WHY THE COLONEL WAS SO FIRMLY OPPOSED TO MY REASSIGN-MENT.

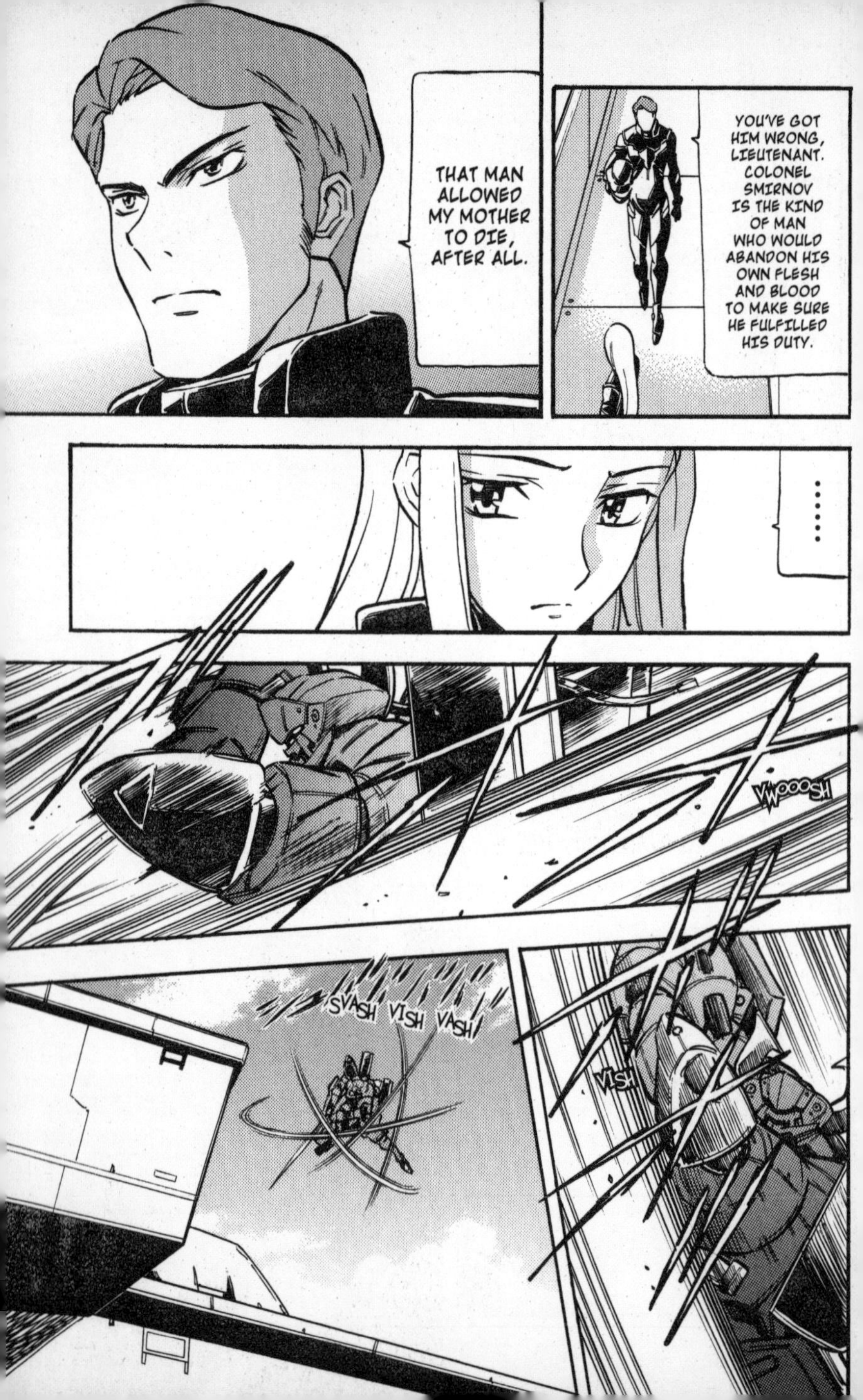
YOU'VE GOT HIM WRONG, LIEUTENANT. COLONEL SMIRNOV IS THE KIND OF MAN WHO WOULD ABANDON HIS OWN FLESH AND BLOOD TO MAKE SURE HE FULFILLED HIS DUTY.
THAT MAN ALLOWED MY MOTHER TO DIE, AFTER ALL.
......
VWOOOSH
VISH
SVASH VISH VASH

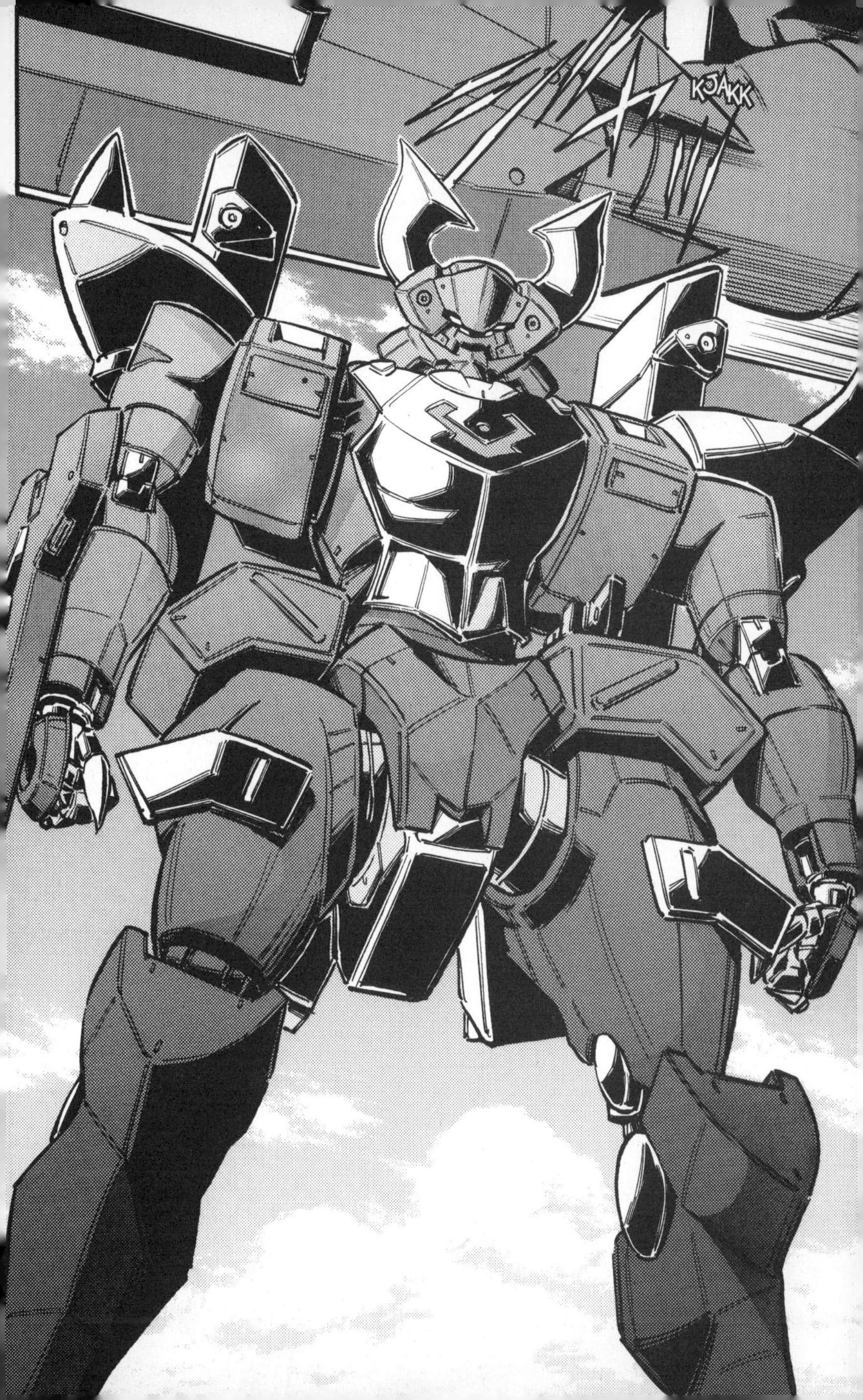
KJAKK

WHAT DO YOU THINK YOU'RE DOING, MR. BUSHIDO?

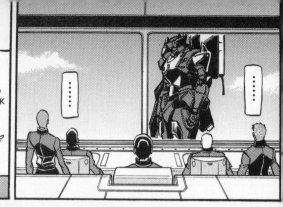

I'LL DEAL WITH THE "DOUBLE POWERED" GUNDAM WITH THE SHOULDER ENGINES MYSELF.

NO ONE IS TO ASSIST OR INTERFERE WITH ME!

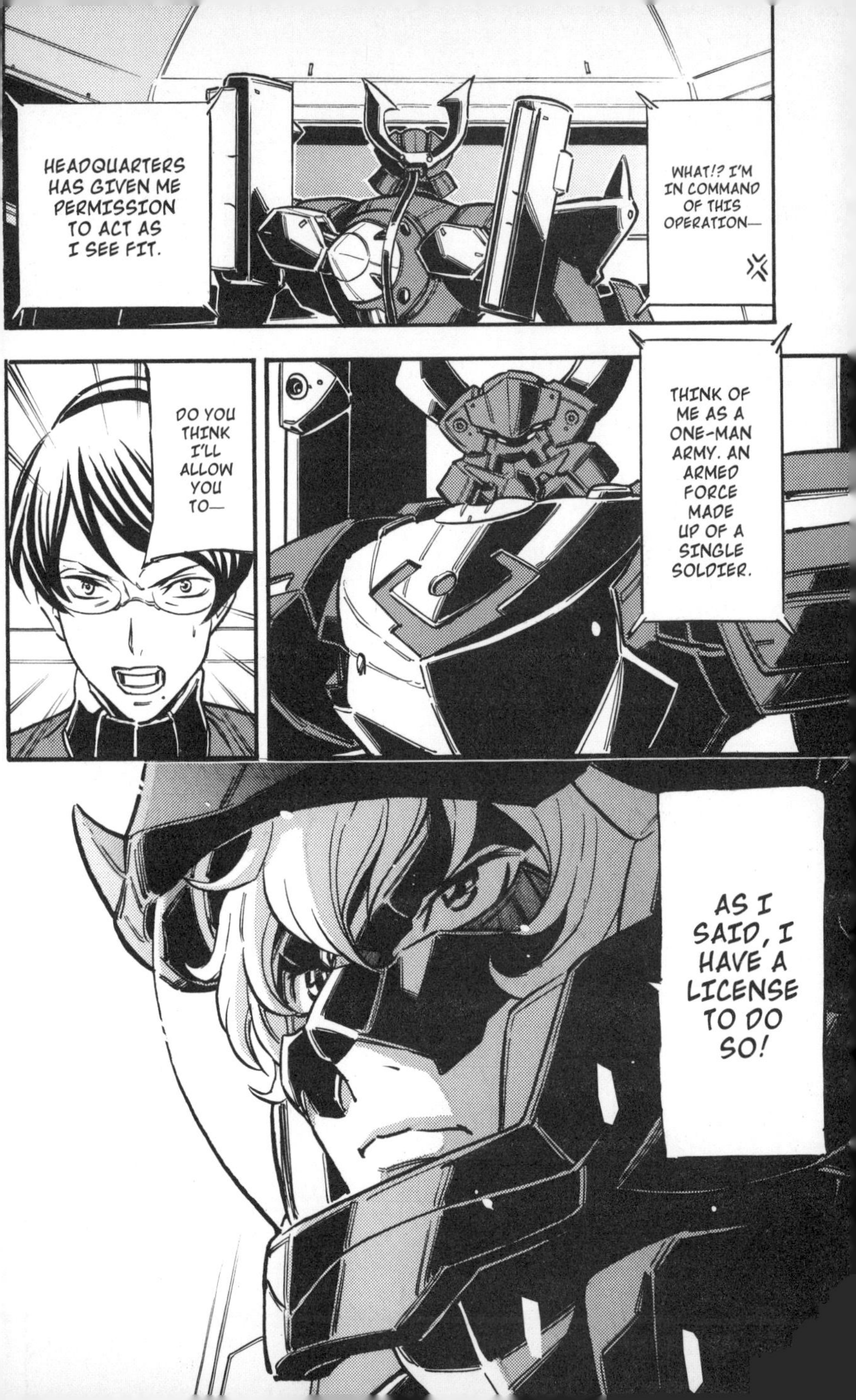
WHAT!? I'M IN COMMAND OF THIS OPERATION—
HEADQUARTERS HAS GIVEN ME PERMISSION TO ACT AS I SEE FIT.
THINK OF ME AS A ONE-MAN ARMY. AN ARMED FORCE MADE UP OF A SINGLE SOLDIER.
DO YOU THINK I'LL ALLOW YOU TO—
AS I SAID, I HAVE A LICENSE TO DO SO!

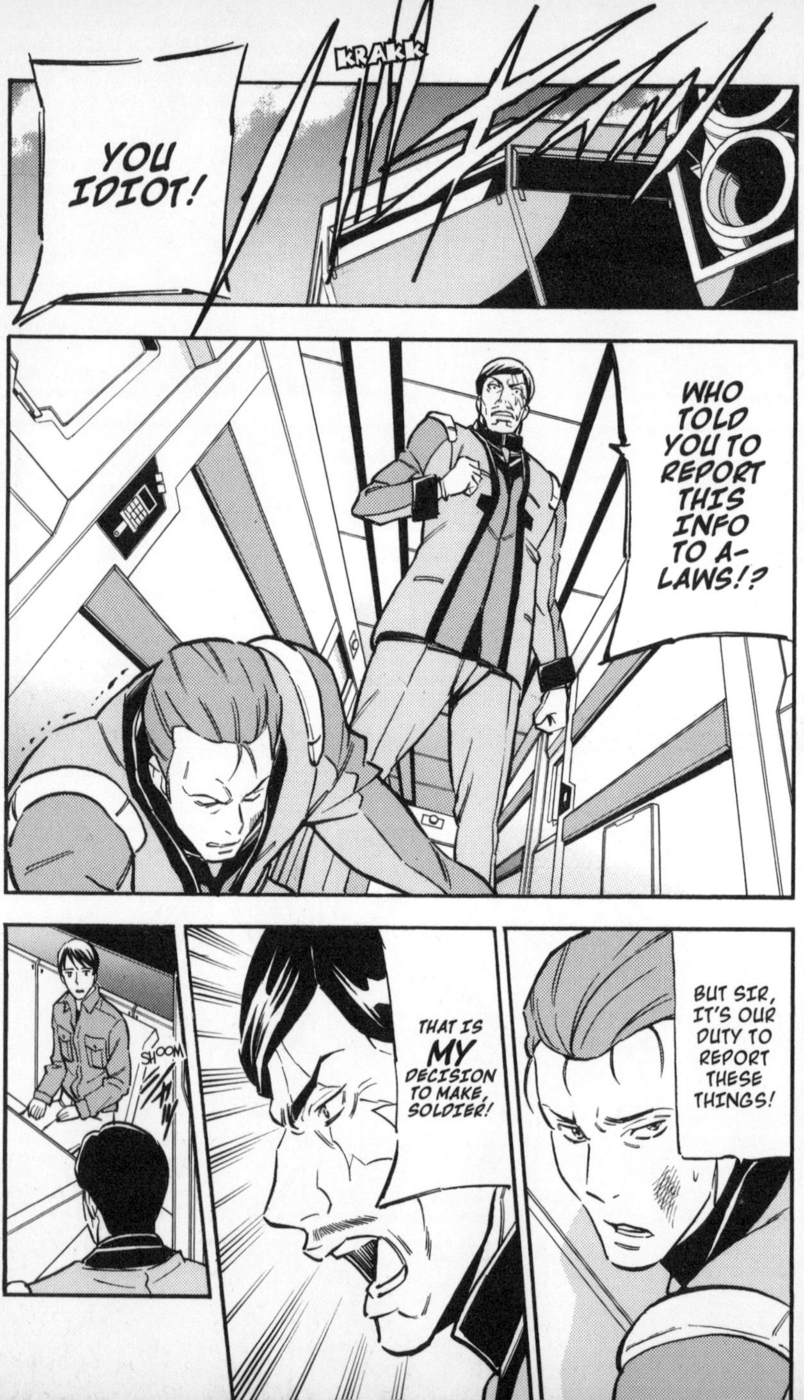
KRAKK
YOU IDIOT!
WHO TOLD YOU TO REPORT THIS INFO TO A-LAWS!?
BUT SIR, IT'S OUR DUTY TO REPORT THESE THINGS!
THAT IS MY DECISION TO MAKE, SOLDIER!
SHOOM

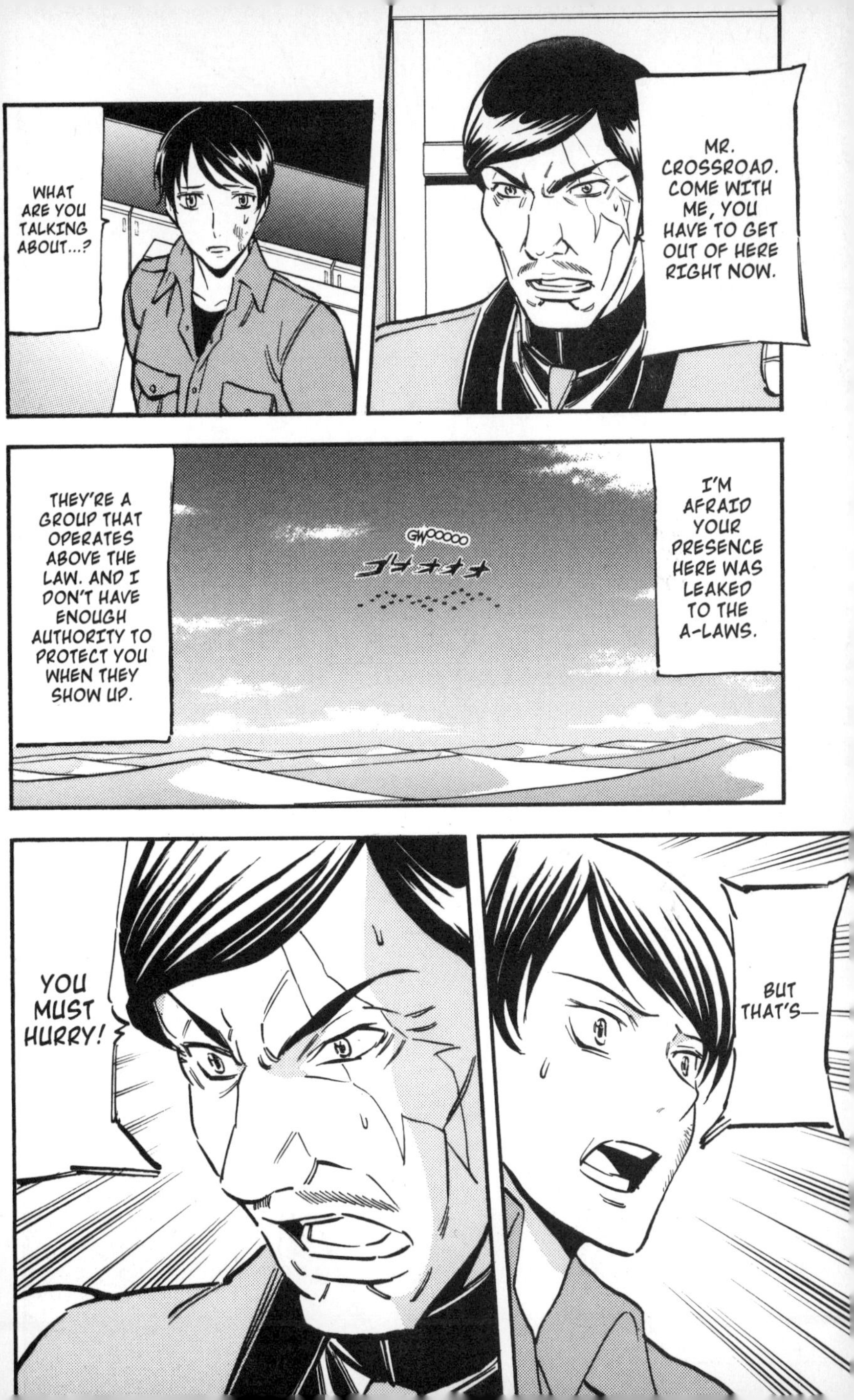
MR. CROSSROAD. COME WITH ME, YOU HAVE TO GET OUT OF HERE RIGHT NOW.
WHAT ARE YOU TALKING ABOUT...?
I'M AFRAID YOUR PRESENCE HERE WAS LEAKED TO THE A-LAWS.
GWOOOOO
THEY'RE A GROUP THAT OPERATES ABOVE THE LAW. AND I DON'T HAVE ENOUGH AUTHORITY TO PROTECT YOU WHEN THEY SHOW UP.
BUT THAT'S—
YOU MUST HURRY!

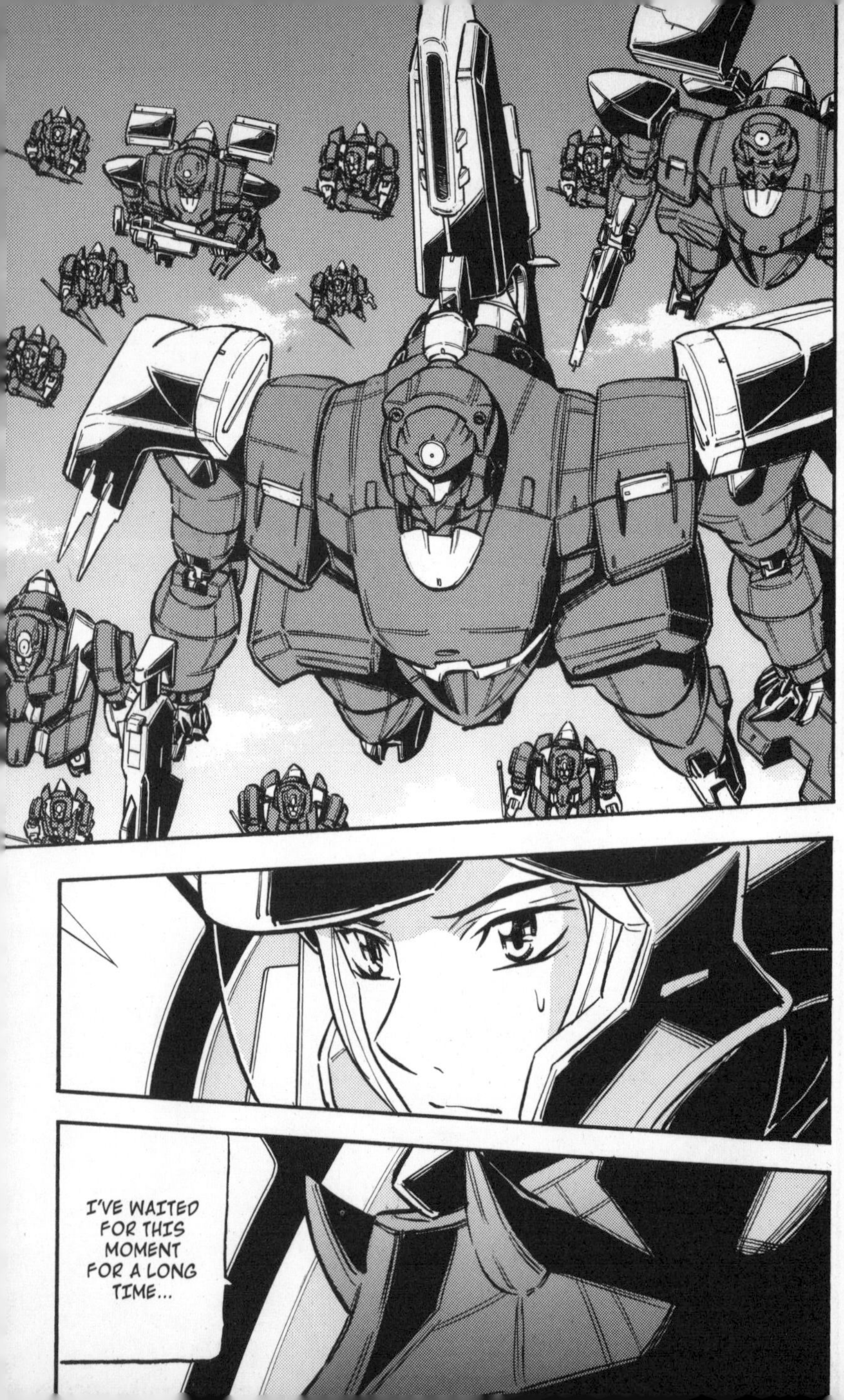
I'VE WAITED FOR THIS MOMENT FOR A LONG TIME...

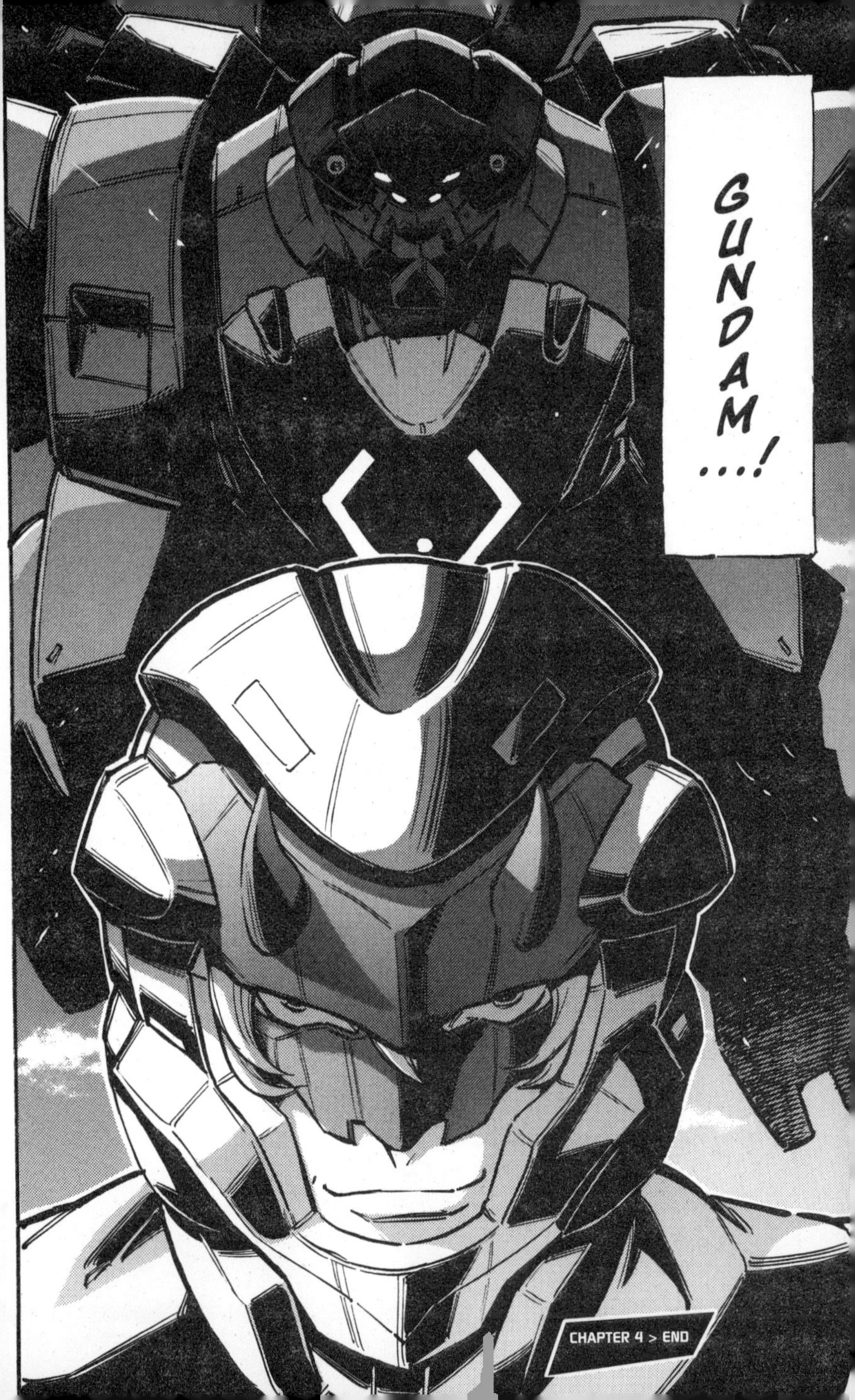
GUNDAM ...!
CHAPTER 4 > END

MOBILE SUIT GUNDAM 00 DOUBLE-O

機動戦士ガンダム

SECOND SEASON

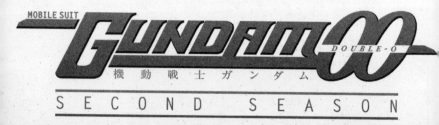

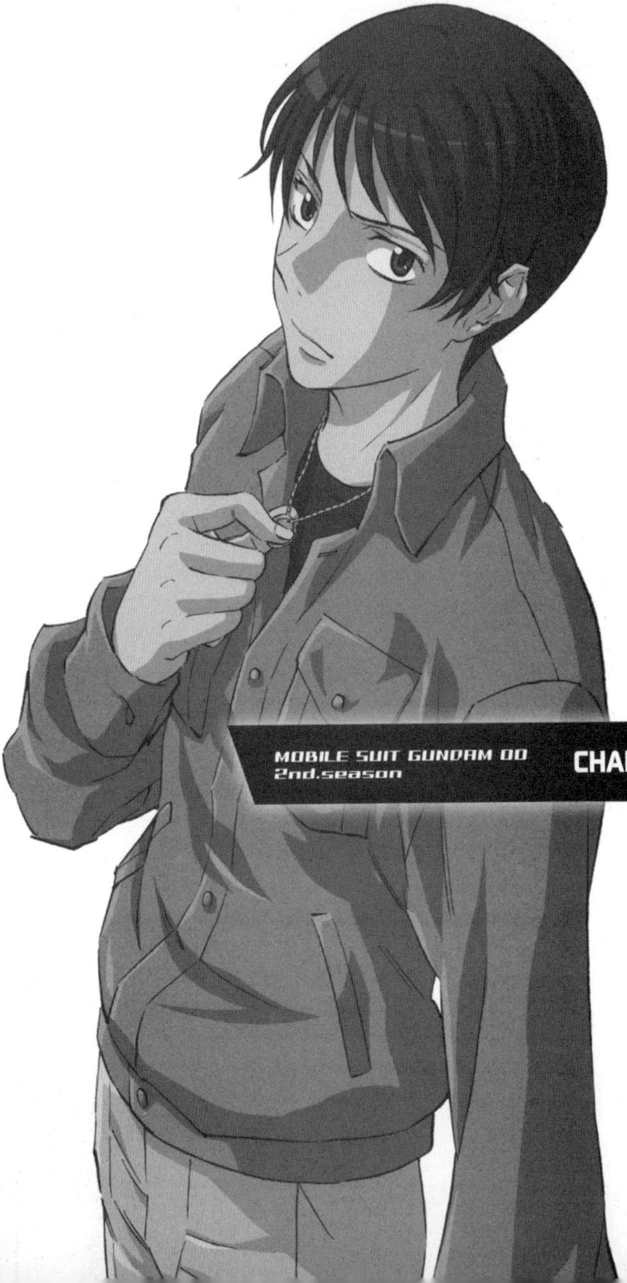

MOBILE SUIT GUNDAM 00
2nd.season

CHAPTER 5 > SCARS

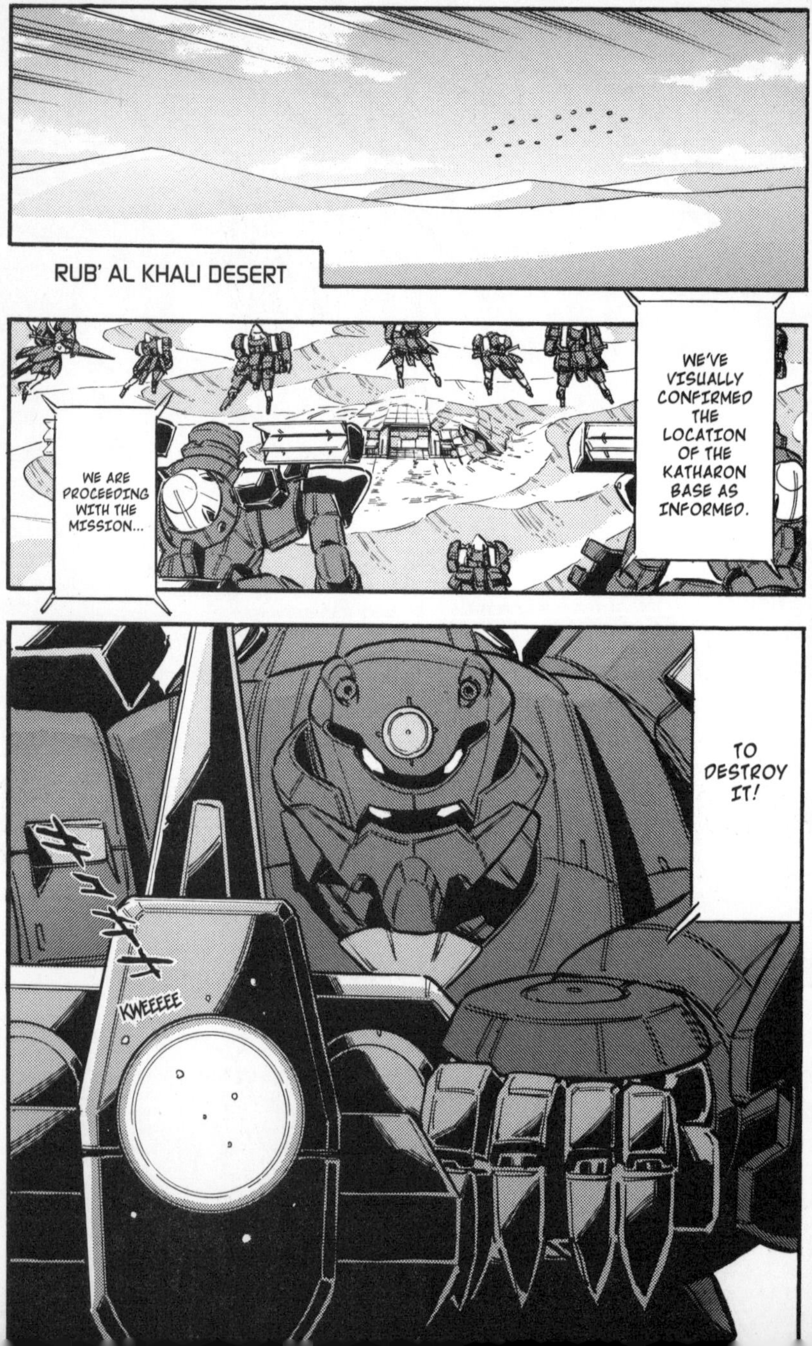
RUB' AL KHALI DESERT
WE'VE VISUALLY CONFIRMED THE LOCATION OF THE KATHARON BASE AS INFORMED.
WE ARE PROCEEDING WITH THE MISSION...
TO DESTROY IT!
KWEEEEE

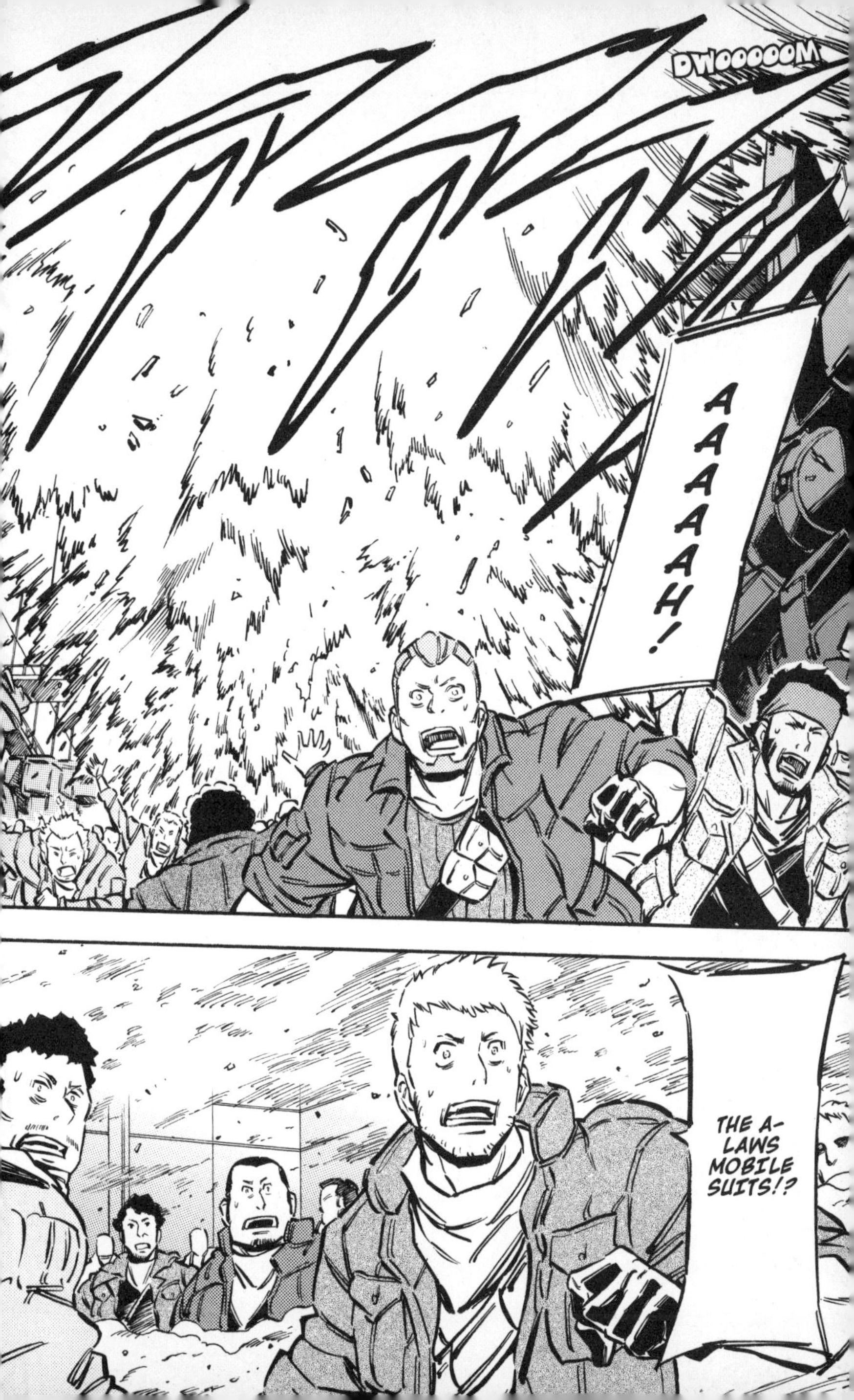
DWOOOOOM
AAAAAAH!
THE A-LAWS MOBILE SUITS!?

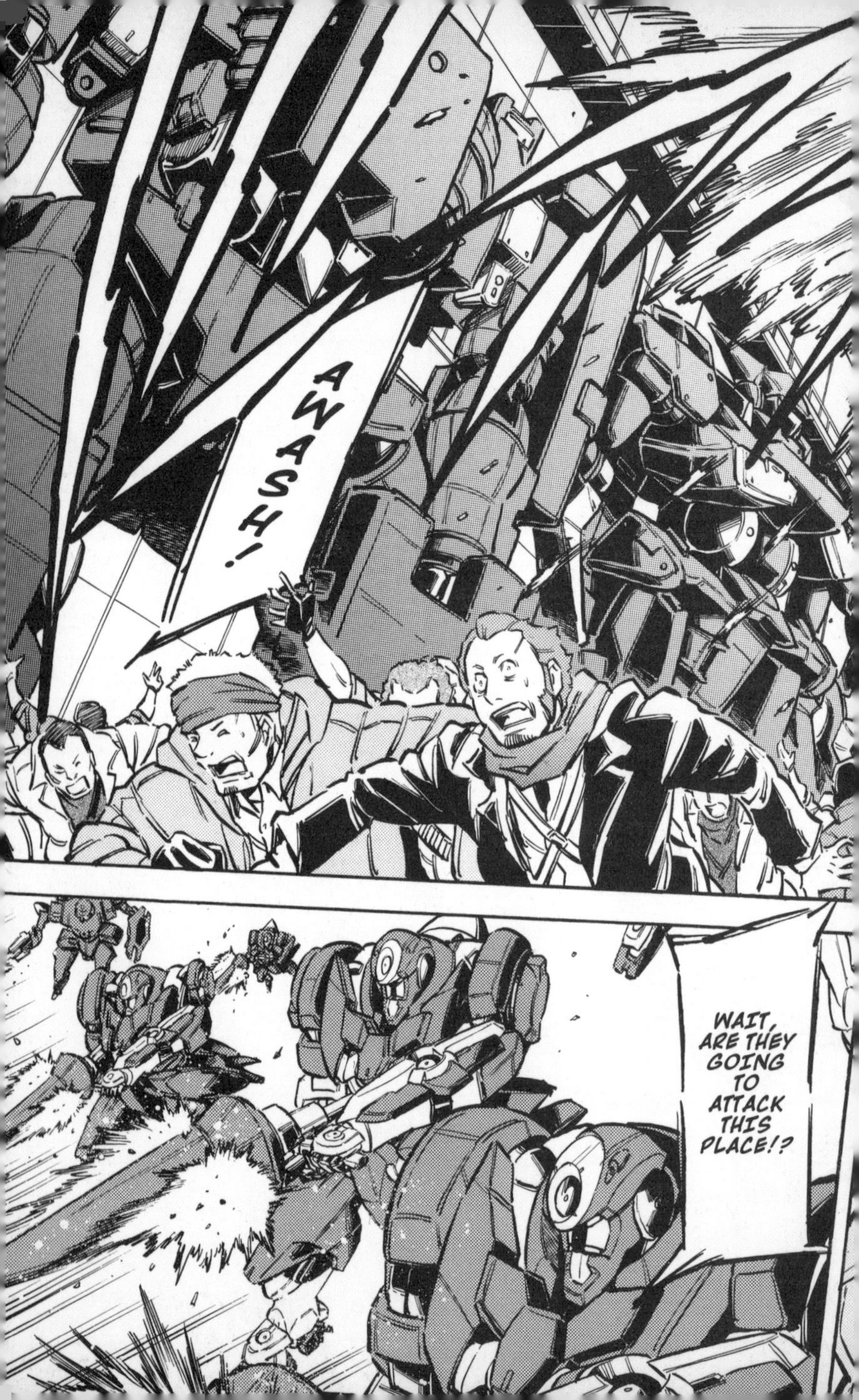
AWASH!
WAIT, ARE THEY GOING TO ATTACK THIS PLACE!?

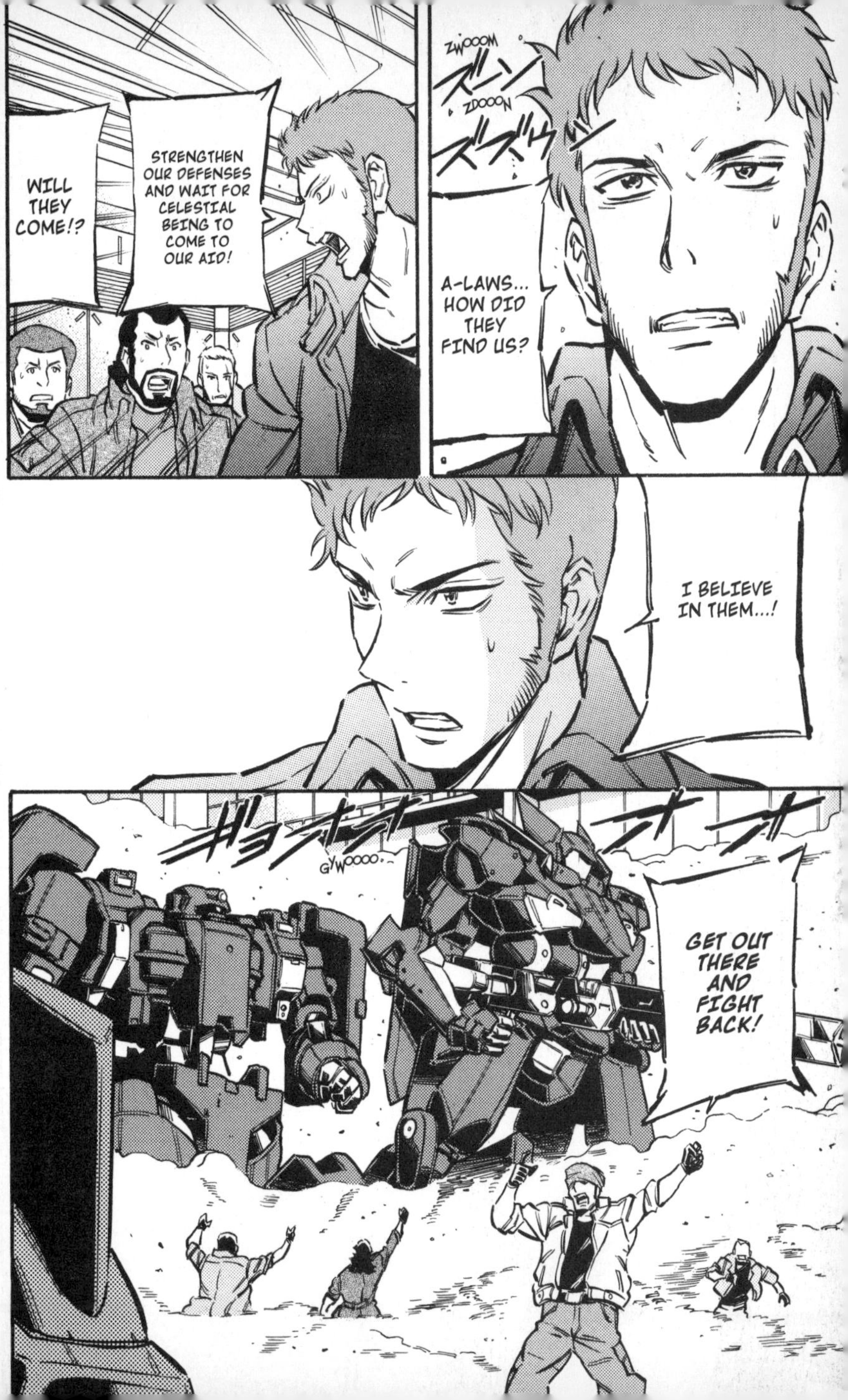
ZWOOOM
ズーン
ZDOOON
A-LAWS... HOW DID THEY FIND US?
STRENGTHEN OUR DEFENSES AND WAIT FOR CELESTIAL BEING TO COME TO OUR AID!
WILL THEY COME!?
I BELIEVE IN THEM...!
GYWOOOO...
GET OUT THERE AND FIGHT BACK!

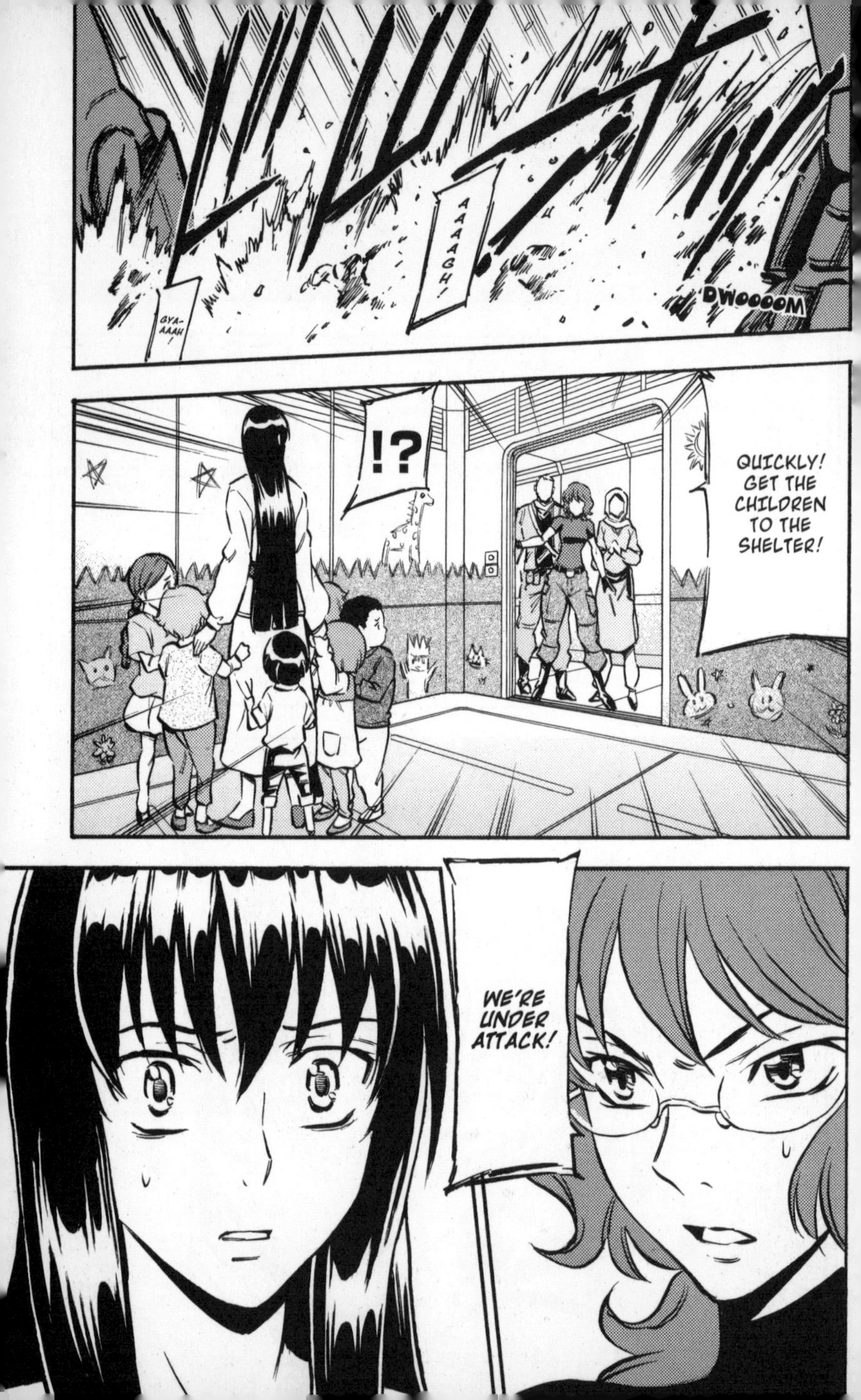
DWOOOOM
AAAAGH!
GYA-AAAH!
QUICKLY! GET THE CHILDREN TO THE SHELTER!
!?
WE'RE UNDER ATTACK!

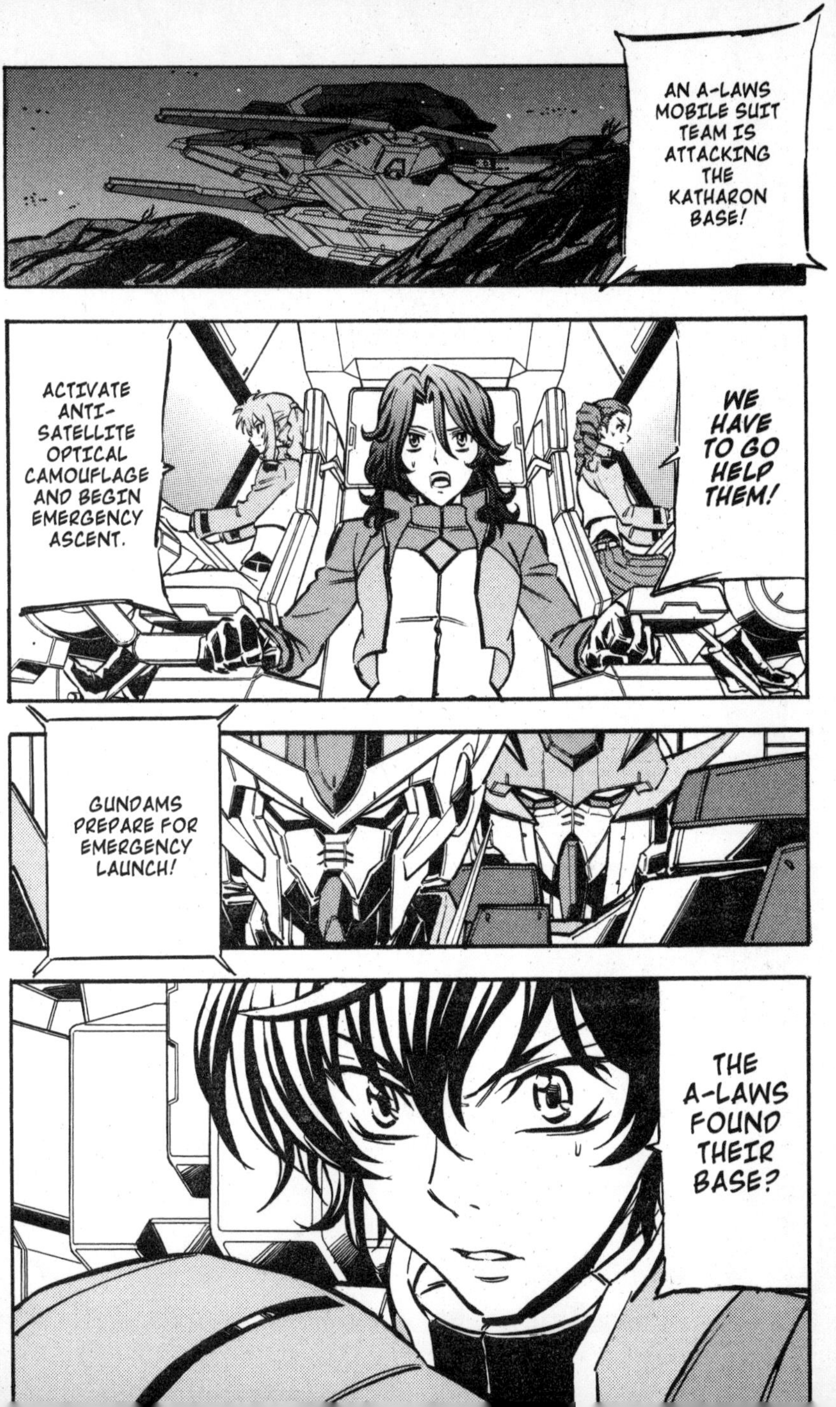
AN A-LAWS MOBILE SUIT TEAM IS ATTACKING THE KATHARON BASE!
WE HAVE TO GO HELP THEM!
ACTIVATE ANTI-SATELLITE OPTICAL CAMOUFLAGE AND BEGIN EMERGENCY ASCENT.
GUNDAMS PREPARE FOR EMERGENCY LAUNCH!
THE A-LAWS FOUND THEIR BASE?

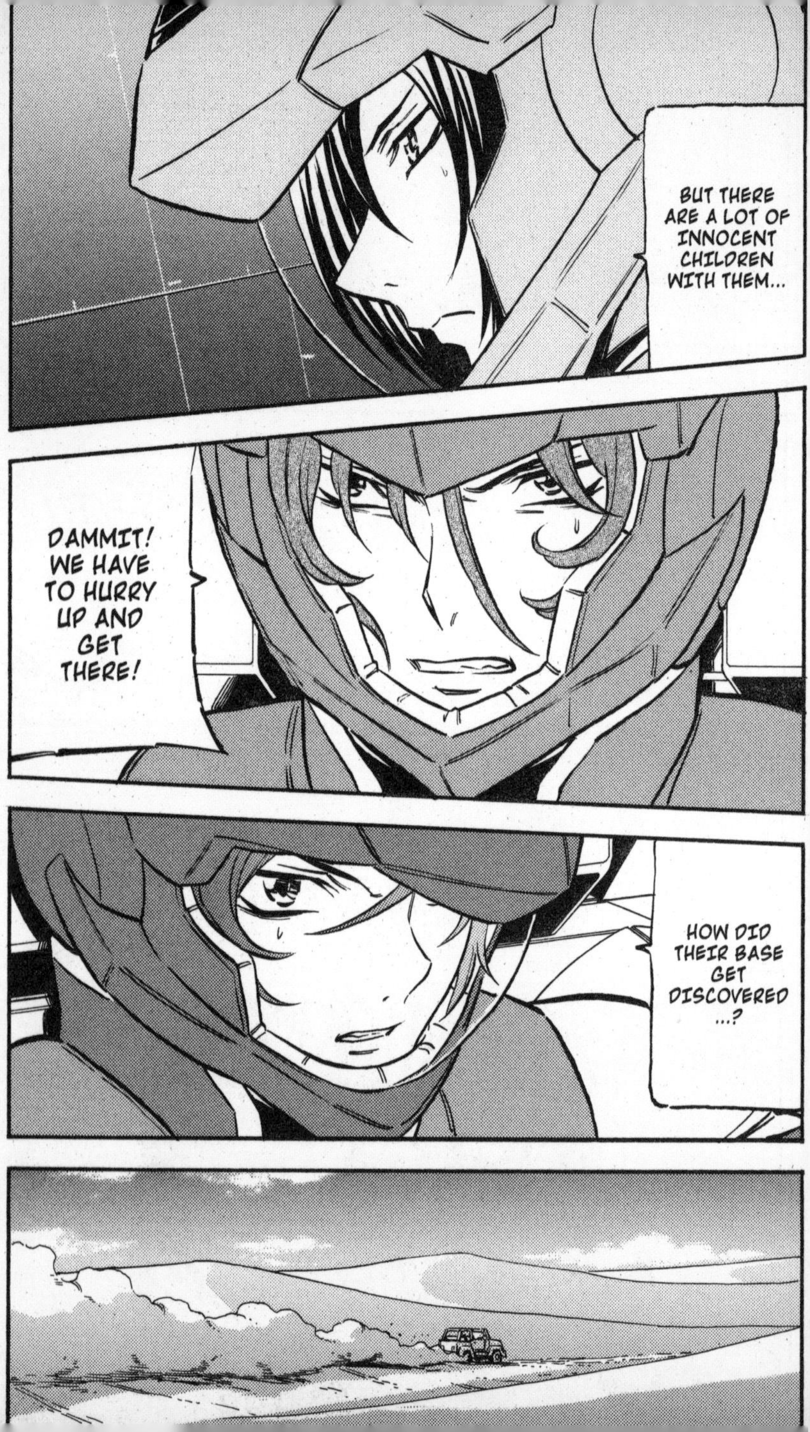
BUT THERE ARE A LOT OF INNOCENT CHILDREN WITH THEM...
DAMMIT! WE HAVE TO HURRY UP AND GET THERE!
HOW DID THEIR BASE GET DISCOVERED ...?

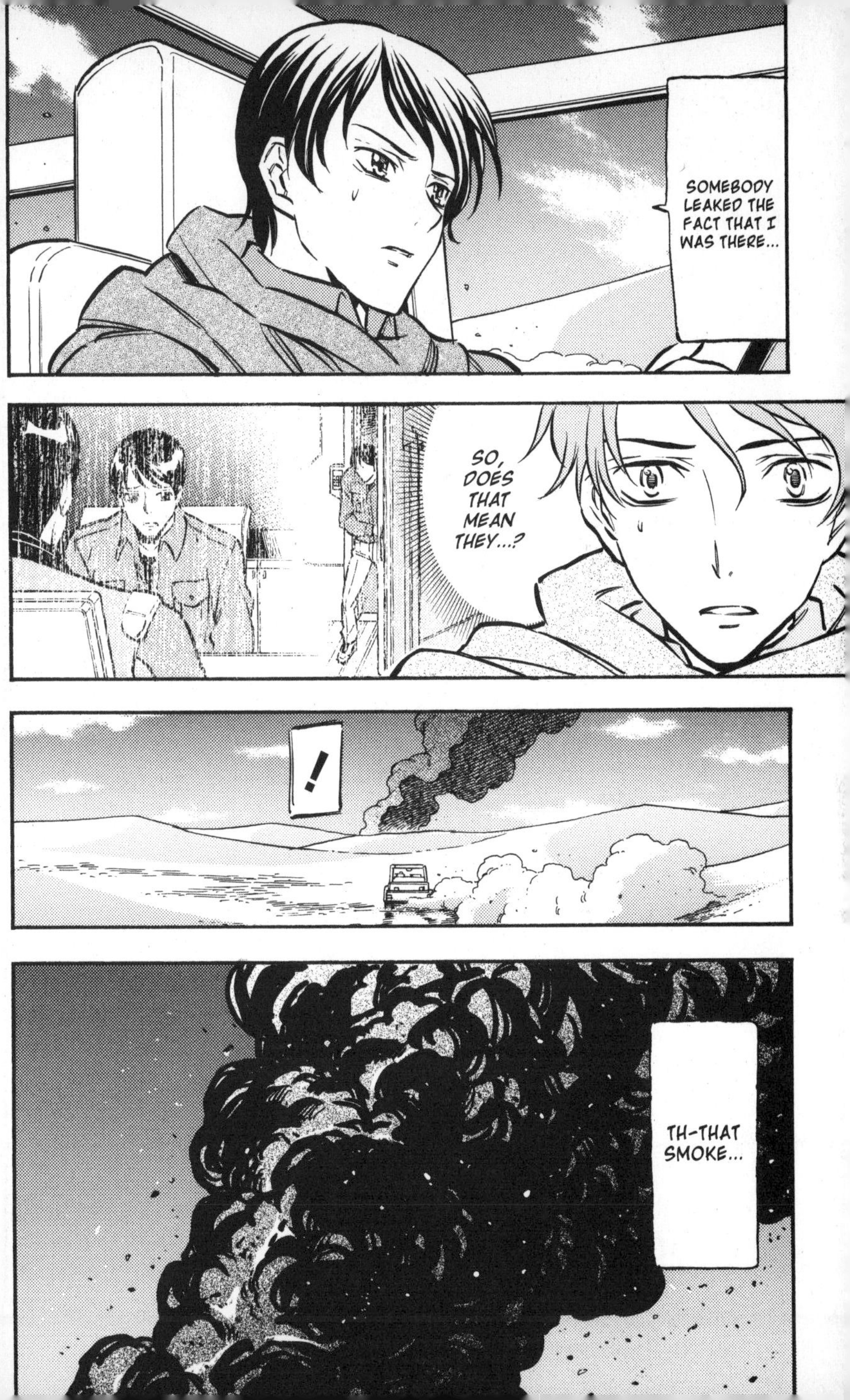
SOMEBODY LEAKED THE FACT THAT I WAS THERE...
SO, DOES THAT MEAN THEY...?
!
TH-THAT SMOKE...

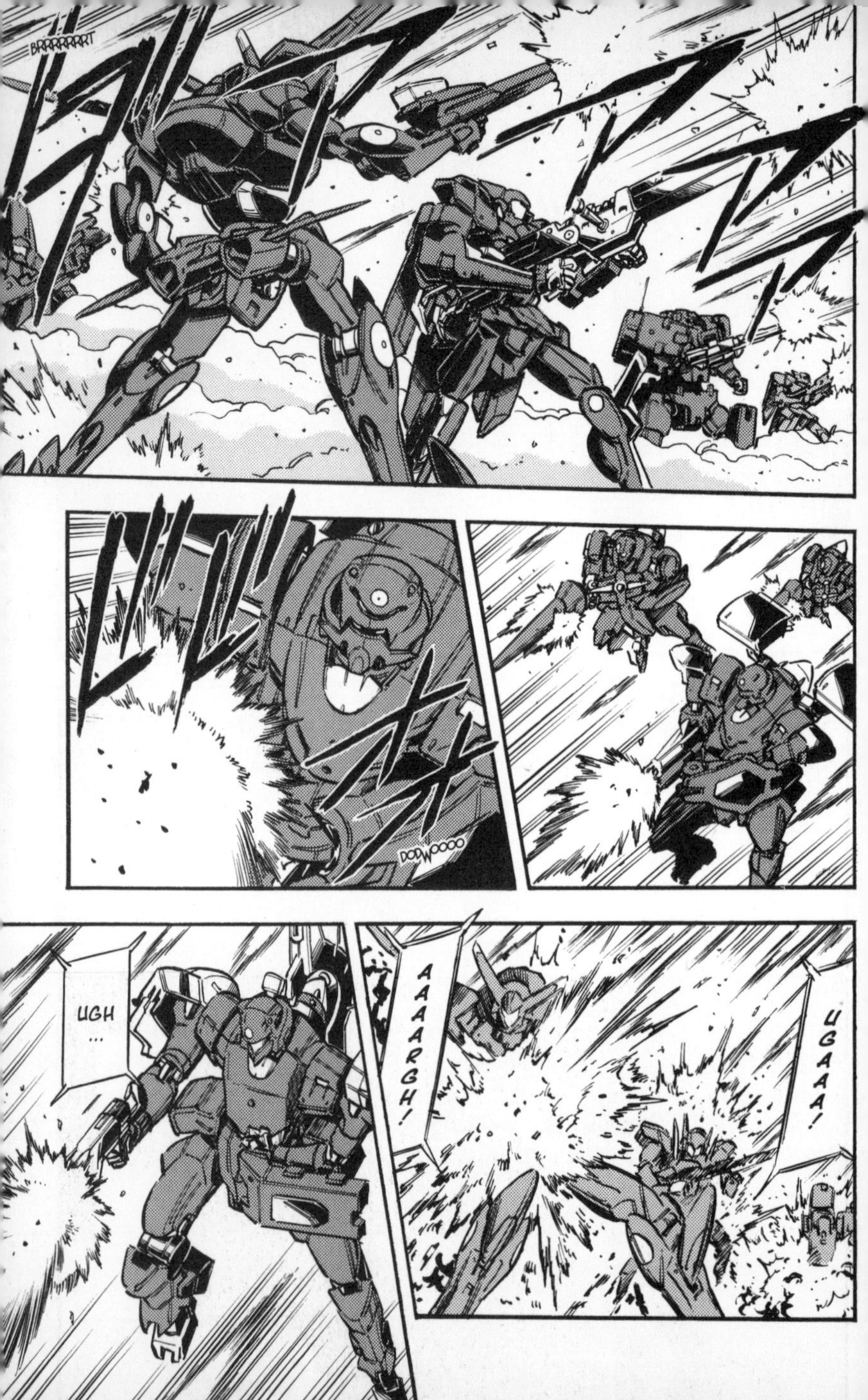
BRRRRRRRT
DODWOOOO
UGAAAA!
AAAARGH!
UGH ...

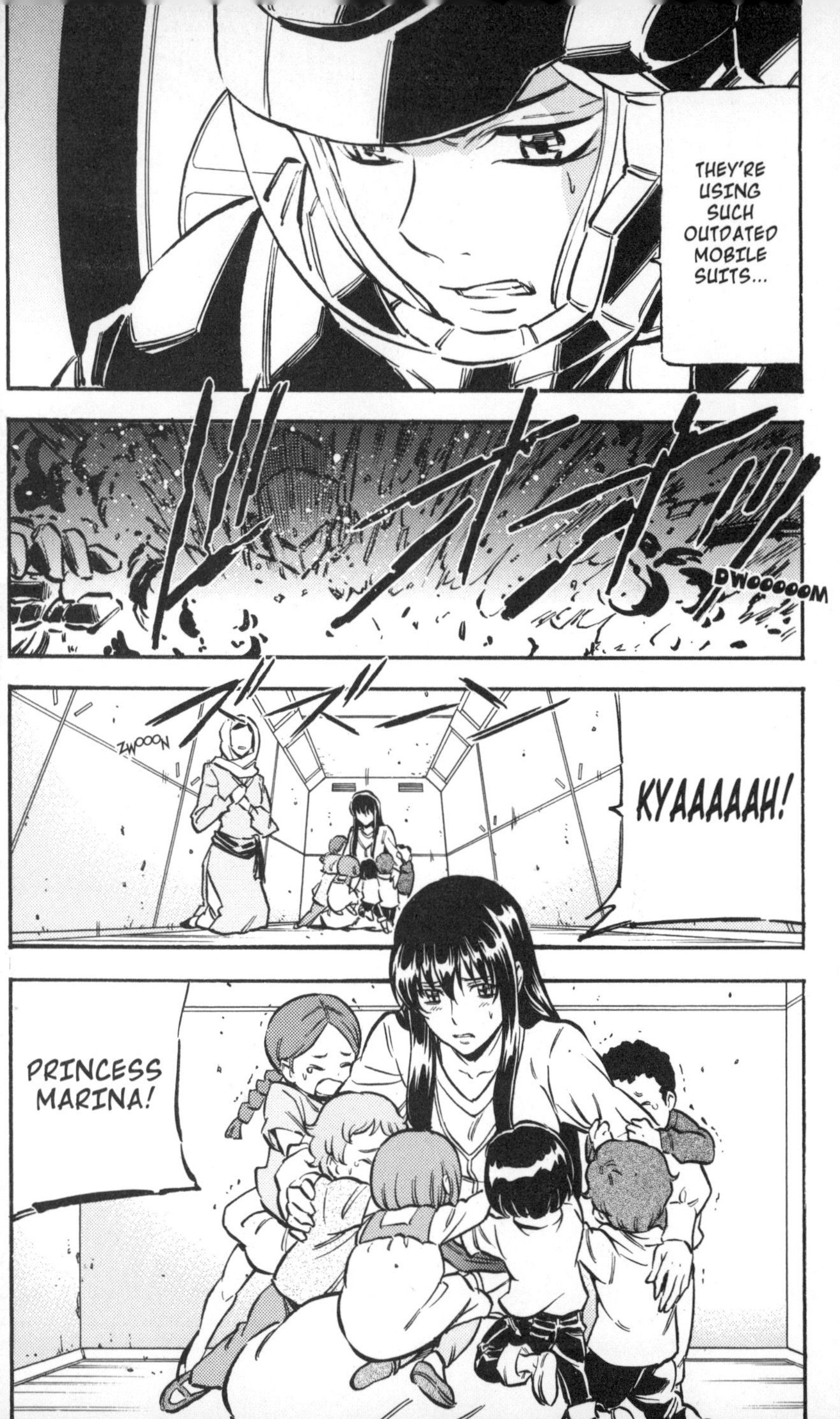
THEY'RE USING SUCH OUTDATED MOBILE SUITS...
DWOOOOOM
KYAAAAAH!
ZWOOON
PRINCESS MARINA!

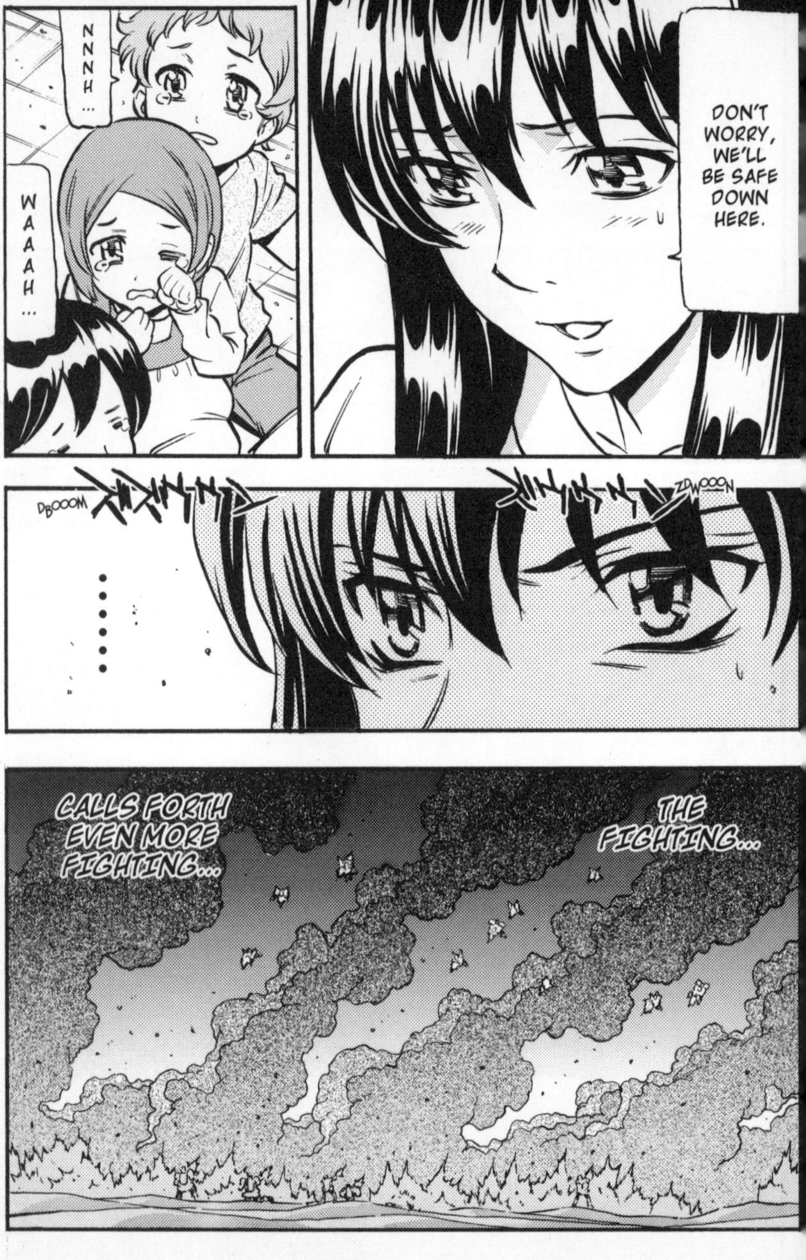
DON'T WORRY, WE'LL BE SAFE DOWN HERE.
NNNH...
WAAAAH...
ZDWOOON
DBOOOM
......
THE FIGHTING...
CALLS FORTH EVEN MORE FIGHTING...

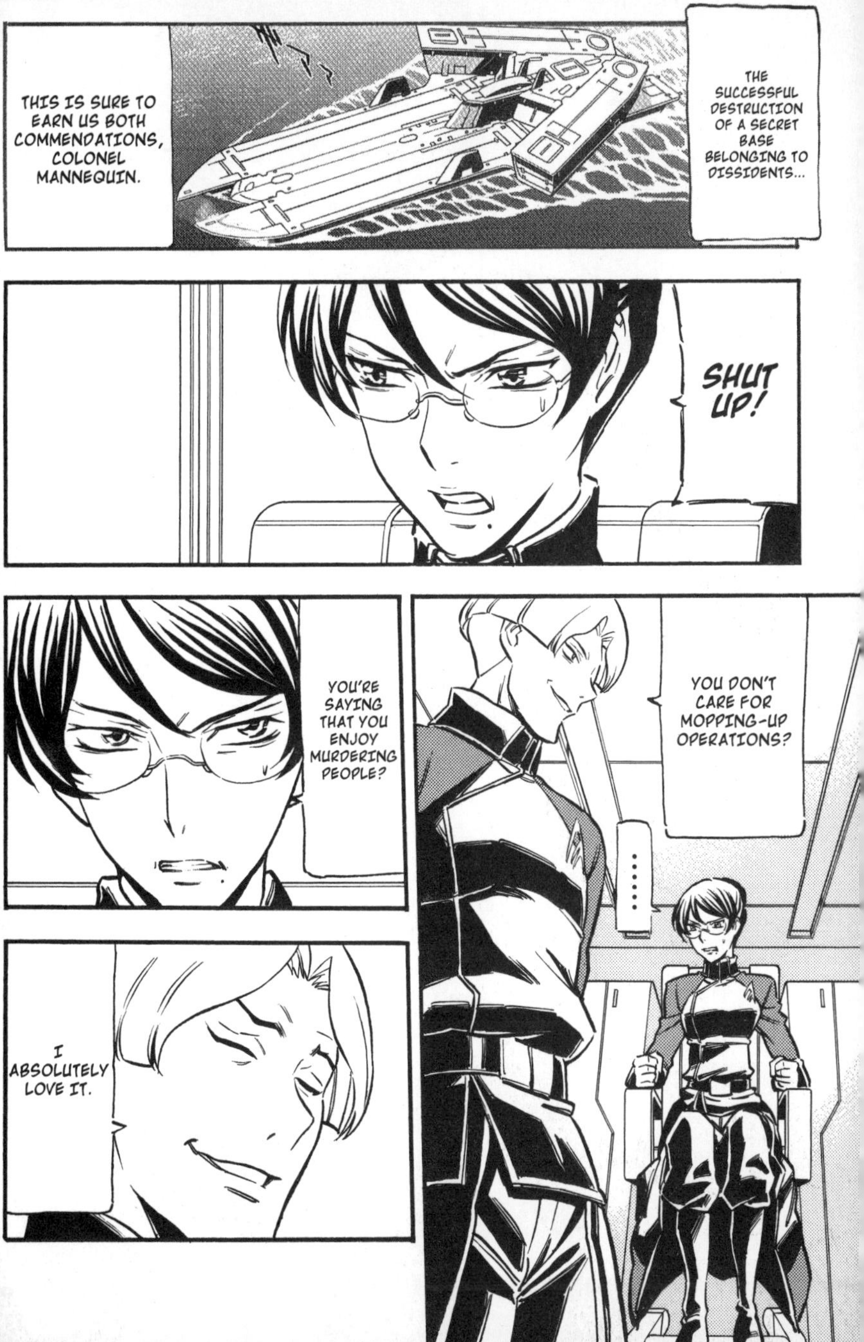
THE SUCCESSFUL DESTRUCTION OF A SECRET BASE BELONGING TO DISSIDENTS...
THIS IS SURE TO EARN US BOTH COMMENDATIONS, COLONEL MANNEQUIN.
SHUT UP!
YOU DON'T CARE FOR MOPPING-UP OPERATIONS?
......
YOU'RE SAYING THAT YOU ENJOY MURDERING PEOPLE?
I ABSOLUTELY LOVE IT.

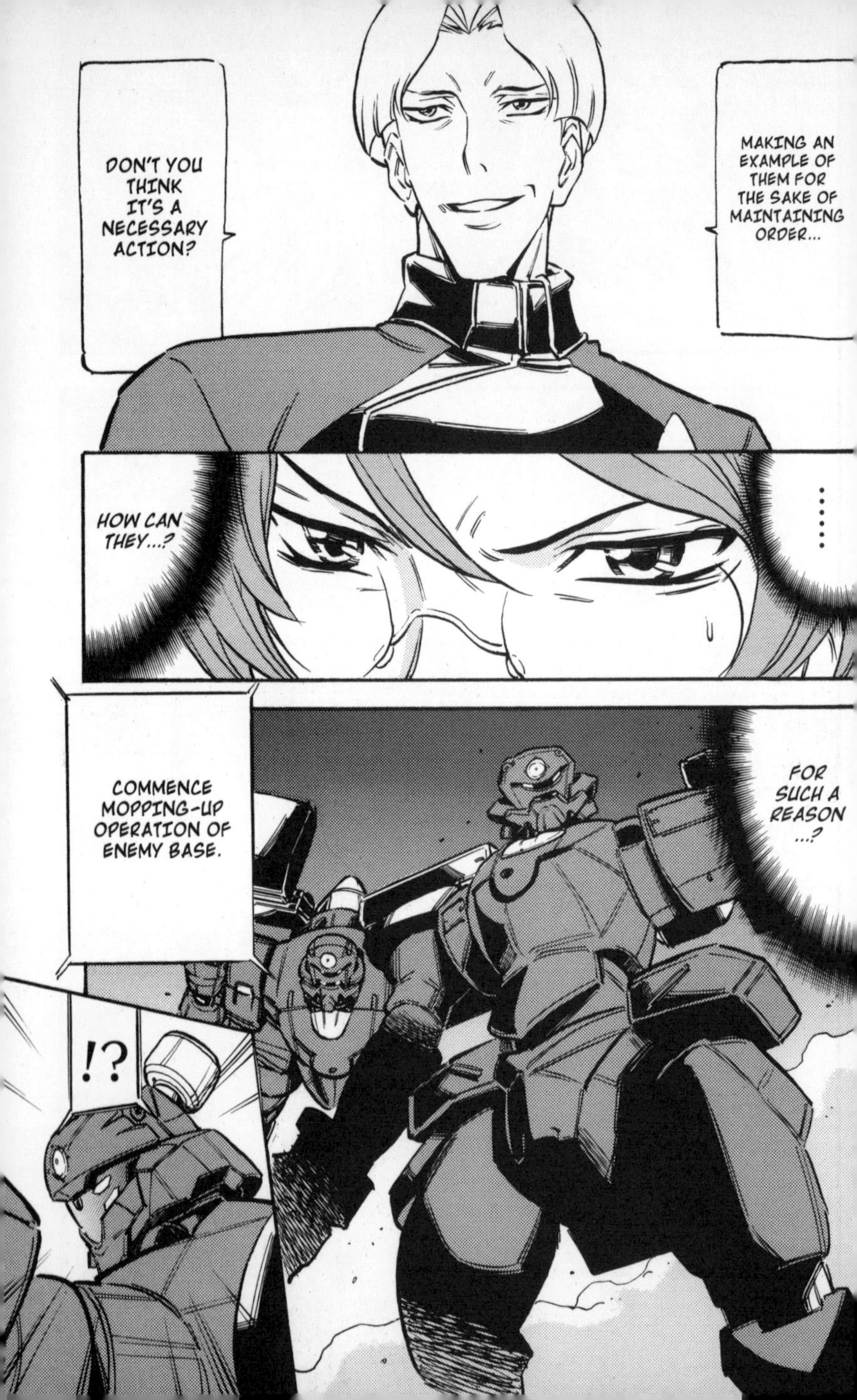
MAKING AN EXAMPLE OF THEM FOR THE SAKE OF MAINTAINING ORDER...
DON'T YOU THINK IT'S A NECESSARY ACTION?
......
HOW CAN THEY...?
FOR SUCH A REASON ...?
COMMENCE MOPPING-UP OPERATION OF ENEMY BASE.
!?

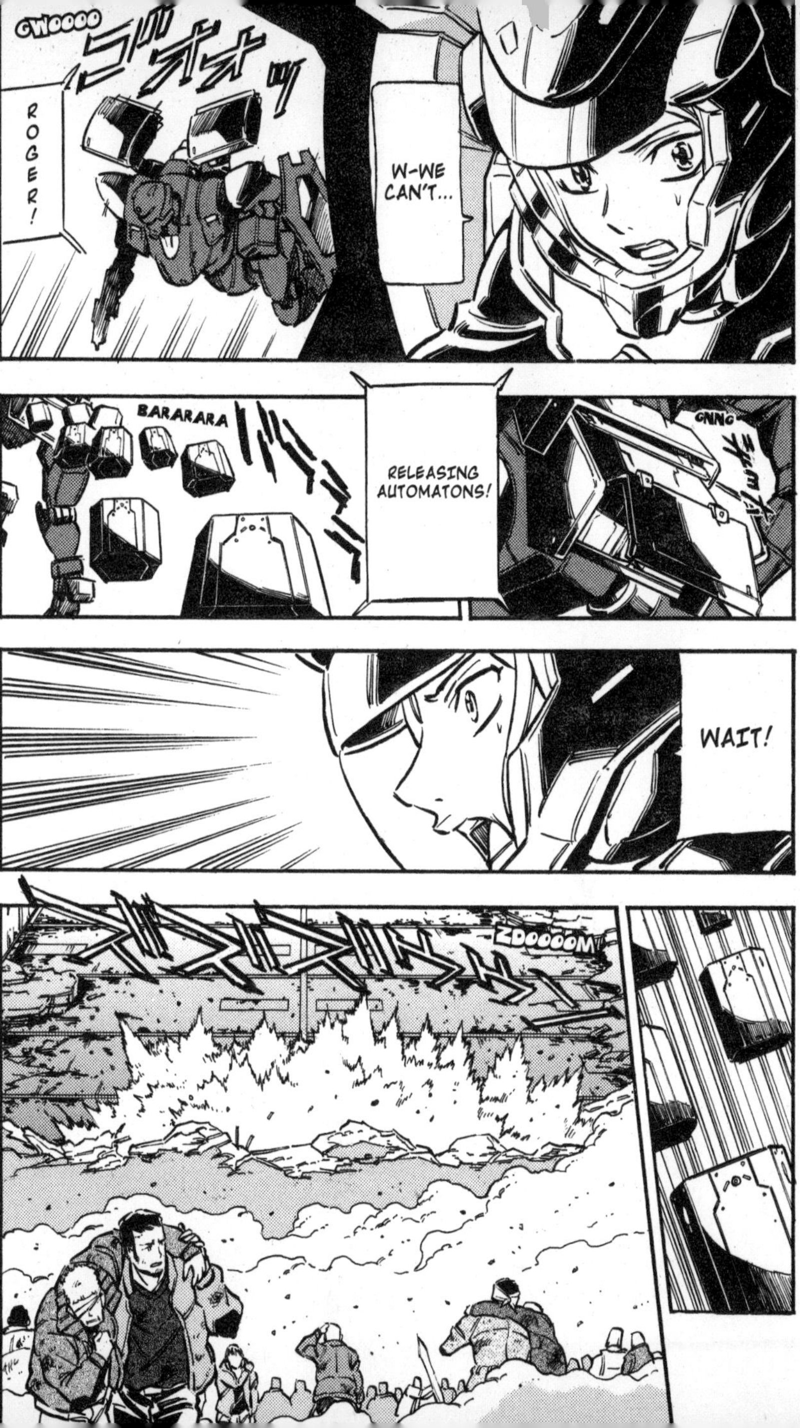
W-WE CAN'T...
GWOOOO
ROGER!
GNNG
RELEASING AUTOMATONS!
BARARARA
WAIT!
ZDOOOOM

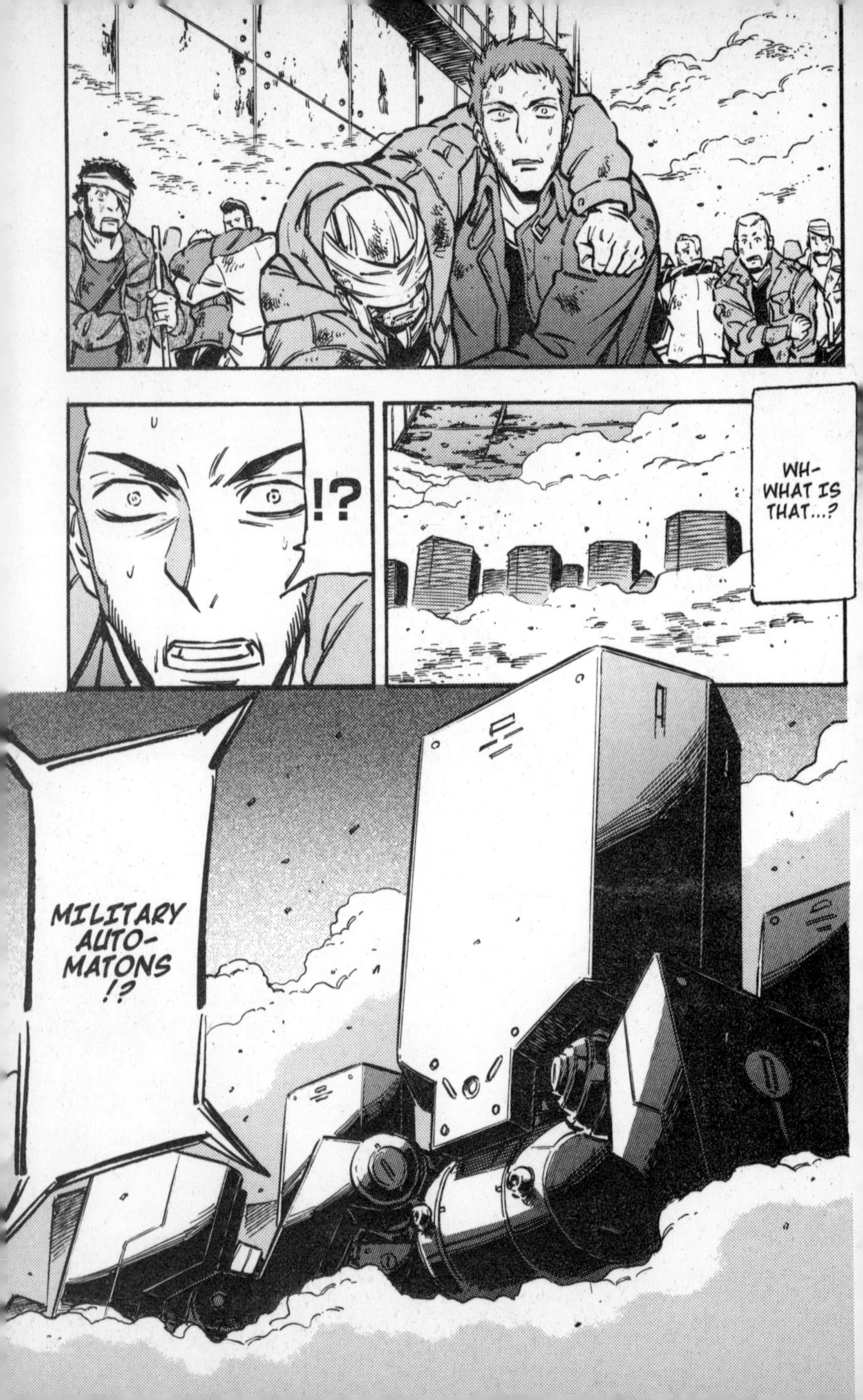
WH- WHAT IS THAT...?
!?
MILITARY AUTO-MATONS !?

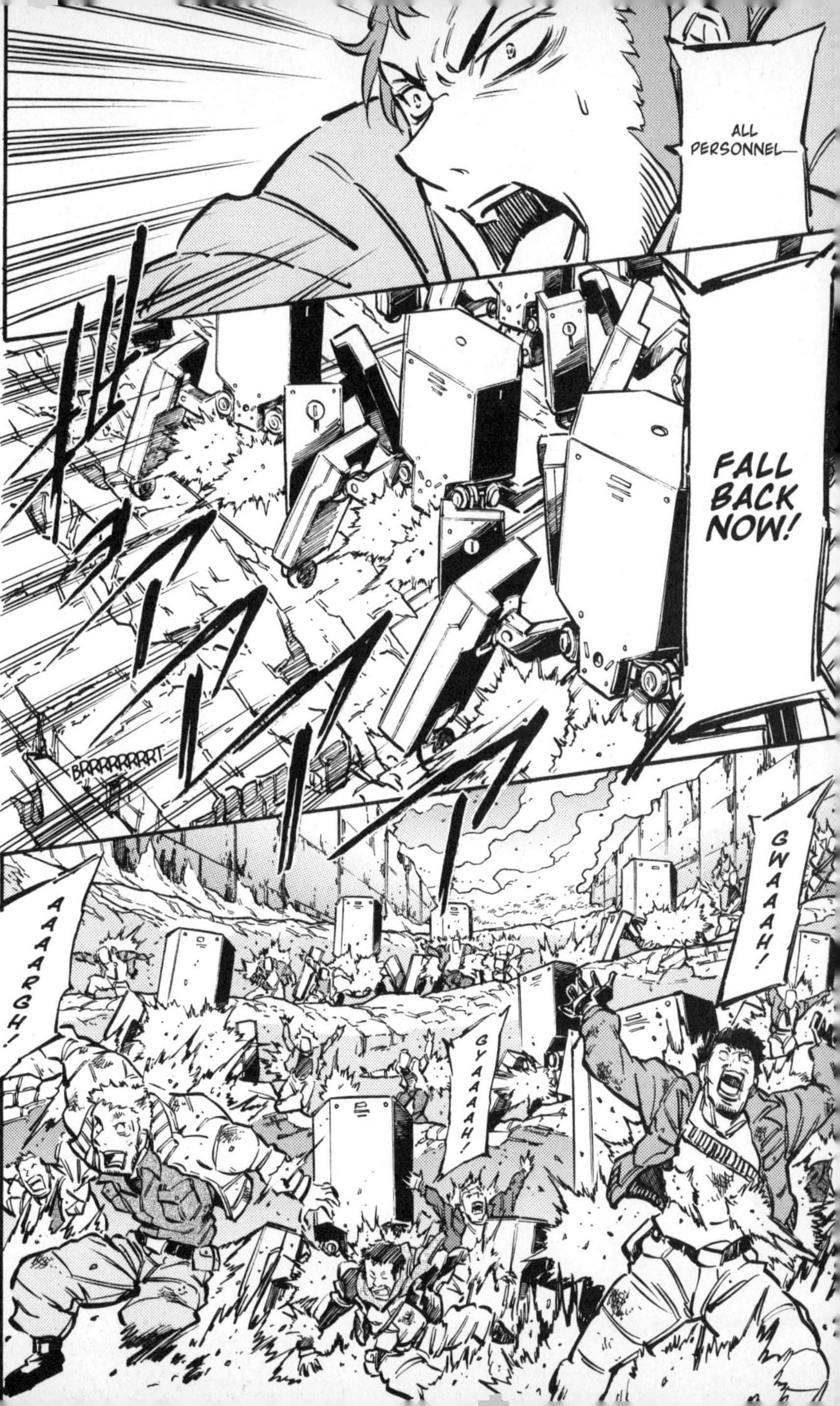
ALL PERSONNEL—
FALL BACK NOW!
BRRRRRRRRRT
GWAAAAH!
GYAAAAH!
AAAAARGH!

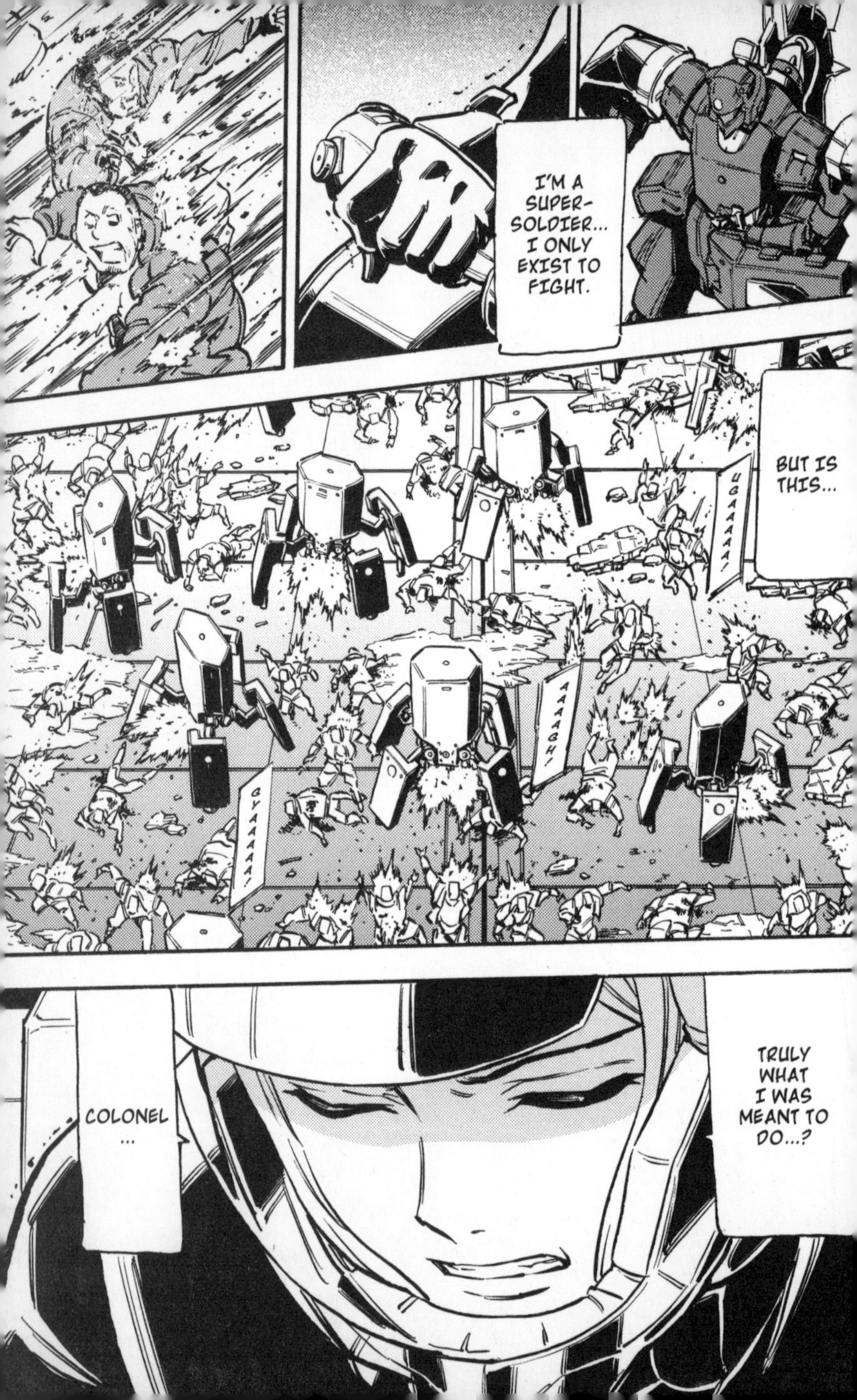
I'M A SUPER-SOLDIER... I ONLY EXIST TO FIGHT.
BUT IS THIS...
UGAAAAAA!
AAAAGH!
GYAAAAAA!
TRULY WHAT I WAS MEANT TO DO...?
COLONEL ...

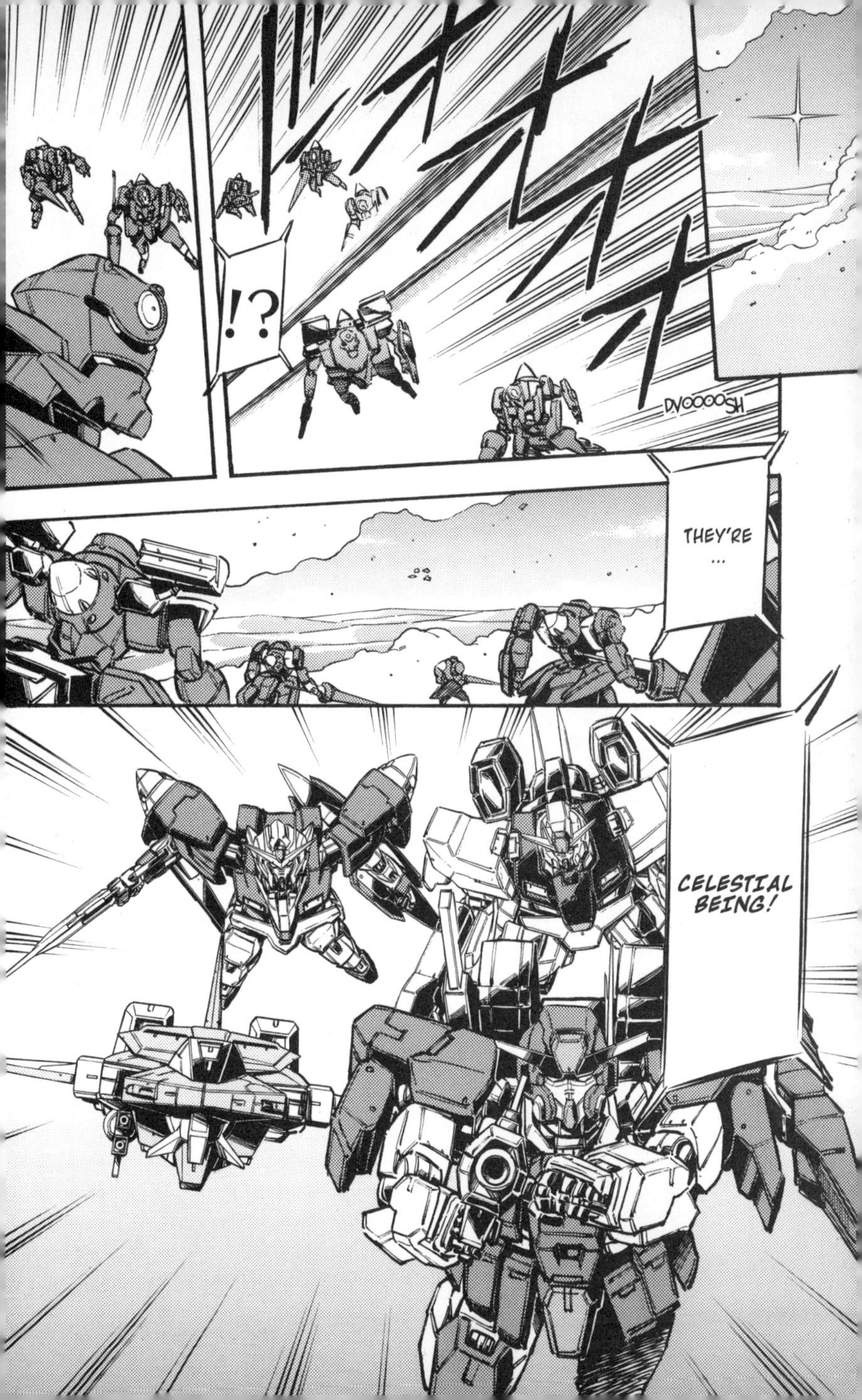
!?
DVOOOOSH
THEY'RE ...
CELESTIAL BEING!

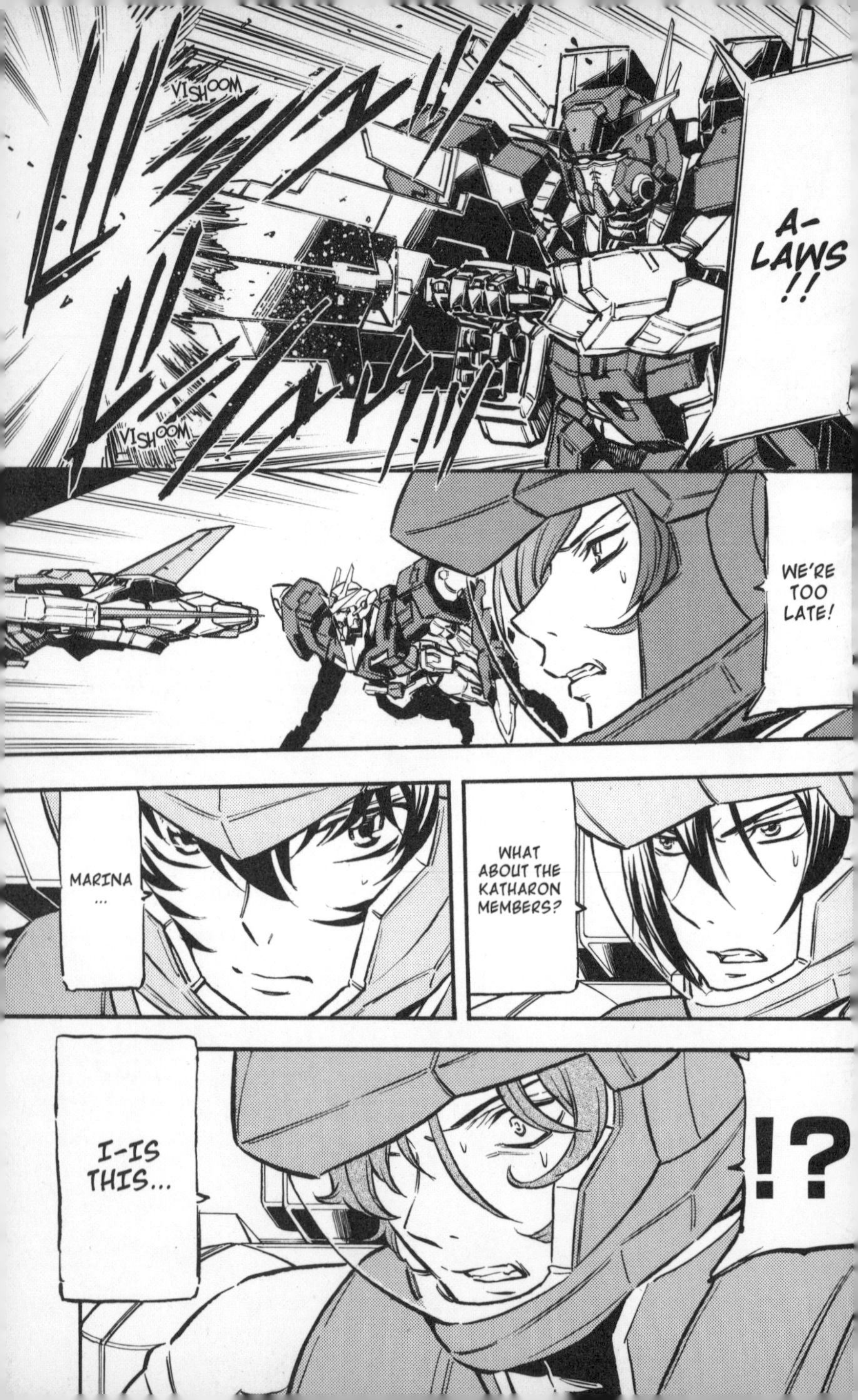
VISHOOM
A-LAWS!!
VISHOOM
WE'RE TOO LATE!
WHAT ABOUT THE KATHARON MEMBERS?
MARINA ...
!?
I-IS THIS...

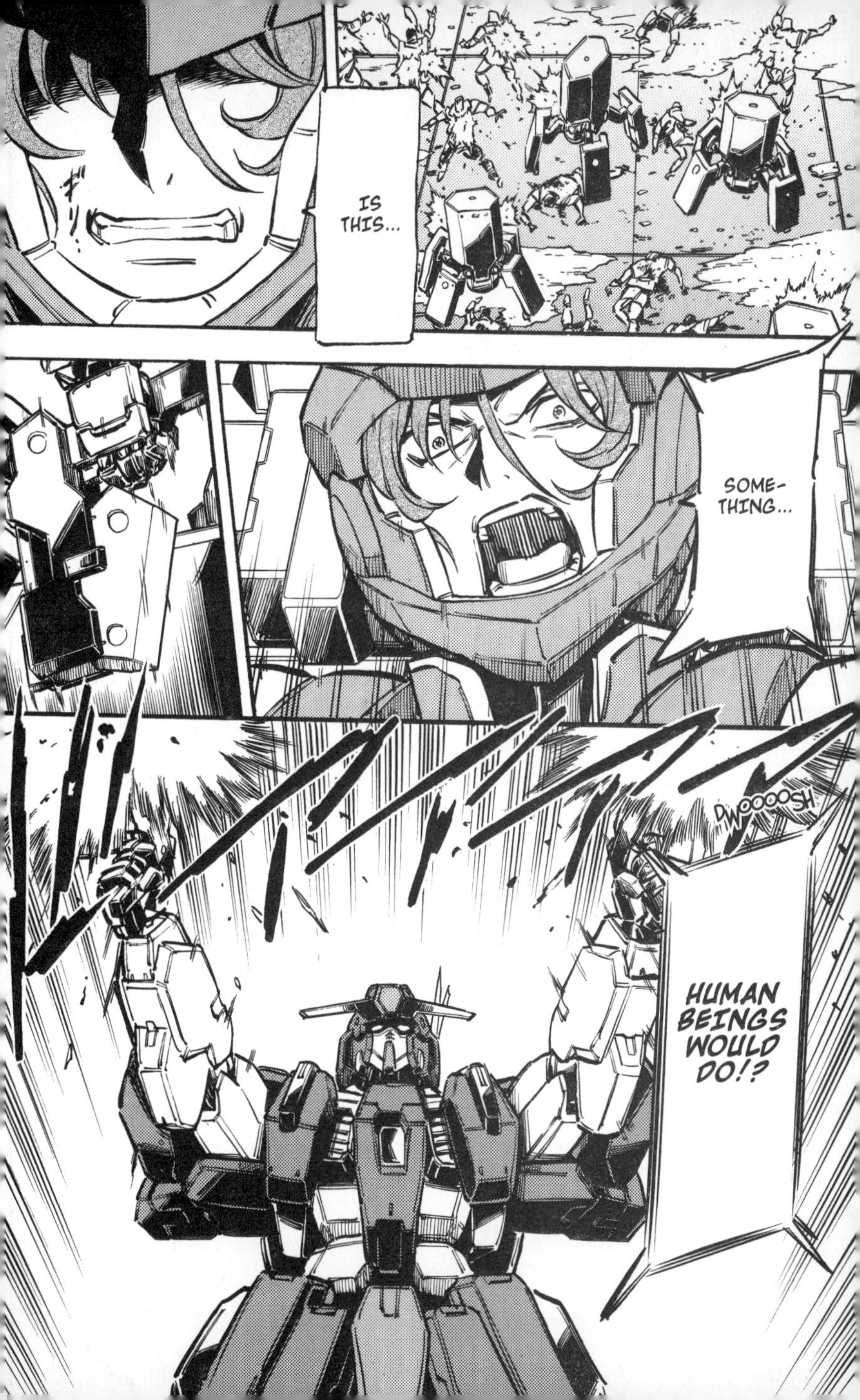
IS THIS...
SOME-THING...
DWOOOOSH
HUMAN BEINGS WOULD DO!?

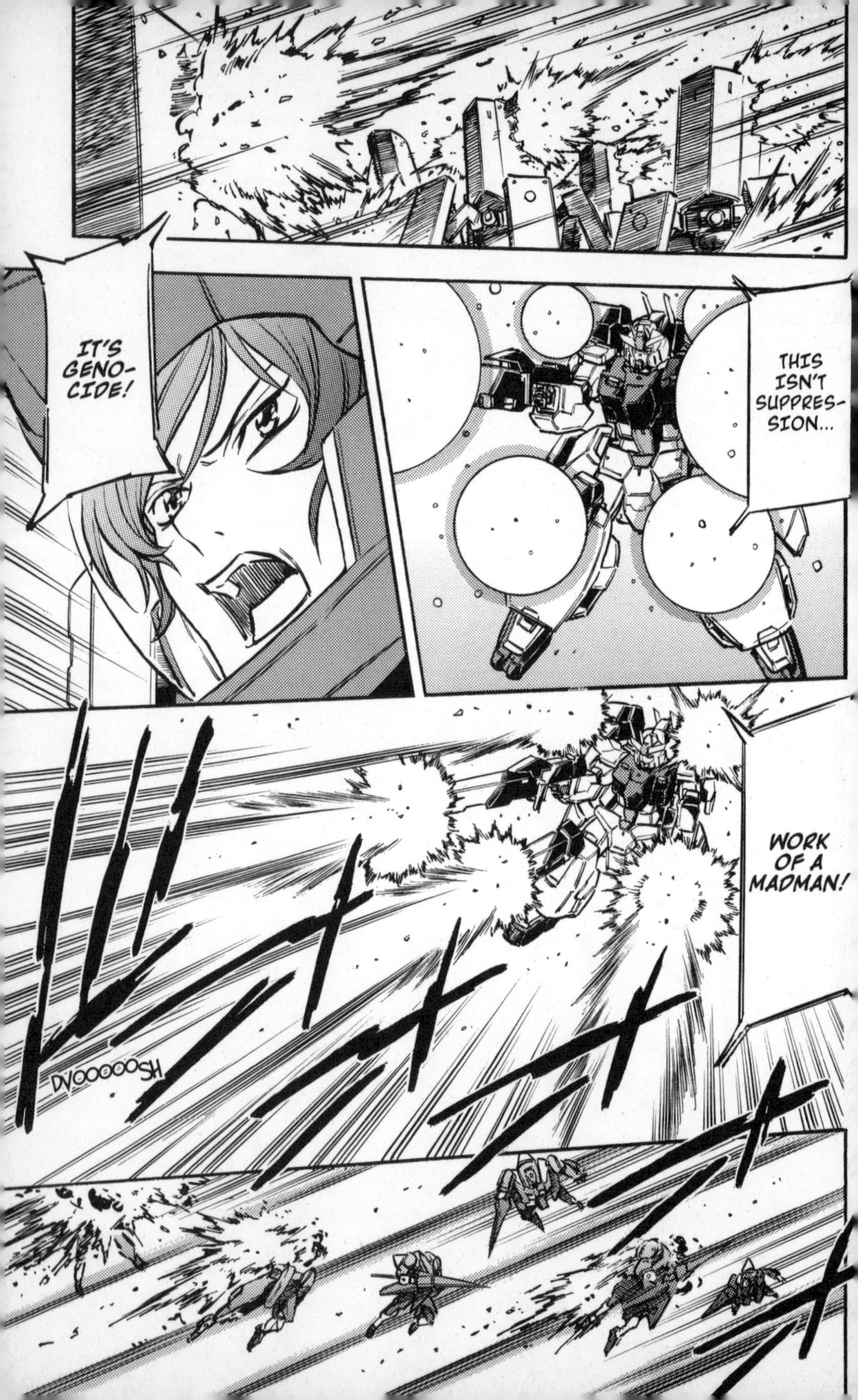
THIS ISN'T SUPPRESSION...
IT'S GENOCIDE!
WORK OF A MADMAN!
DVOOOOOSH

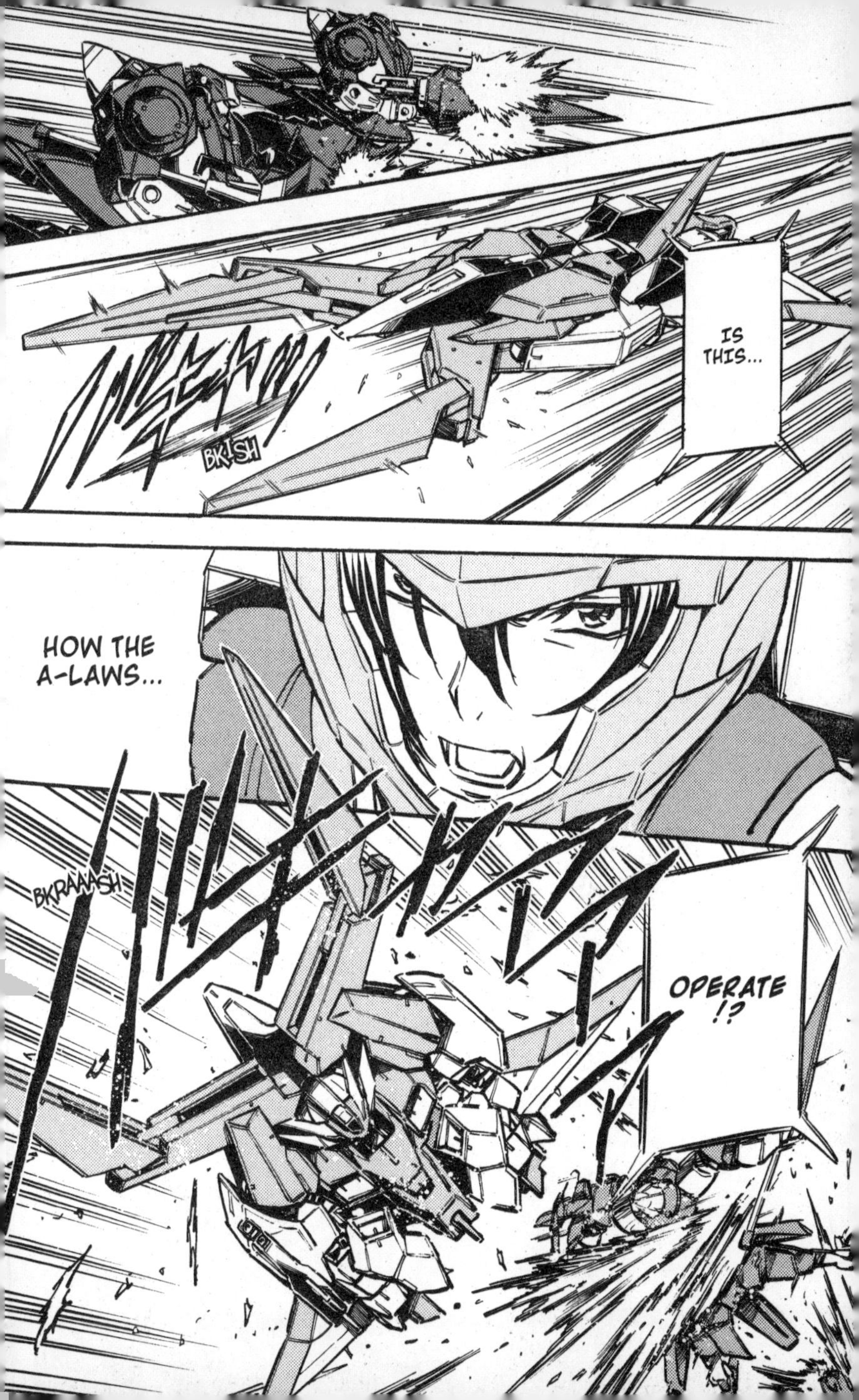
IS THIS...
BK-ISH
HOW THE A-LAWS...
OPERATE !?
BKRAAASH

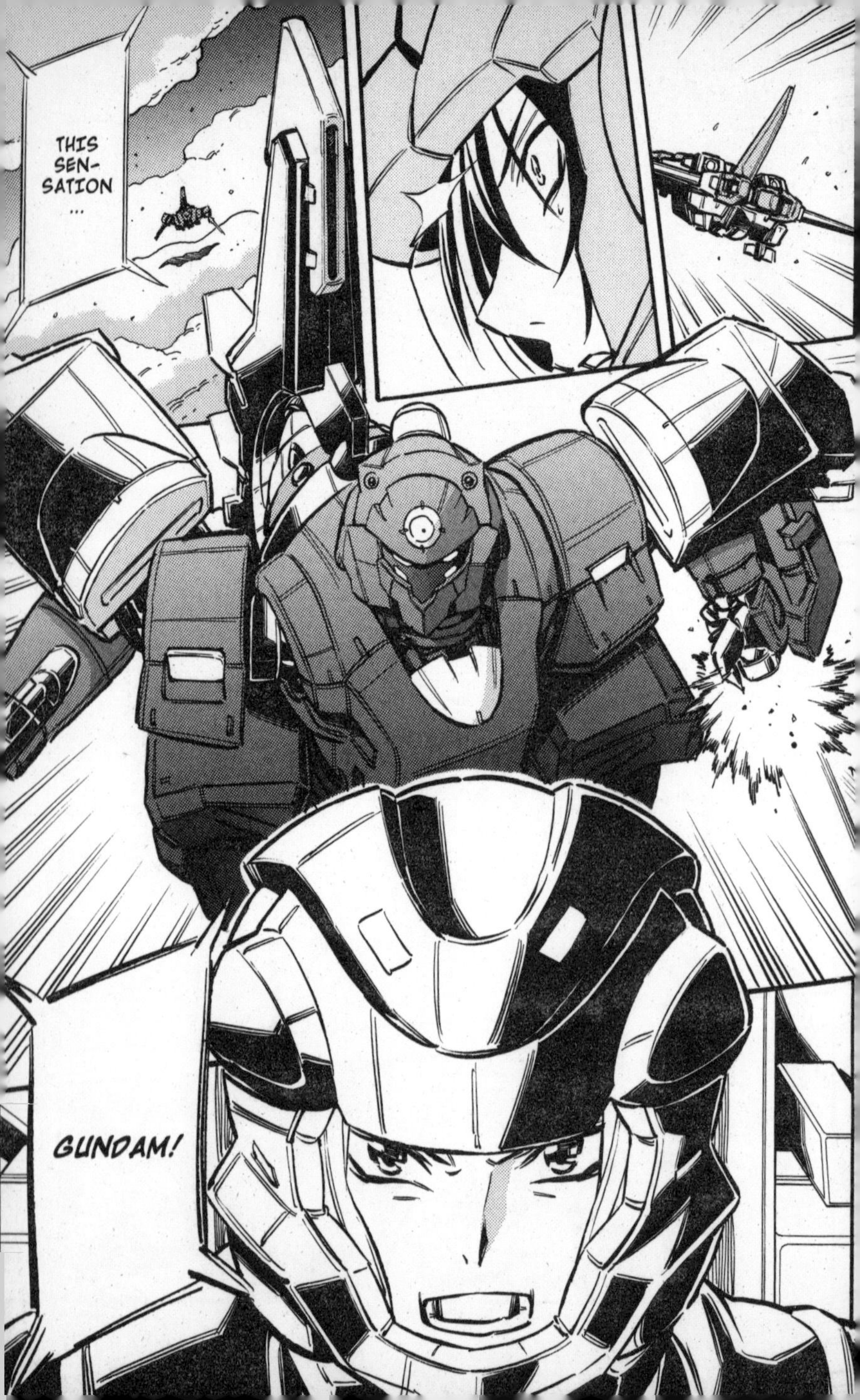
THIS SEN-SATION ...
GUNDAM!

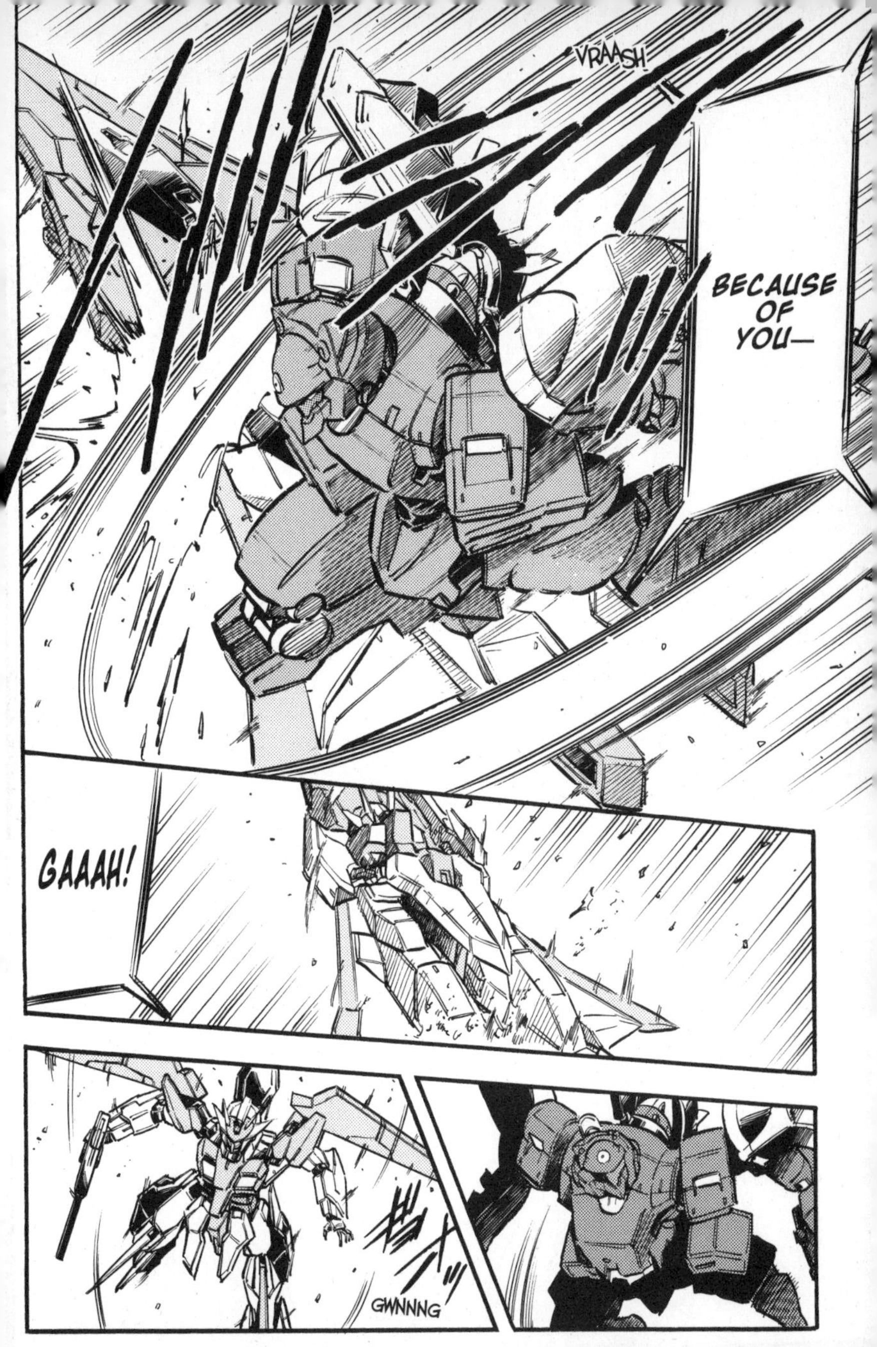
VRAASH
BECAUSE OF YOU—
GAAAH!
GWNNNG

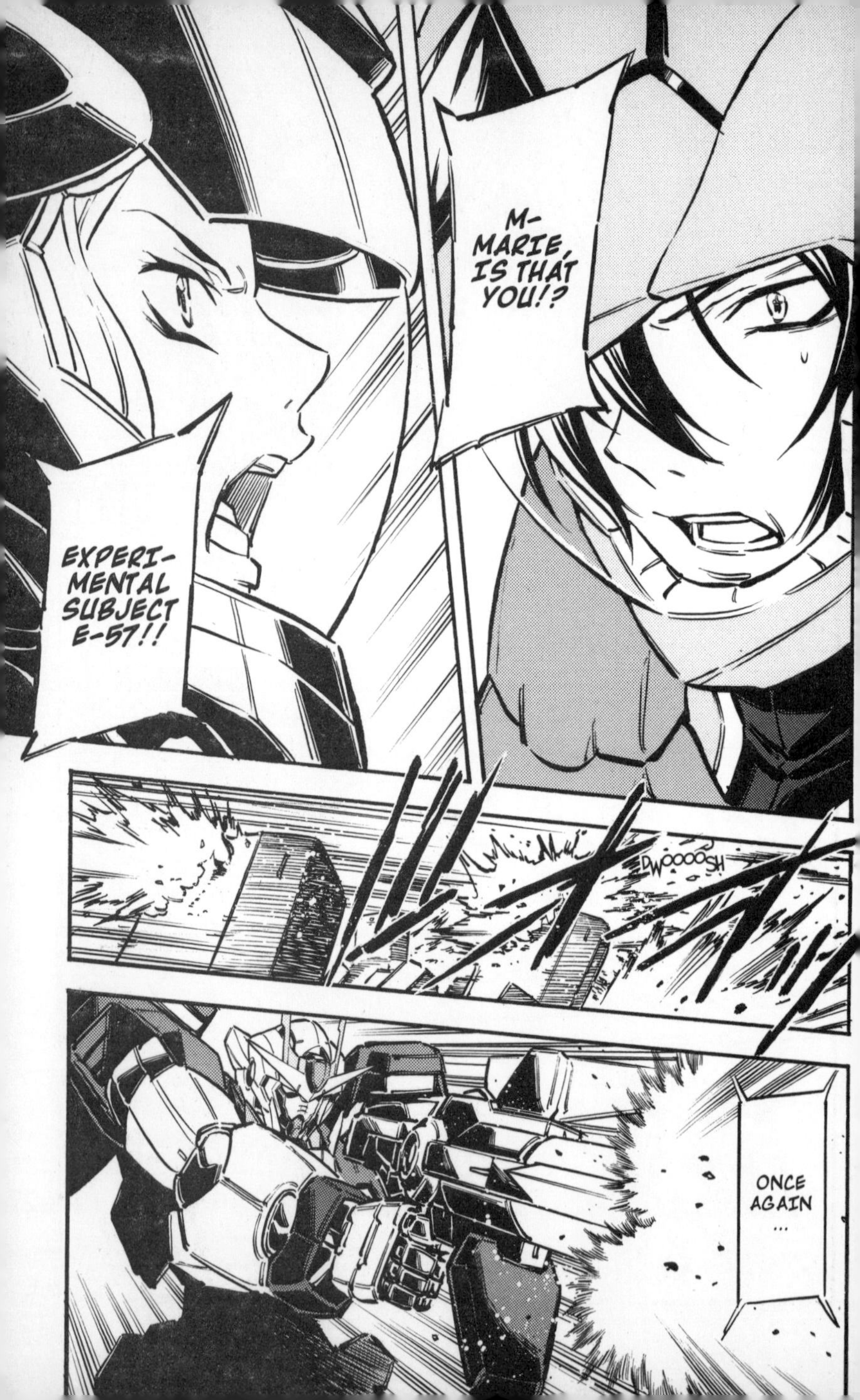
M-MARIE, IS THAT YOU!?
EXPERI-MENTAL SUBJECT E-57!!
DWOOOOSH
ONCE AGAIN ...

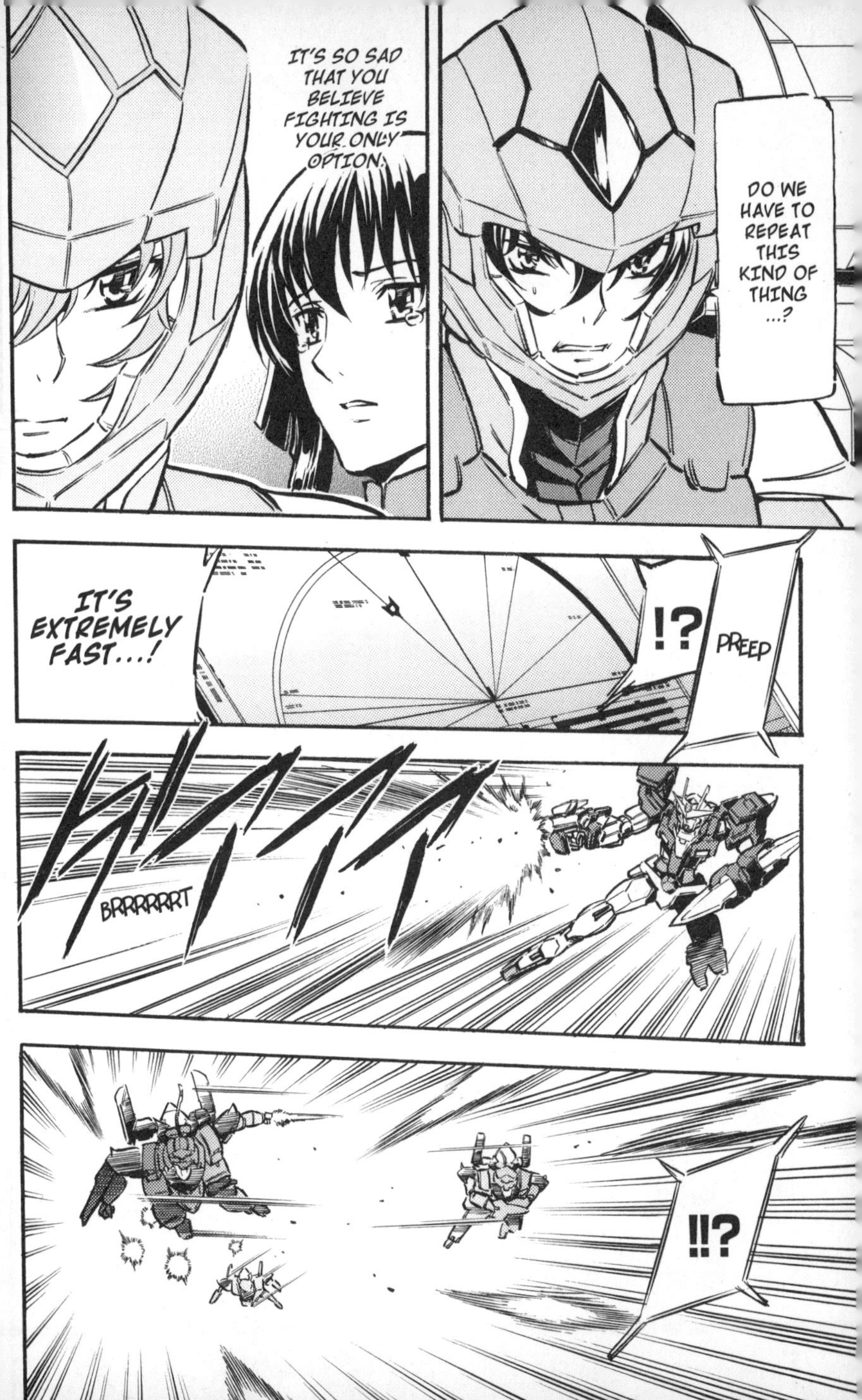
DO WE HAVE TO REPEAT THIS KIND OF THING ...?
IT'S SO SAD THAT YOU BELIEVE FIGHTING IS YOUR ONLY OPTION.
!?
PREEP
IT'S EXTREMELY FAST...!
BRRRRRRT
!!?

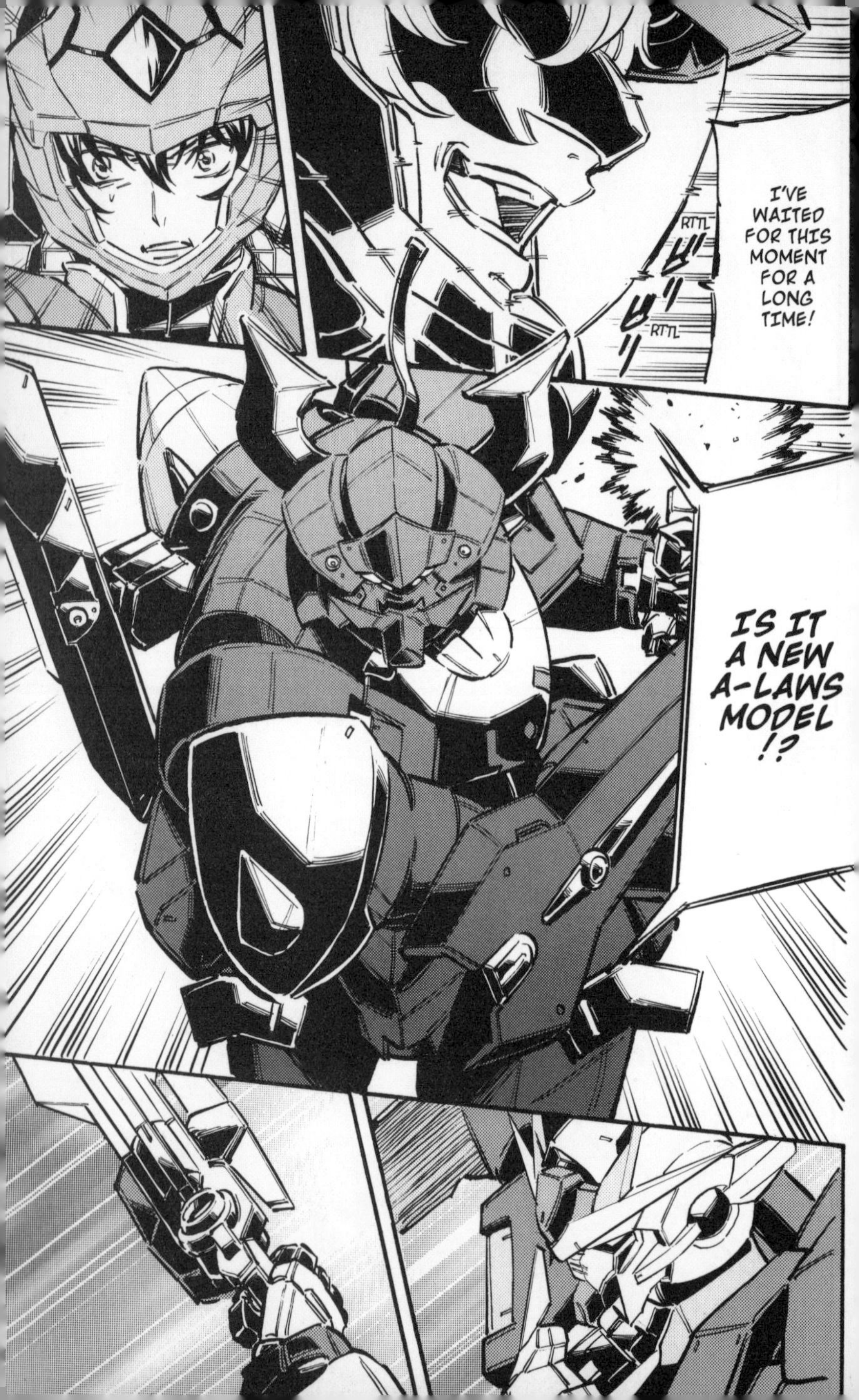

I'VE WAITED FOR THIS MOMENT FOR A LONG TIME!
RTTL
RTTL
IS IT A NEW A-LAWS MODEL!?

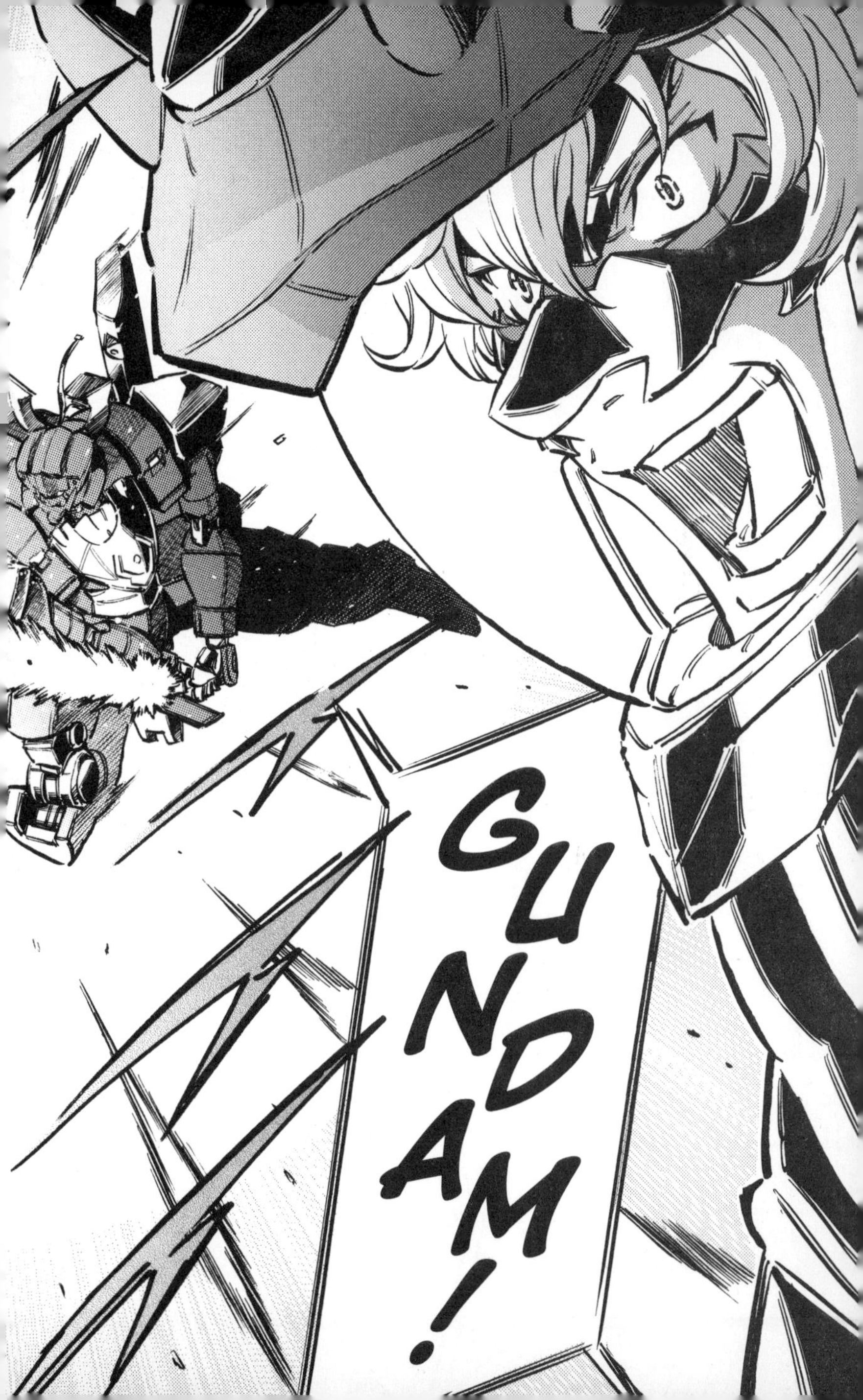
GUNDAM!

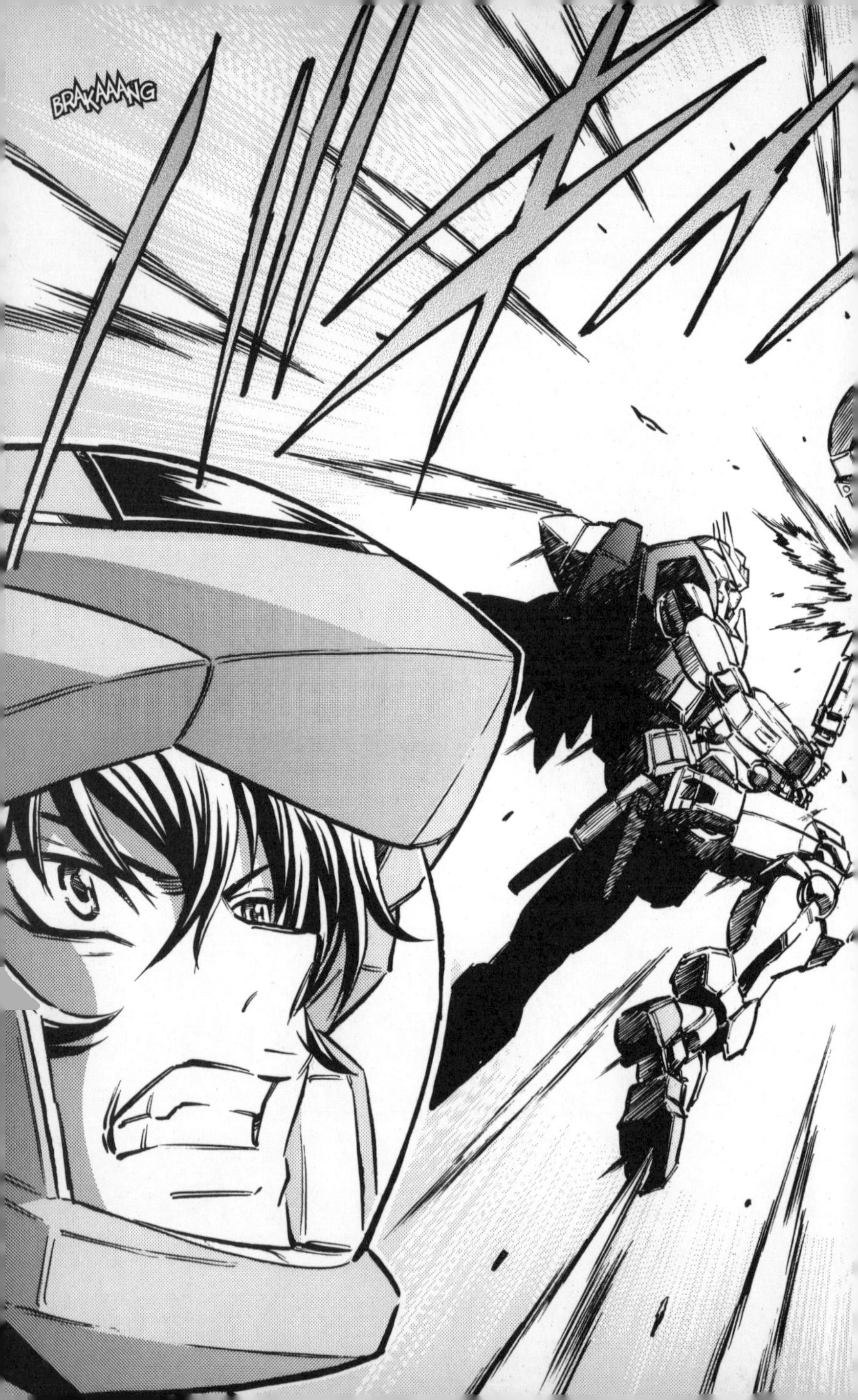
BRAKAAANG

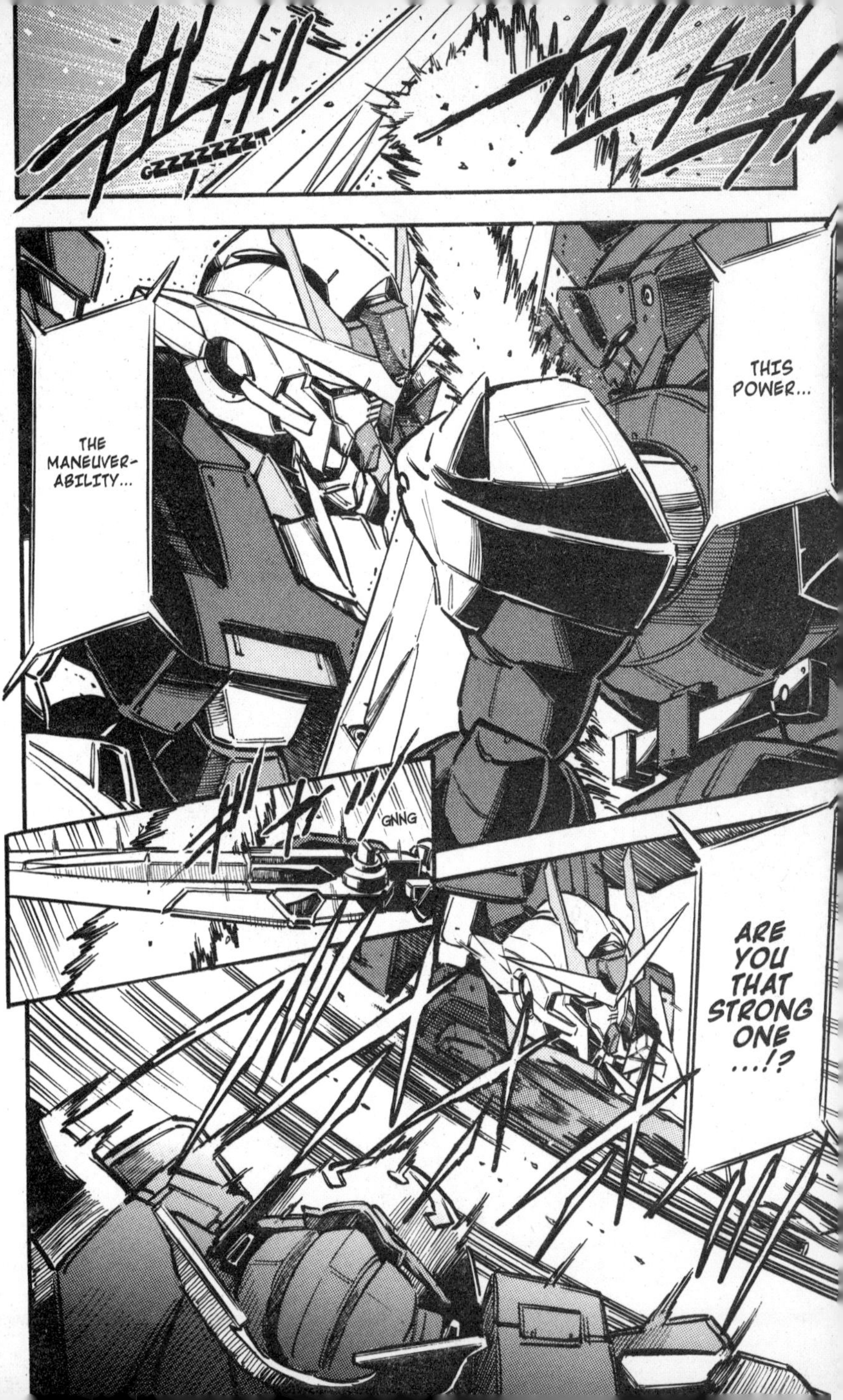
GZZZZZZZT
THIS POWER...
THE MANEUVER-ABILITY...
GNNG
ARE YOU THAT STRONG ONE ...!?

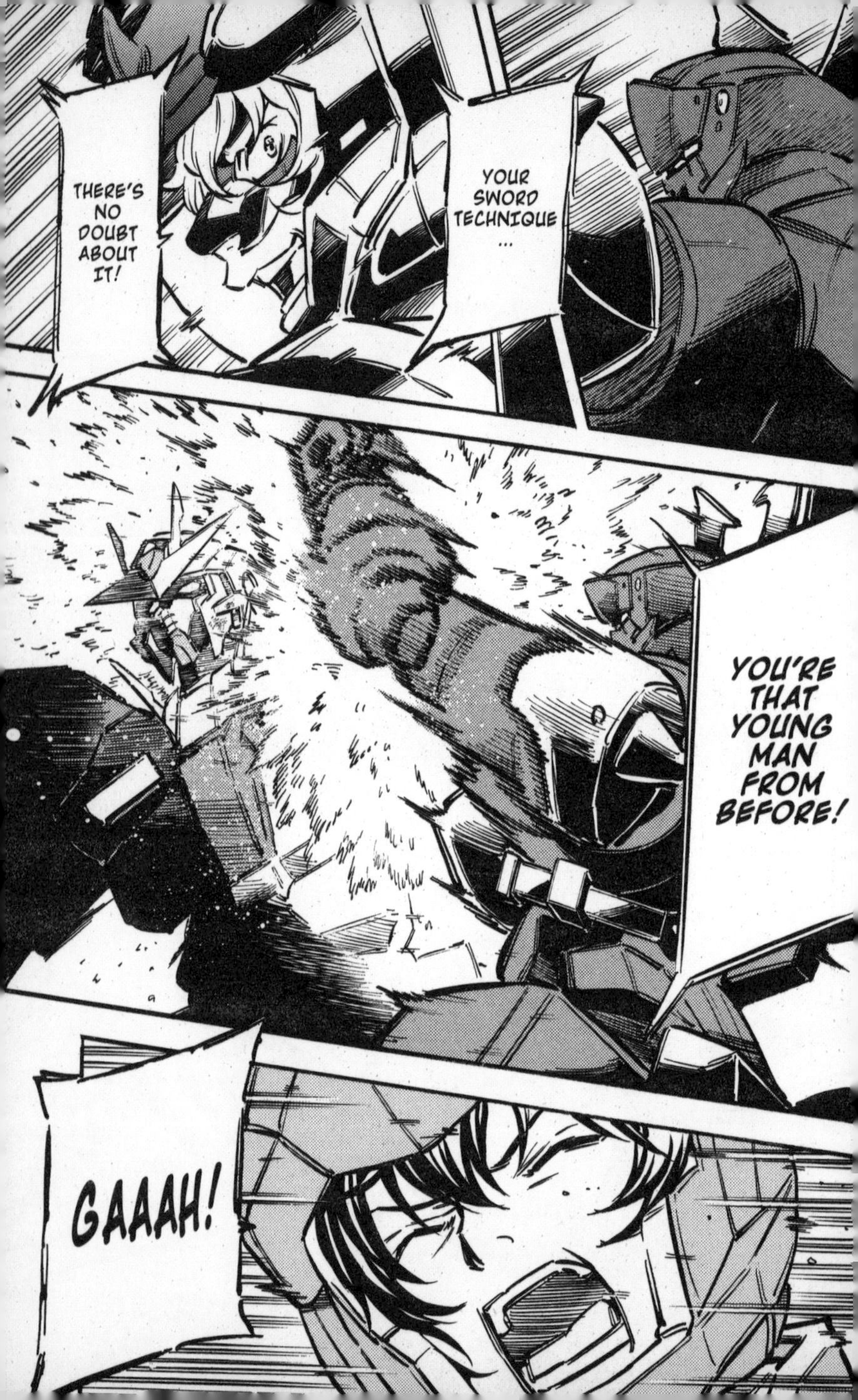
YOUR SWORD TECHNIQUE ...
THERE'S NO DOUBT ABOUT IT!
YOU'RE THAT YOUNG MAN FROM BEFORE!
GAAAH!

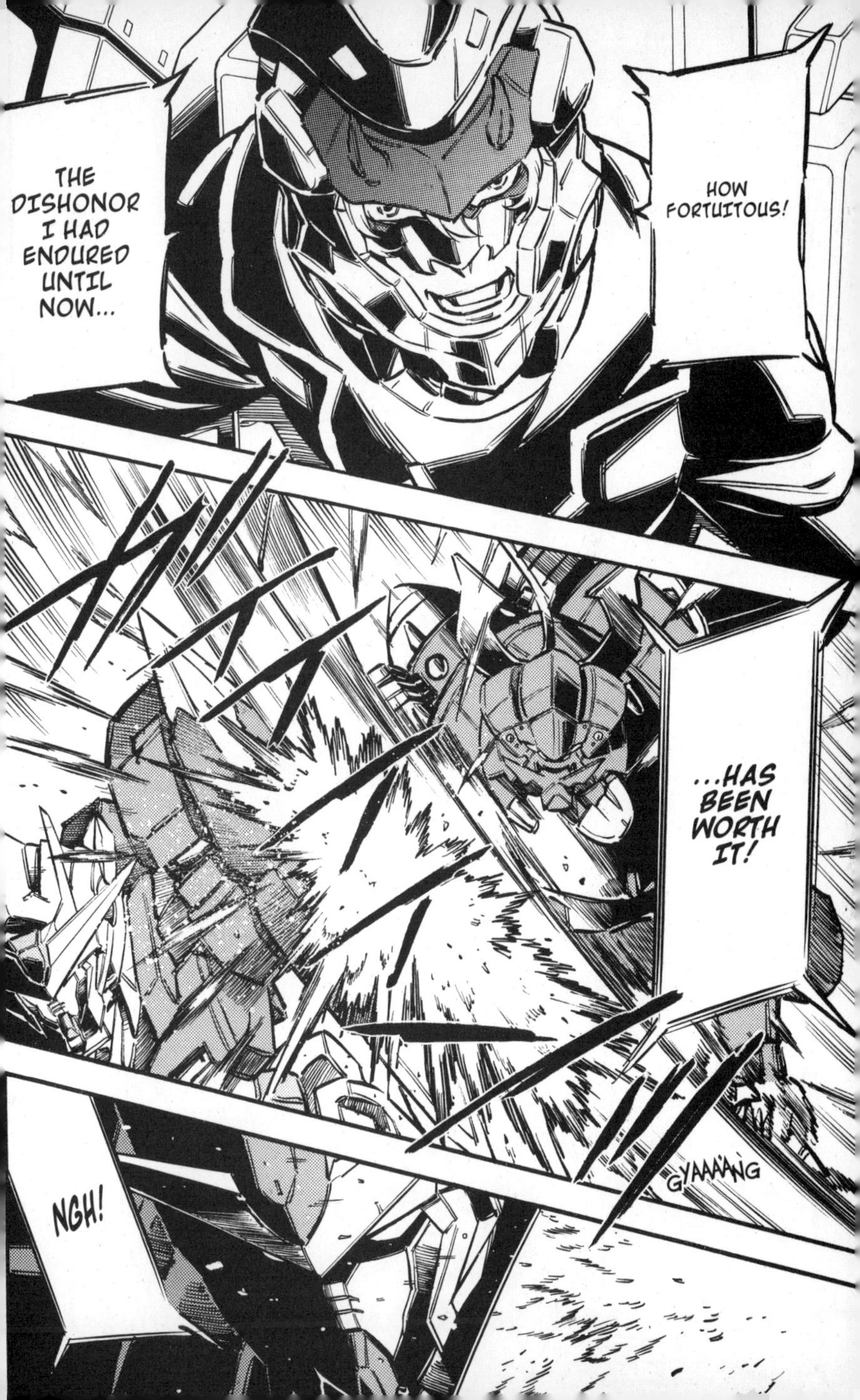
HOW FORTUITOUS!
THE DISHONOR I HAD ENDURED UNTIL NOW...
...HAS BEEN WORTH IT!
GYAAAANG
NGH!

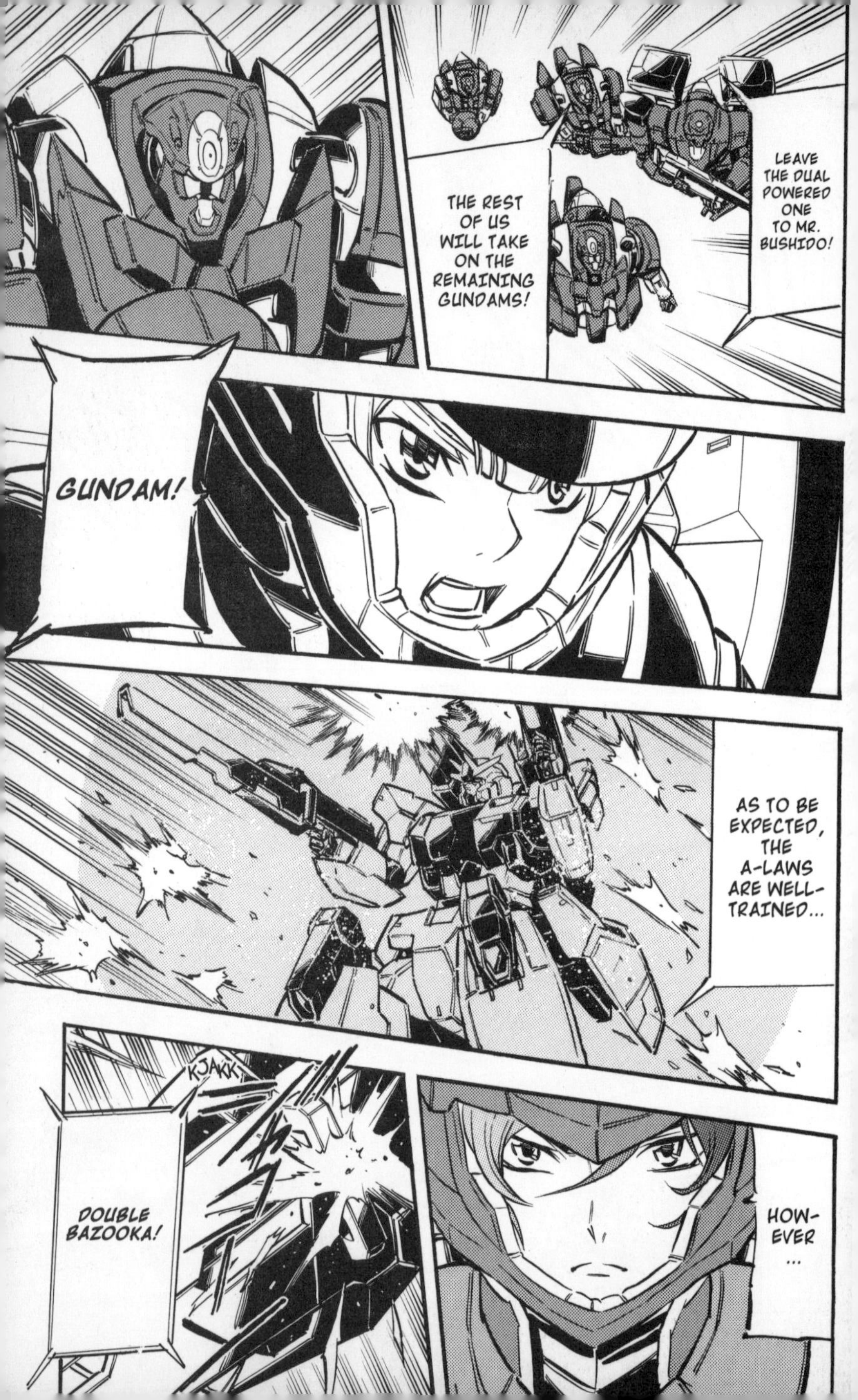
LEAVE THE DUAL POWERED ONE TO MR. BUSHIDO!
THE REST OF US WILL TAKE ON THE REMAINING GUNDAMS!
GUNDAM!
AS TO BE EXPECTED, THE A-LAWS ARE WELL-TRAINED...
HOW-EVER ...
KJAKK
DOUBLE BAZOOKA!

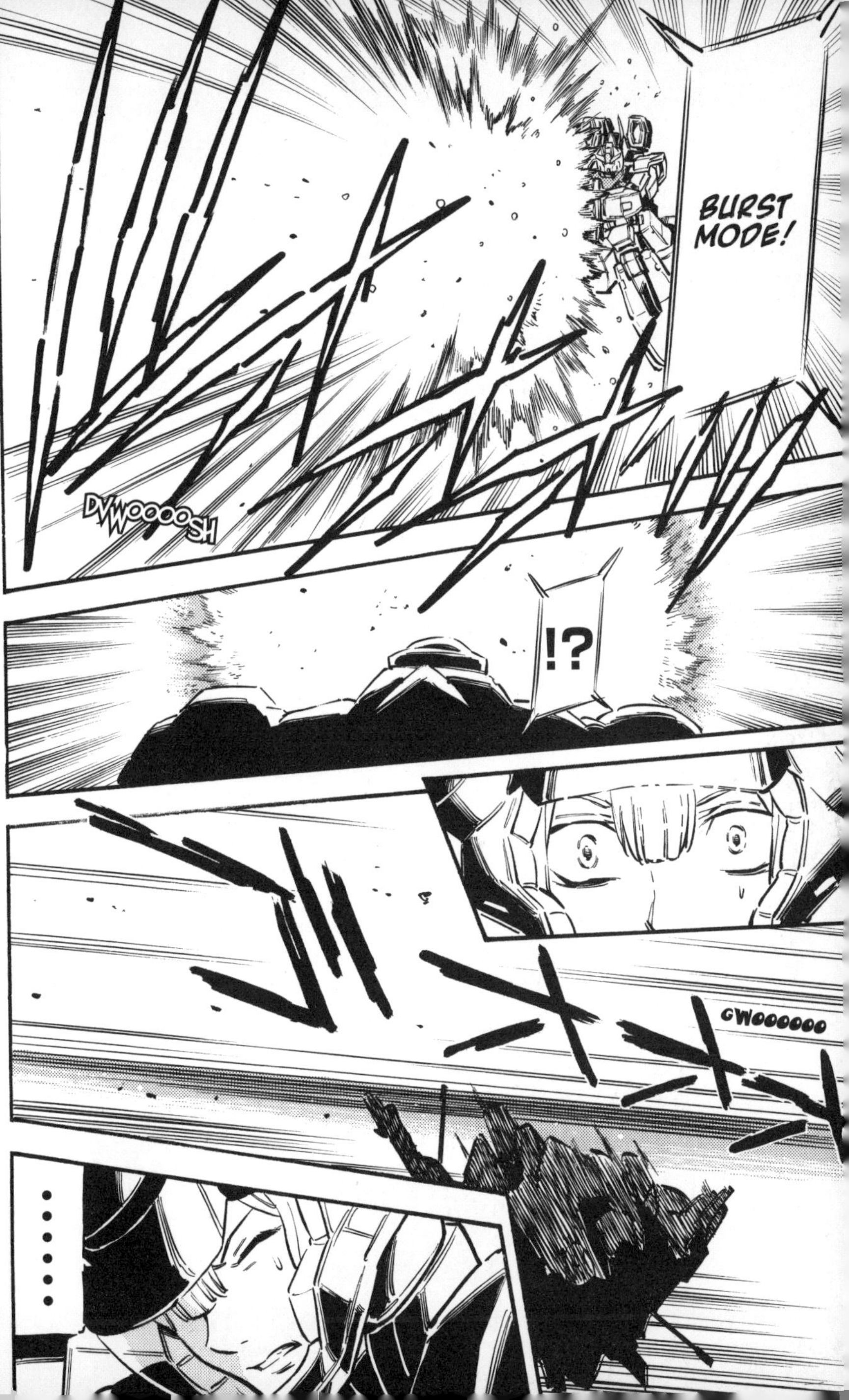
BURST MODE!
DVWOOOOSH
!?
GWOOOOOO
......

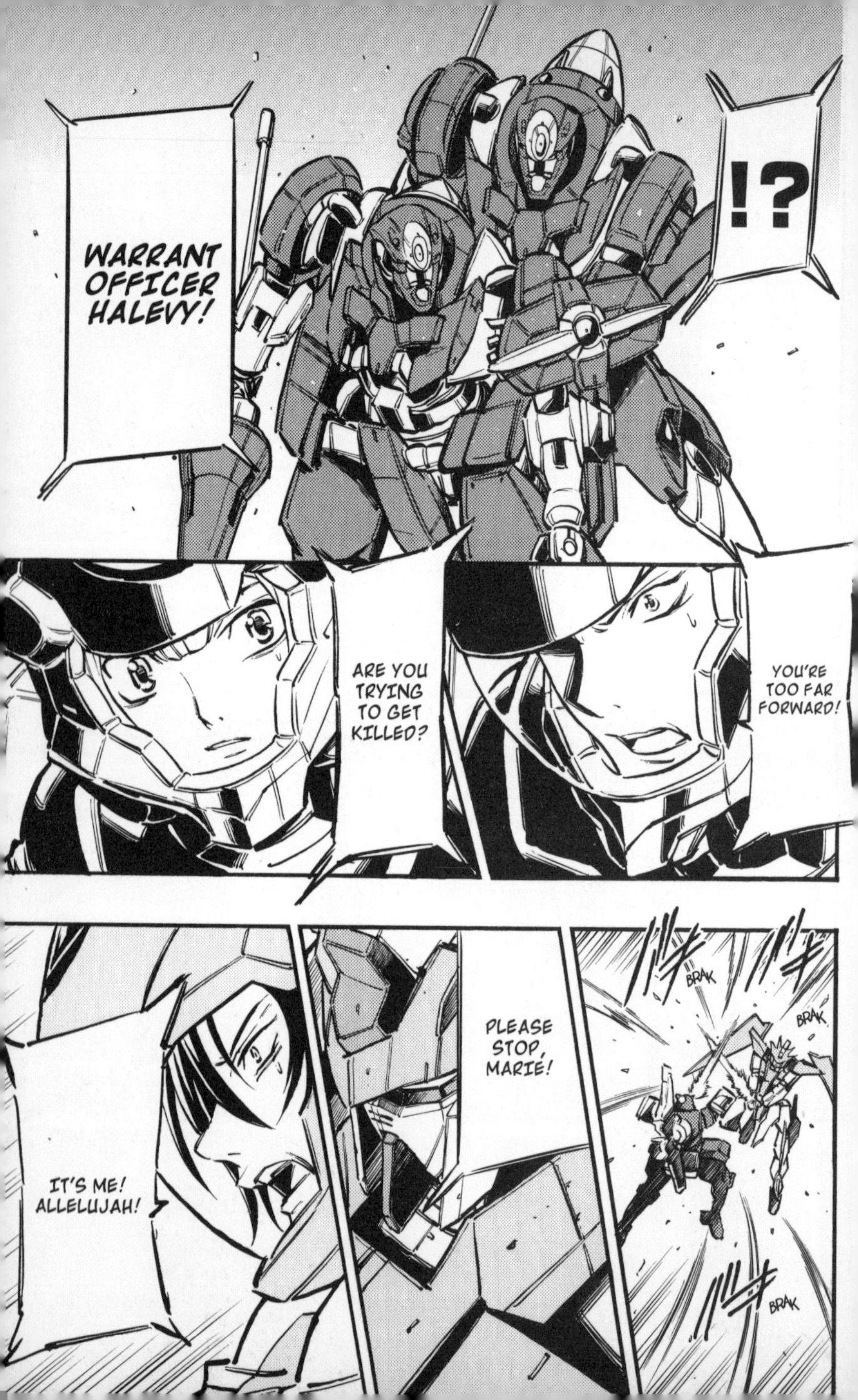
!?
WARRANT OFFICER HALEVY!
YOU'RE TOO FAR FORWARD!
ARE YOU TRYING TO GET KILLED?
BRAK
BRAK
BRAK
PLEASE STOP, MARIE!
IT'S ME! ALLELUJAH!

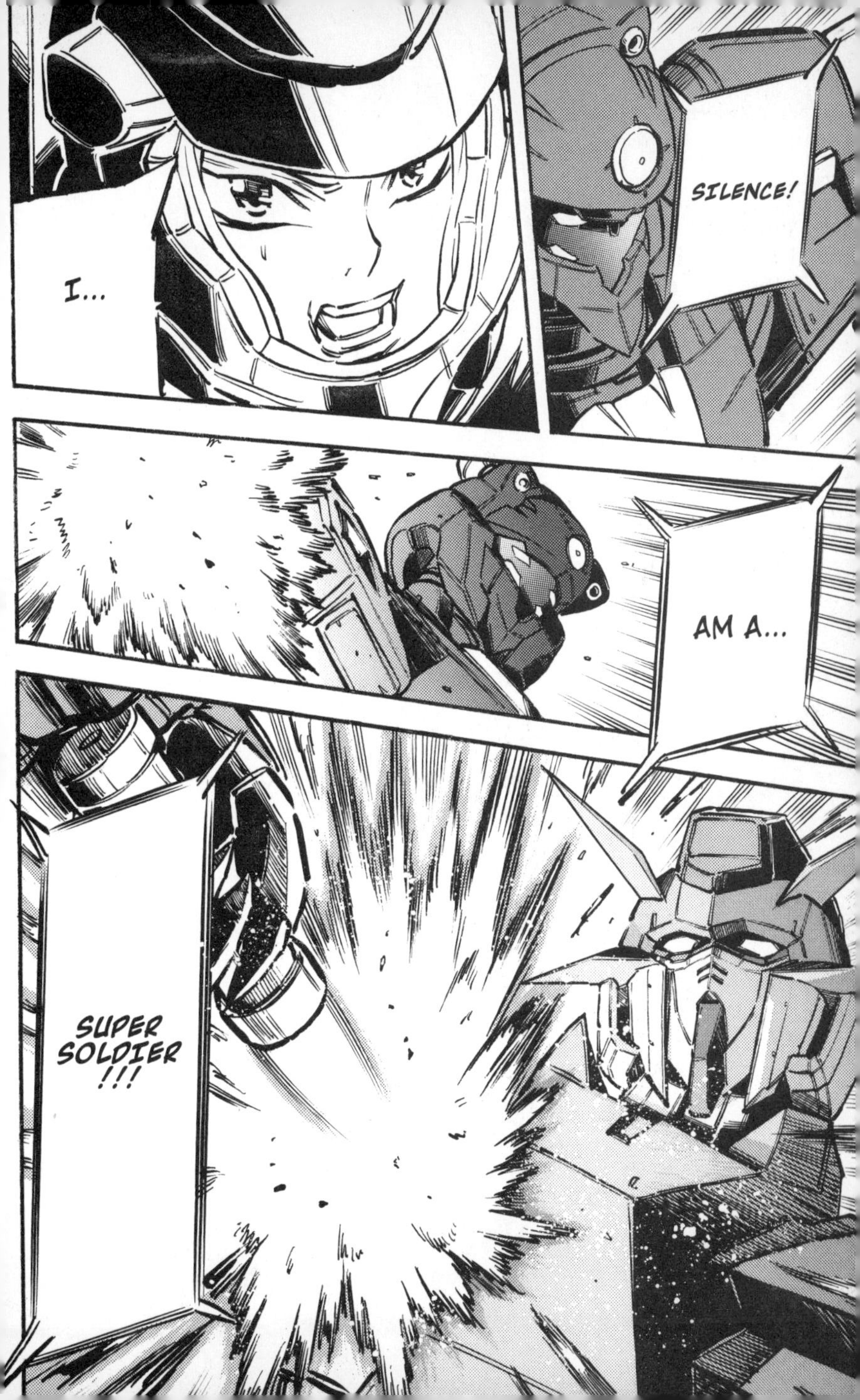
SILENCE!
I...
AM A...
SUPER SOLDIER !!!

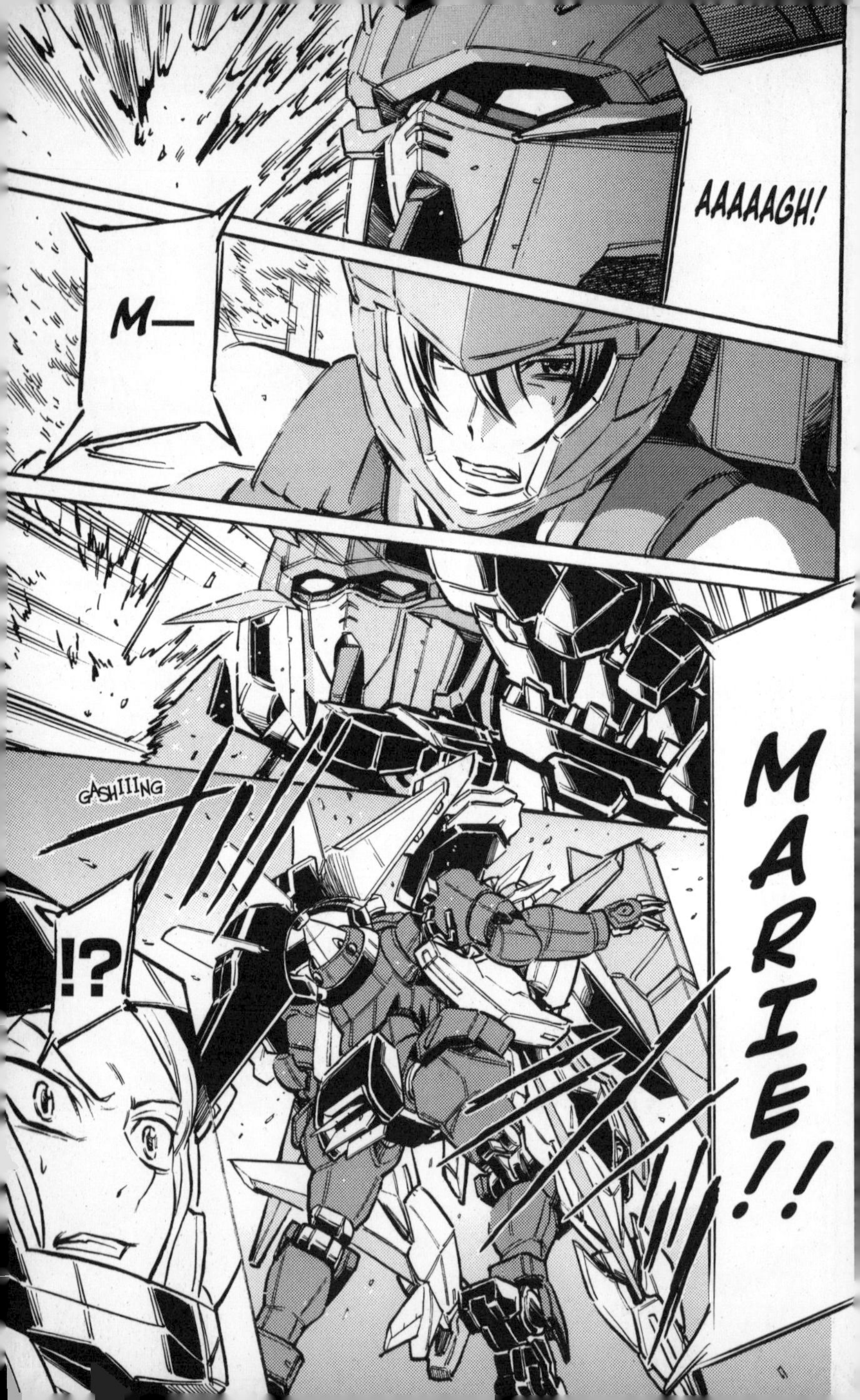
AAAAAGH!
M—
MARIE!!
GASHIIING
!?

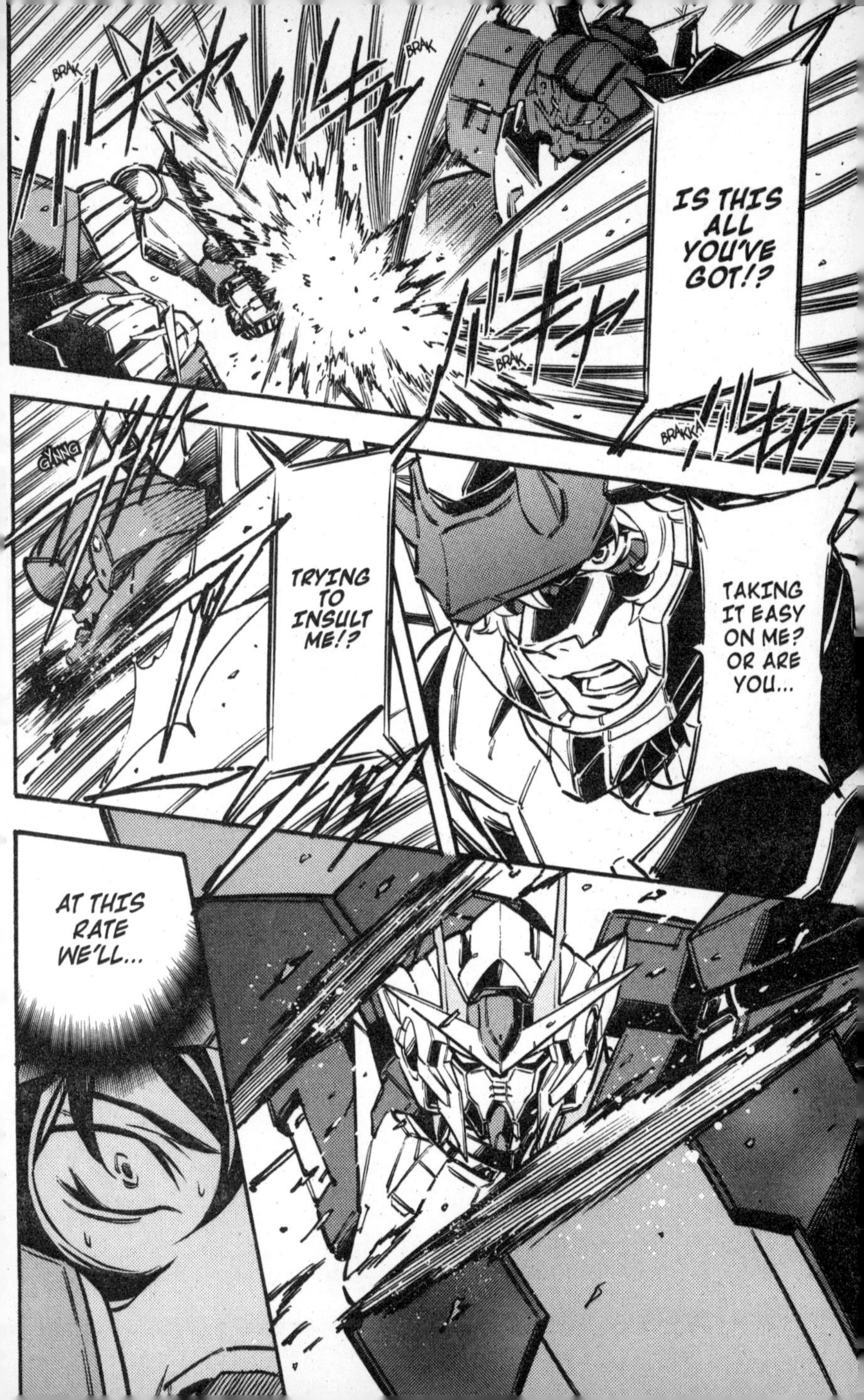
BRAK
IS THIS ALL YOU'VE GOT!?
BRAK
BRAK
BRAKKA
TAKING IT EASY ON ME? OR ARE YOU...
TRYING TO INSULT ME!?
GYNNG
AT THIS RATE WE'LL...

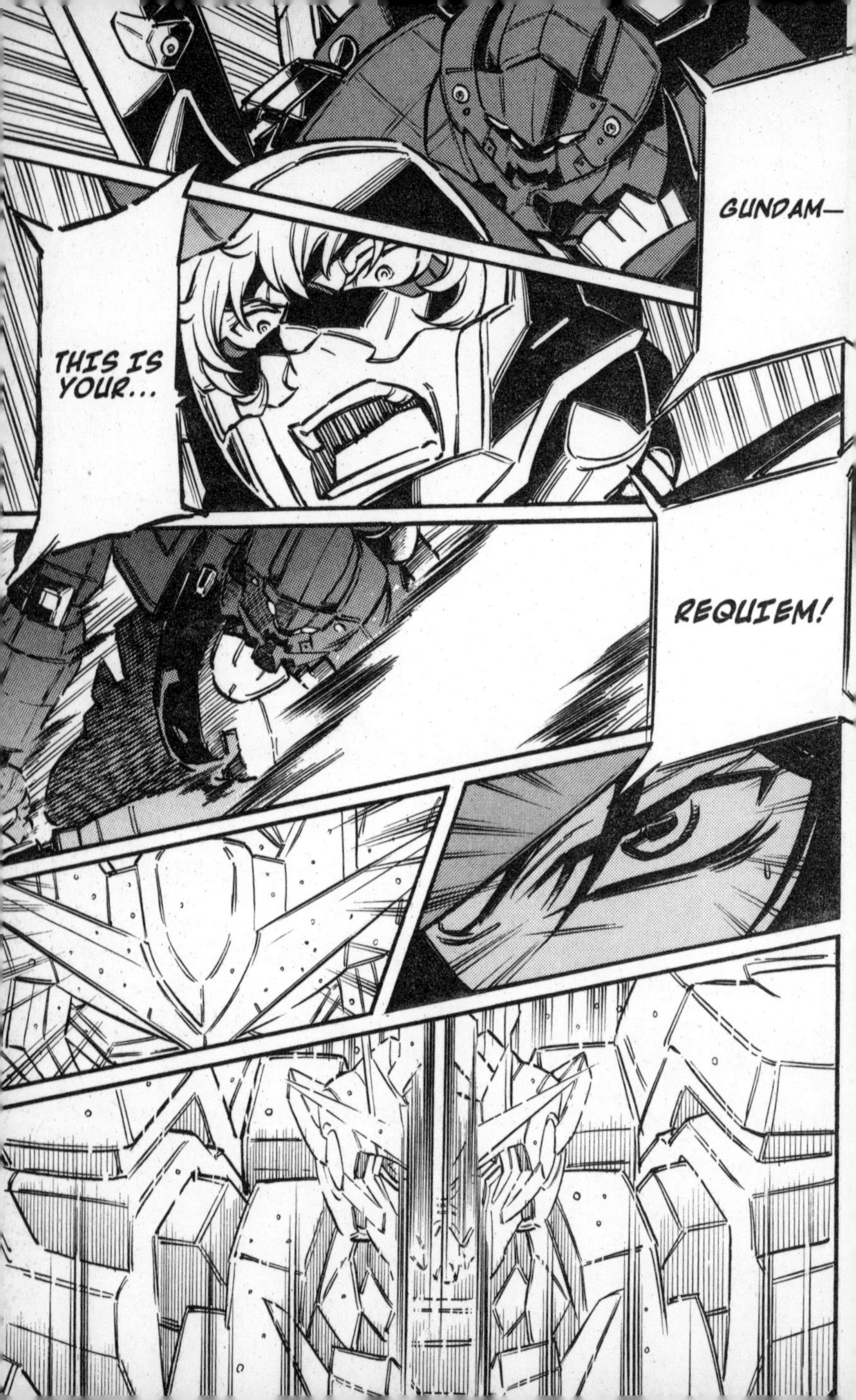
GUNDAM—
THIS IS YOUR...
REQUIEM!

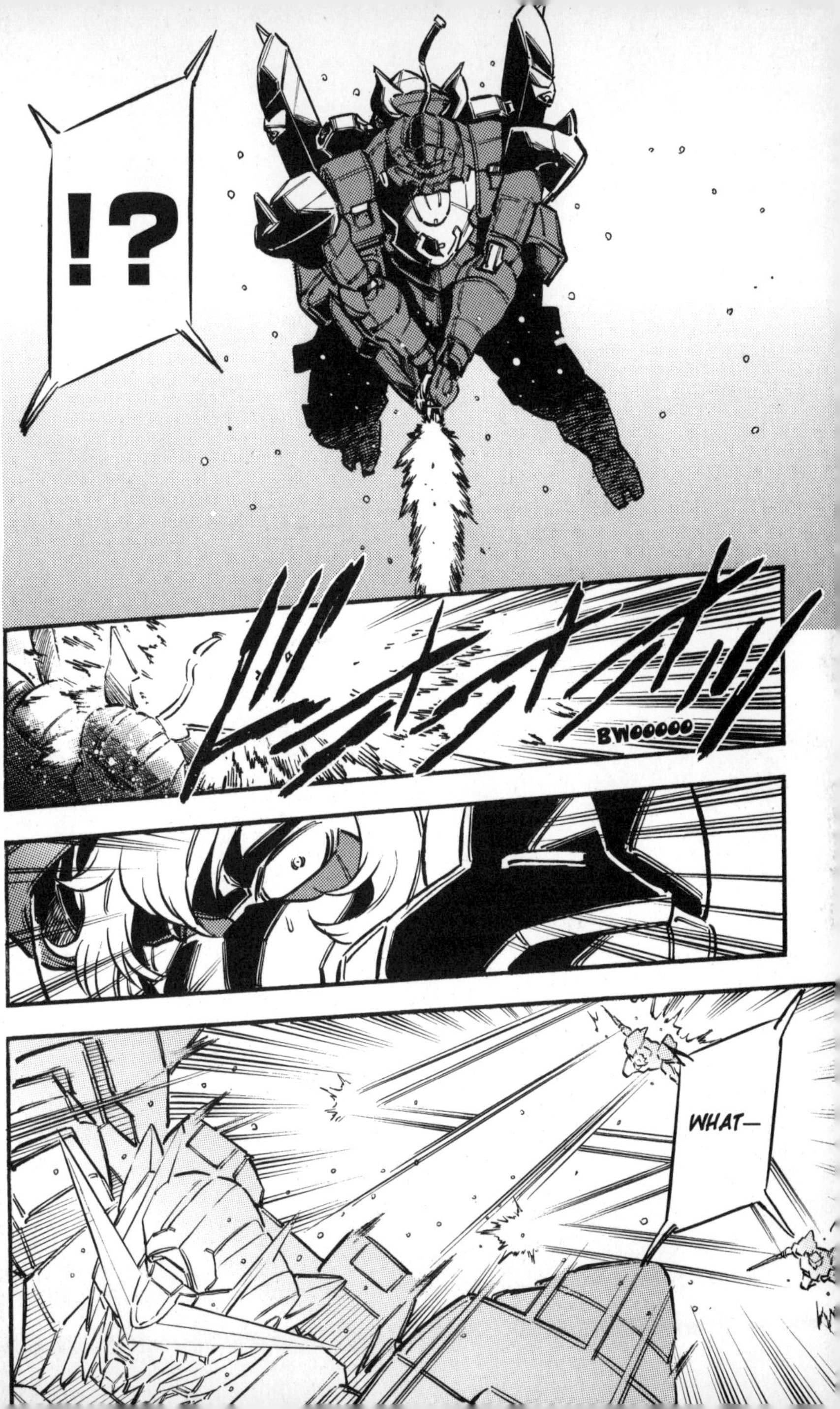
!?
BWOOOOO
WHAT—

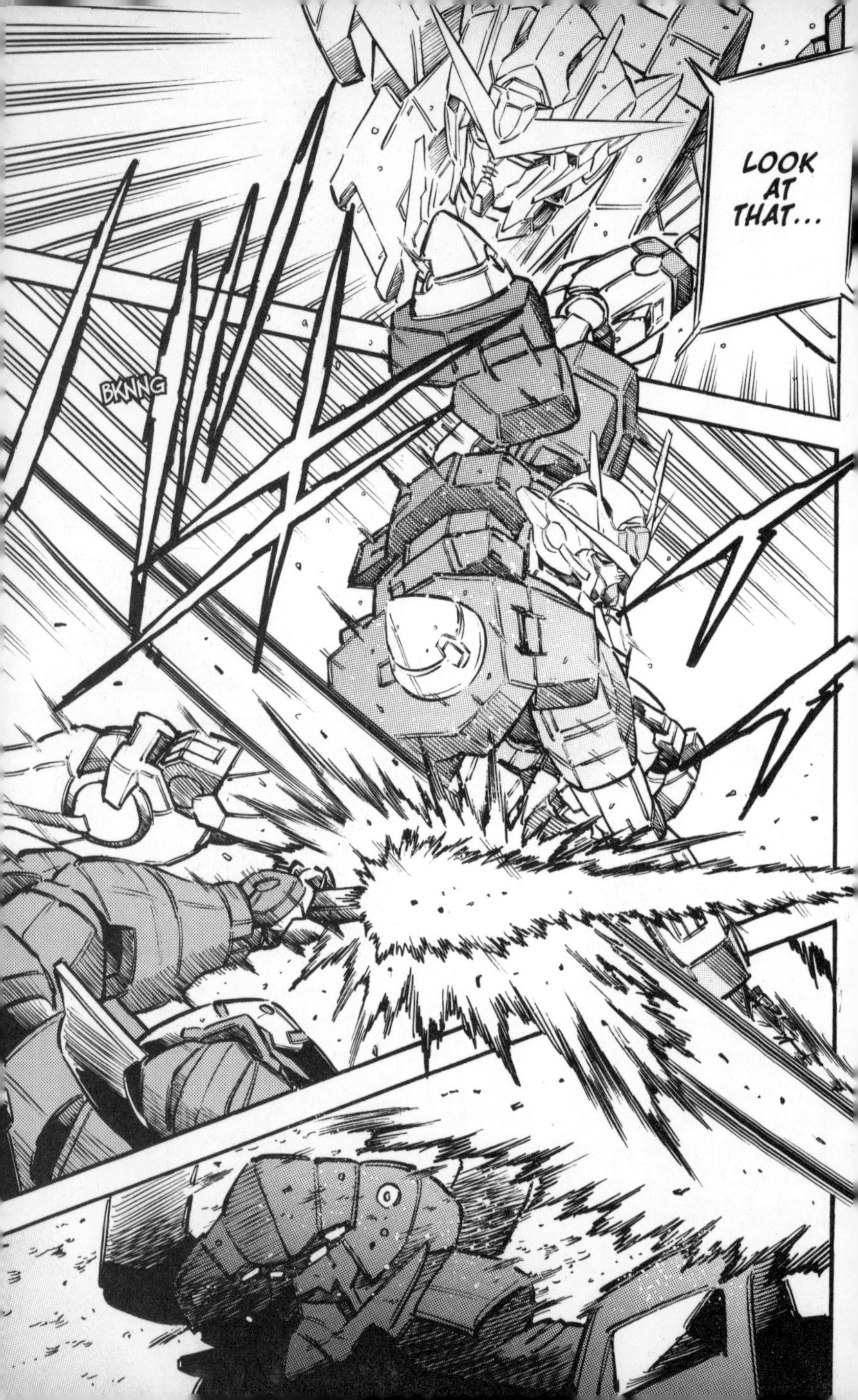
LOOK AT THAT...
BKNNG

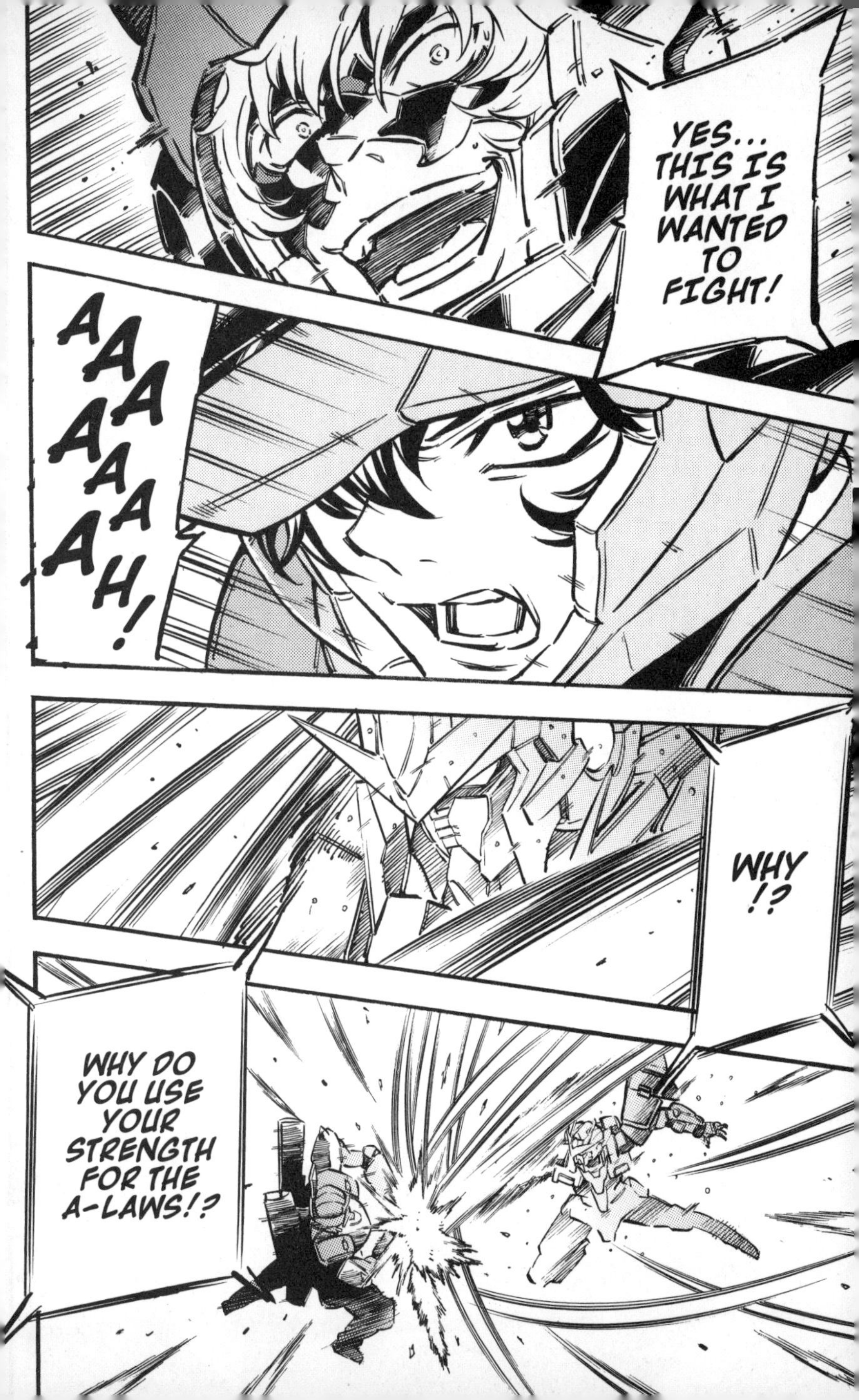
YES... THIS IS WHAT I WANTED TO FIGHT!
AAAAAAAH!
WHY!?
WHY DO YOU USE YOUR STRENGTH FOR THE A-LAWS!?

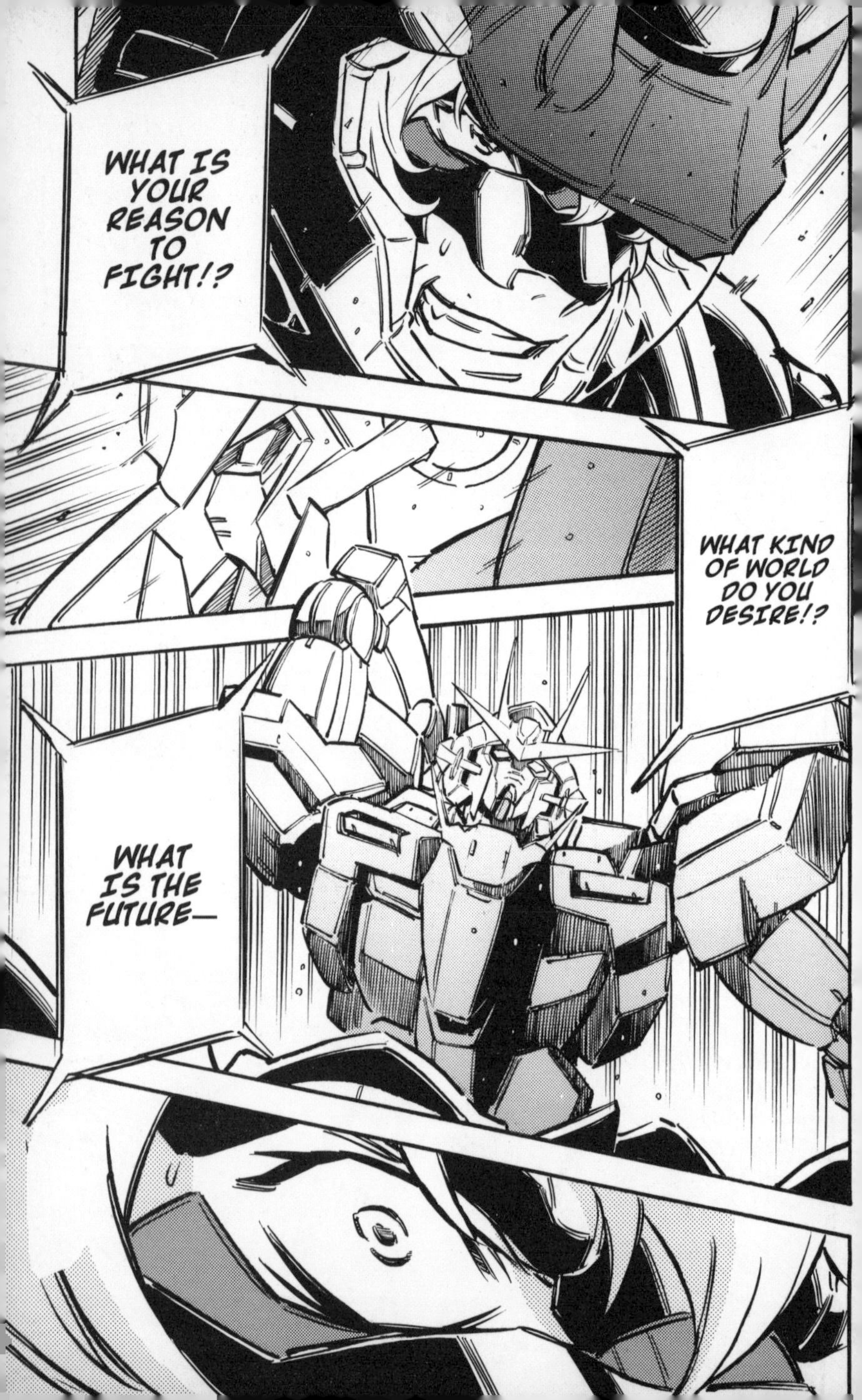
WHAT IS YOUR REASON TO FIGHT!?
WHAT KIND OF WORLD DO YOU DESIRE!?
WHAT IS THE FUTURE—

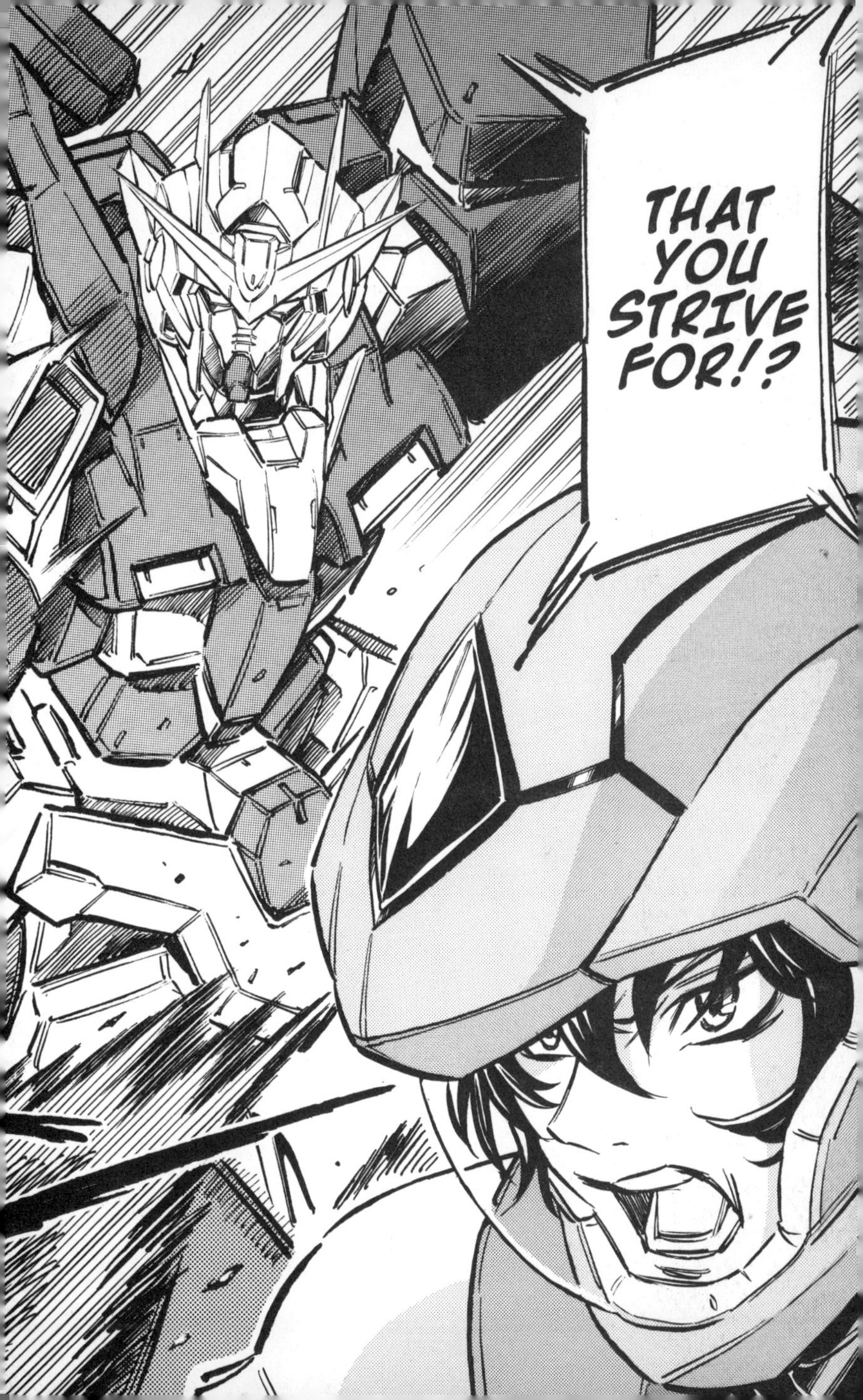
THAT YOU STRIVE FOR!?

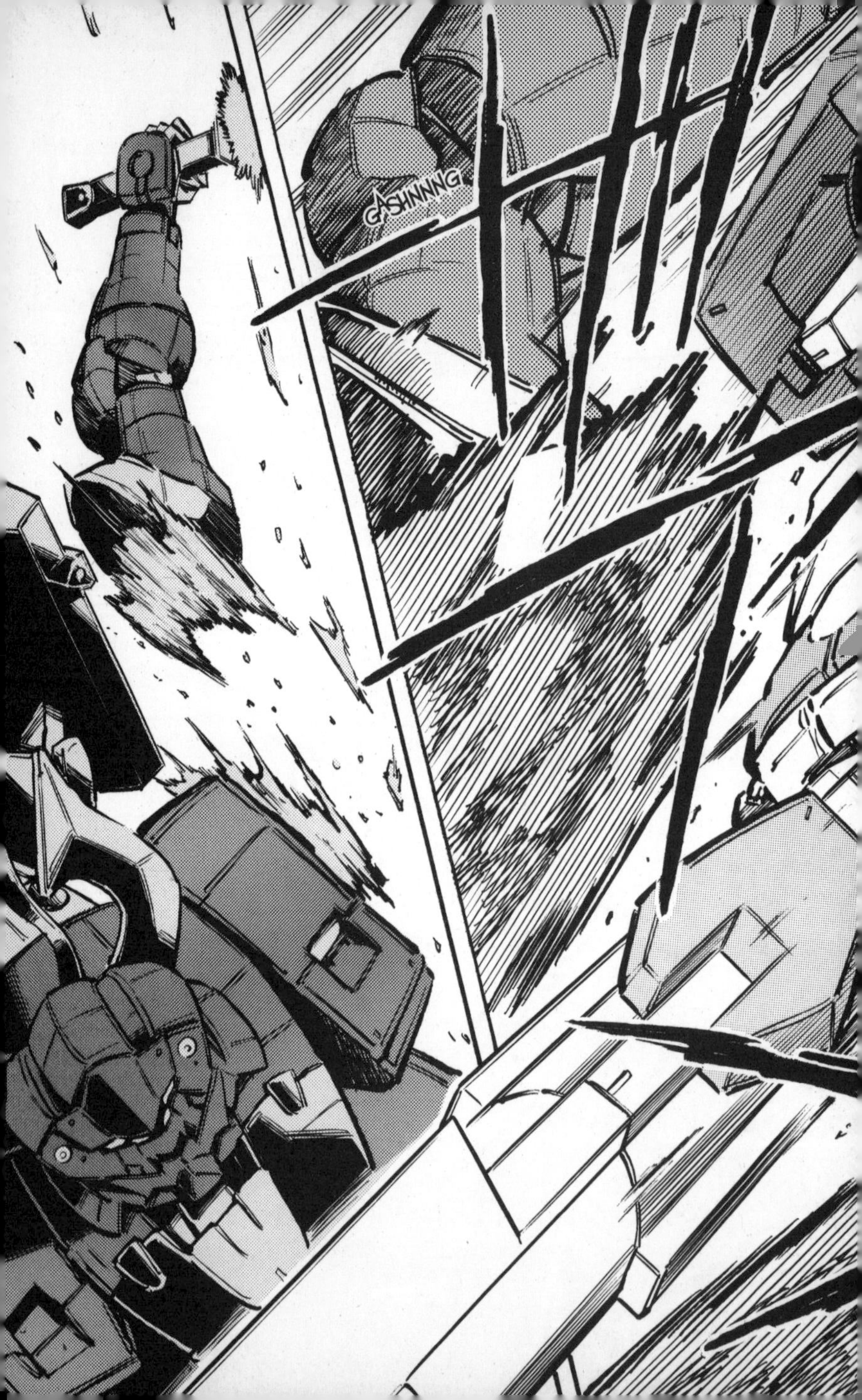
GASHNNNG

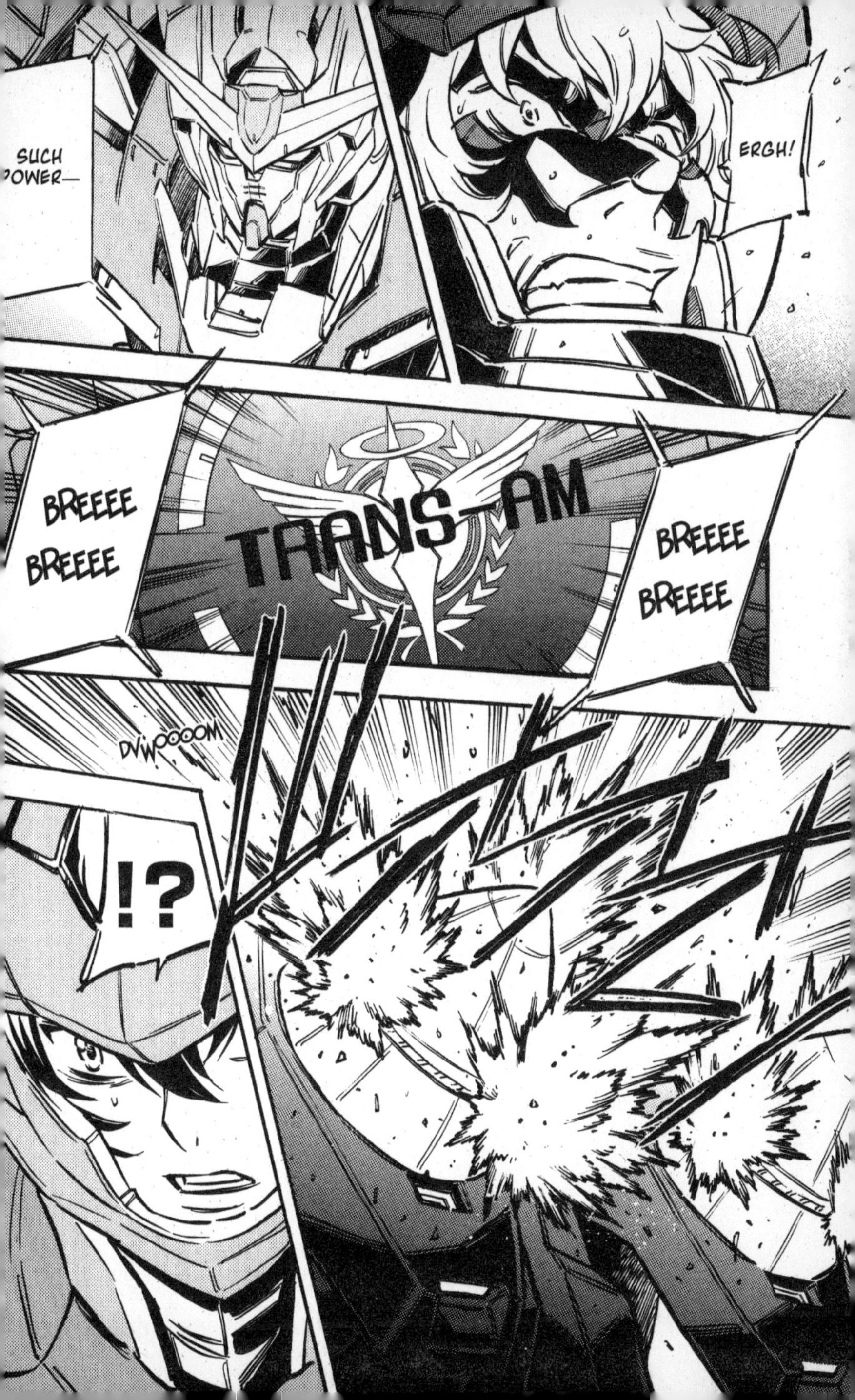
ERGH!
SUCH POWER—
BREEEE BREEEE
TRANS-AM
BREEEE BREEEE
DVWOOOOM
!?

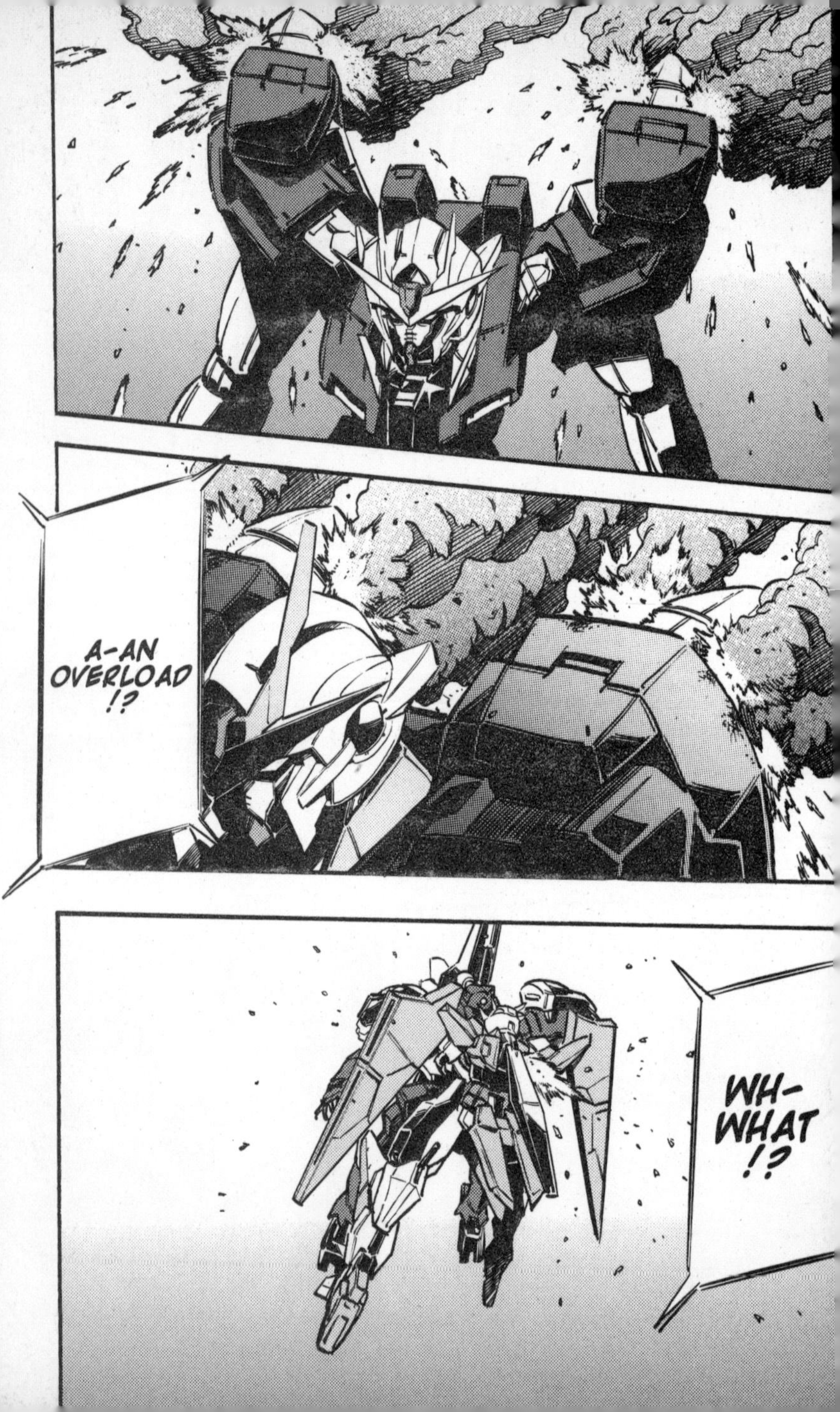
A-AN OVERLOAD !?
WH- WHAT !?

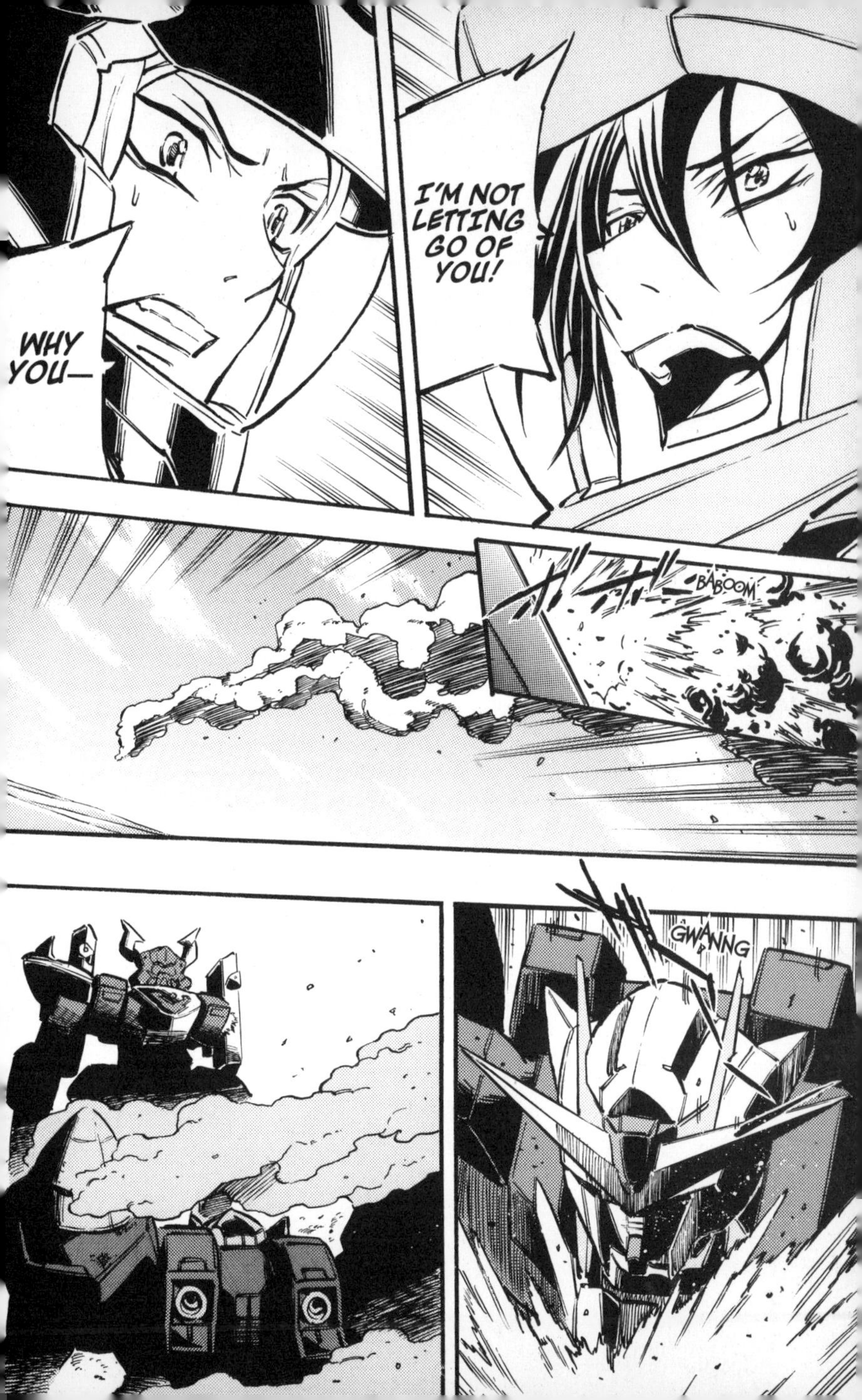
I'M NOT LETTING GO OF YOU!
WHY YOU—
BABOOM
GWANNG

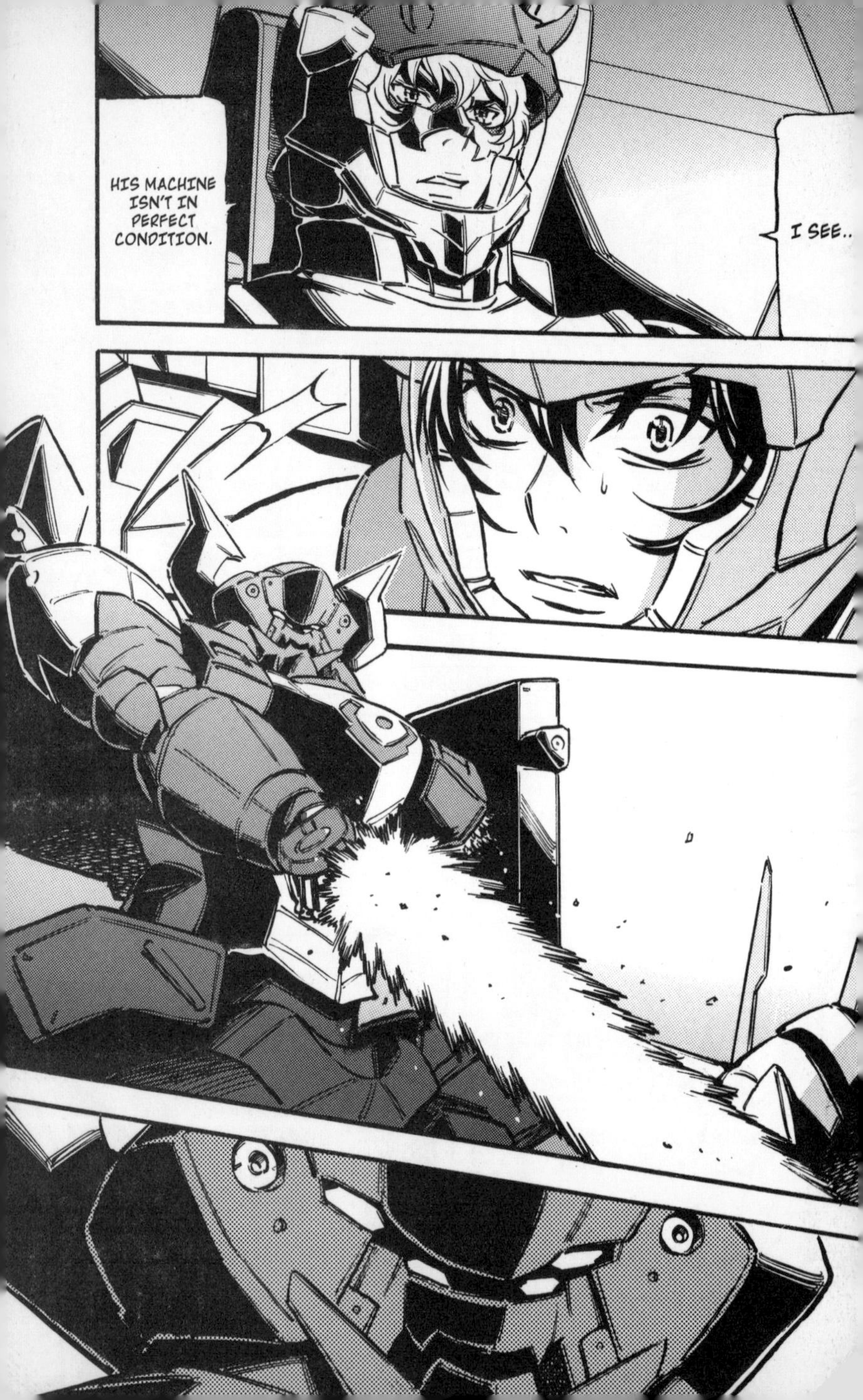
I SEE..
HIS MACHINE ISN'T IN PERFECT CONDITION.

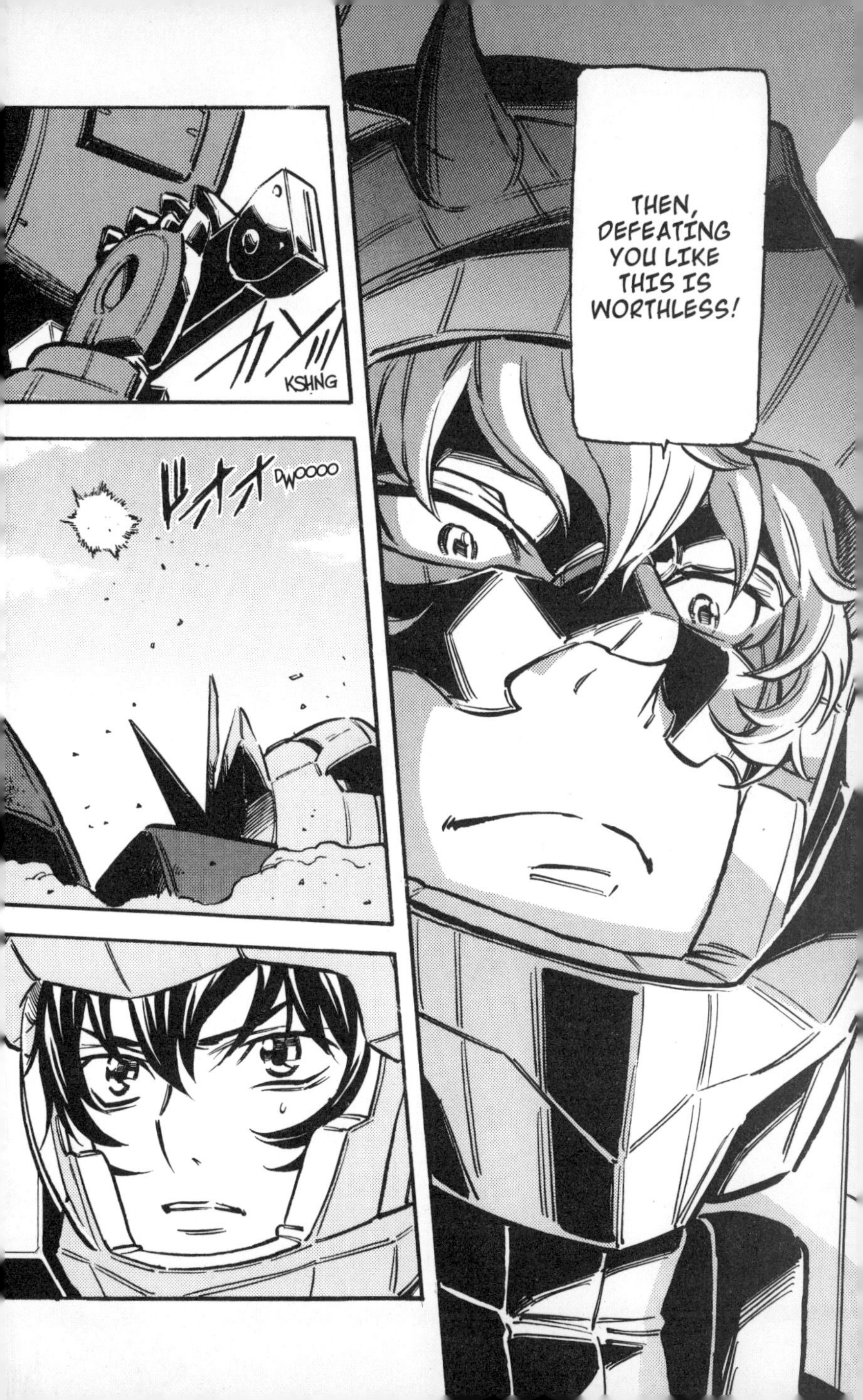
THEN, DEFEATING YOU LIKE THIS IS WORTHLESS!
KSHNG
DWOOOO

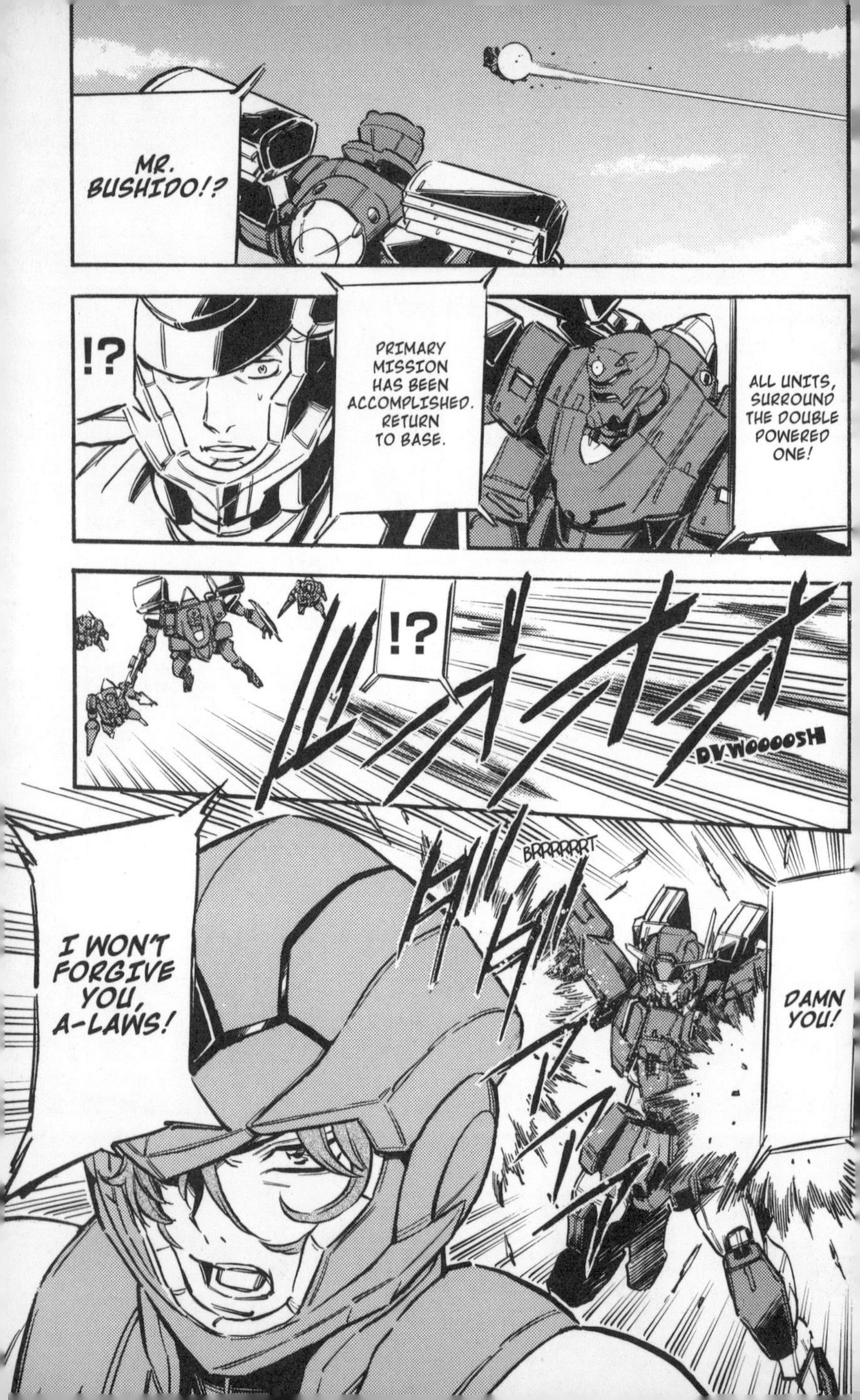
MR. BUSHIDO!?
ALL UNITS, SURROUND THE DOUBLE POWERED ONE!
PRIMARY MISSION HAS BEEN ACCOMPLISHED. RETURN TO BASE.
!?
DV WOOOOSH
!?
DAMN YOU!
BRRRRRRT
I WON'T FORGIVE YOU, A-LAWS!

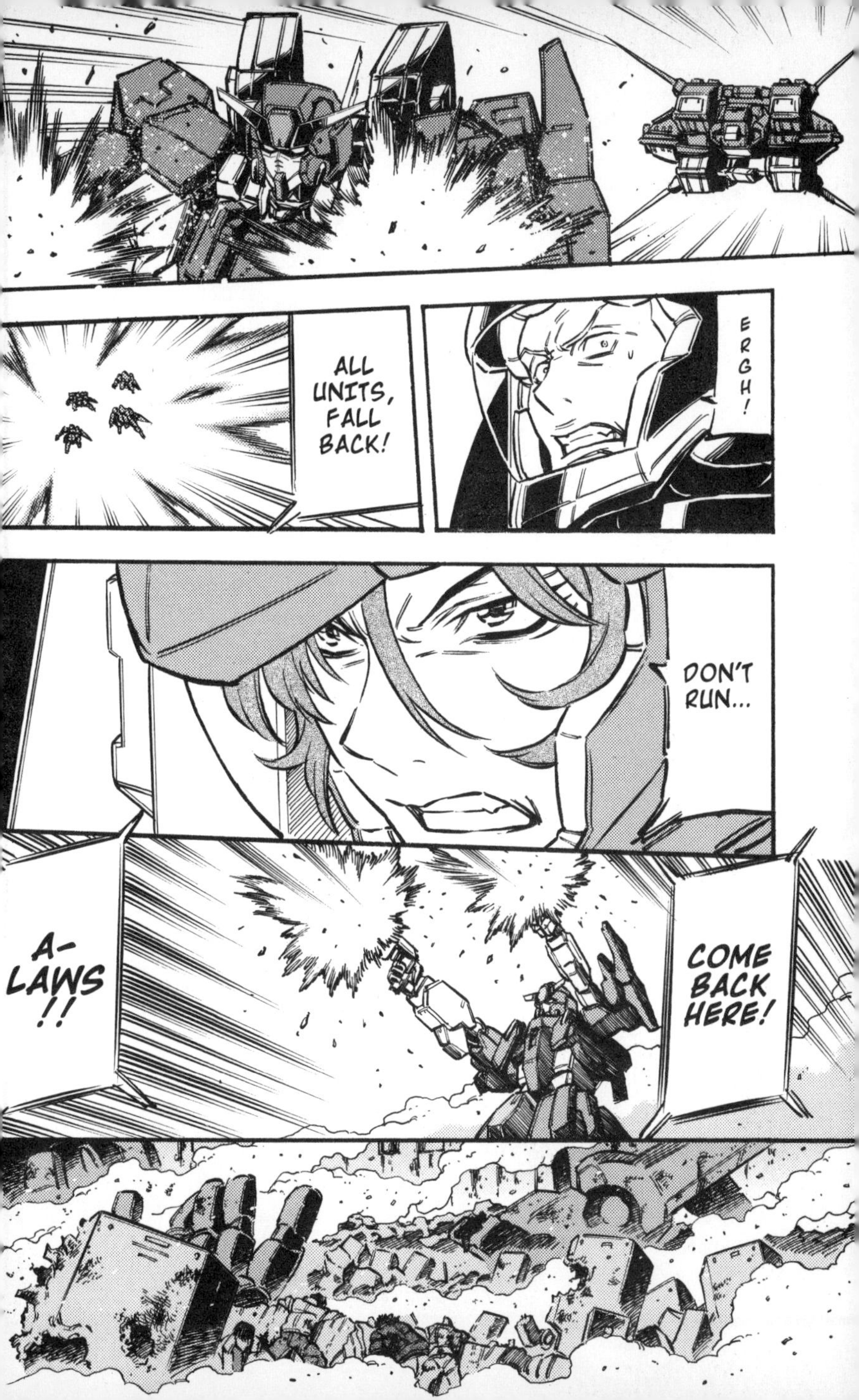
ERGH!
ALL UNITS, FALL BACK!
DON'T RUN...
COME BACK HERE!
A-LAWS!!

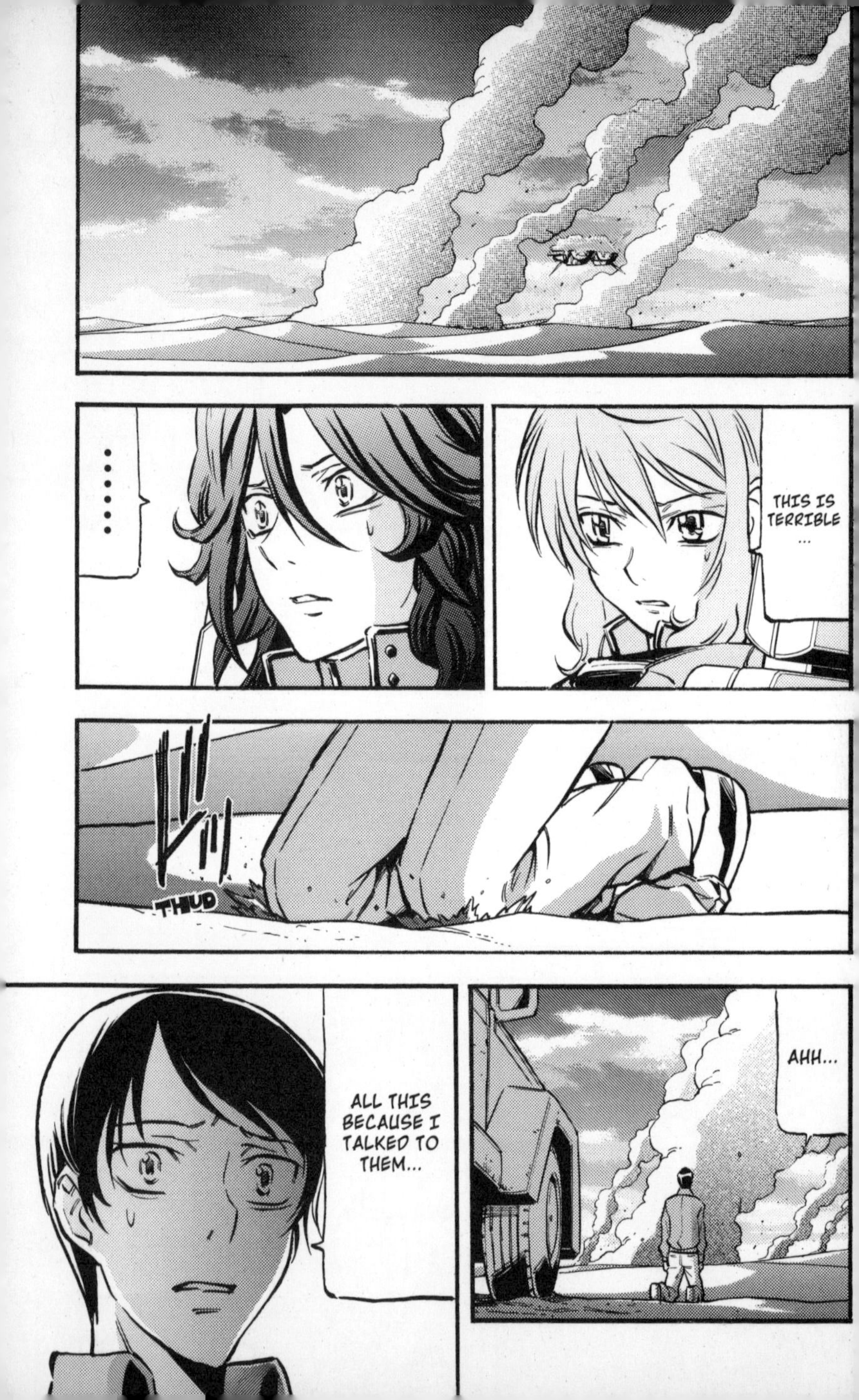
THIS IS TERRIBLE ...
......
THUD
AHH...
ALL THIS BECAUSE I TALKED TO THEM...

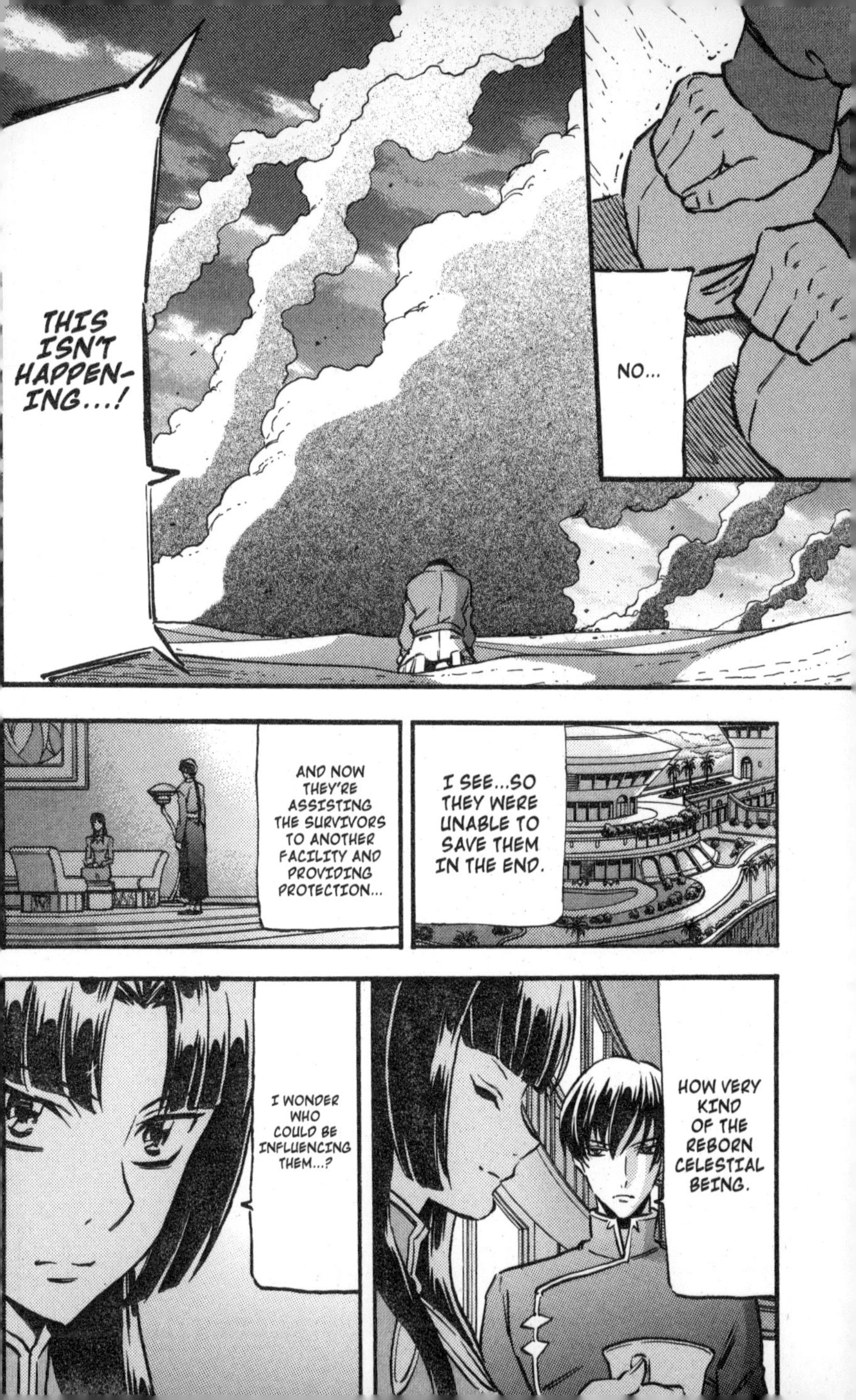
NO...
THIS ISN'T HAPPEN-ING...!
I SEE...SO THEY WERE UNABLE TO SAVE THEM IN THE END.
AND NOW THEY'RE ASSISTING THE SURVIVORS TO ANOTHER FACILITY AND PROVIDING PROTECTION...
HOW VERY KIND OF THE REBORN CELESTIAL BEING.
I WONDER WHO COULD BE INFLUENCING THEM...?

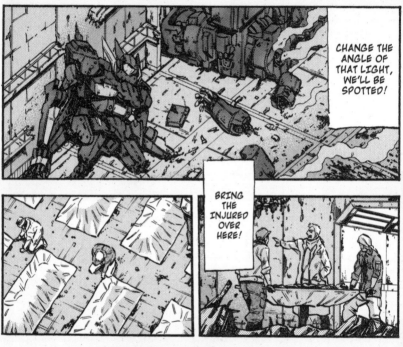

CHANGE THE ANGLE OF THAT LIGHT, WE'LL BE SPOTTED!

BRING THE INJURED OVER HERE!

PLEASE TELL MARINA TO KEEP THE CHILDREN IN THE SHELTER...

IT'S SO BAD ...

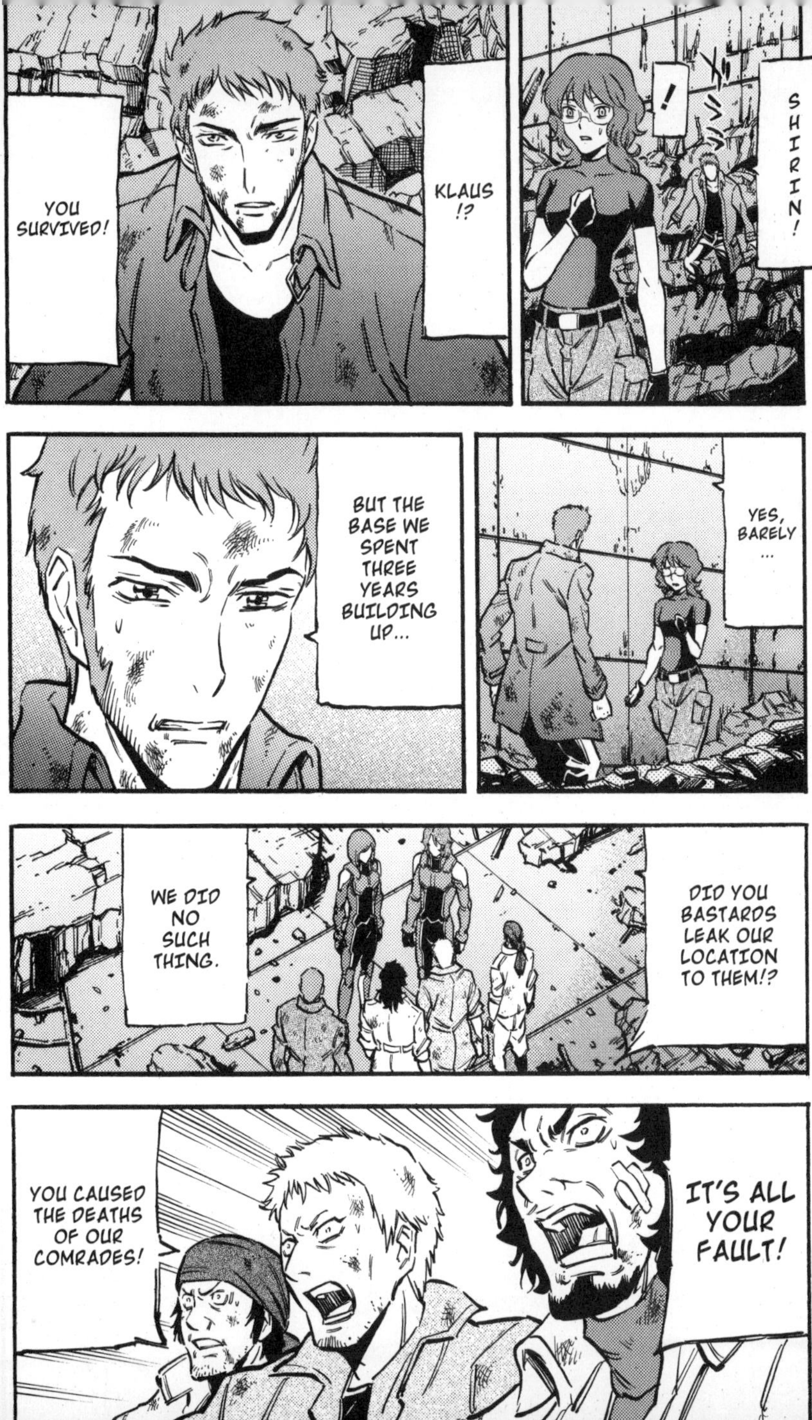
SHIRIN!
!
KLAUS!?
YOU SURVIVED!
YES, BARELY...
BUT THE BASE WE SPENT THREE YEARS BUILDING UP...
DID YOU BASTARDS LEAK OUR LOCATION TO THEM!?
WE DID NO SUCH THING.
IT'S ALL YOUR FAULT!
YOU CAUSED THE DEATHS OF OUR COMRADES!

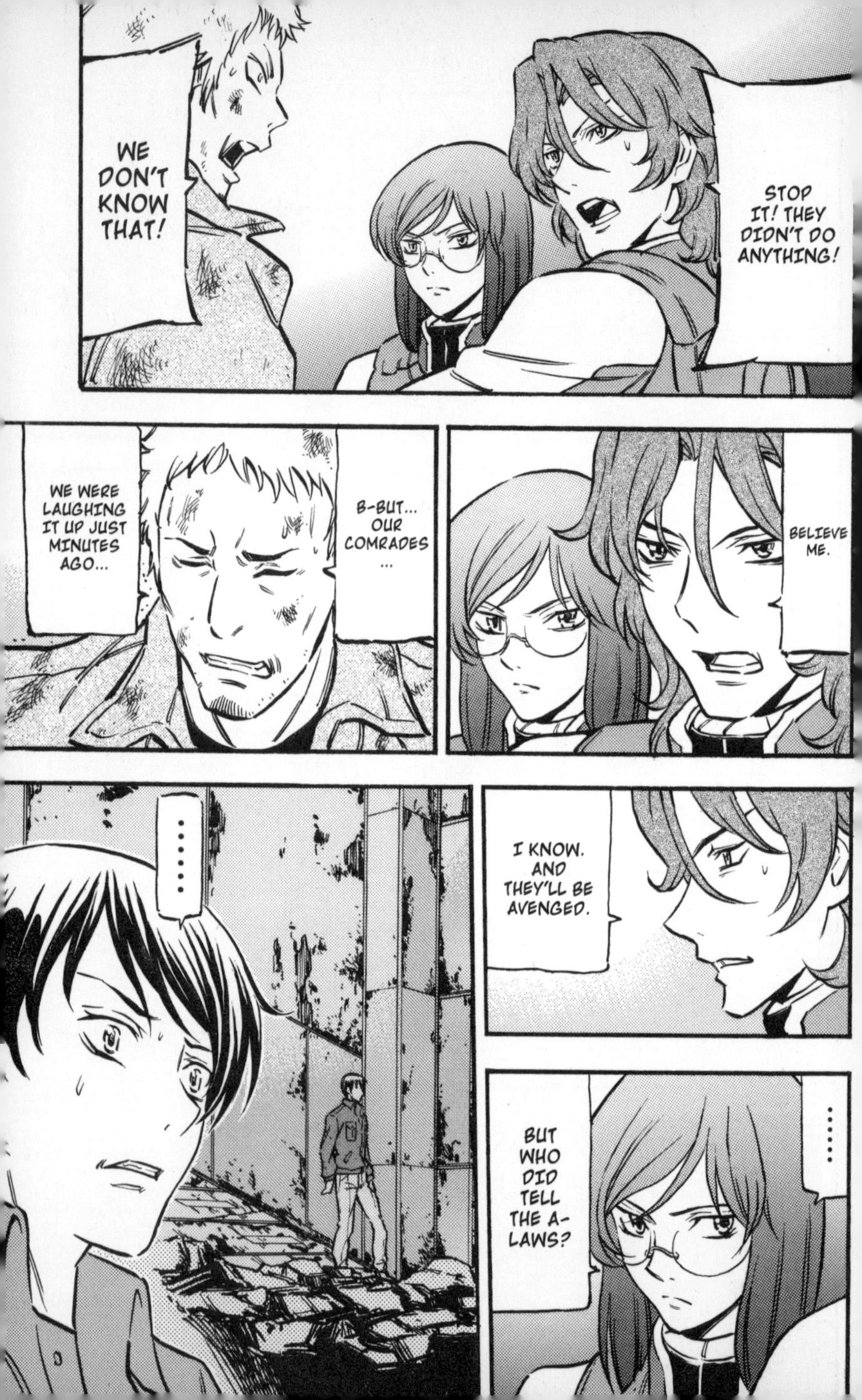
STOP IT! THEY DIDN'T DO ANYTHING!
WE DON'T KNOW THAT!
BELIEVE ME.
B-BUT... OUR COMRADES ...
WE WERE LAUGHING IT UP JUST MINUTES AGO...
I KNOW. AND THEY'LL BE AVENGED.
......
BUT WHO DID TELL THE A-LAWS?
......

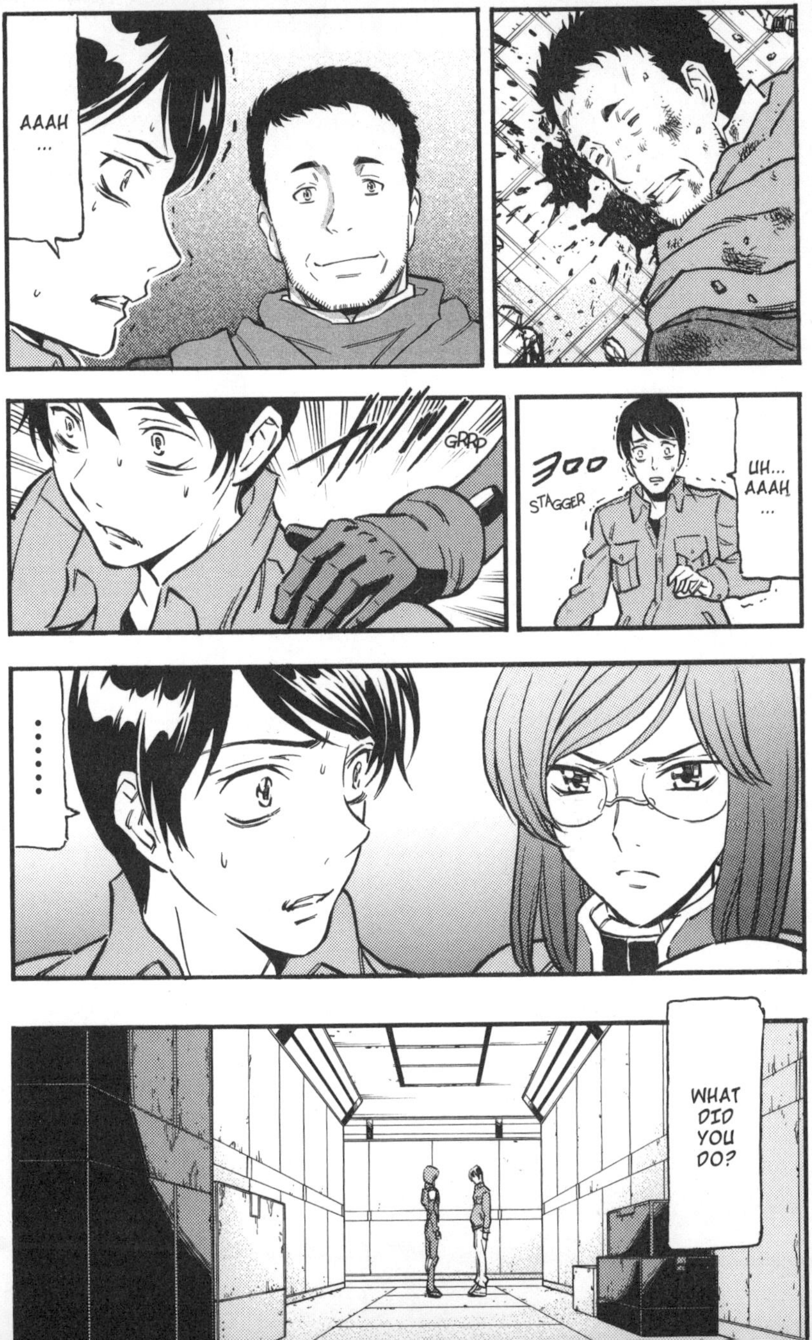
AAAH ...
UH... AAAH ...
ヨロロ
STAGGER
GRRP
......
WHAT DID YOU DO?

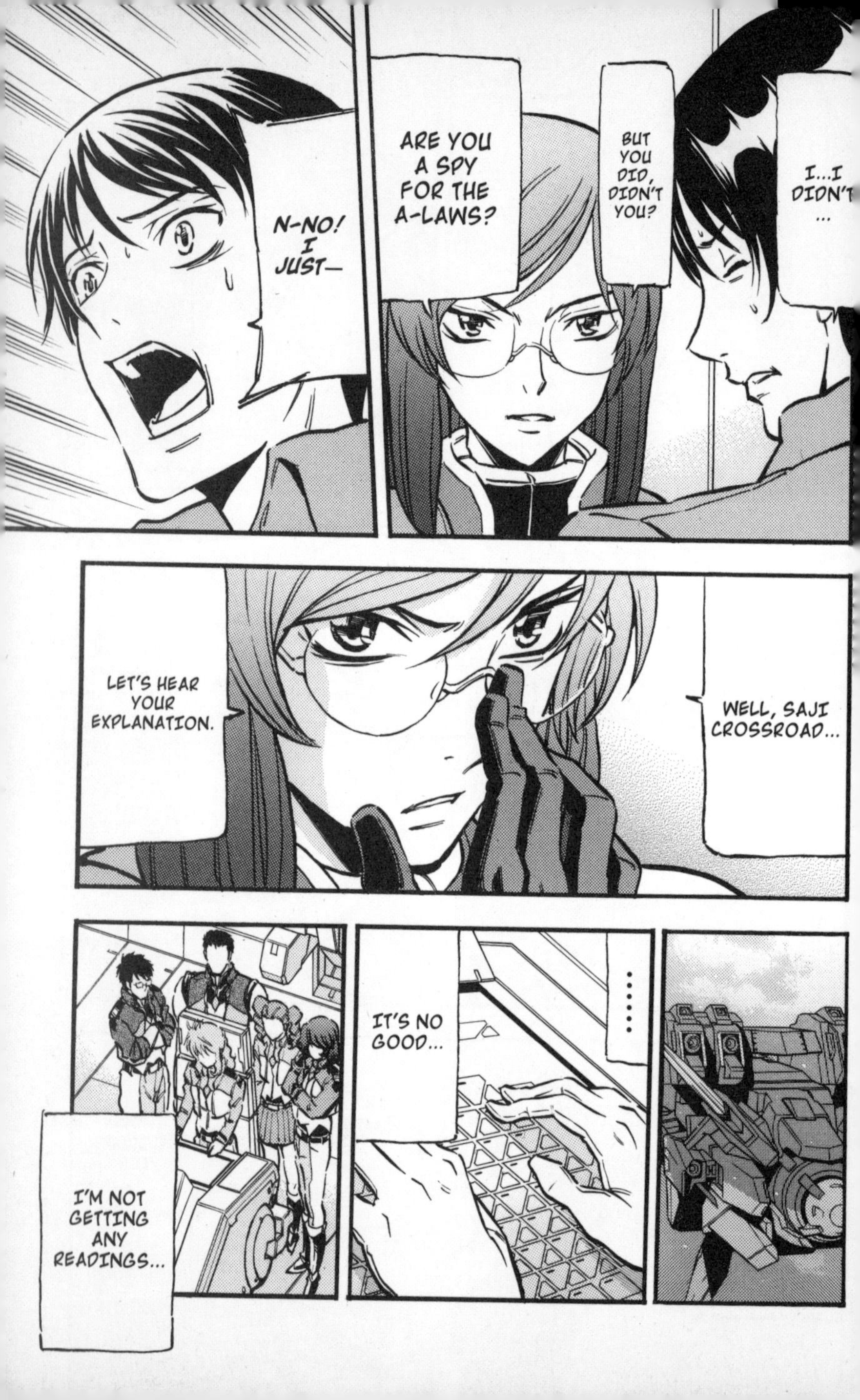
I...I DIDN'T ...
BUT YOU DID, DIDN'T YOU?
ARE YOU A SPY FOR THE A-LAWS?
N-NO! I JUST—
WELL, SAJI CROSSROAD...
LET'S HEAR YOUR EXPLANATION.
......
IT'S NO GOOD...
I'M NOT GETTING ANY READINGS...

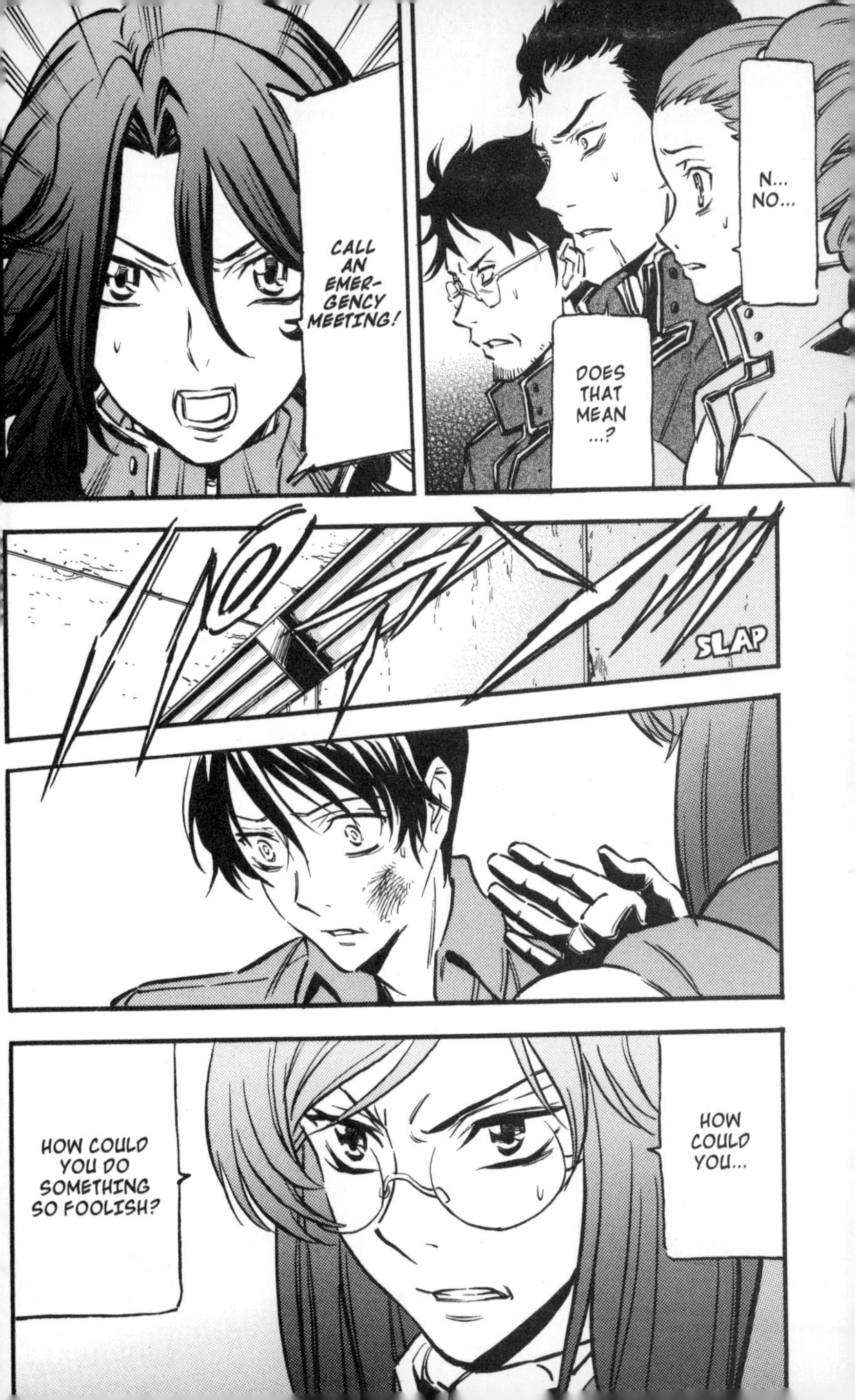
N... NO...
DOES THAT MEAN ...?
CALL AN EMERGENCY MEETING!
SLAP
HOW COULD YOU...
HOW COULD YOU DO SOMETHING SO FOOLISH?

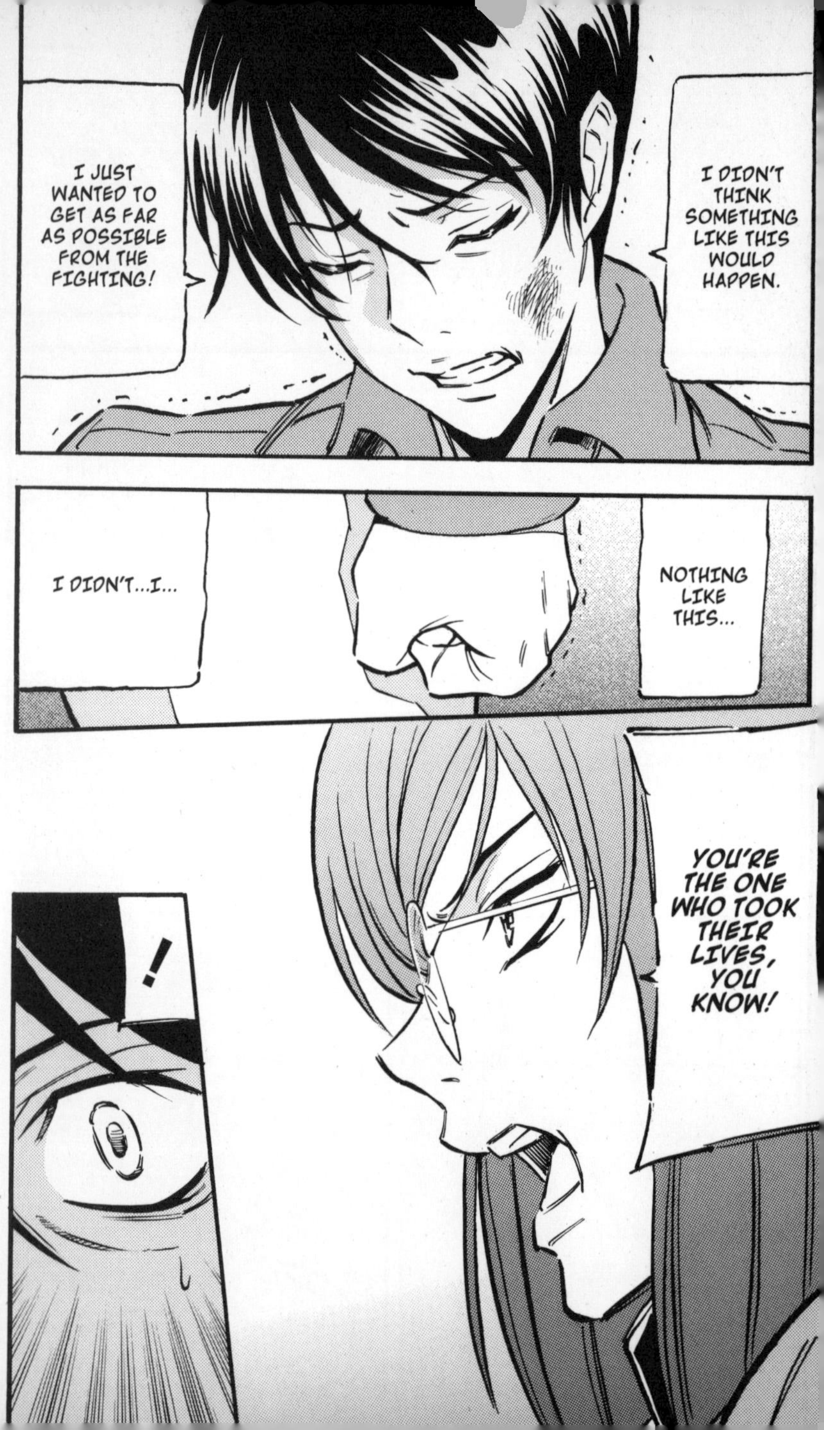
I DIDN'T THINK SOMETHING LIKE THIS WOULD HAPPEN.
I JUST WANTED TO GET AS FAR AS POSSIBLE FROM THE FIGHTING!
NOTHING LIKE THIS...
I DIDN'T...I...
YOU'RE THE ONE WHO TOOK THEIR LIVES, YOU KNOW!
!

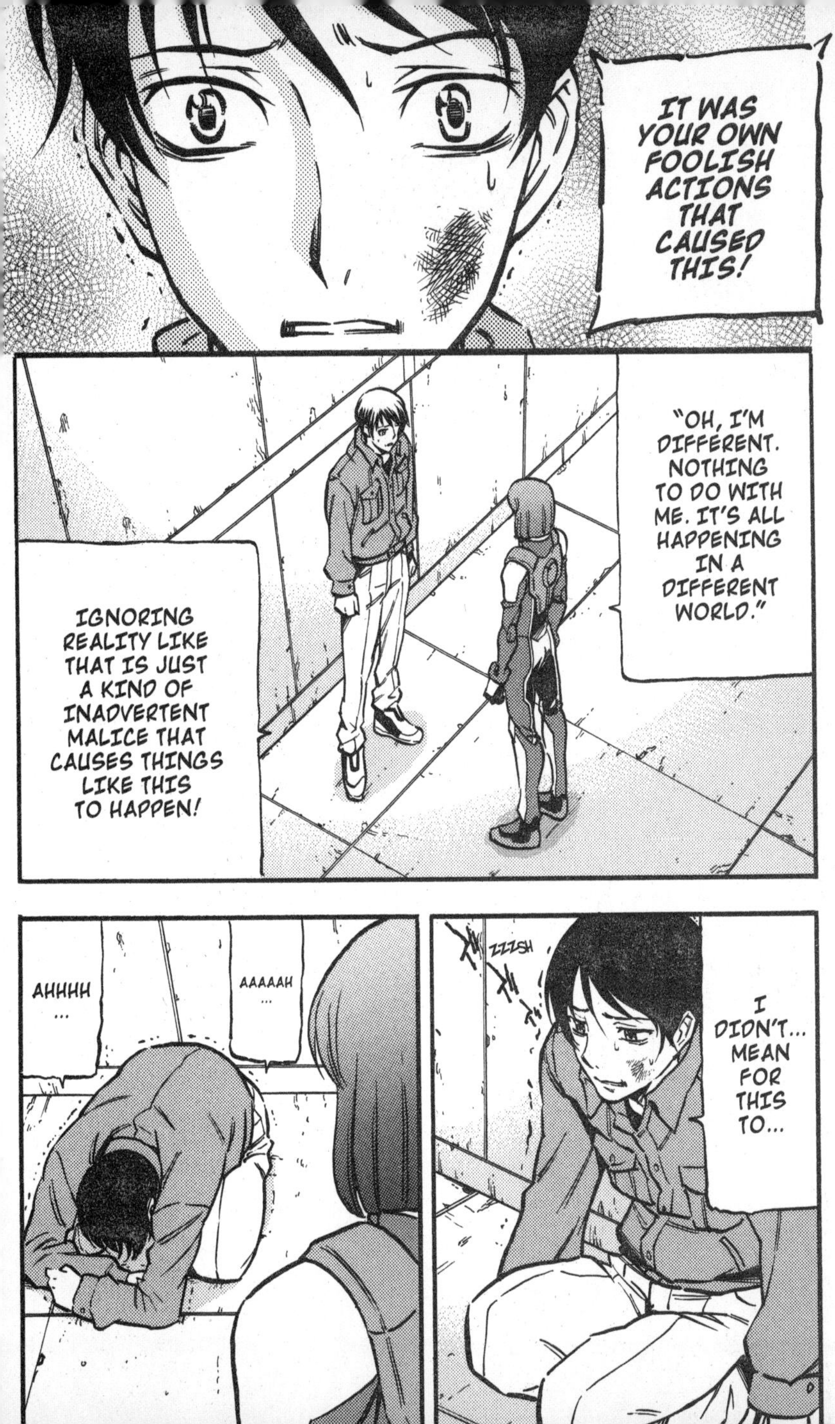
IT WAS YOUR OWN FOOLISH ACTIONS THAT CAUSED THIS!
"OH, I'M DIFFERENT. NOTHING TO DO WITH ME. IT'S ALL HAPPENING IN A DIFFERENT WORLD."
IGNORING REALITY LIKE THAT IS JUST A KIND OF INADVERTENT MALICE THAT CAUSES THINGS LIKE THIS TO HAPPEN!
ZZZSH
I DIDN'T... MEAN FOR THIS TO...
AAAAAH...
AHHHH...

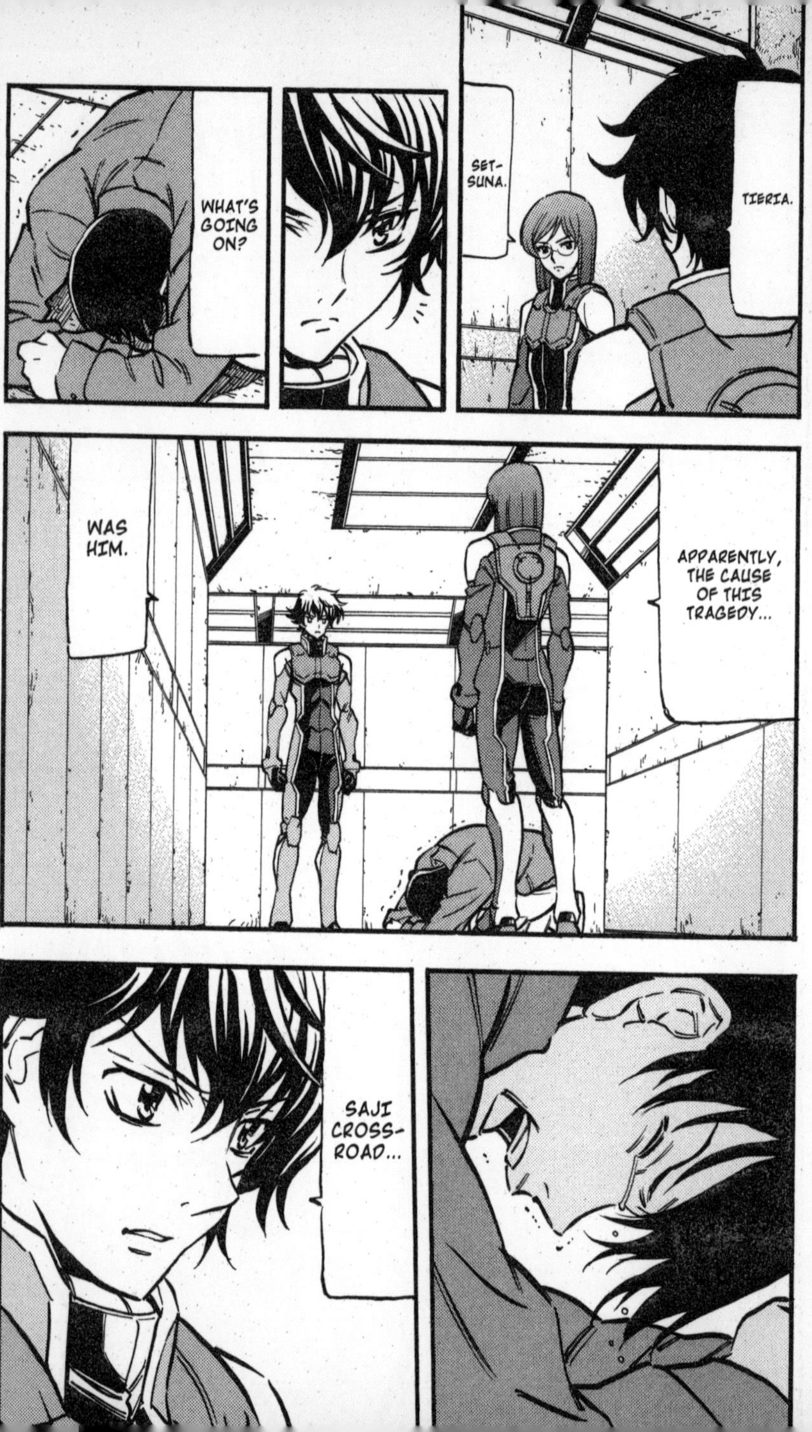
TIERIA.
SET-SUNA.
WHAT'S GOING ON?
APPARENTLY, THE CAUSE OF THIS TRAGEDY...
WAS HIM.
SAJI CROSS-ROAD...

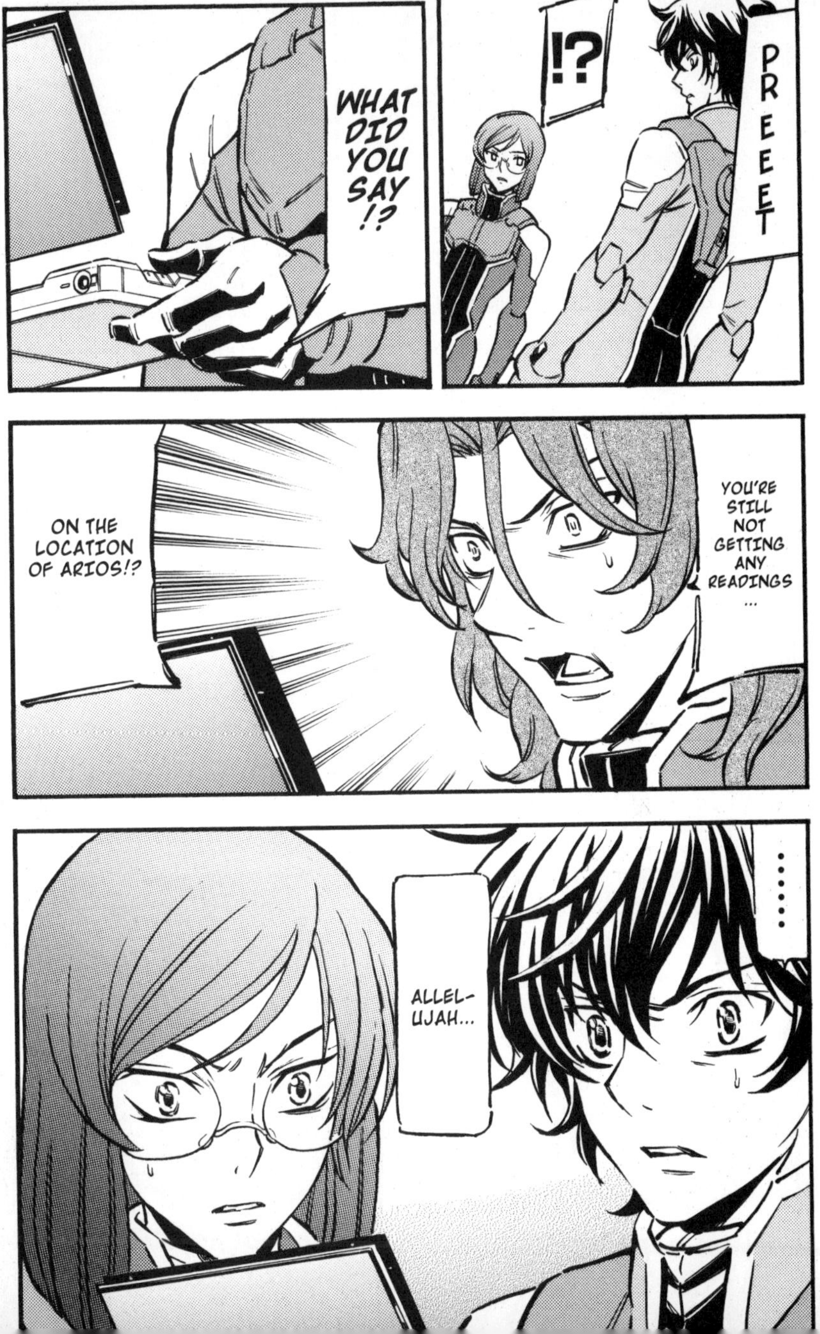
PREEET
!?
WHAT DID YOU SAY!?
YOU'RE STILL NOT GETTING ANY READINGS...
ON THE LOCATION OF ARIOS!?
......
ALLEL-UJAH...

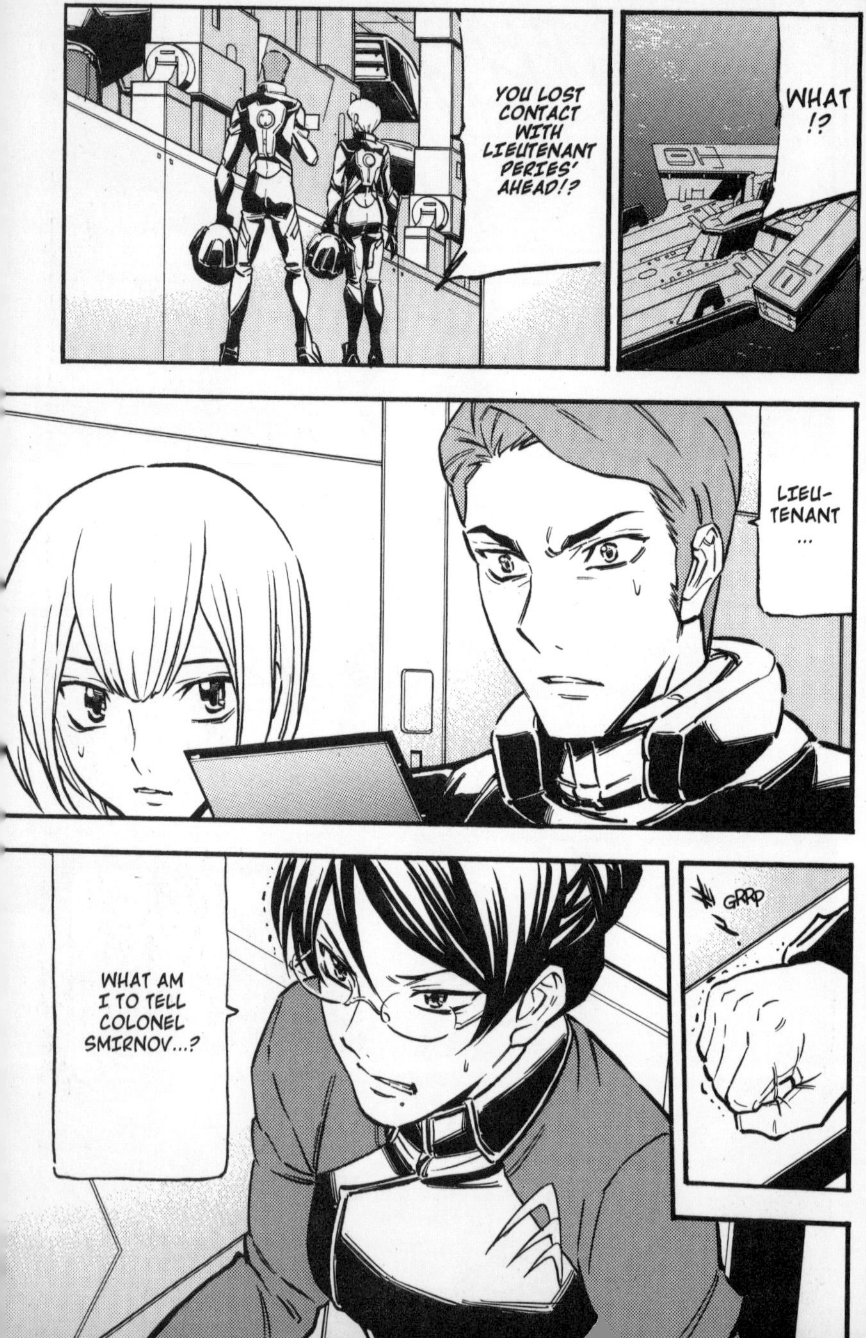
WHAT !?
YOU LOST CONTACT WITH LIEUTENANT PERIES' AHEAD!?
LIEU-TENANT ...
GRRP
WHAT AM I TO TELL COLONEL SMIRNOV...?

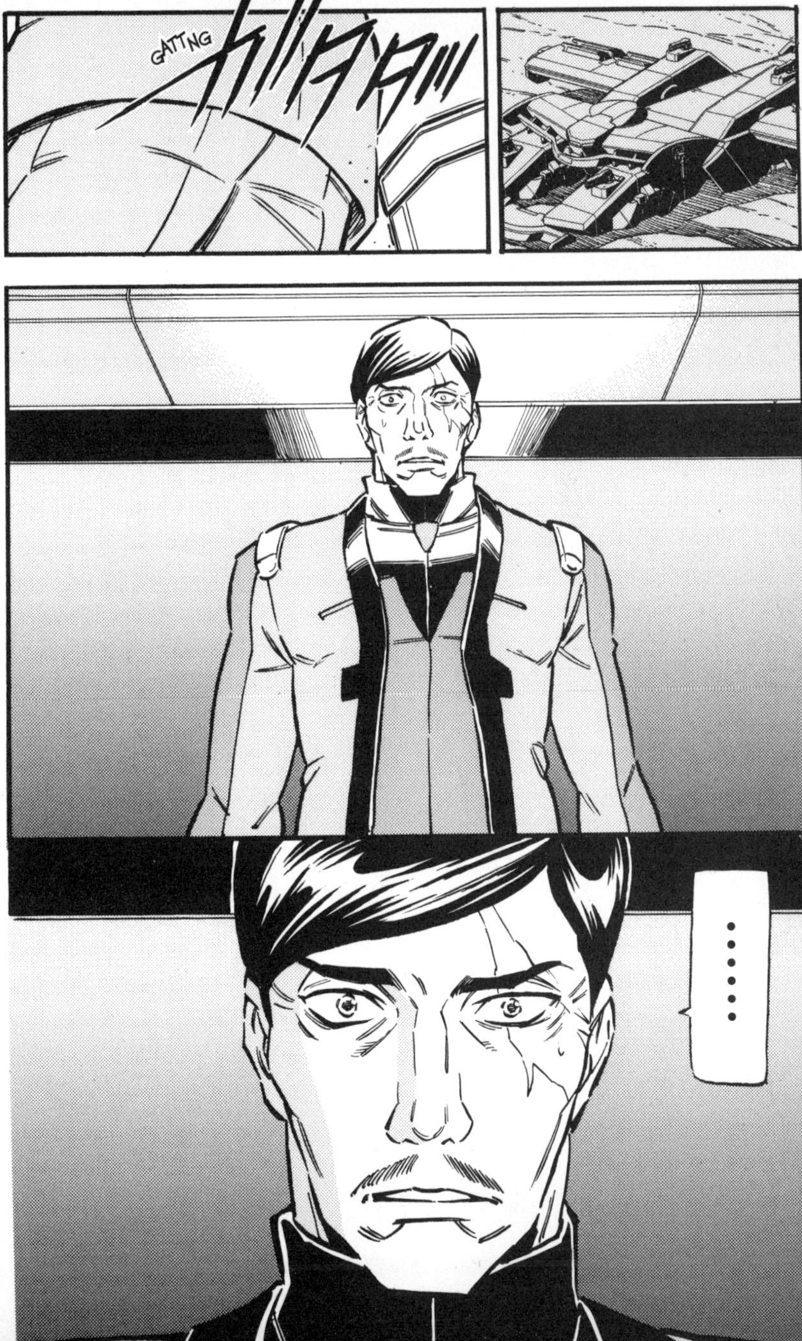
GATTNG
......

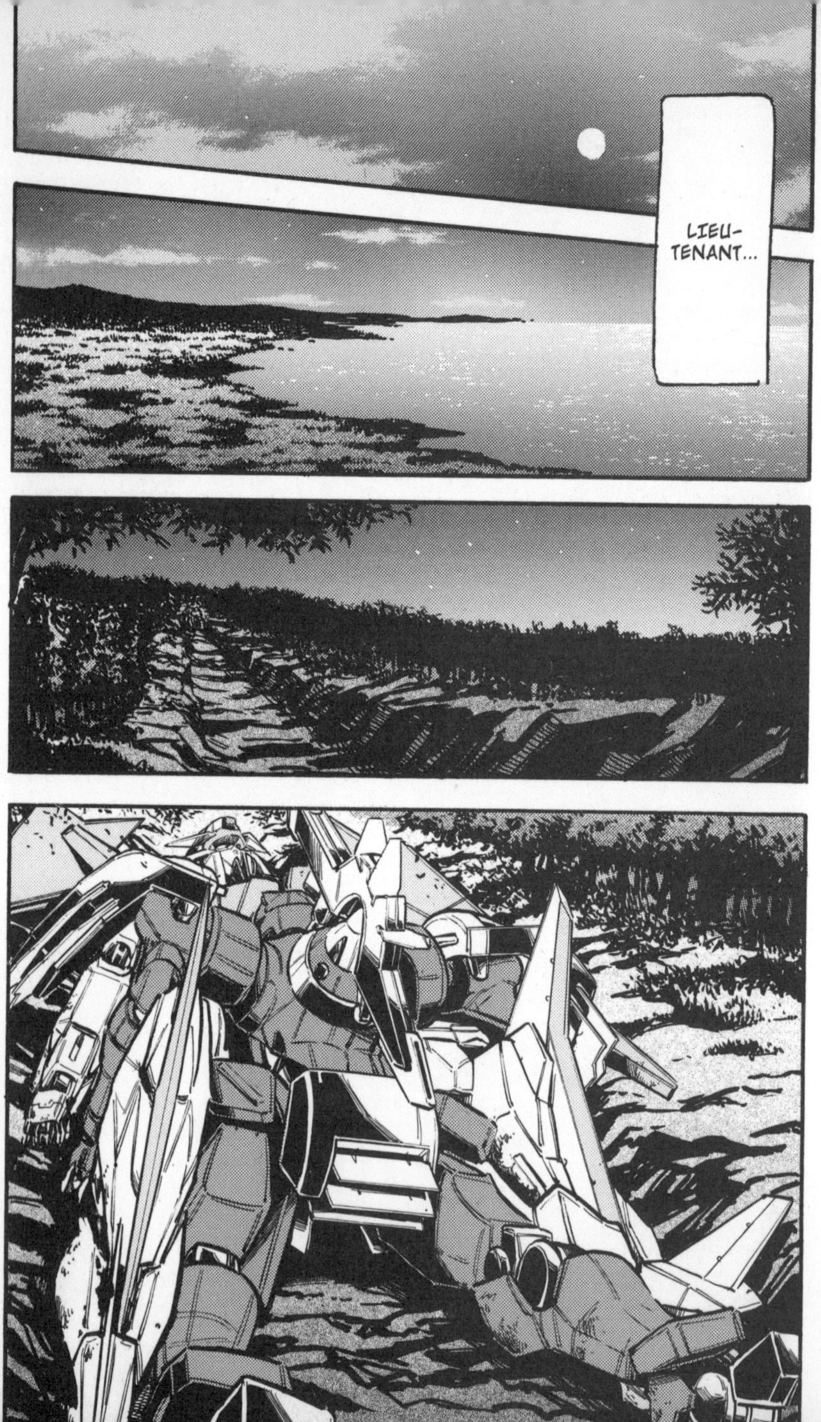
LIEU-
TENANT...

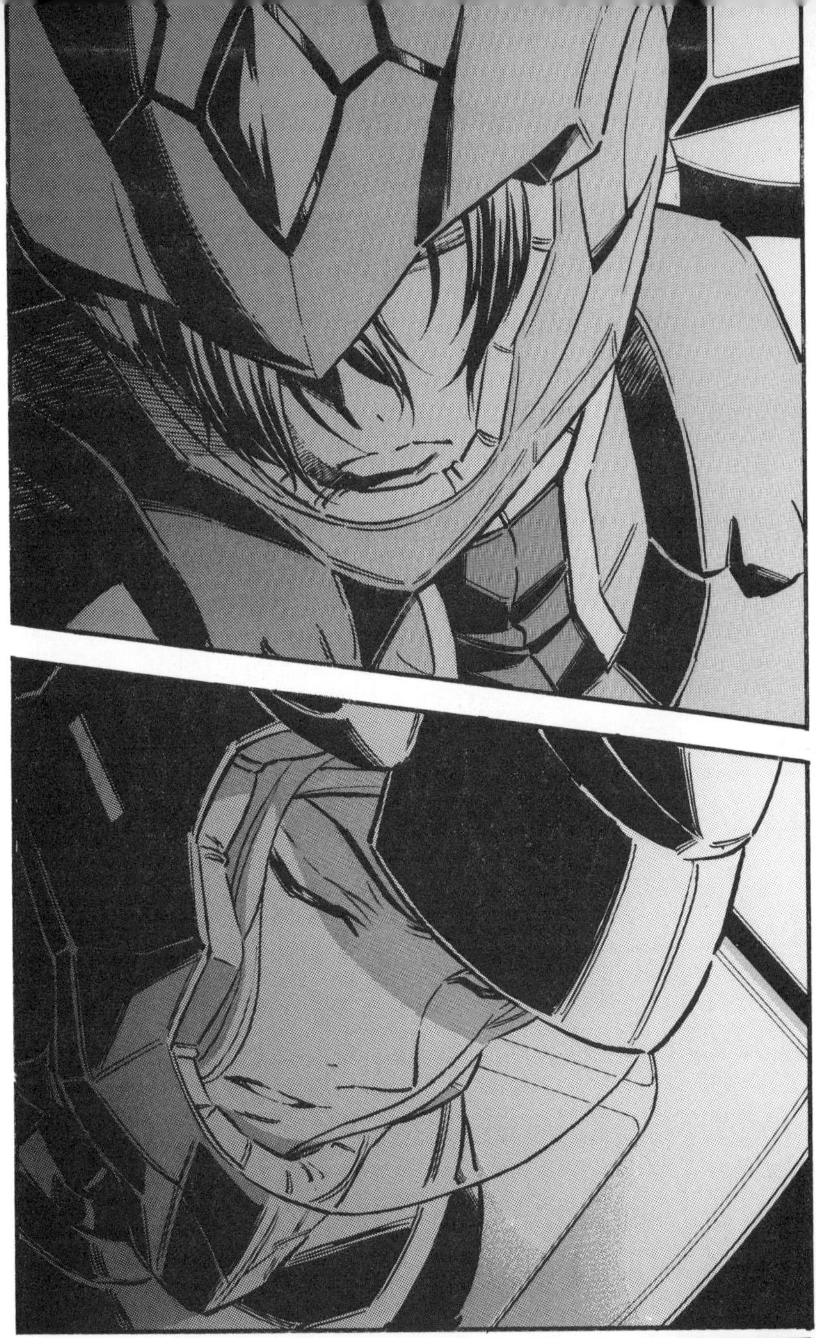

CHAPTER 5 > END

MOBILE SUIT GUNDAM 00 DOUBLE-O
機動戦士ガンダム
SECOND SEASON

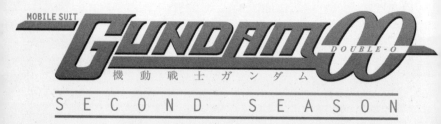

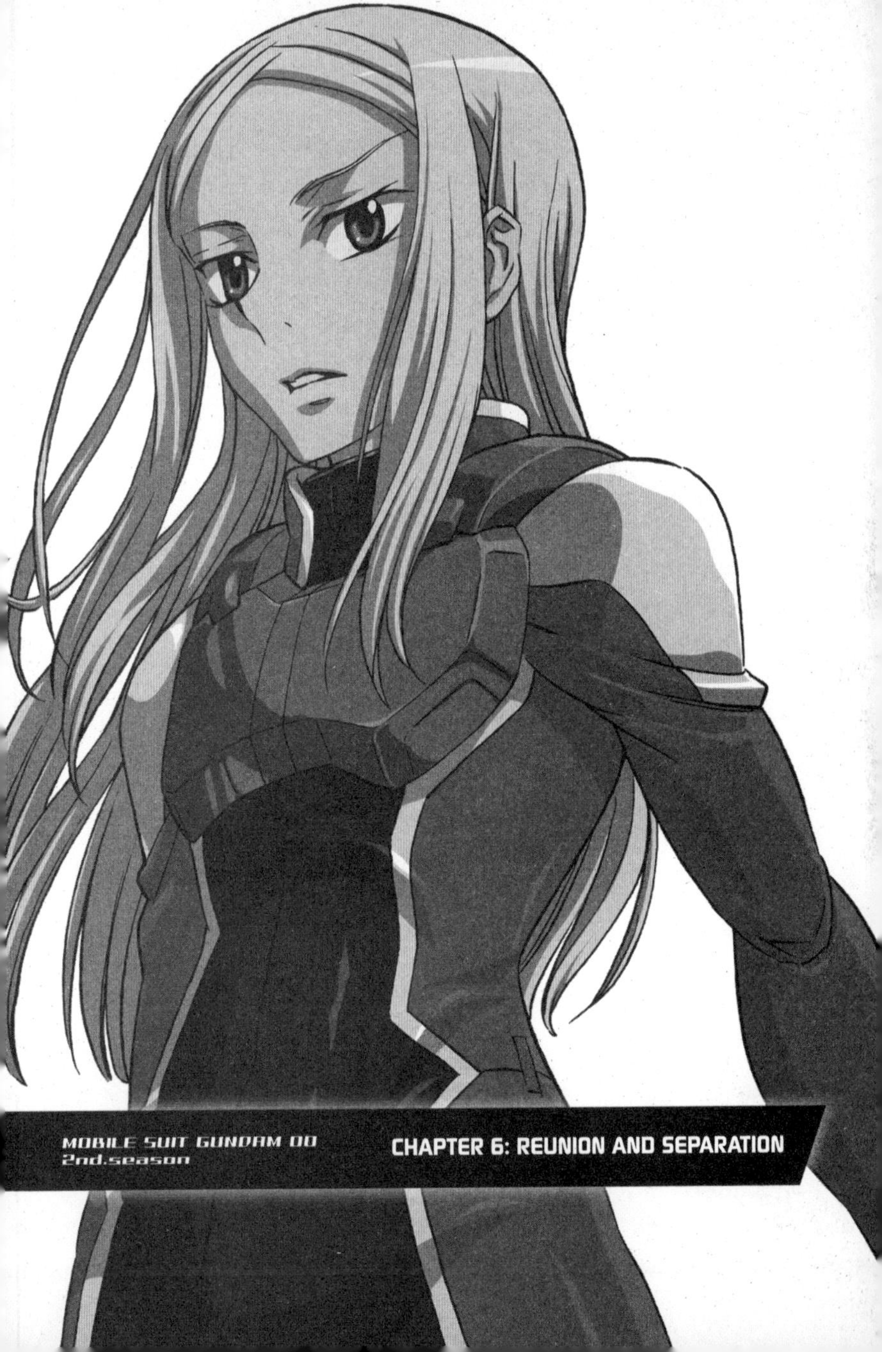

MOBILE SUIT GUNDAM 00
2nd.season

CHAPTER 6: REUNION AND SEPARATION

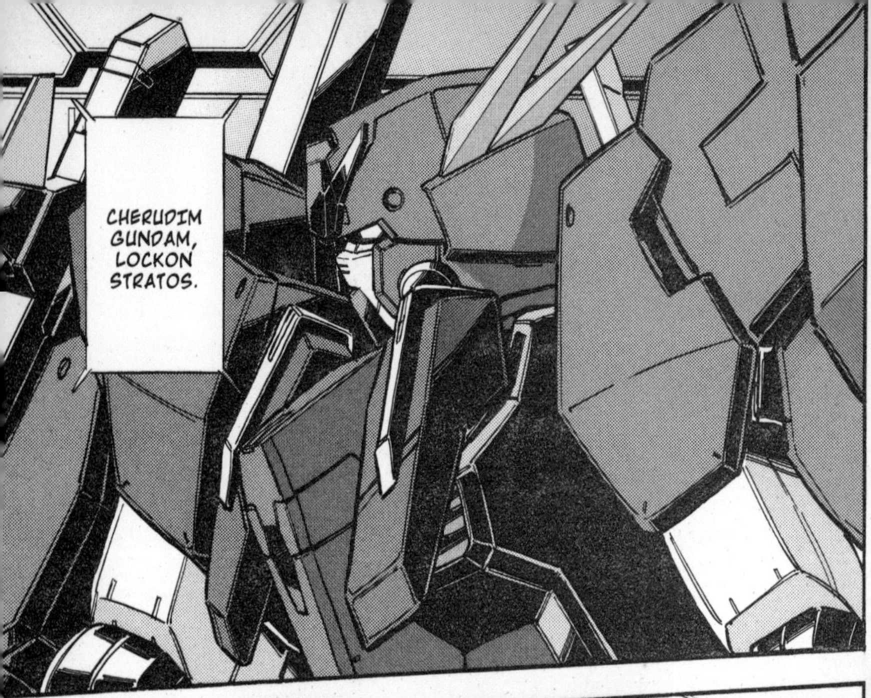
CHERUDIM GUNDAM, LOCKON STRATOS.
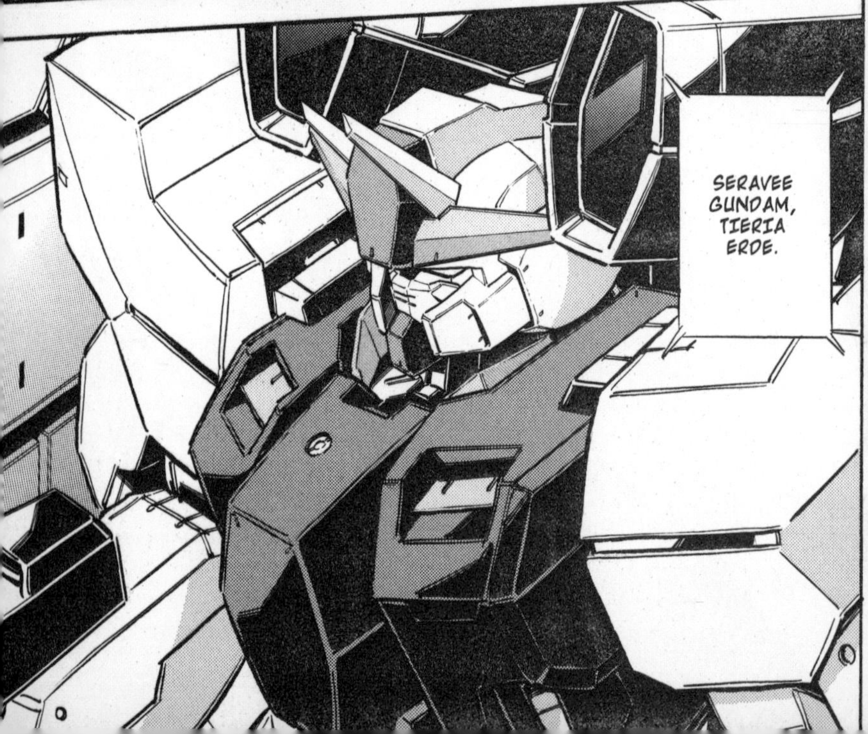
SERAVEE GUNDAM, TIERIA ERDE.

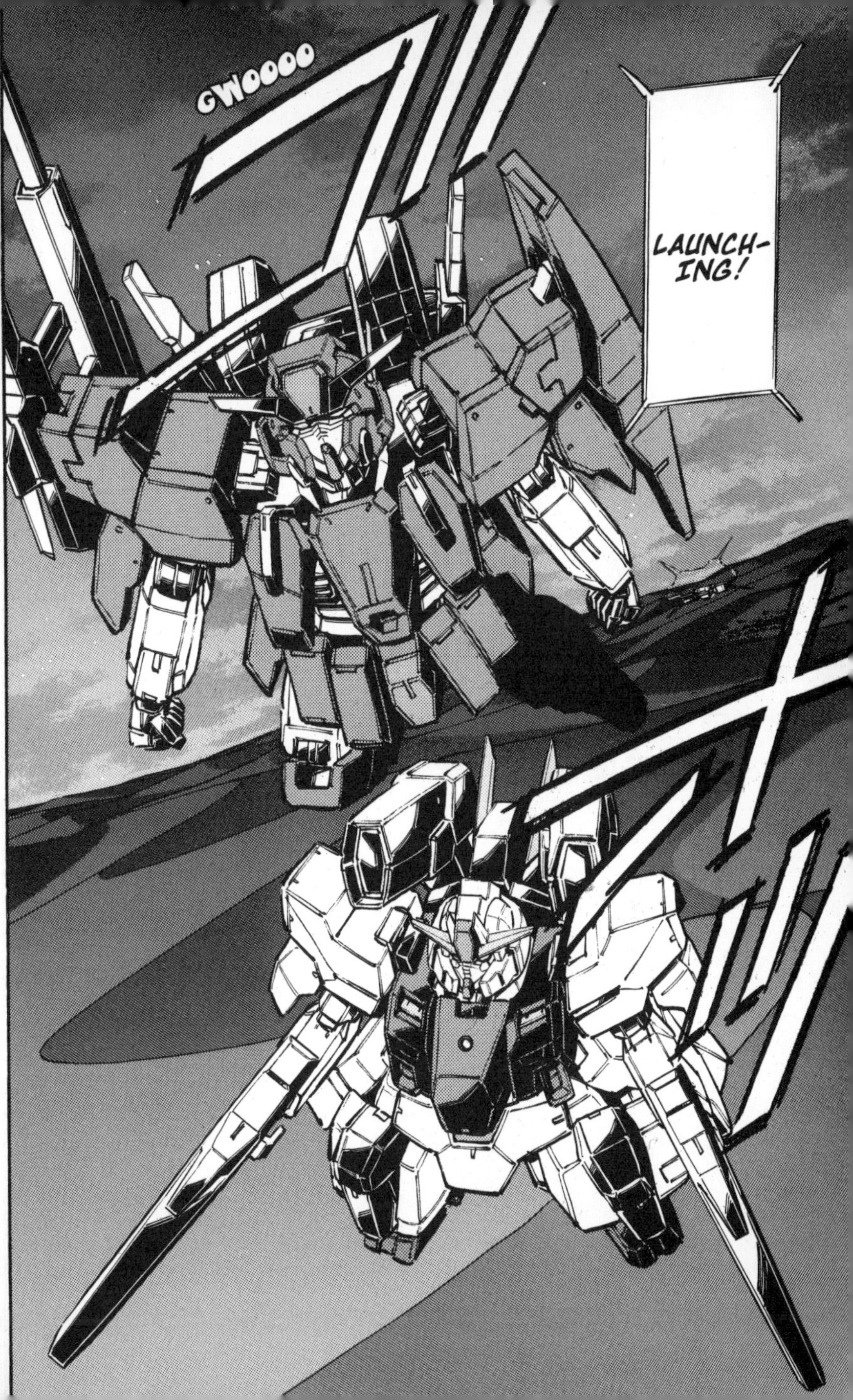
LAUNCH-ING!
GWOOOO

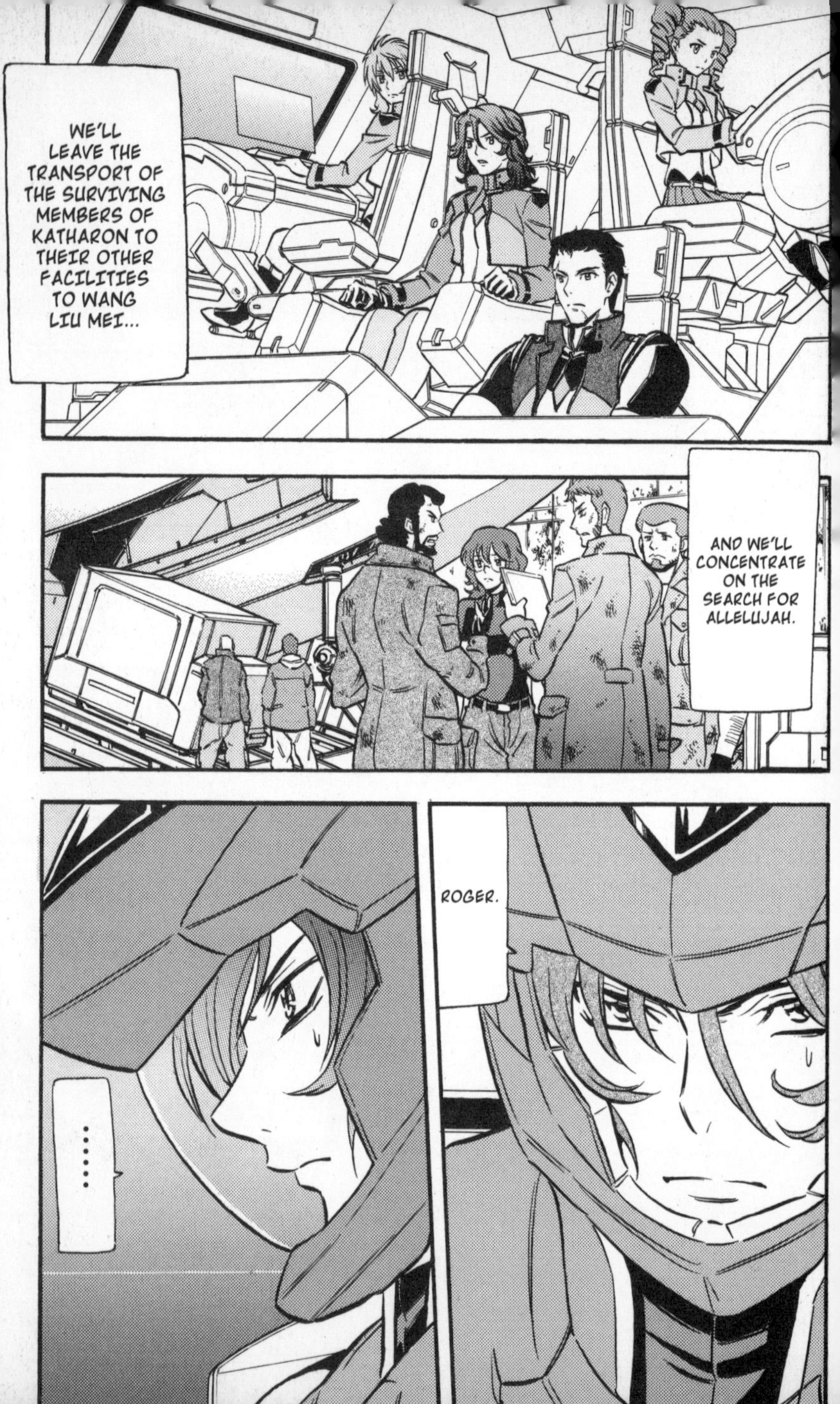
WE'LL LEAVE THE TRANSPORT OF THE SURVIVING MEMBERS OF KATHARON TO THEIR OTHER FACILITIES TO WANG LIU MEI...
AND WE'LL CONCENTRATE ON THE SEARCH FOR ALLELUJAH.
ROGER.
......

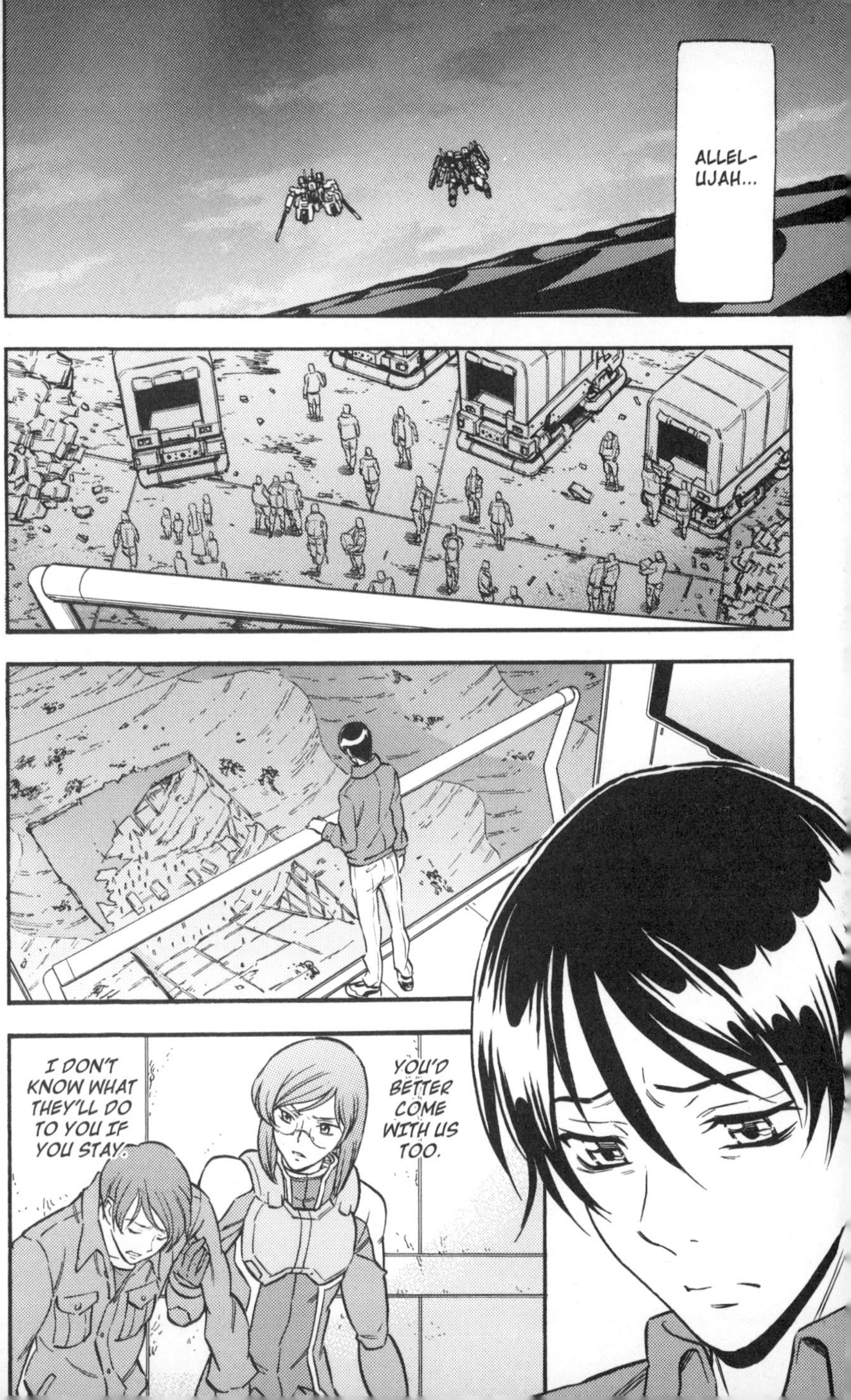
ALLEL-UJAH...
YOU'D BETTER COME WITH US TOO.
I DON'T KNOW WHAT THEY'LL DO TO YOU IF YOU STAY.

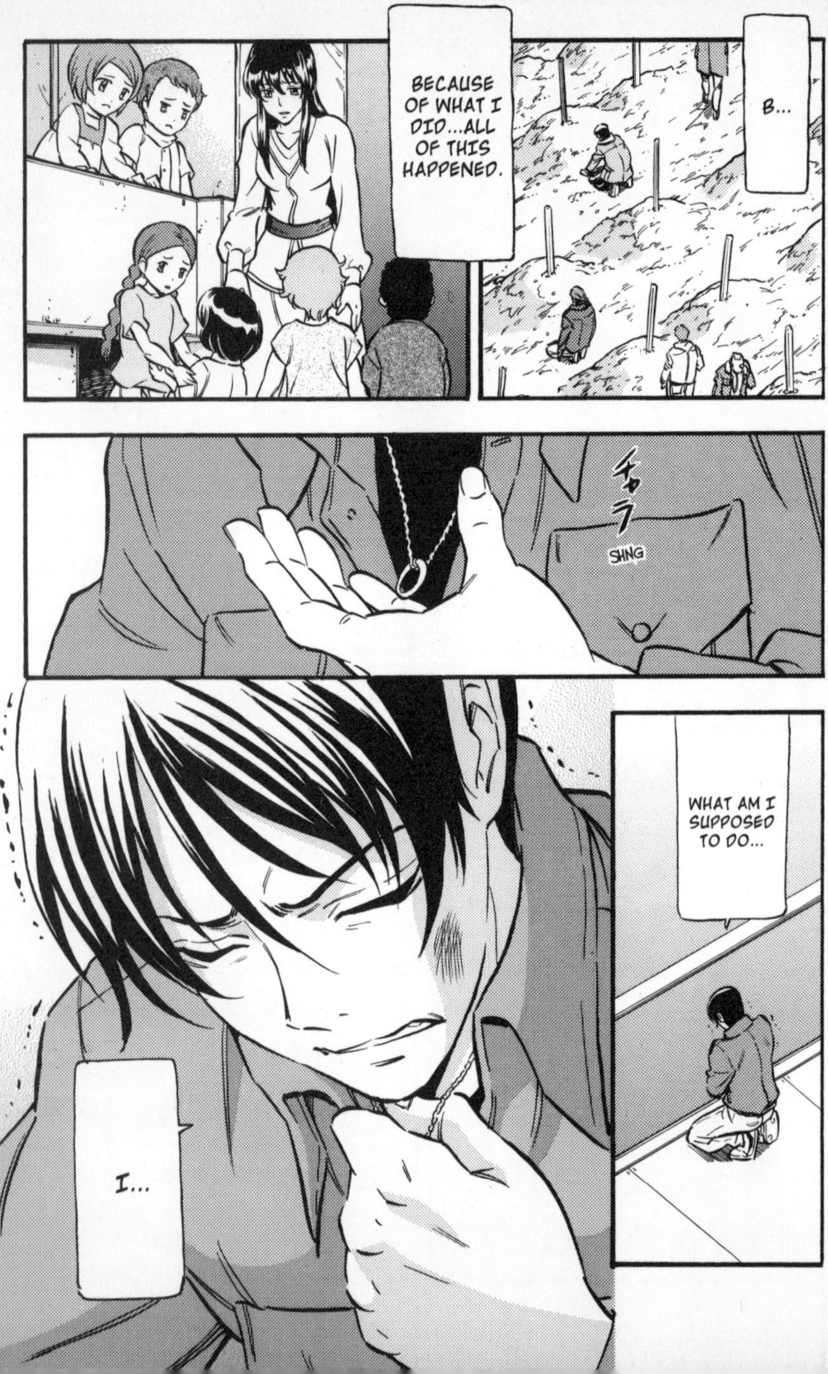
B...
BECAUSE OF WHAT I DID...ALL OF THIS HAPPENED.
チャラ
SHNG
WHAT AM I SUPPOSED TO DO...
I...

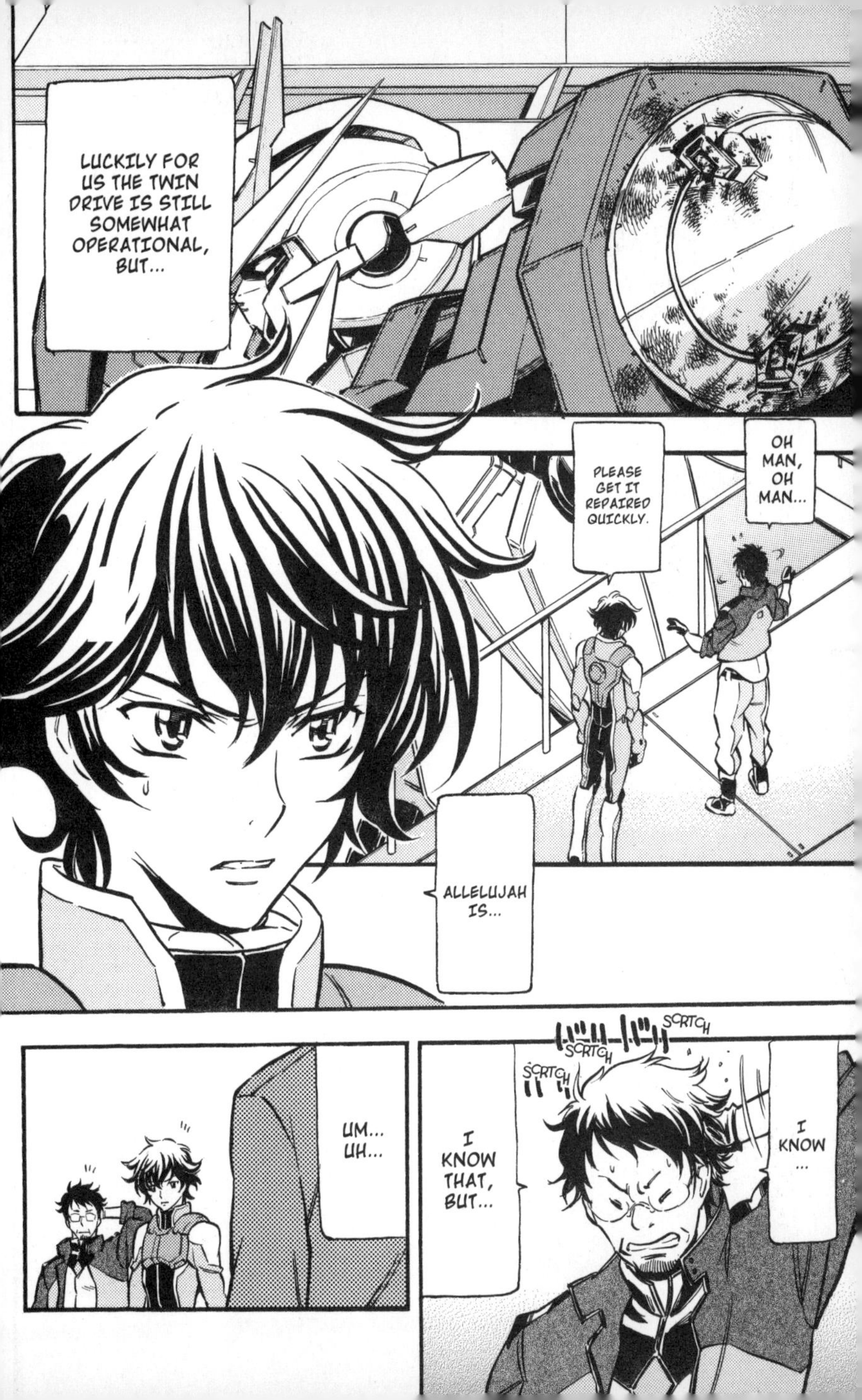
LUCKILY FOR US THE TWIN DRIVE IS STILL SOMEWHAT OPERATIONAL, BUT...
OH MAN, OH MAN...
PLEASE GET IT REPAIRED QUICKLY.
ALLELUJAH IS...
SCRTCH
SCRTCH
SCRTCH
I KNOW...
I KNOW THAT, BUT...
UM... UH...

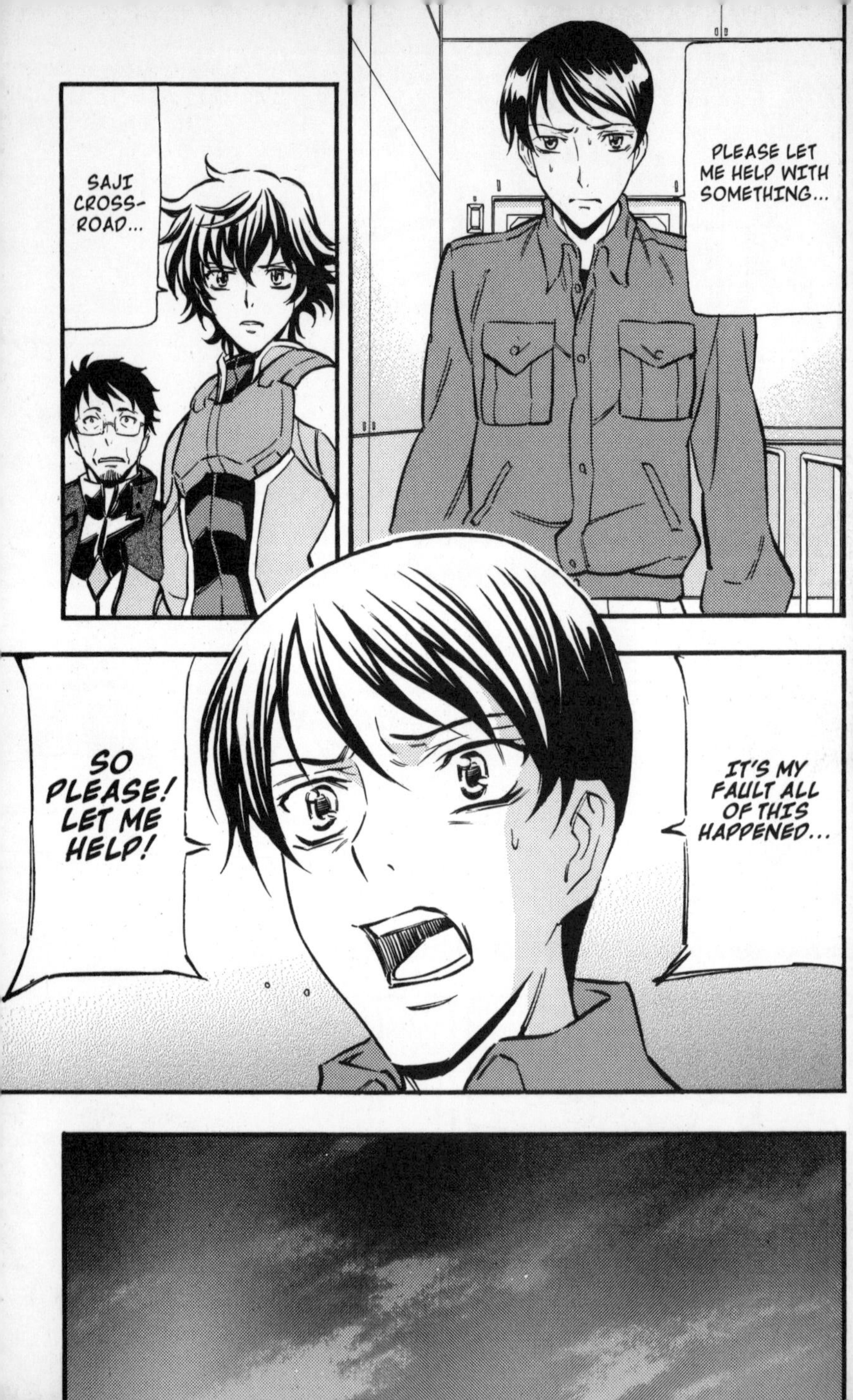
PLEASE LET ME HELP WITH SOMETHING...
SAJI CROSS-ROAD...
IT'S MY FAULT ALL OF THIS HAPPENED...
SO PLEASE! LET ME HELP!

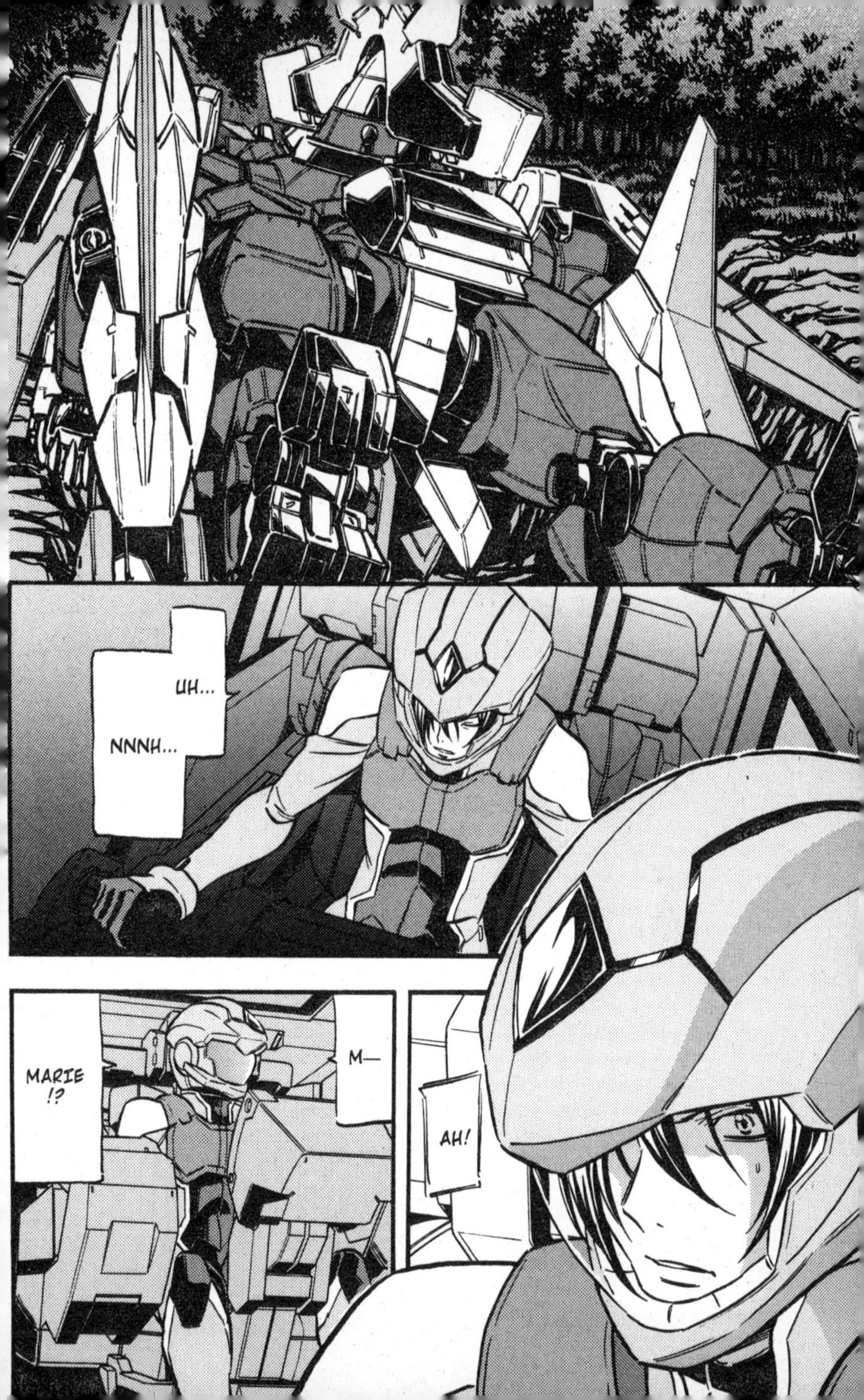
UH...
NNNH...
AH!
M—
MARIE !?

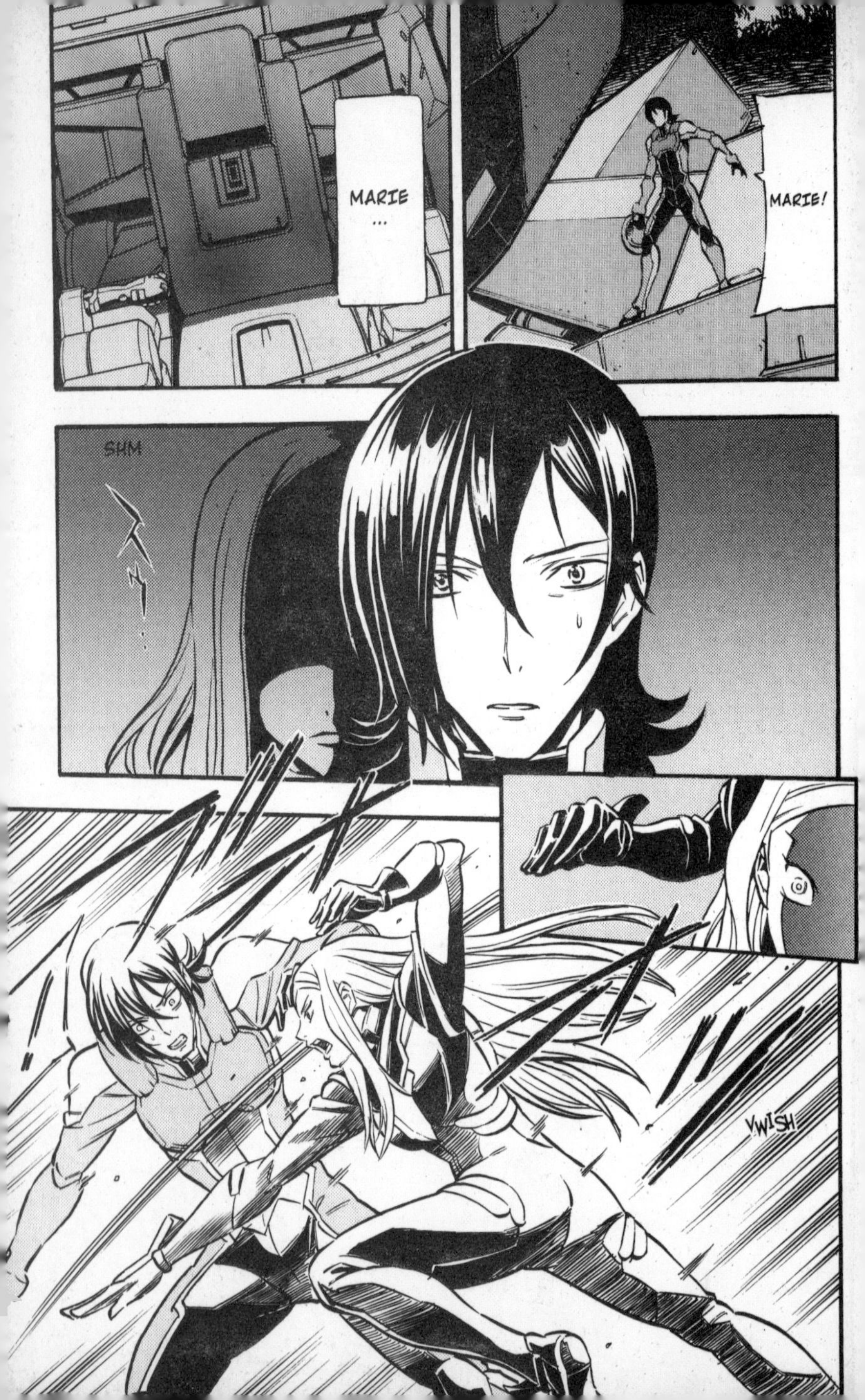
MARIE!
MARIE ...
SHM
VWISH

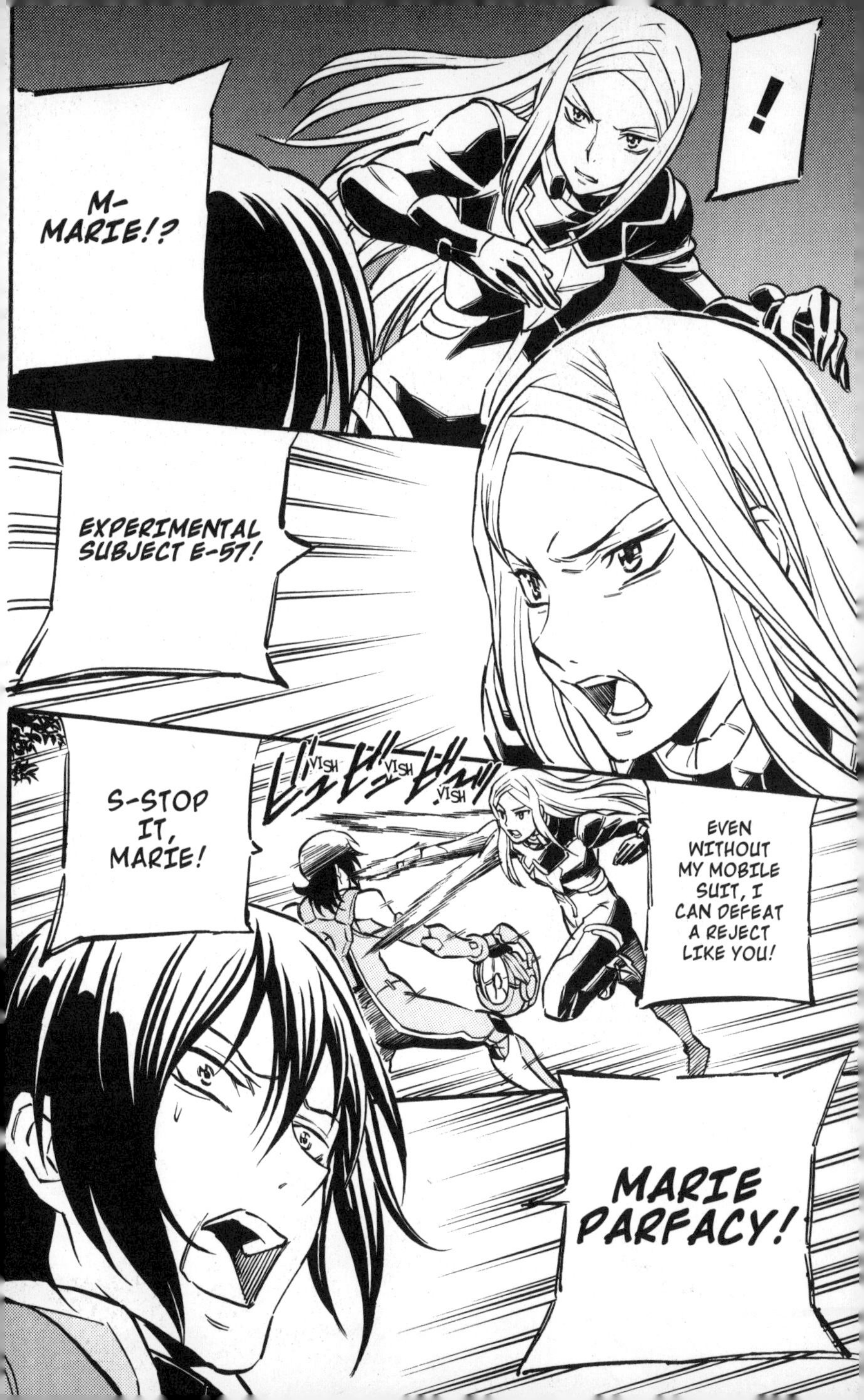
!
M-MARIE!?
EXPERIMENTAL SUBJECT E-57!
VISH
VISH
VISH
EVEN WITHOUT MY MOBILE SUIT, I CAN DEFEAT A REJECT LIKE YOU!
S-STOP IT, MARIE!
MARIE PARFACY!

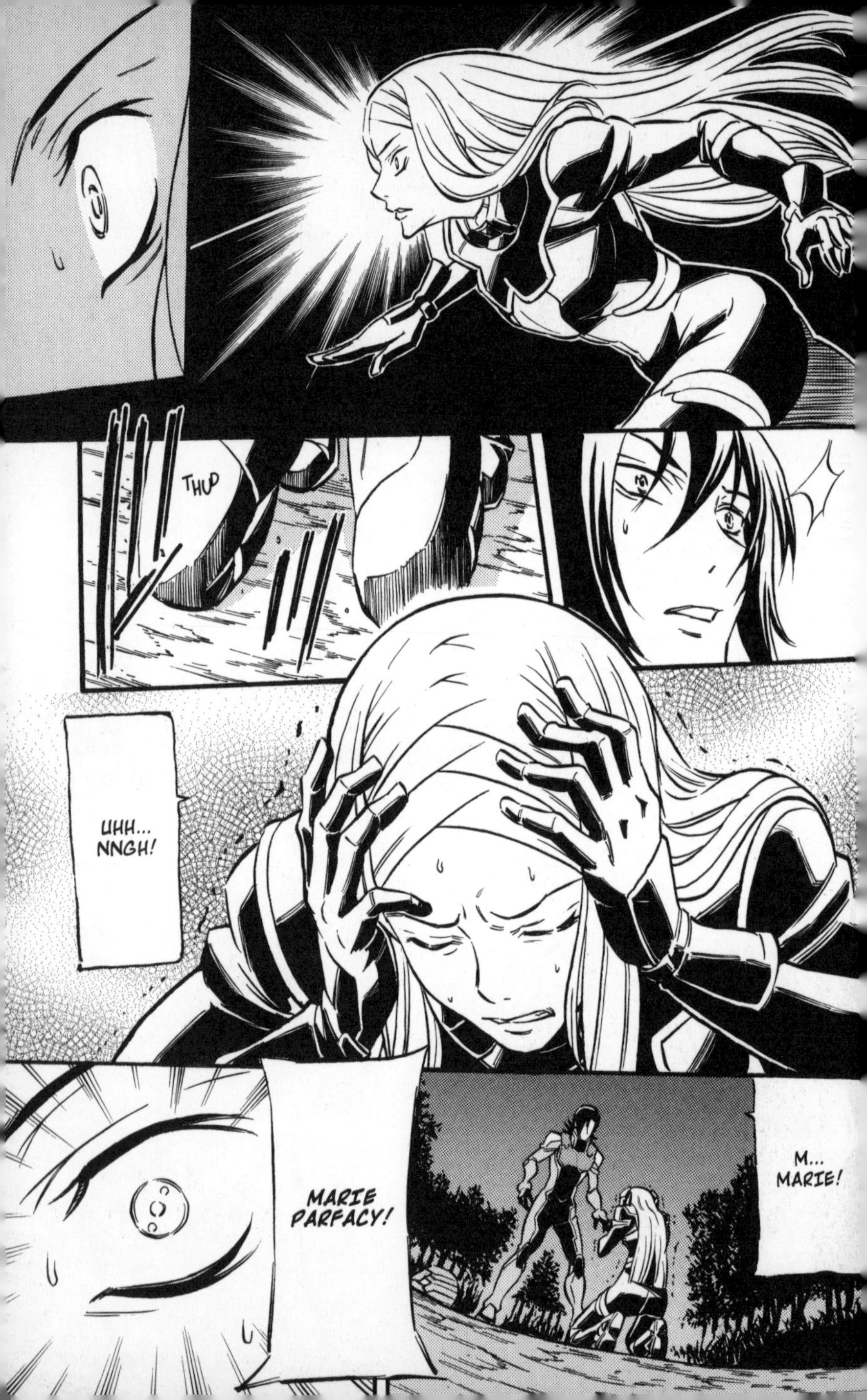
THUD
UHH... NNGH!
M... MARIE!
MARIE PARFACY!

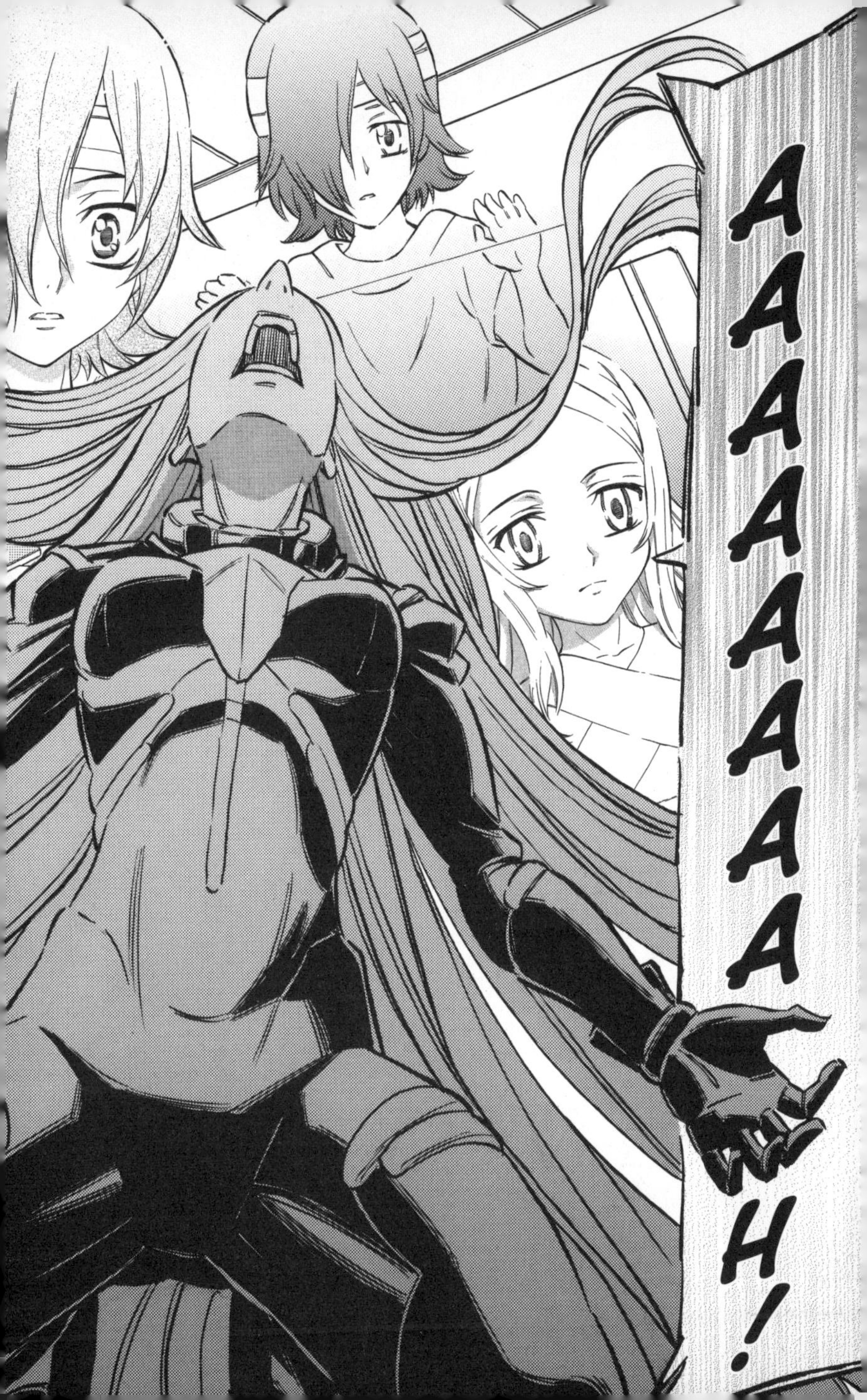
AAAAAAAAH!

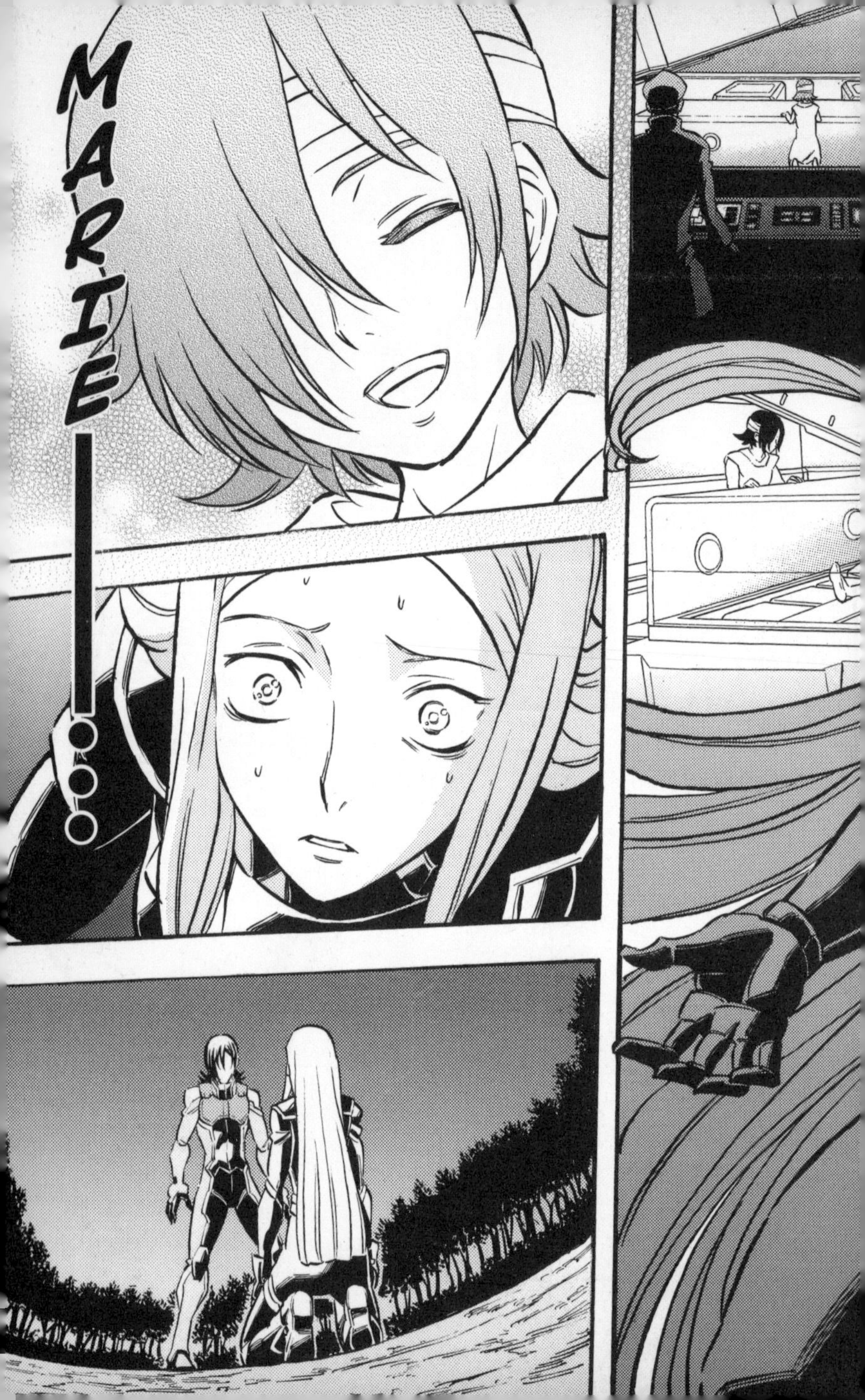
MARIE——...

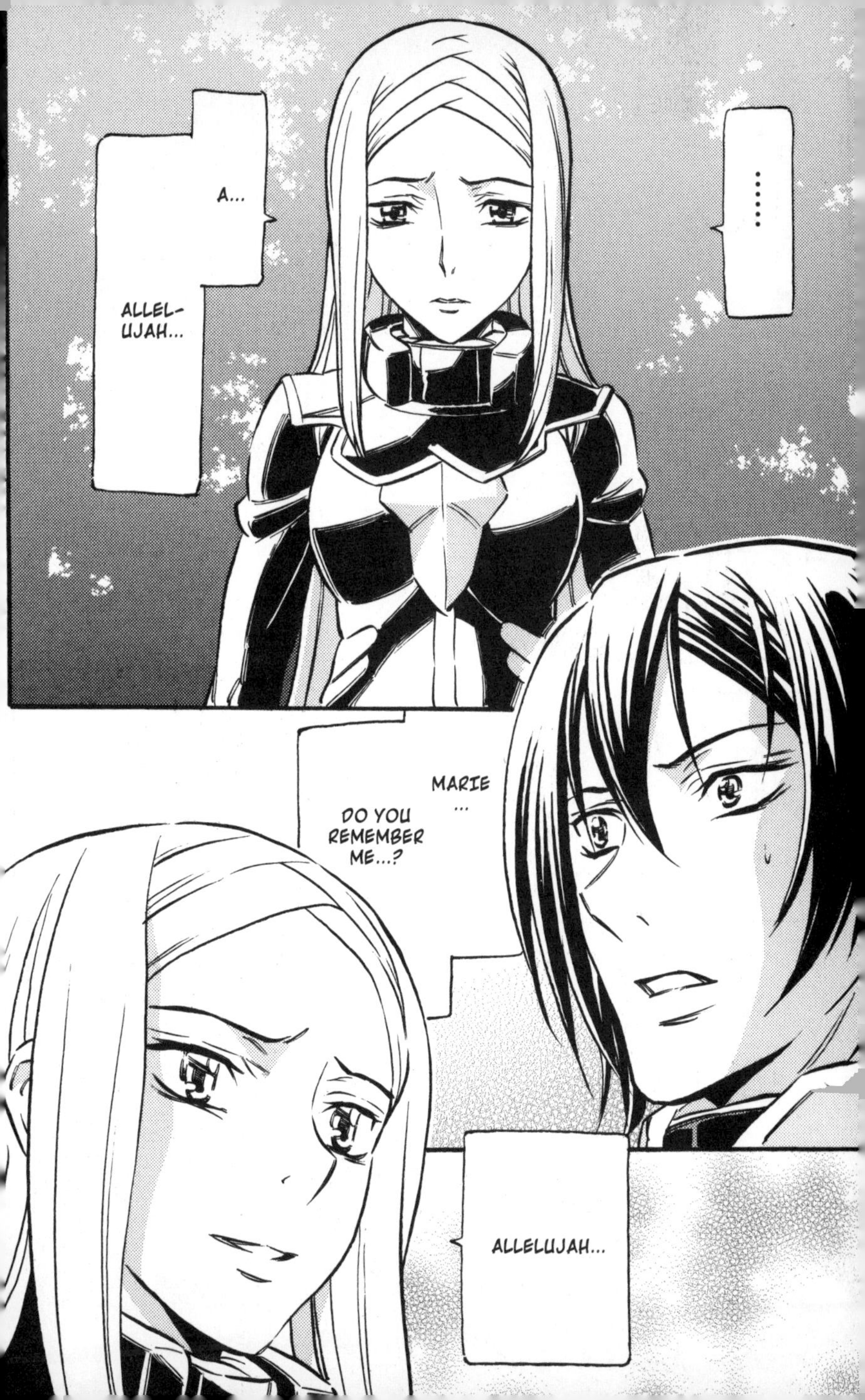
......
A... ALLELUJAH...
MARIE ... DO YOU REMEMBER ME...?
ALLELUJAH...

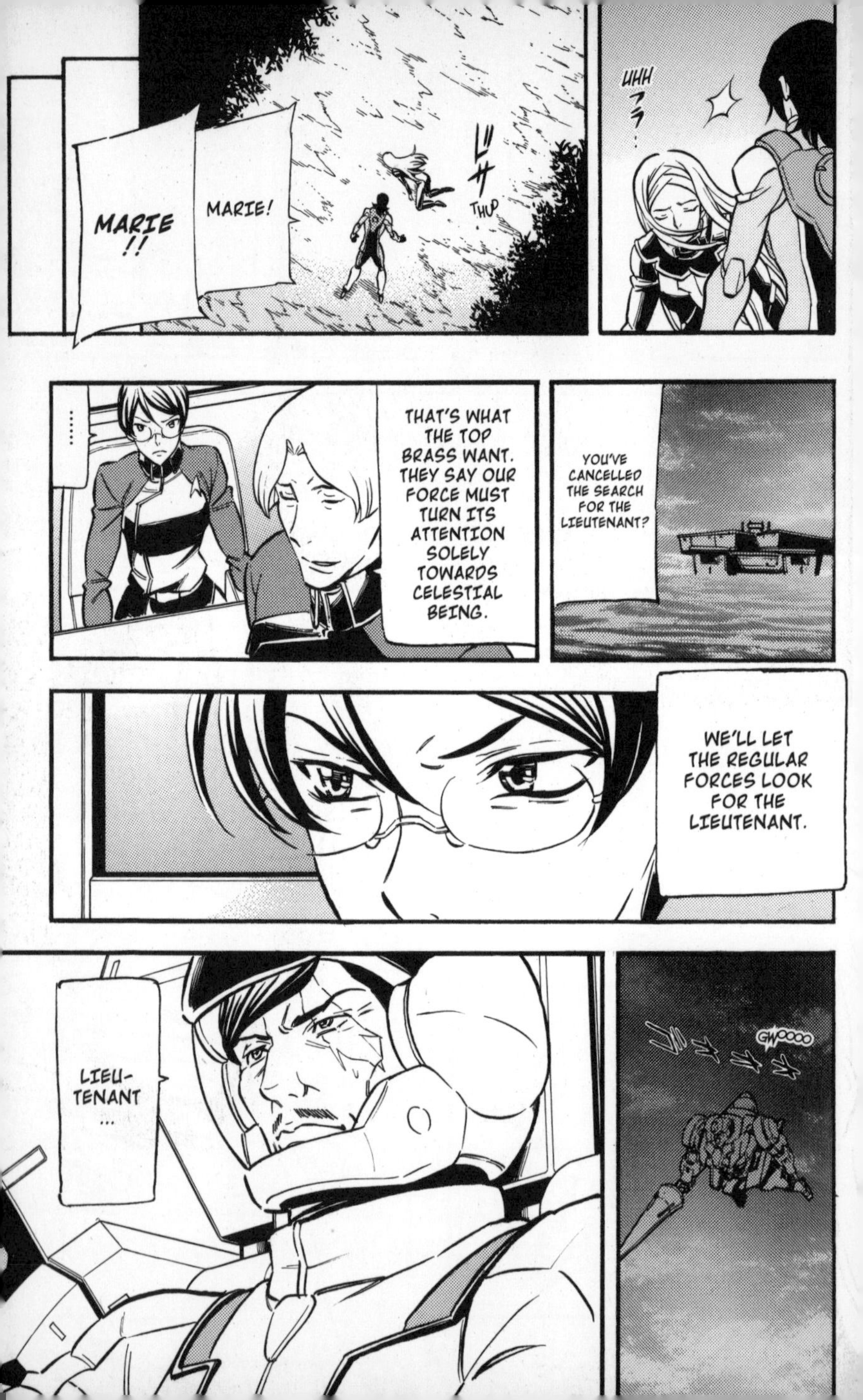

UHH
THUP
MARIE!
MARIE !!
YOU'VE CANCELLED THE SEARCH FOR THE LIEUTENANT?
THAT'S WHAT THE TOP BRASS WANT. THEY SAY OUR FORCE MUST TURN ITS ATTENTION SOLELY TOWARDS CELESTIAL BEING.
……
WE'LL LET THE REGULAR FORCES LOOK FOR THE LIEUTENANT.
GWOOOO
LIEU-TENANT …

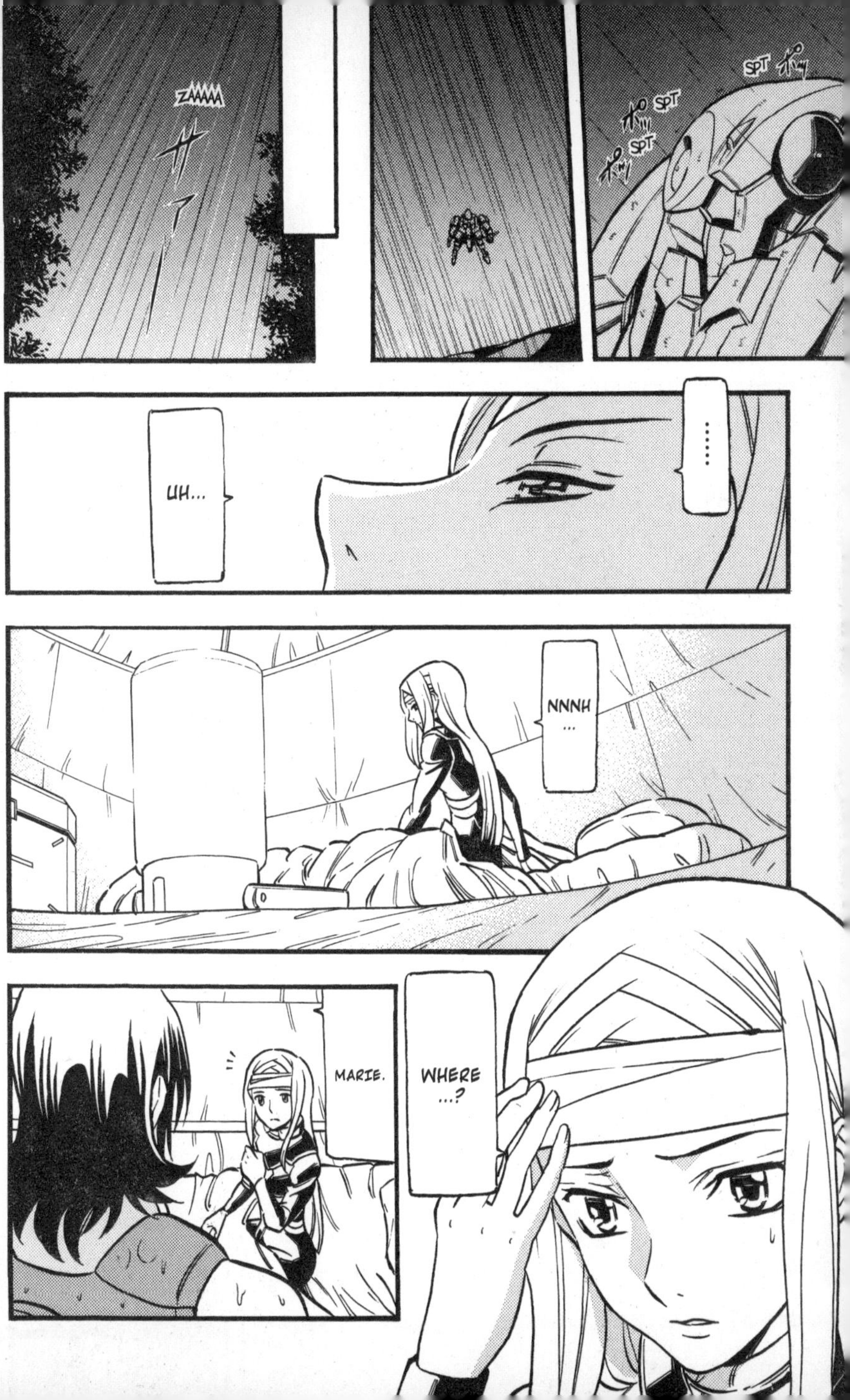
SPT
SPT
SPT
ZAAAAA
ザァー
......
UH...
NNNH...
WHERE...?
MARIE.

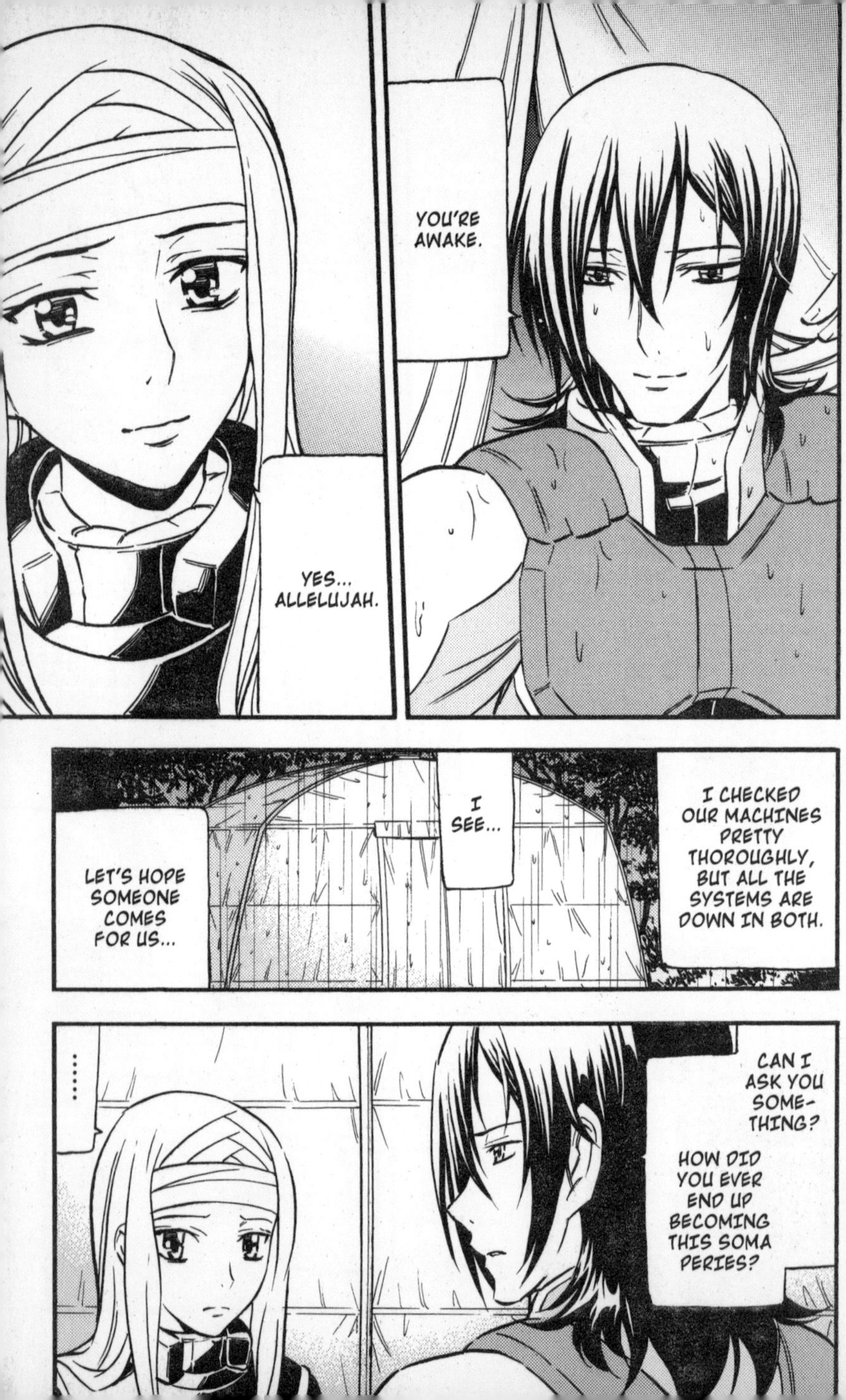
YOU'RE AWAKE.
YES... ALLELUJAH.
I CHECKED OUR MACHINES PRETTY THOROUGHLY, BUT ALL THE SYSTEMS ARE DOWN IN BOTH.
I SEE...
LET'S HOPE SOMEONE COMES FOR US...
CAN I ASK YOU SOME-THING?
HOW DID YOU EVER END UP BECOMING THIS SOMA PERIES?
......

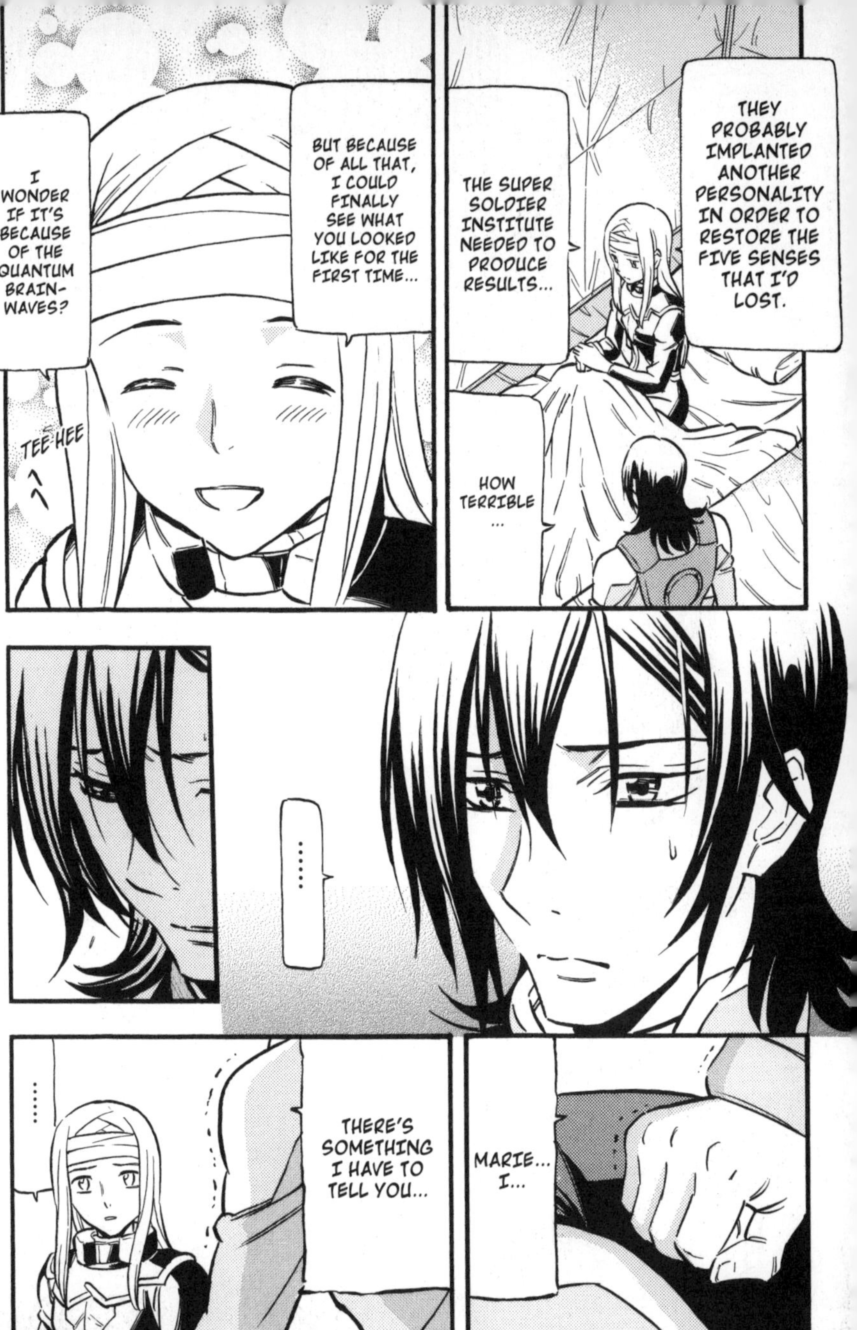
THEY PROBABLY IMPLANTED ANOTHER PERSONALITY IN ORDER TO RESTORE THE FIVE SENSES THAT I'D LOST.
THE SUPER SOLDIER INSTITUTE NEEDED TO PRODUCE RESULTS...
HOW TERRIBLE ...
BUT BECAUSE OF ALL THAT, I COULD FINALLY SEE WHAT YOU LOOKED LIKE FOR THE FIRST TIME...
I WONDER IF IT'S BECAUSE OF THE QUANTUM BRAIN-WAVES?
TEE HEE
......
MARIE... I...
THERE'S SOMETHING I HAVE TO TELL YOU...
......

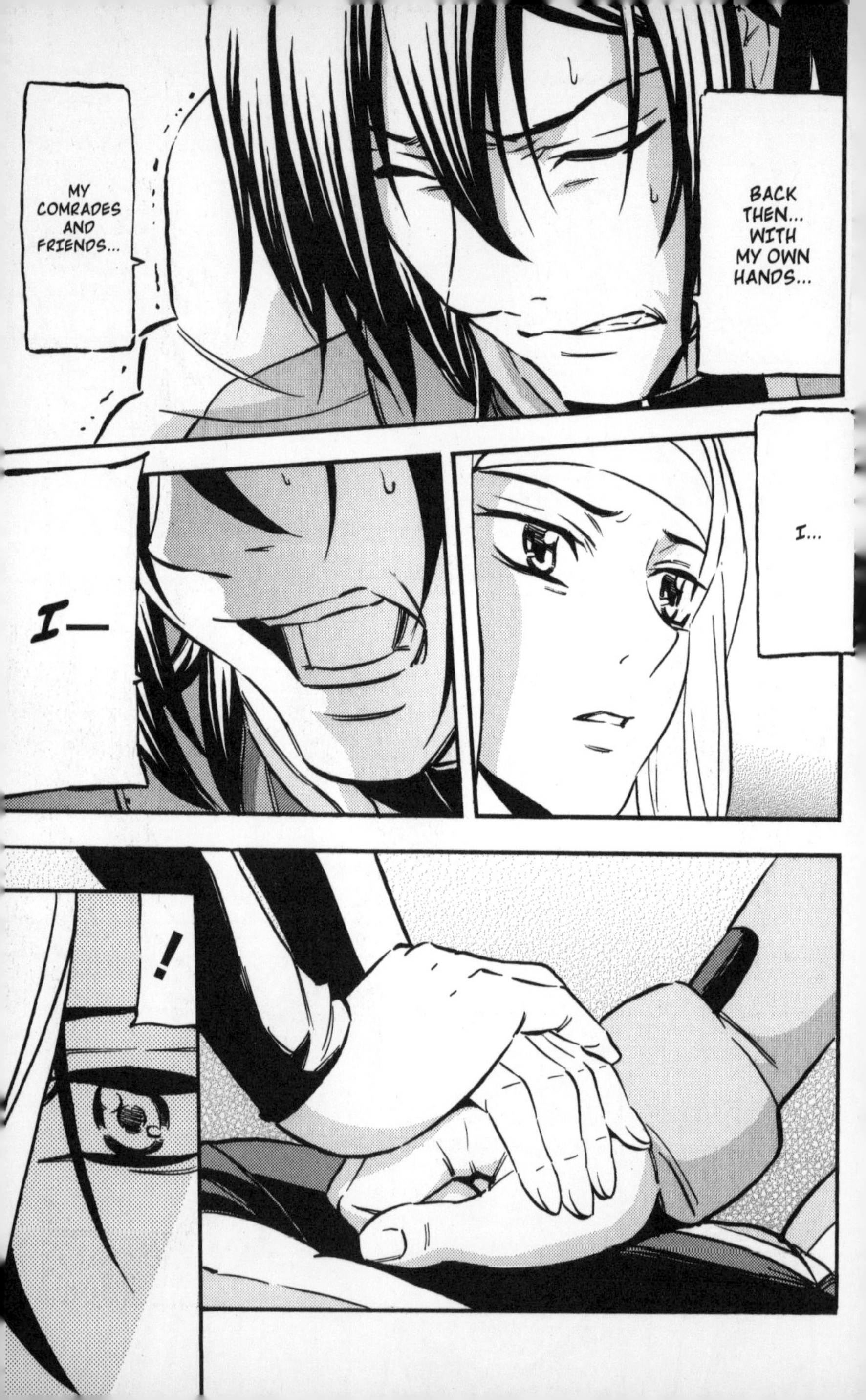
BACK THEN... WITH MY OWN HANDS...
MY COMRADES AND FRIENDS...
I...
I—
!

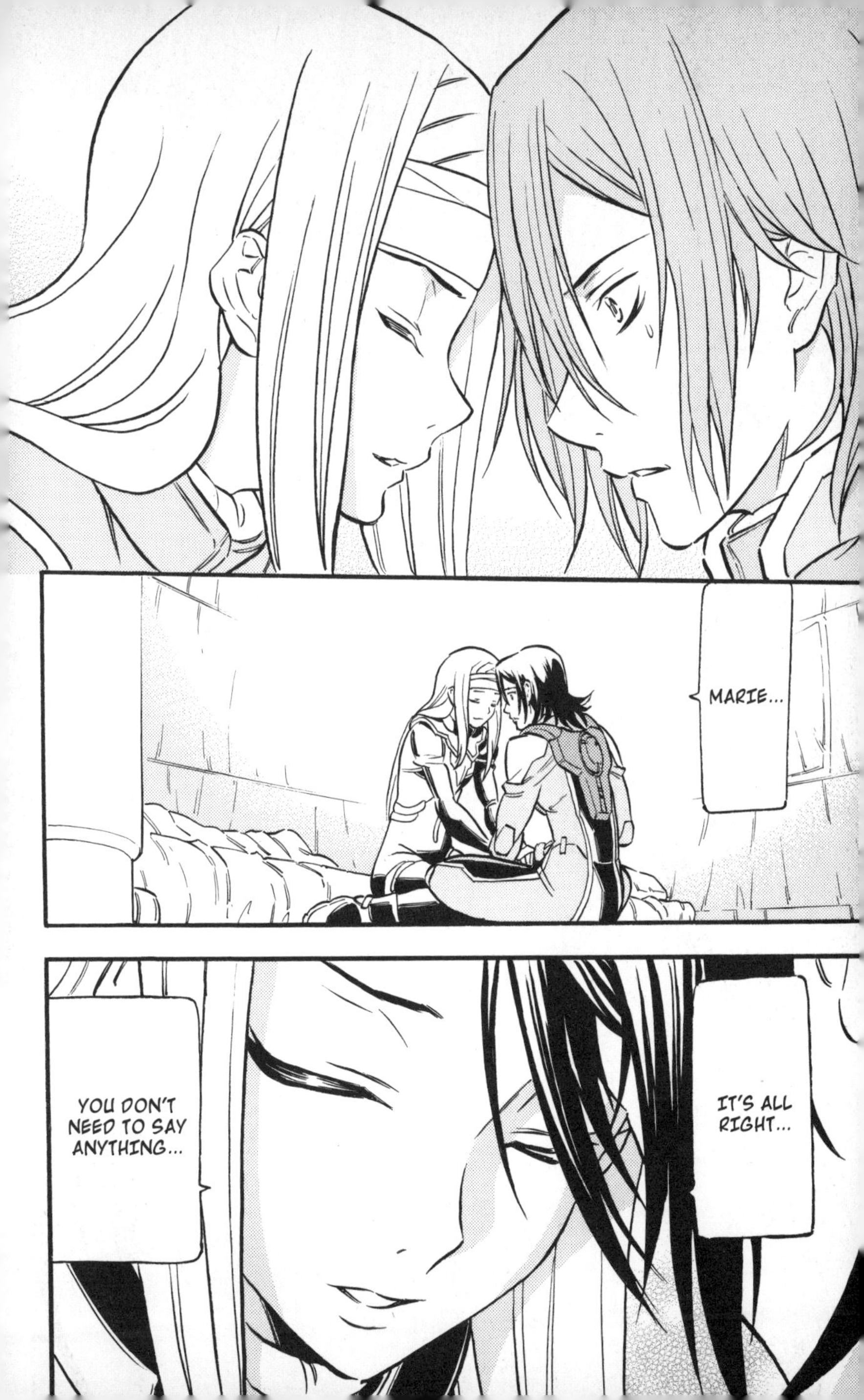
MARIE...
IT'S ALL RIGHT...
YOU DON'T NEED TO SAY ANYTHING...

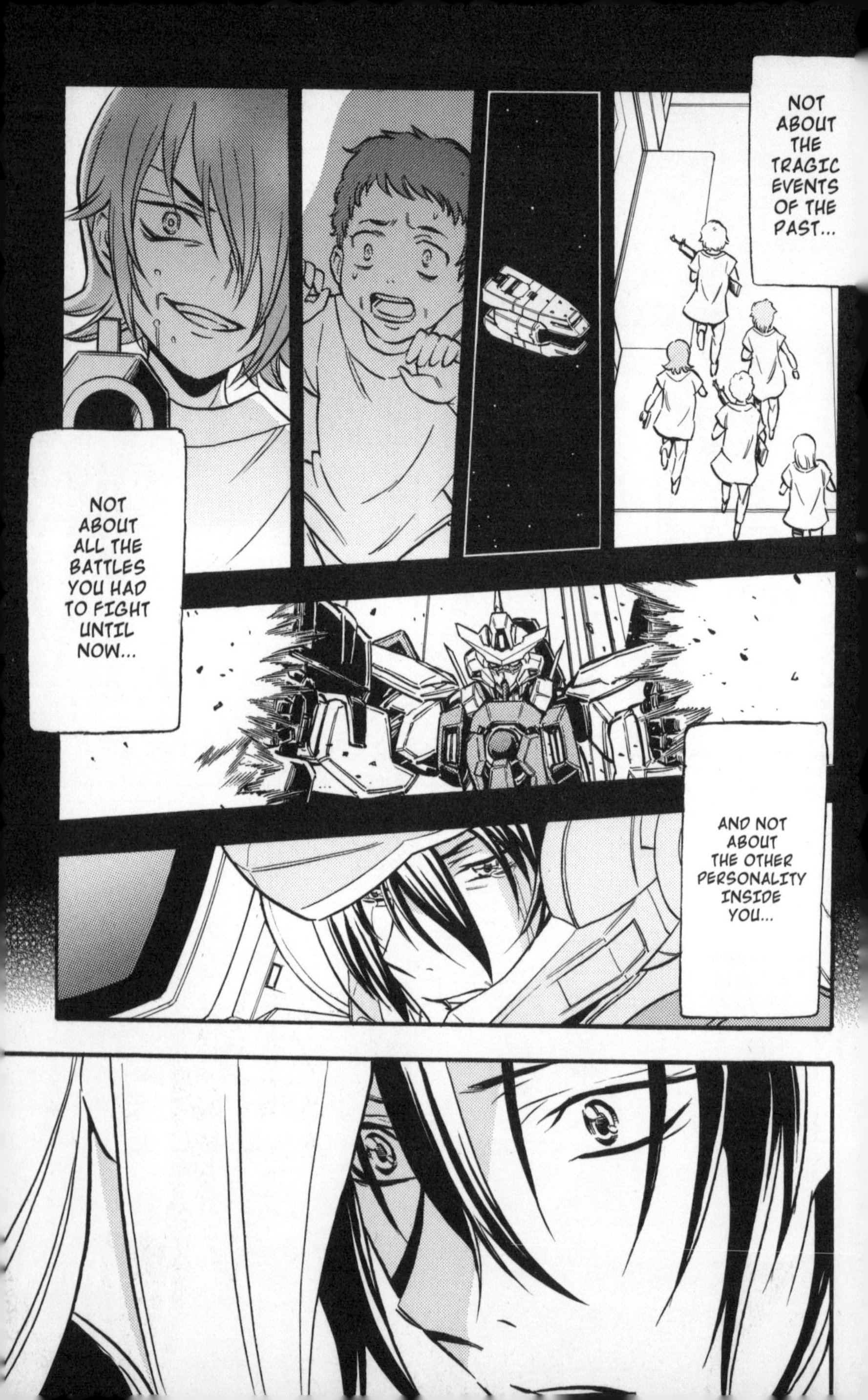
NOT ABOUT THE TRAGIC EVENTS OF THE PAST...
NOT ABOUT ALL THE BATTLES YOU HAD TO FIGHT UNTIL NOW...
AND NOT ABOUT THE OTHER PERSONALITY INSIDE YOU...

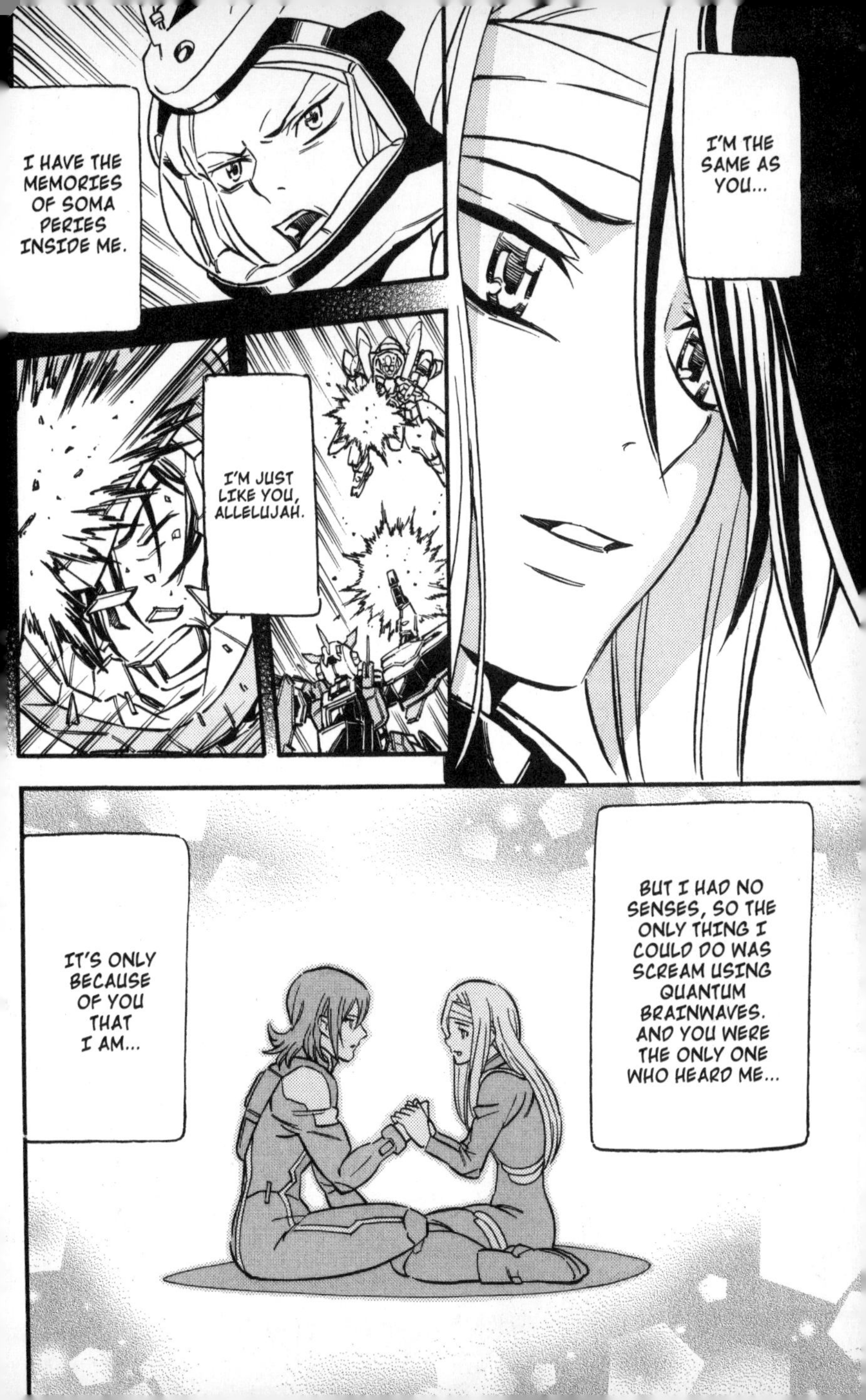
I'M THE SAME AS YOU...
I HAVE THE MEMORIES OF SOMA PERIES INSIDE ME.
I'M JUST LIKE YOU, ALLELUJAH.
BUT I HAD NO SENSES, SO THE ONLY THING I COULD DO WAS SCREAM USING QUANTUM BRAINWAVES. AND YOU WERE THE ONLY ONE WHO HEARD ME...
IT'S ONLY BECAUSE OF YOU THAT I AM...

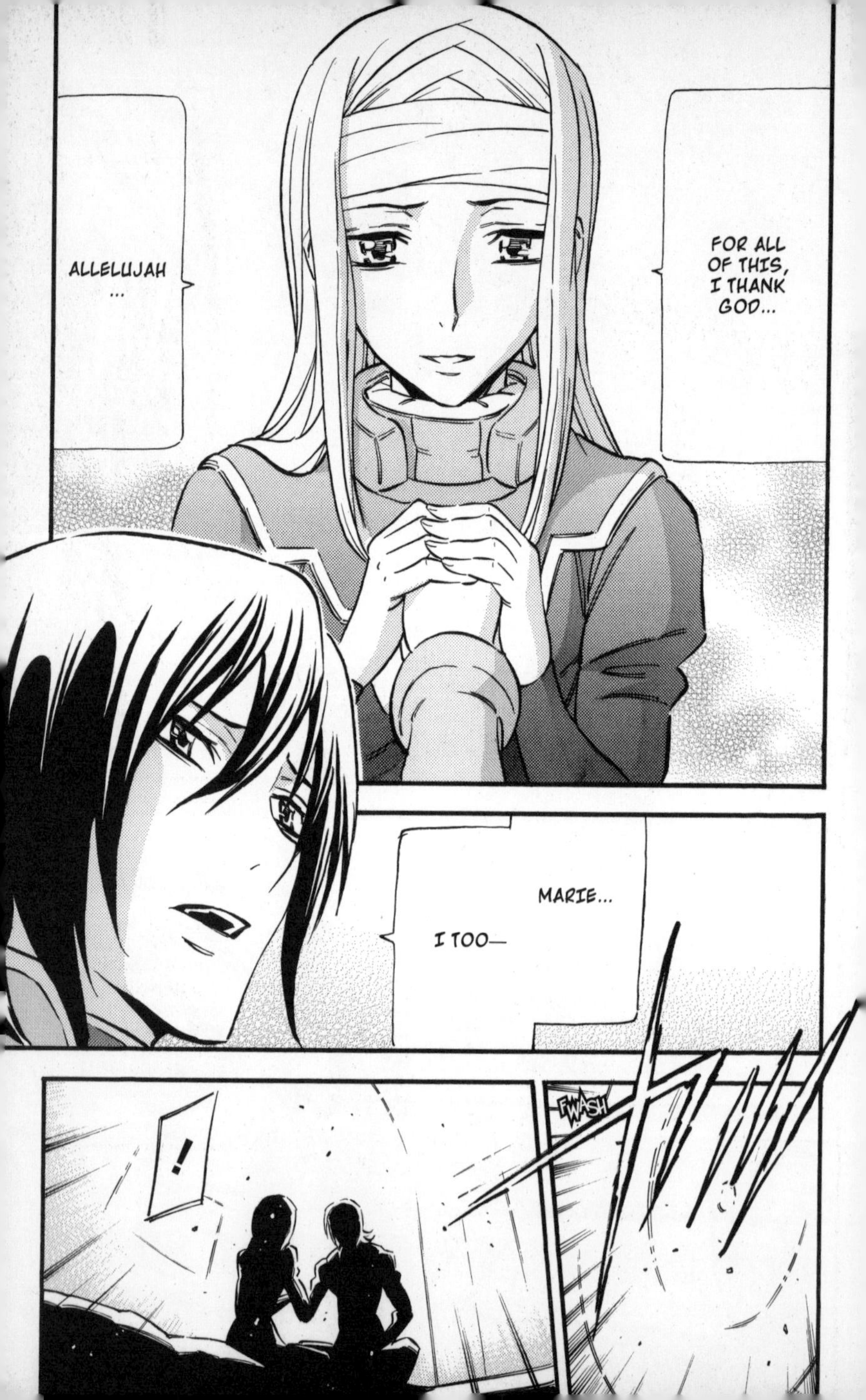
FOR ALL OF THIS, I THANK GOD...
ALLELUJAH ...
MARIE...
I TOO—
FWASH
!

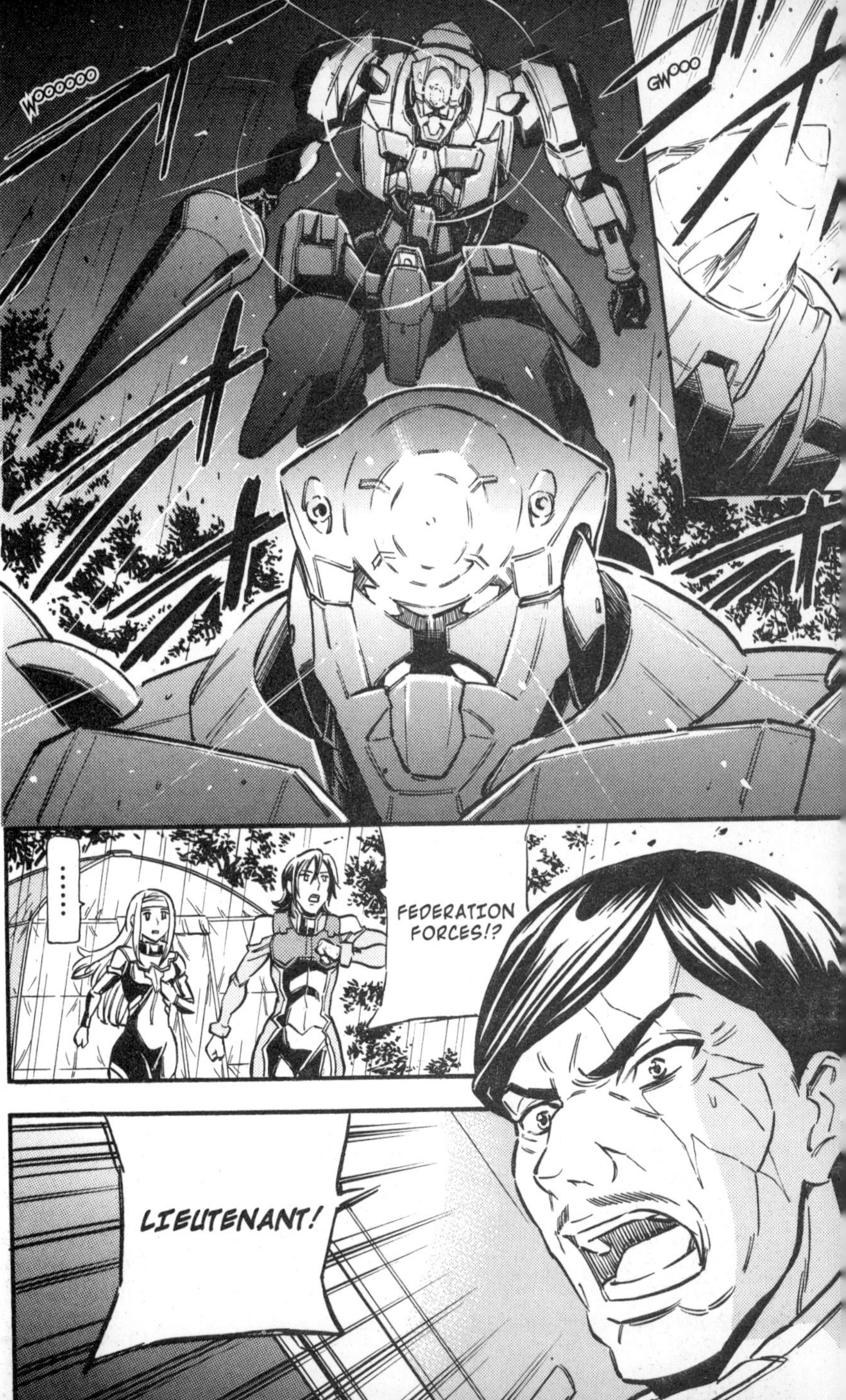
GWOOO
WOOOOOO
FEDERATION FORCES!?
......
LIEUTENANT!

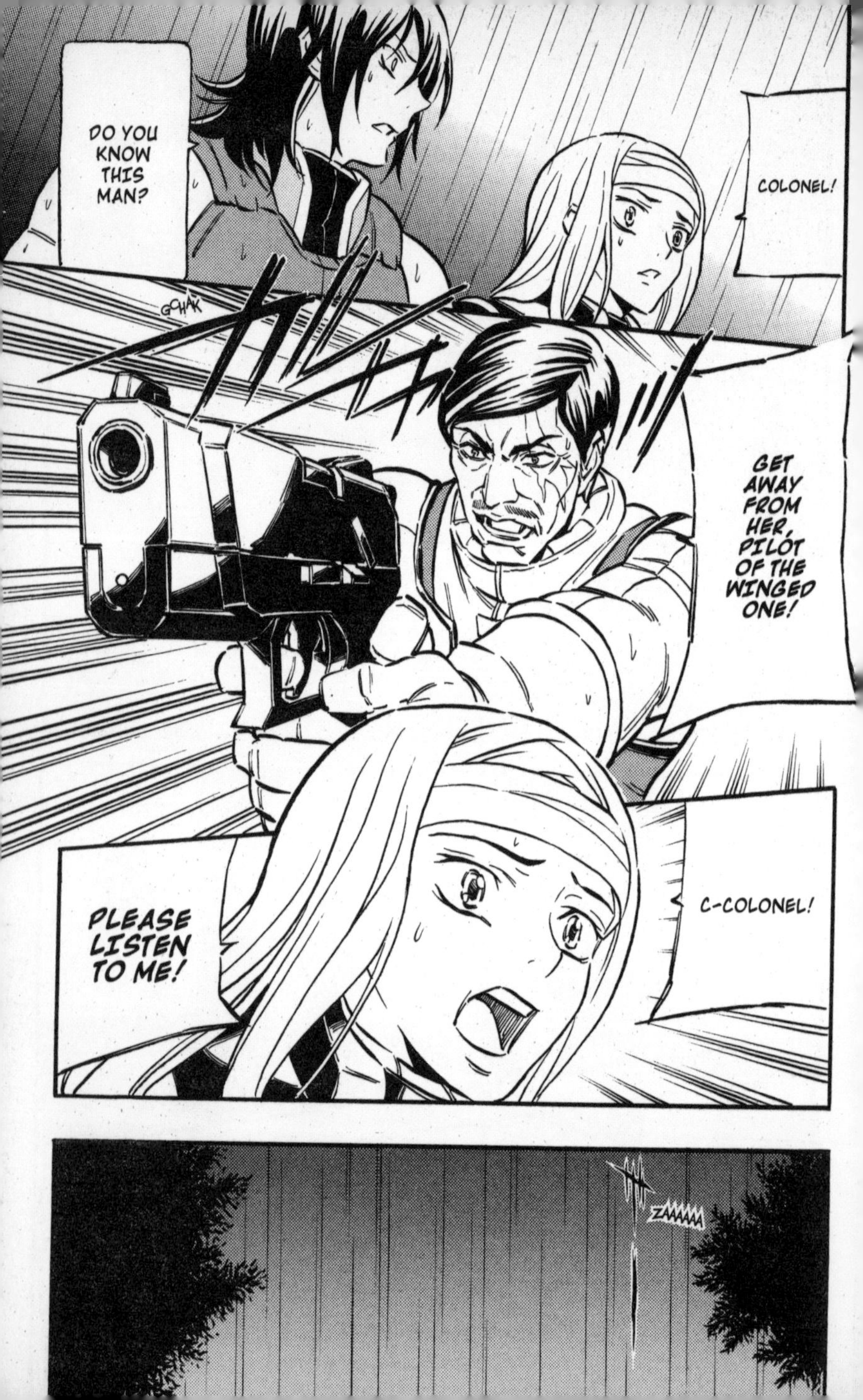
COLONEL!
DO YOU KNOW THIS MAN?
GCHAK
GET AWAY FROM HER, PILOT OF THE WINGED ONE!
C-COLONEL!
PLEASE LISTEN TO ME!
ZAAAAA

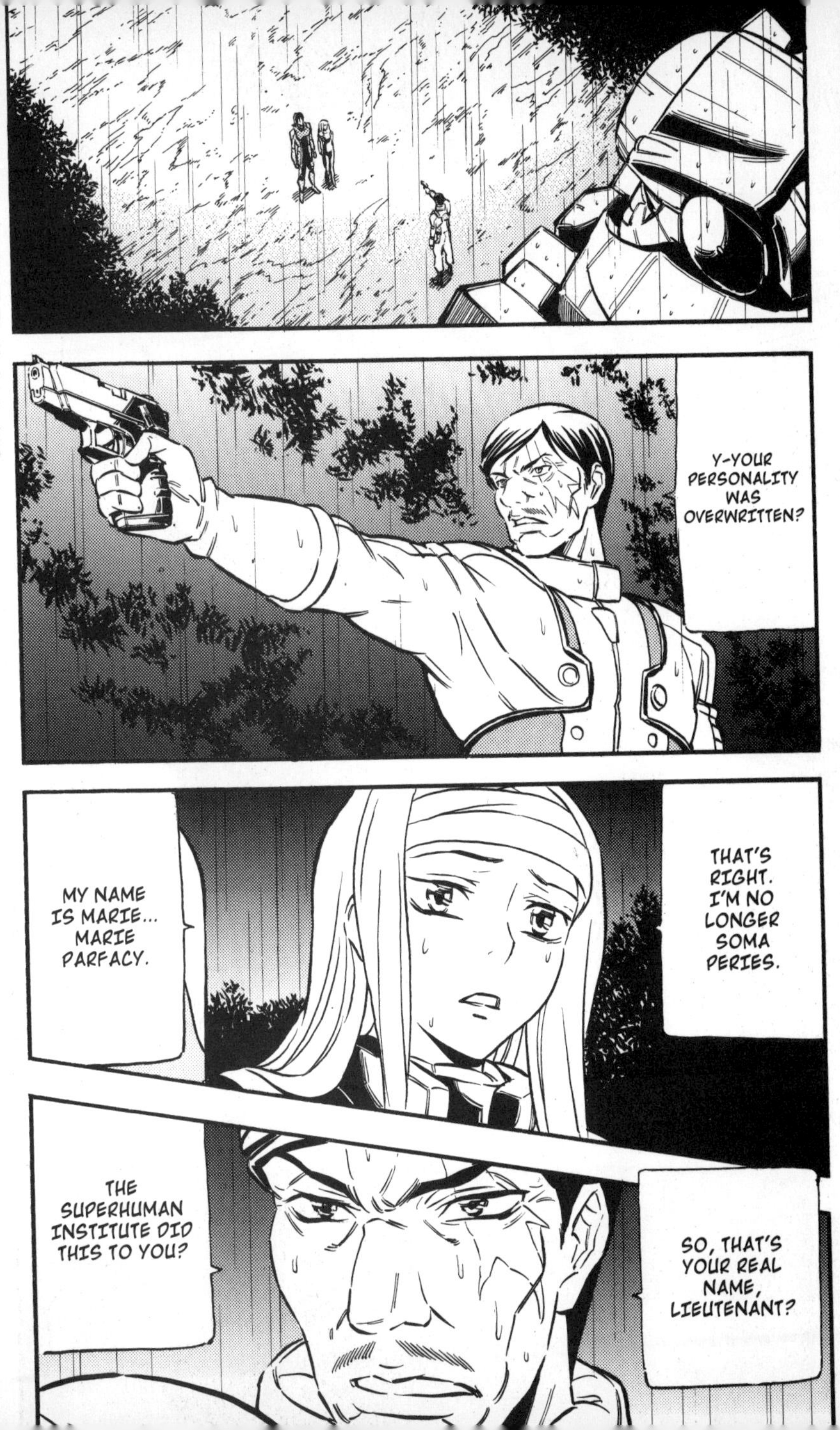
Y-YOUR PERSONALITY WAS OVERWRITTEN?
THAT'S RIGHT. I'M NO LONGER SOMA PERIES.
MY NAME IS MARIE... MARIE PARFACY.
SO, THAT'S YOUR REAL NAME, LIEUTENANT?
THE SUPERHUMAN INSTITUTE DID THIS TO YOU?

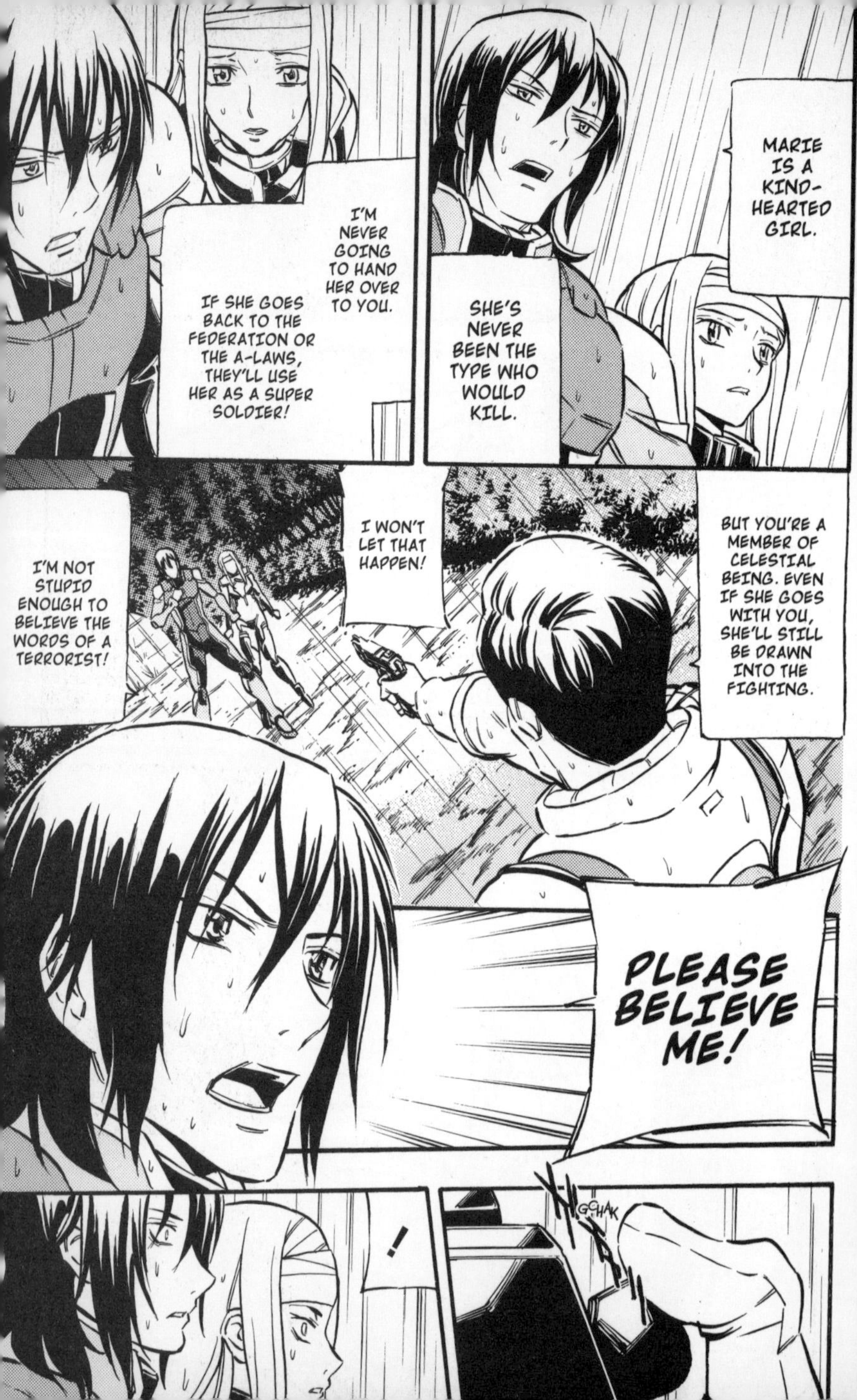
MARIE IS A KIND-HEARTED GIRL.
SHE'S NEVER BEEN THE TYPE WHO WOULD KILL.
I'M NEVER GOING TO HAND HER OVER TO YOU.
IF SHE GOES BACK TO THE FEDERATION OR THE A-LAWS, THEY'LL USE HER AS A SUPER SOLDIER!
BUT YOU'RE A MEMBER OF CELESTIAL BEING. EVEN IF SHE GOES WITH YOU, SHE'LL STILL BE DRAWN INTO THE FIGHTING.
I WON'T LET THAT HAPPEN!
I'M NOT STUPID ENOUGH TO BELIEVE THE WORDS OF A TERRORIST!
PLEASE BELIEVE ME!
GCHAK
!

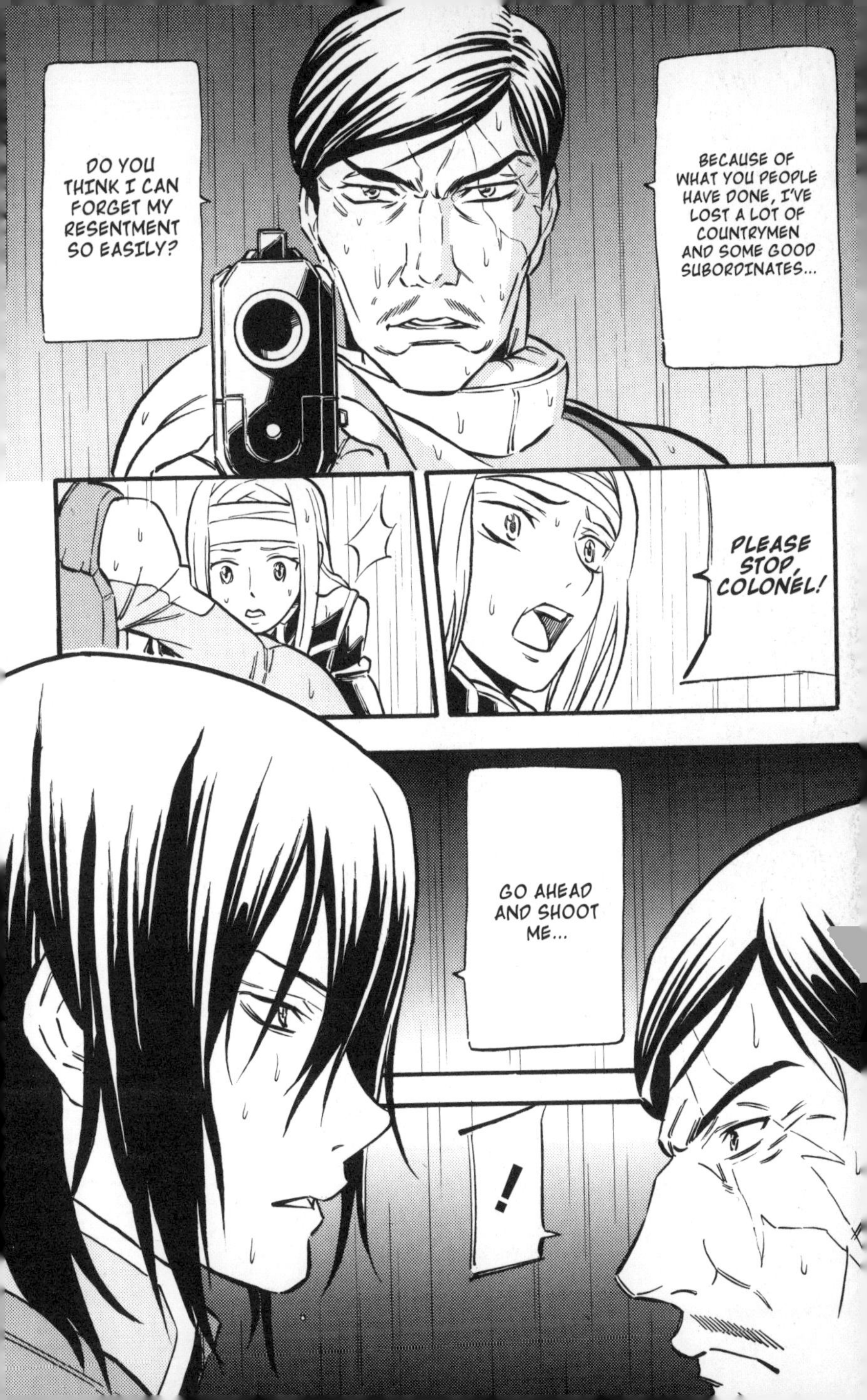
BECAUSE OF WHAT YOU PEOPLE HAVE DONE, I'VE LOST A LOT OF COUNTRYMEN AND SOME GOOD SUBORDINATES...
DO YOU THINK I CAN FORGET MY RESENTMENT SO EASILY?
PLEASE STOP, COLONEL!
GO AHEAD AND SHOOT ME...
!

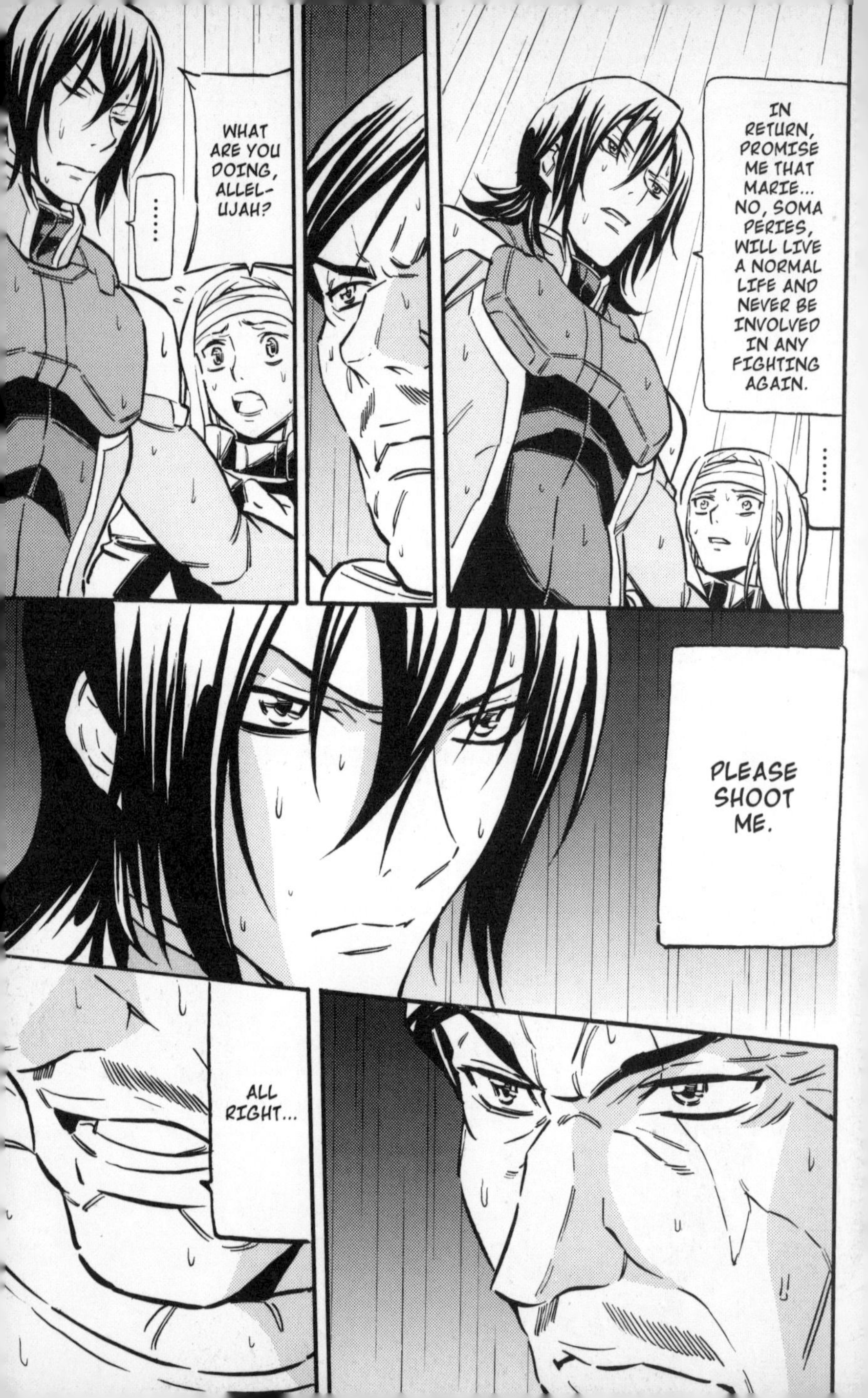
IN RETURN, PROMISE ME THAT MARIE... NO, SOMA PERIES, WILL LIVE A NORMAL LIFE AND NEVER BE INVOLVED IN ANY FIGHTING AGAIN.
......
WHAT ARE YOU DOING, ALLEL-UJAH?
......
PLEASE SHOOT ME.
ALL RIGHT...

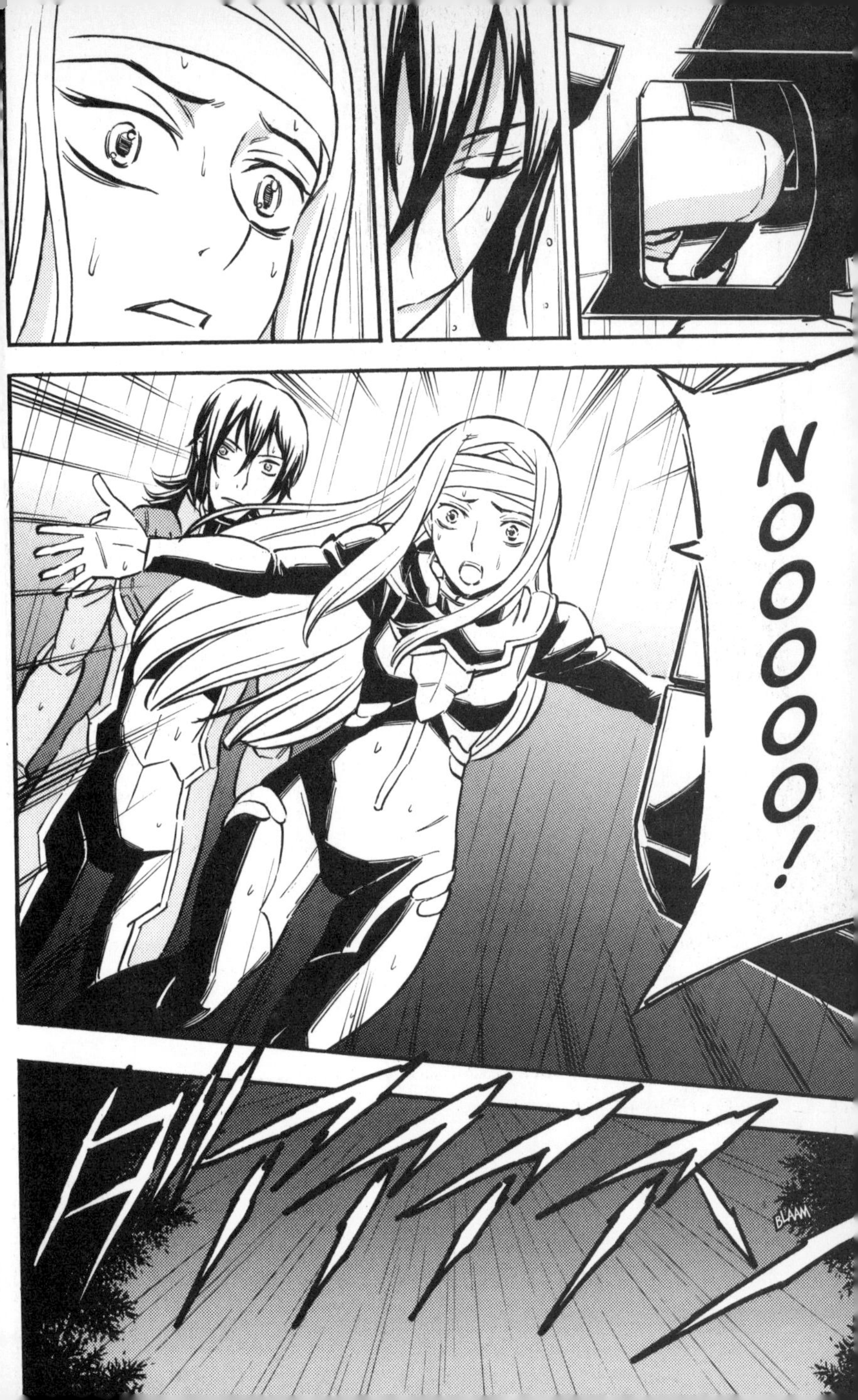
NOOOOOO!
BLAAM

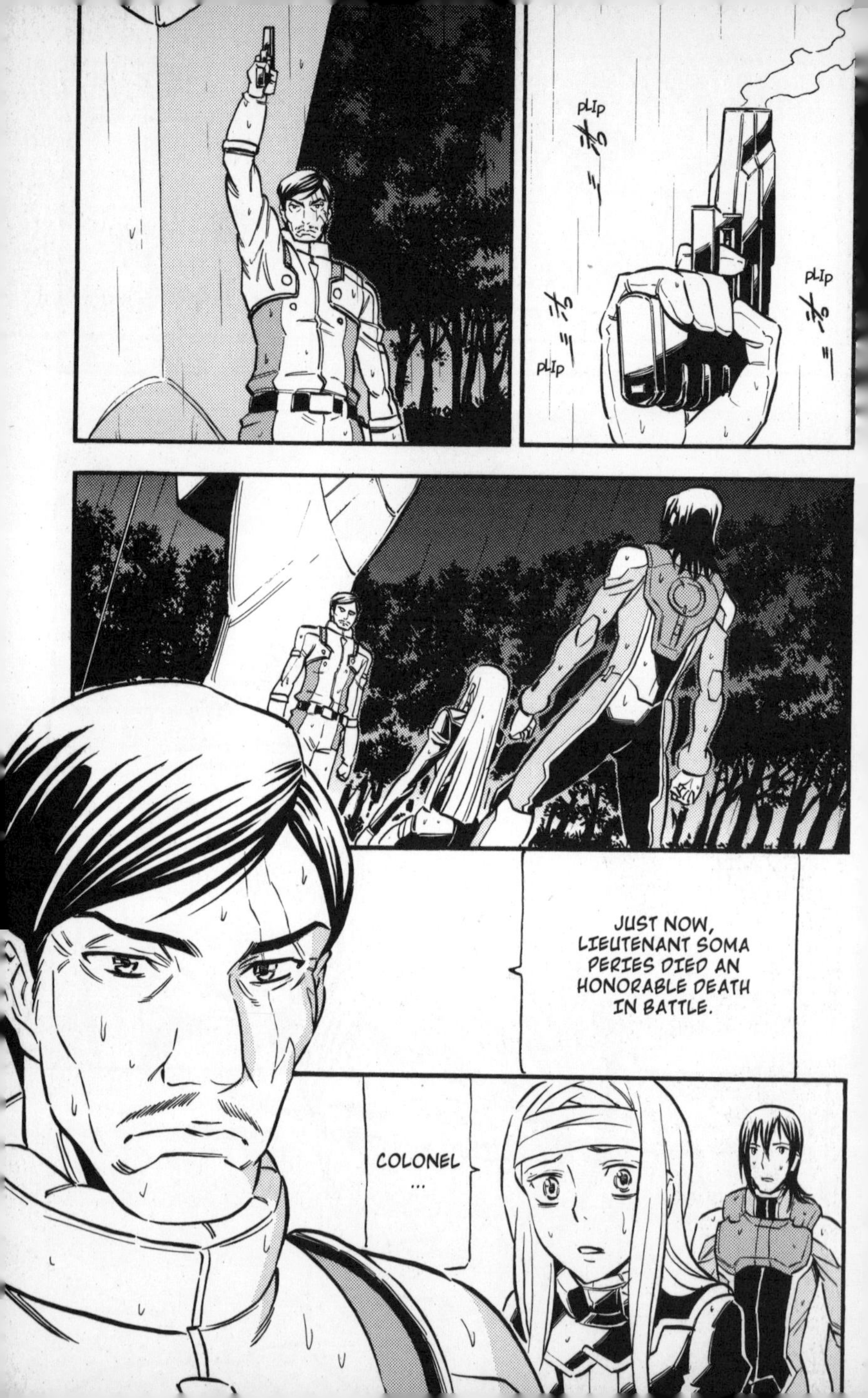
pLIp
pLIp
pLIp
JUST NOW, LIEUTENANT SOMA PERIES DIED AN HONORABLE DEATH IN BATTLE.
COLONEL ...

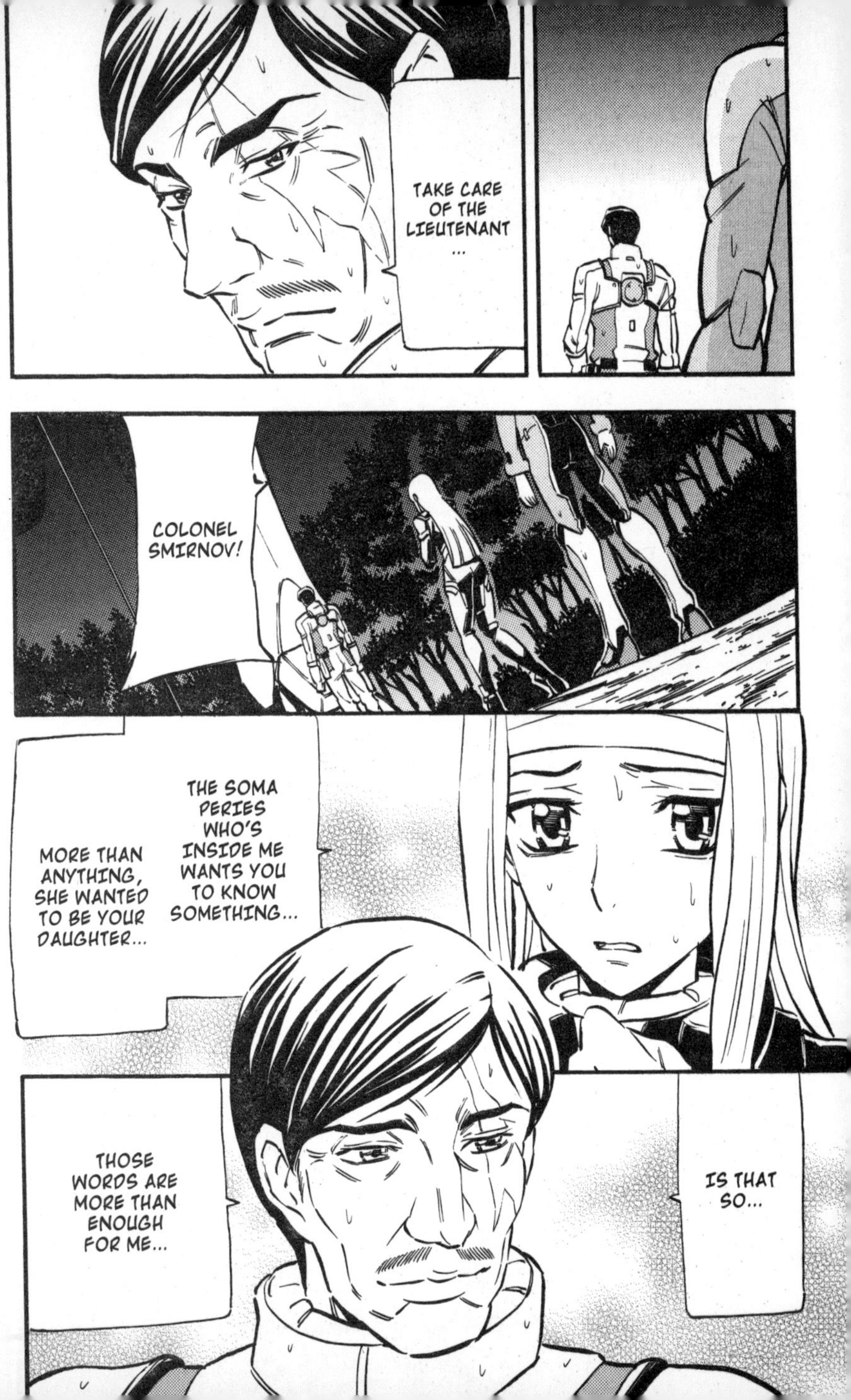
TAKE CARE OF THE LIEUTENANT ...
COLONEL SMIRNOV!
THE SOMA PERIES WHO'S INSIDE ME WANTS YOU TO KNOW SOMETHING...
MORE THAN ANYTHING, SHE WANTED TO BE YOUR DAUGHTER...
IS THAT SO...
THOSE WORDS ARE MORE THAN ENOUGH FOR ME...

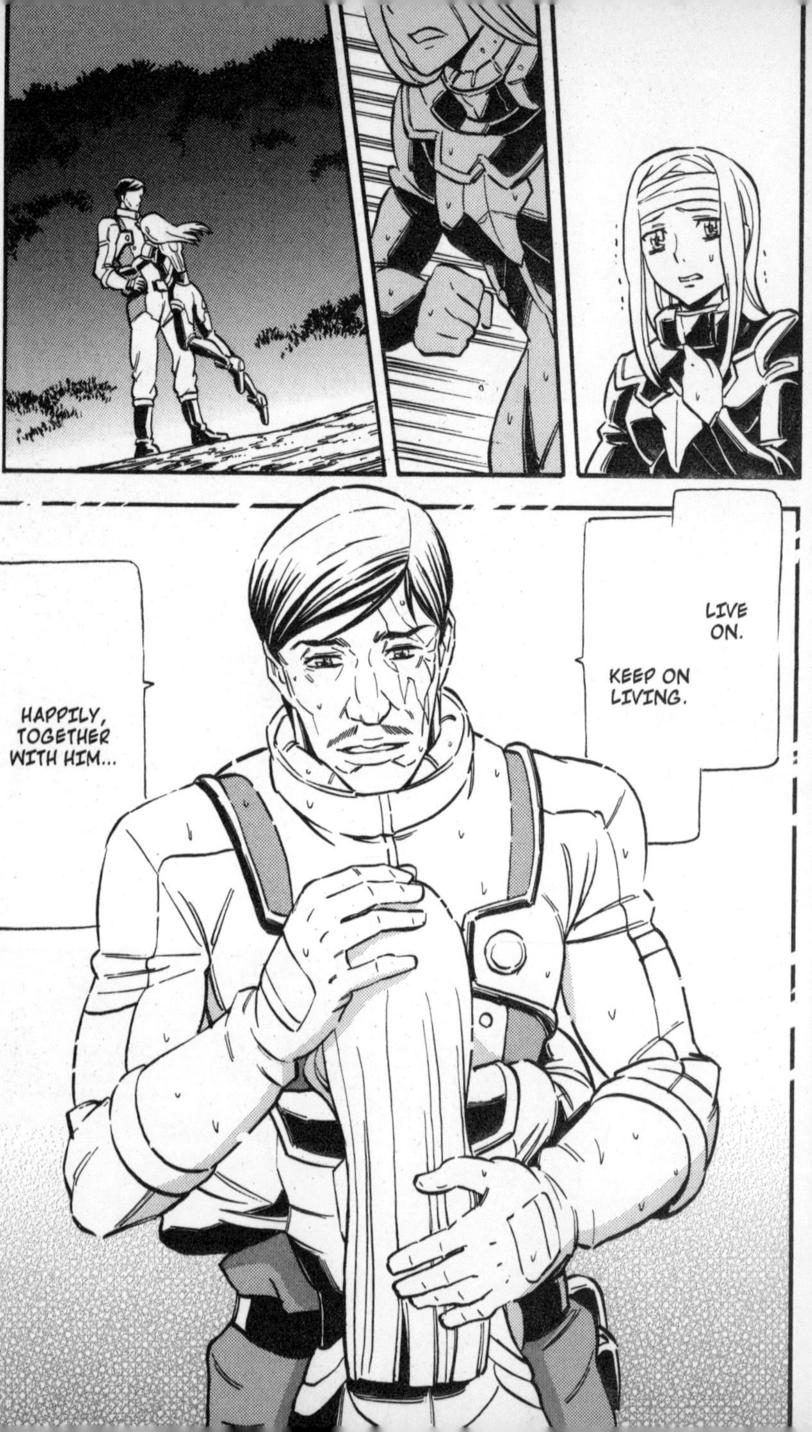
LIVE ON.
KEEP ON LIVING.
HAPPILY, TOGETHER WITH HIM...

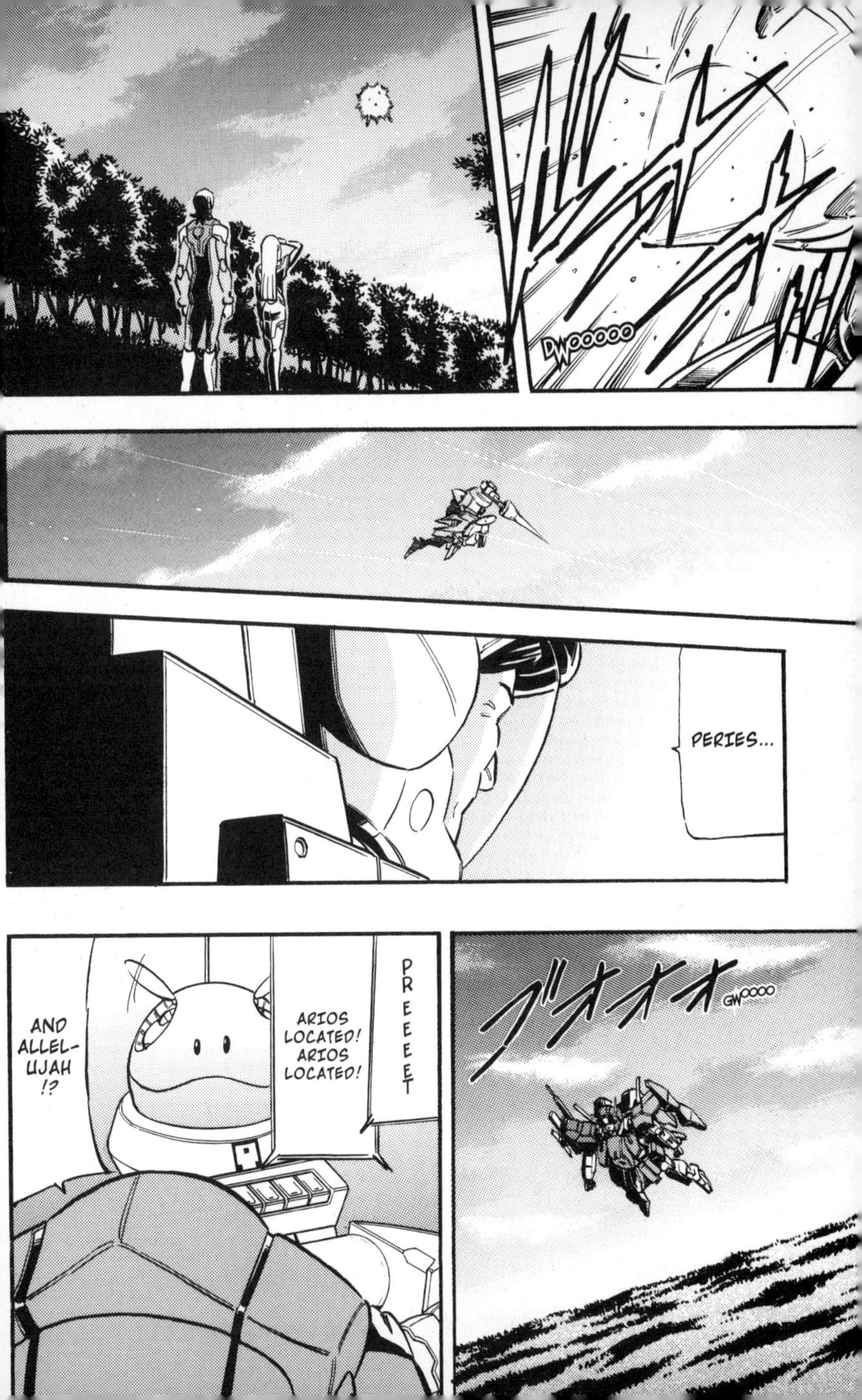
DWOOOOO
PERIES...
GWOOOO
PREEEET
ARIOS LOCATED! ARIOS LOCATED!
AND ALLELUJAH!?

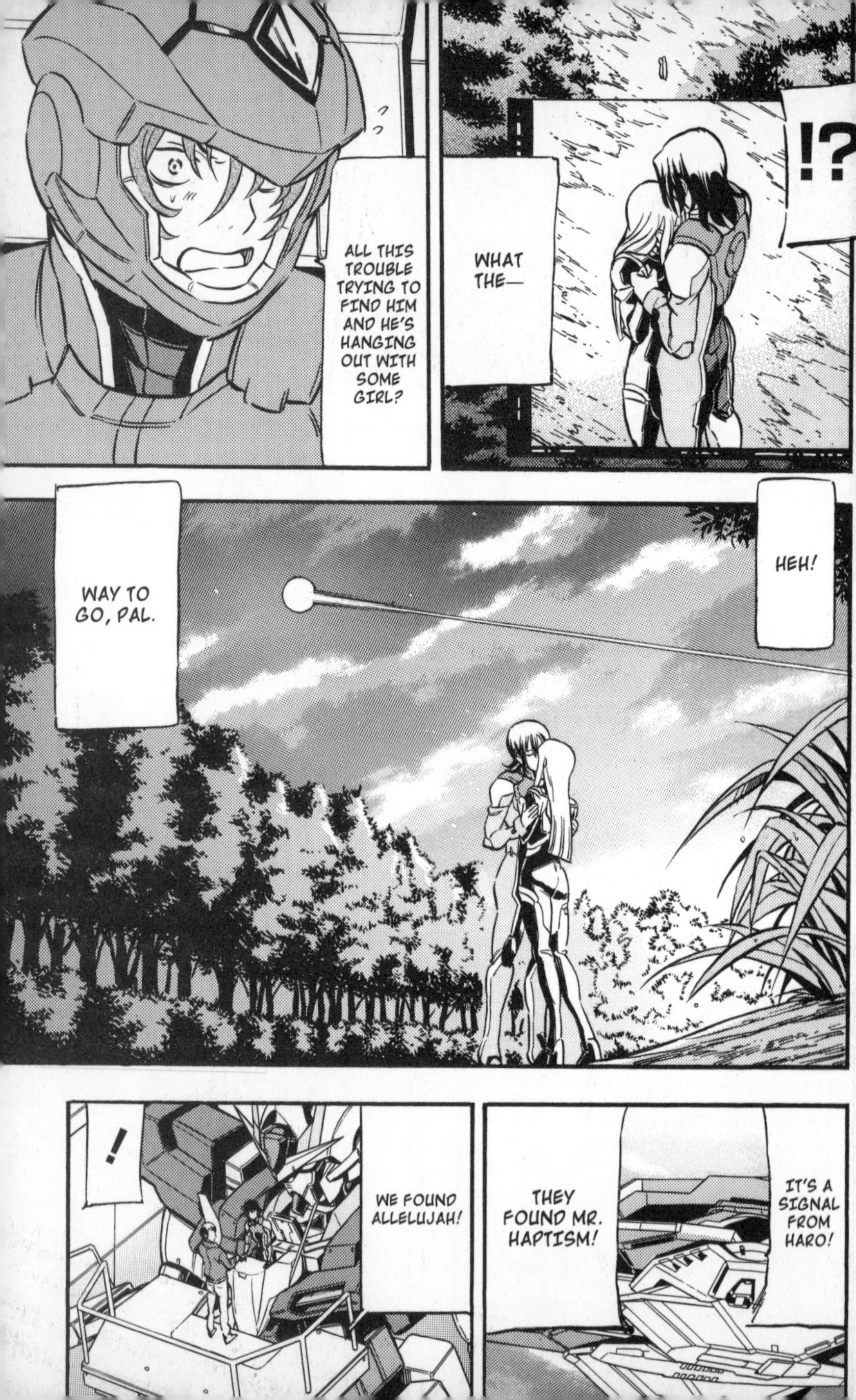
!?
WHAT THE—
ALL THIS TROUBLE TRYING TO FIND HIM AND HE'S HANGING OUT WITH SOME GIRL?
HEH!
WAY TO GO, PAL.
IT'S A SIGNAL FROM HARO!
THEY FOUND MR. HAPTISM!
WE FOUND ALLELUJAH!
!

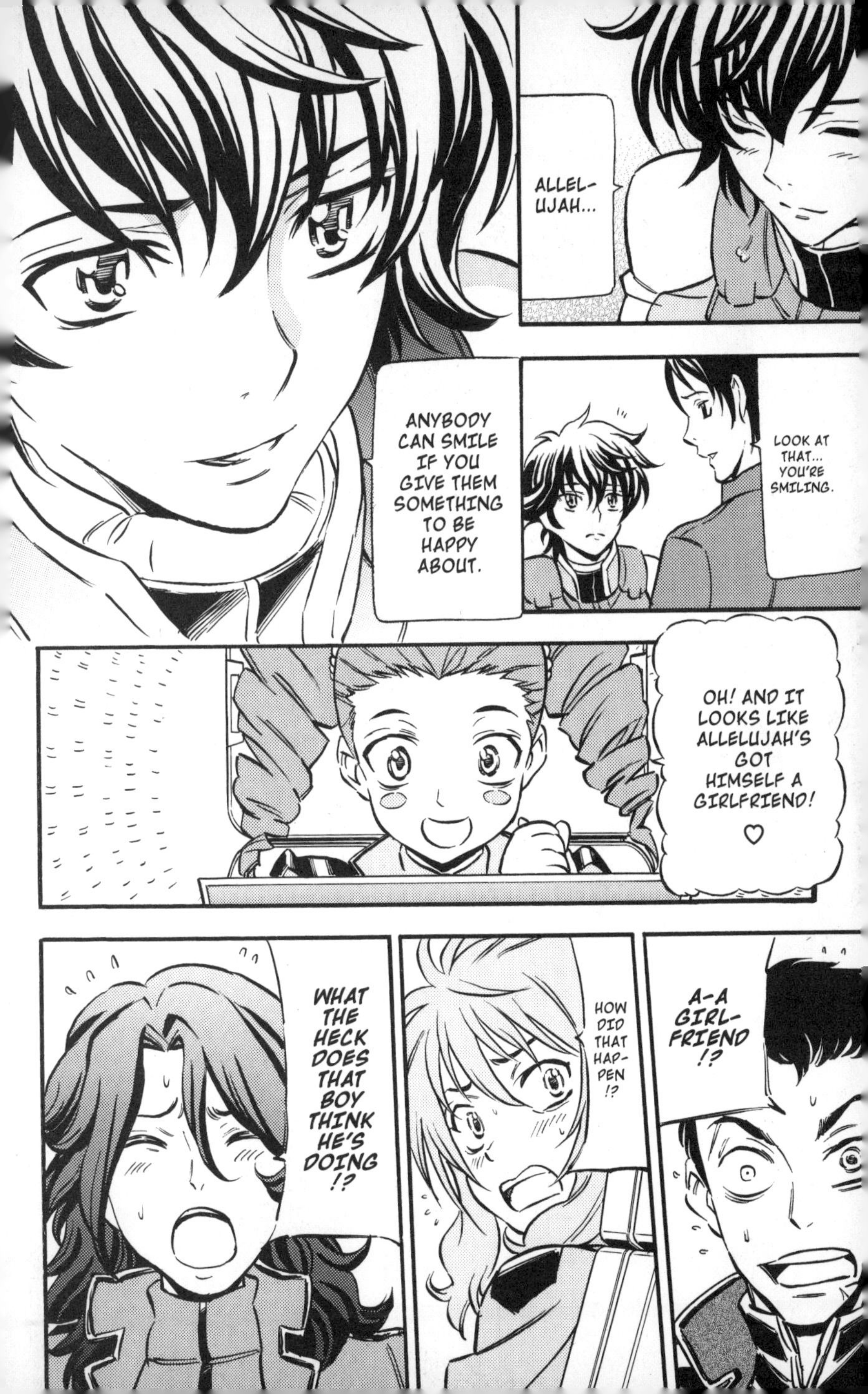
ALLELUJAH...
LOOK AT THAT... YOU'RE SMILING.
ANYBODY CAN SMILE IF YOU GIVE THEM SOMETHING TO BE HAPPY ABOUT.
OH! AND IT LOOKS LIKE ALLELUJAH'S GOT HIMSELF A GIRLFRIEND! ♡
A-A GIRLFRIEND!?
HOW DID THAT HAPPEN!?
WHAT THE HECK DOES THAT BOY THINK HE'S DOING!?

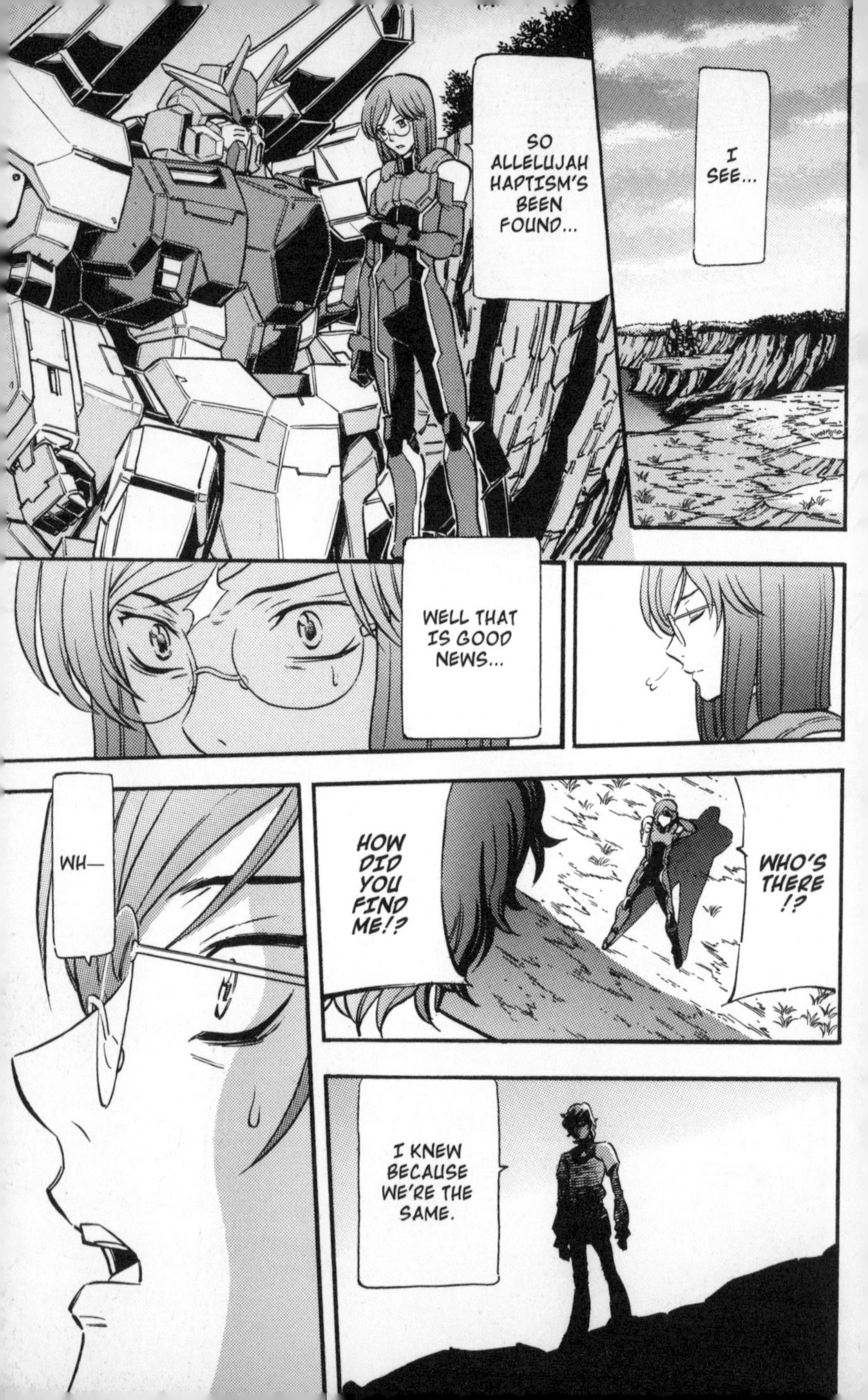
I SEE...
SO ALLELUJAH HAPTISM'S BEEN FOUND...
WELL THAT IS GOOD NEWS...
WHO'S THERE!?
HOW DID YOU FIND ME!?
I KNEW BECAUSE WE'RE THE SAME.
WH—

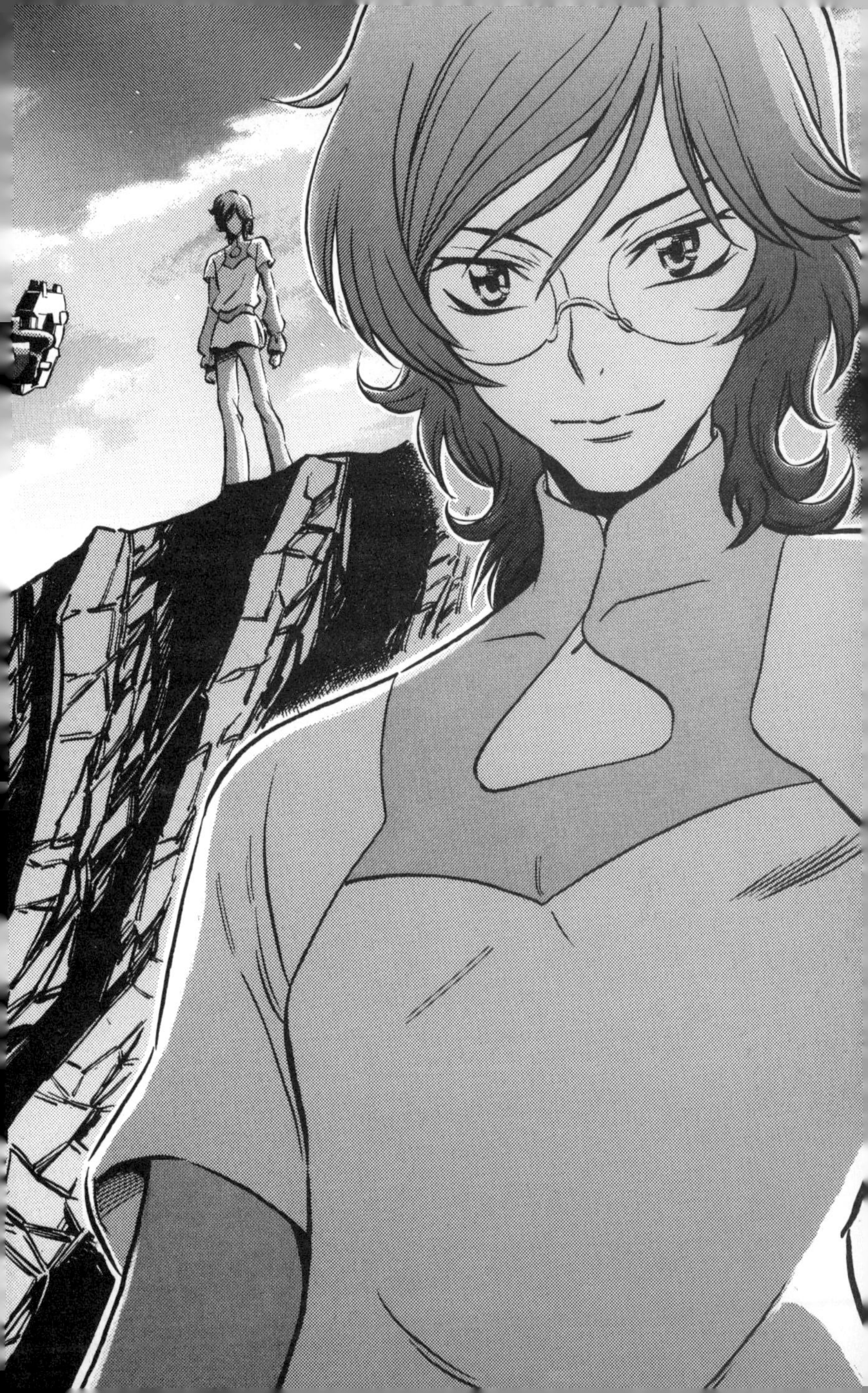

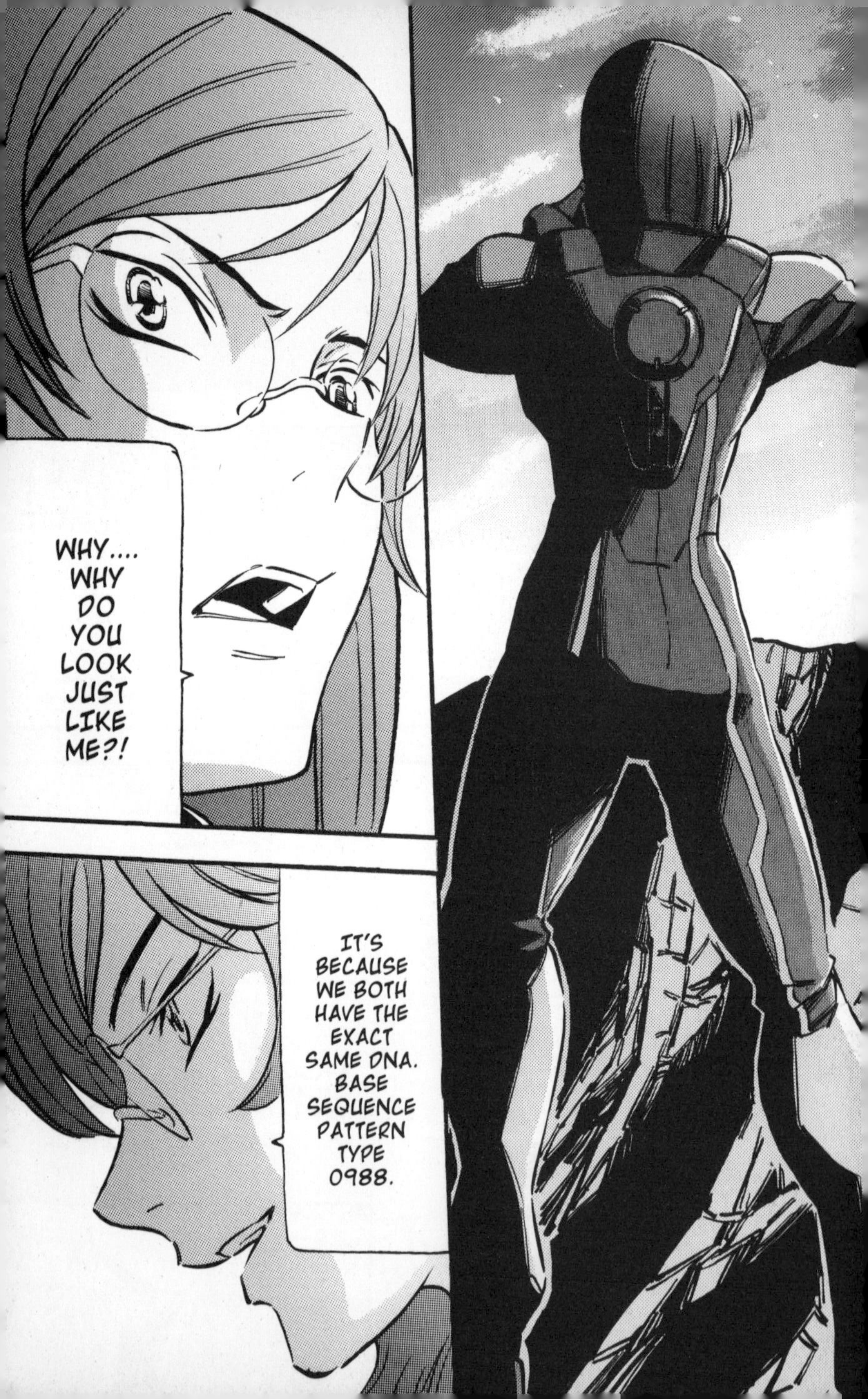
WHY.... WHY DO YOU LOOK JUST LIKE ME?!
IT'S BECAUSE WE BOTH HAVE THE EXACT SAME DNA. BASE SEQUENCE PATTERN TYPE 0988.

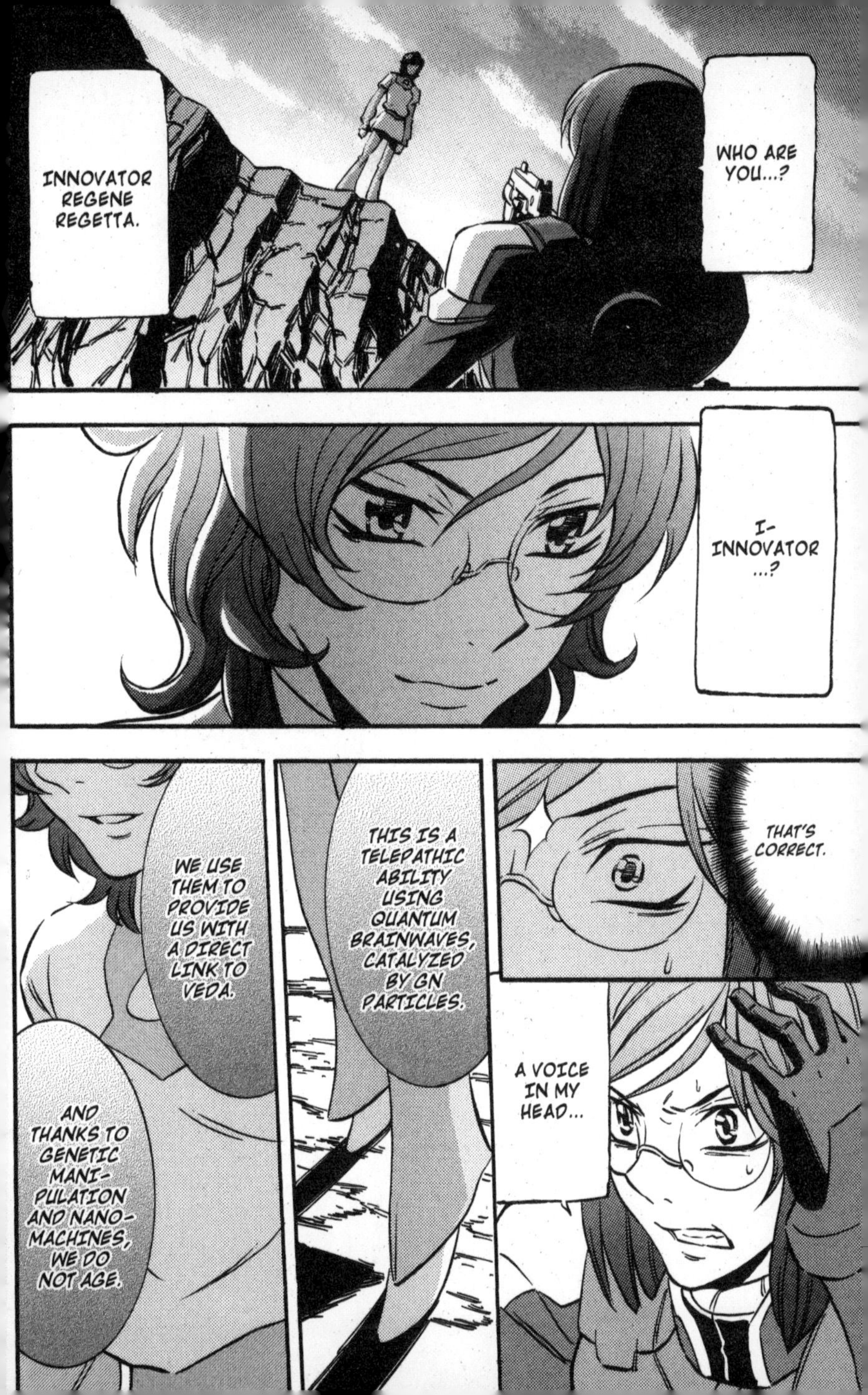
WHO ARE YOU...?
INNOVATOR REGENE REGETTA.
I-INNOVATOR ...?
THAT'S CORRECT.
A VOICE IN MY HEAD...
THIS IS A TELEPATHIC ABILITY USING QUANTUM BRAINWAVES, CATALYZED BY GN PARTICLES.
WE USE THEM TO PROVIDE US WITH A DIRECT LINK TO VEDA.
AND THANKS TO GENETIC MANI-PULATION AND NANO-MACHINES, WE DO NOT AGE.

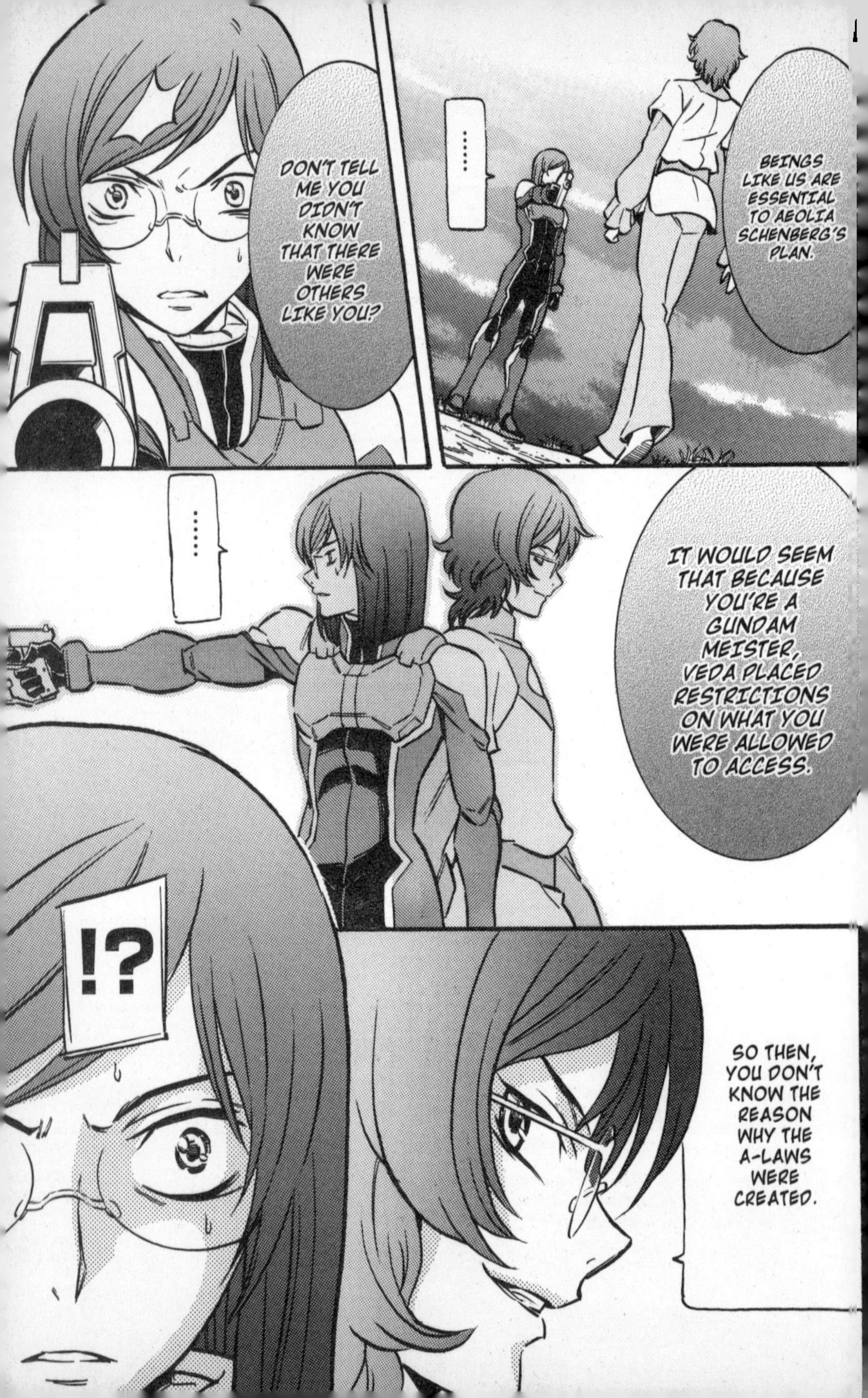
BEINGS LIKE US ARE ESSENTIAL TO AEOLIA SCHENBERG'S PLAN.
......
DON'T TELL ME YOU DIDN'T KNOW THAT THERE WERE OTHERS LIKE YOU?
IT WOULD SEEM THAT BECAUSE YOU'RE A GUNDAM MEISTER, VEDA PLACED RESTRICTIONS ON WHAT YOU WERE ALLOWED TO ACCESS.
......
SO THEN, YOU DON'T KNOW THE REASON WHY THE A-LAWS WERE CREATED.
!?

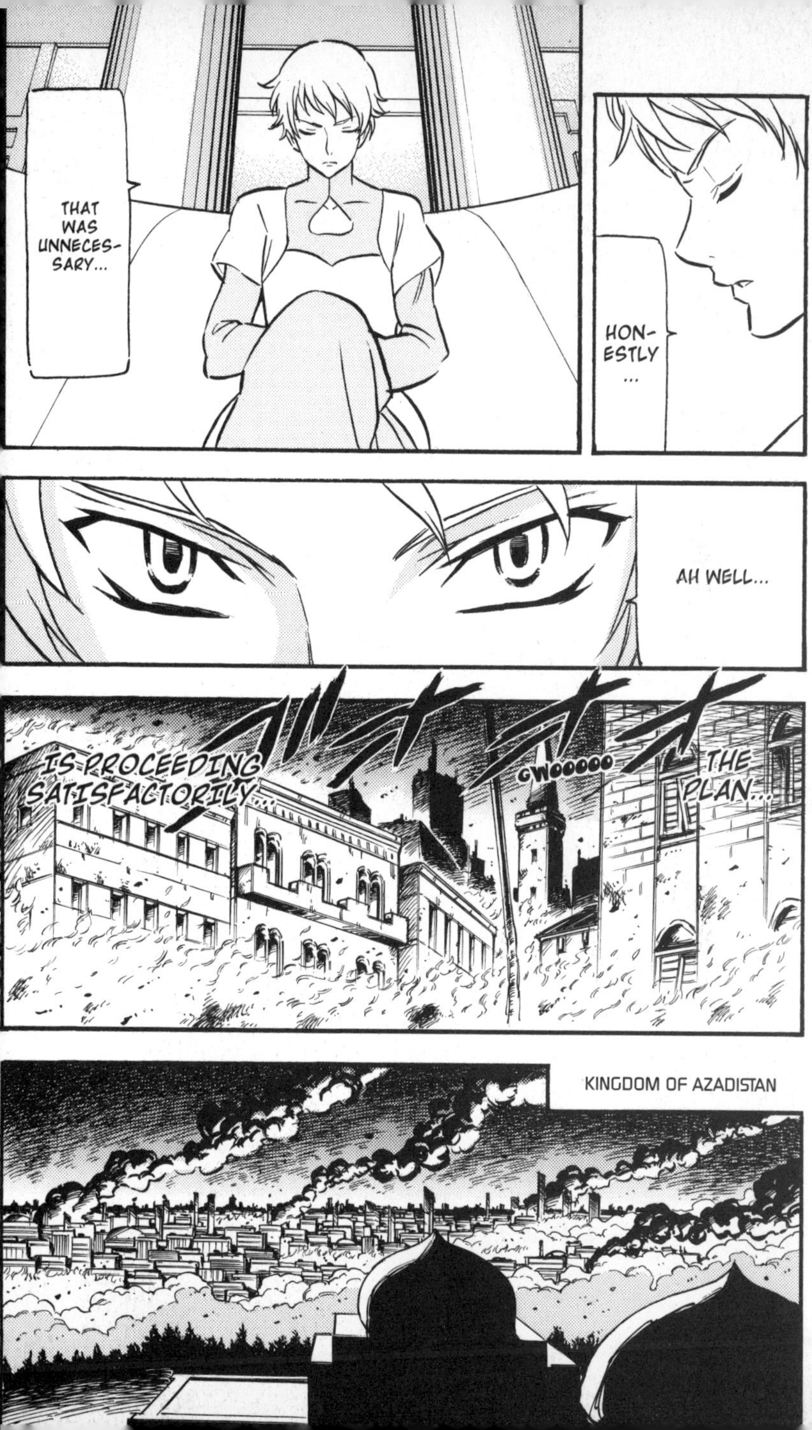
HON-ESTLY ...
THAT WAS UNNECES-SARY...
AH WELL...
THE PLAN...
GWOOOOO
IS PROCEEDING SATISFACTORILY...
KINGDOM OF AZADISTAN

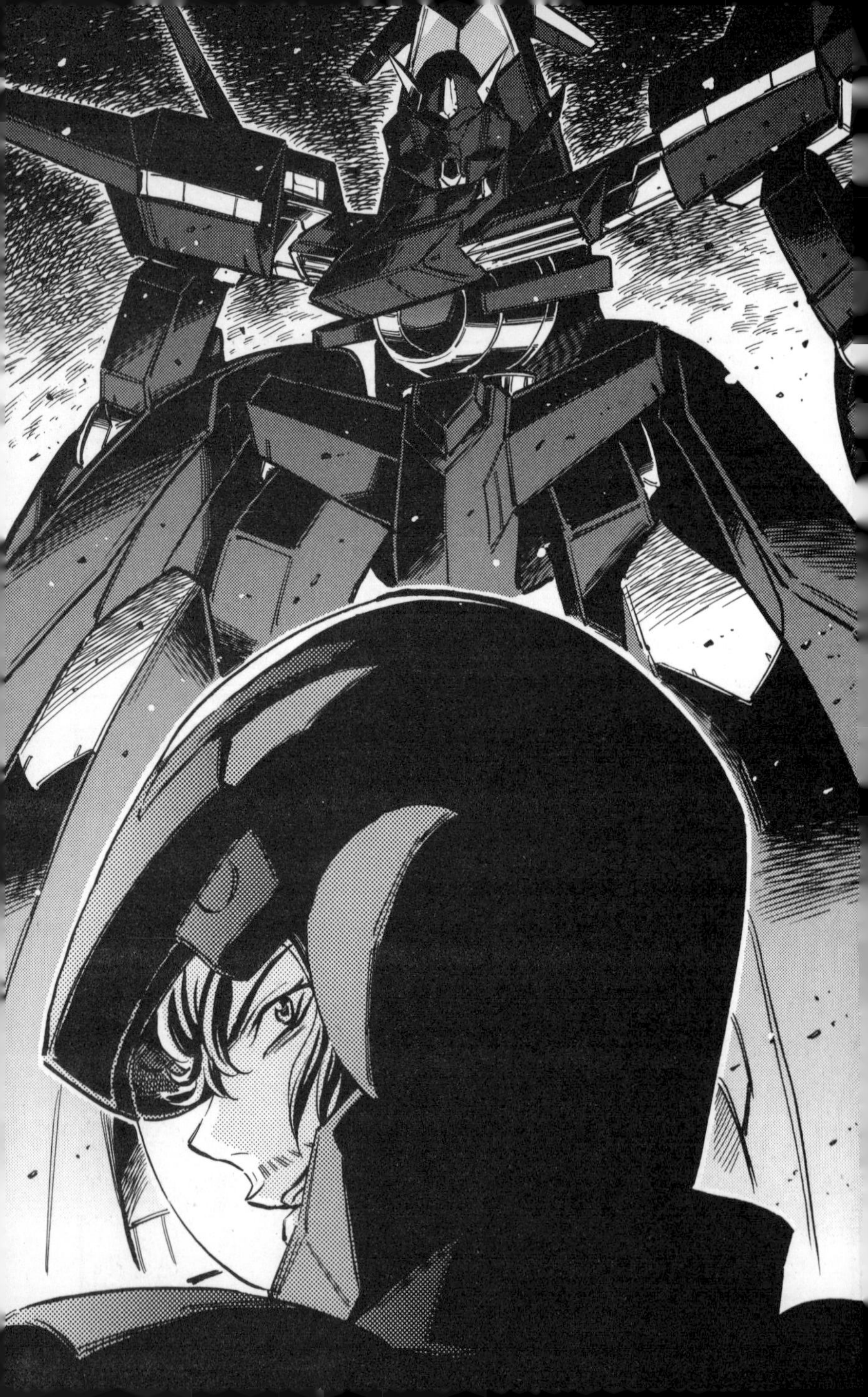

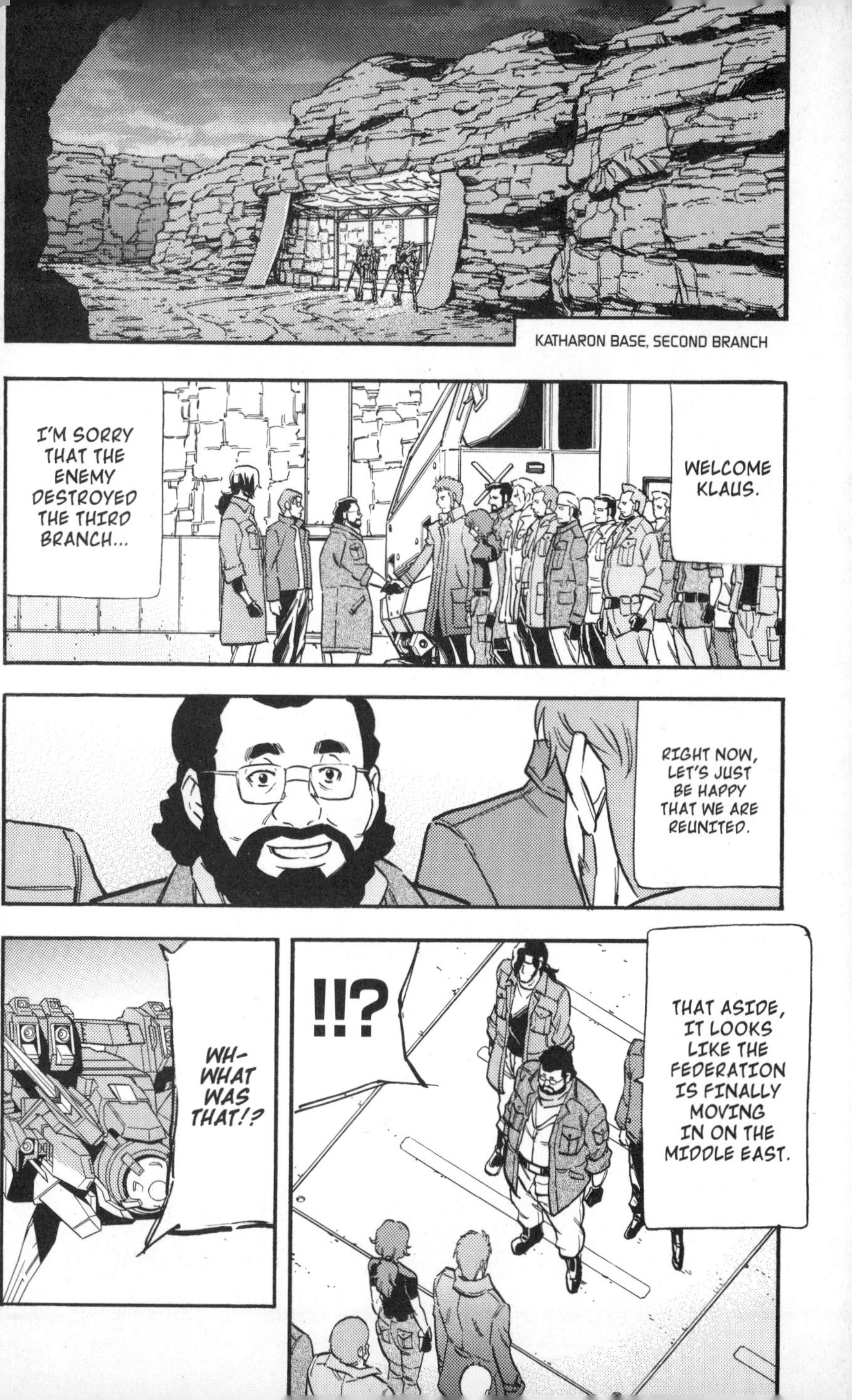
KATHARON BASE, SECOND BRANCH
WELCOME KLAUS.
I'M SORRY THAT THE ENEMY DESTROYED THE THIRD BRANCH...
RIGHT NOW, LET'S JUST BE HAPPY THAT WE ARE REUNITED.
THAT ASIDE, IT LOOKS LIKE THE FEDERATION IS FINALLY MOVING IN ON THE MIDDLE EAST.
!!?
WH-WHAT WAS THAT!?

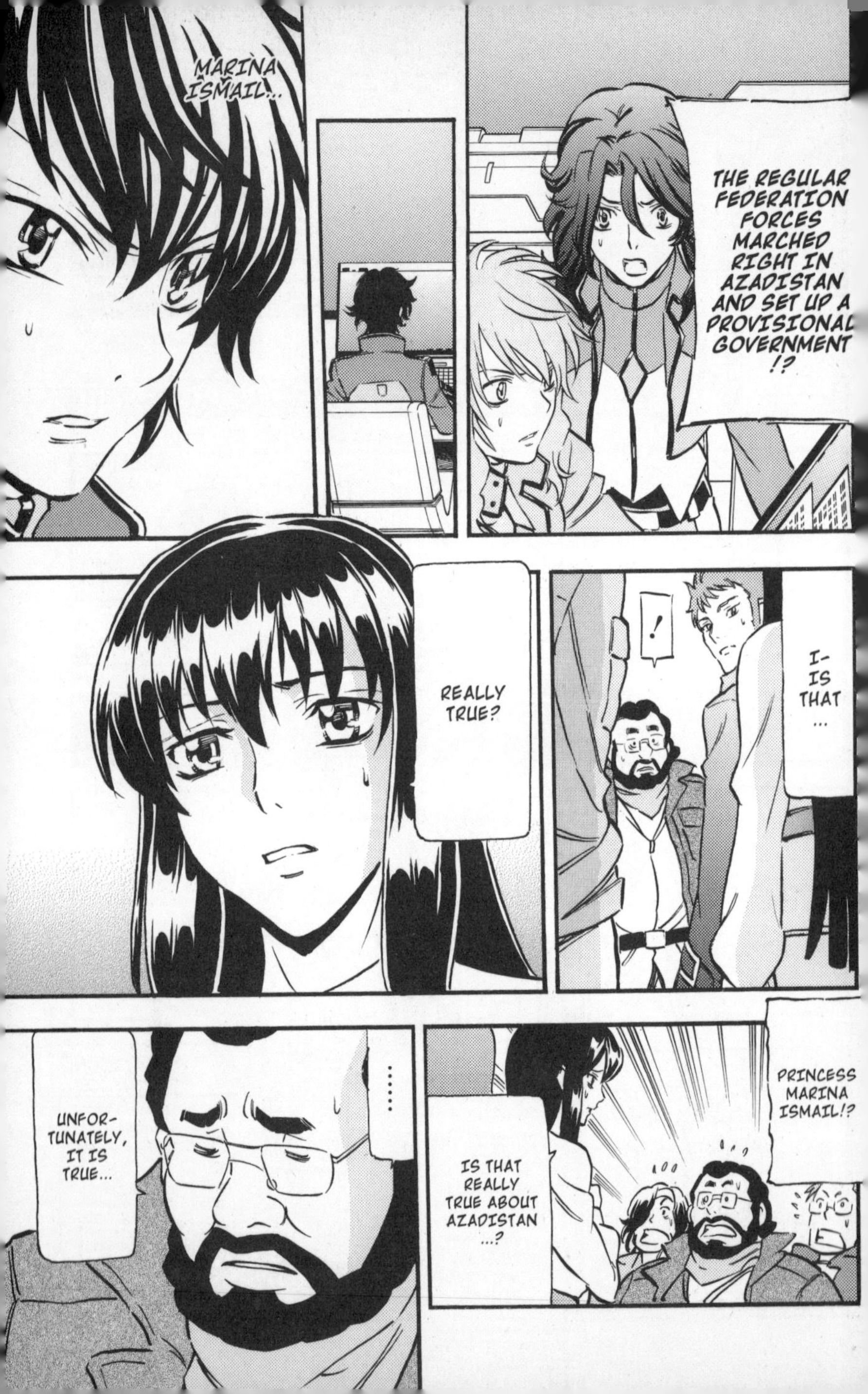
THE REGULAR FEDERATION FORCES MARCHED RIGHT IN AZADISTAN AND SET UP A PROVISIONAL GOVERNMENT !?
MARINA ISMAIL...
!
I- IS THAT ...
REALLY TRUE?
PRINCESS MARINA ISMAIL!?
IS THAT REALLY TRUE ABOUT AZADISTAN ...?
......
UNFOR-TUNATELY, IT IS TRUE...

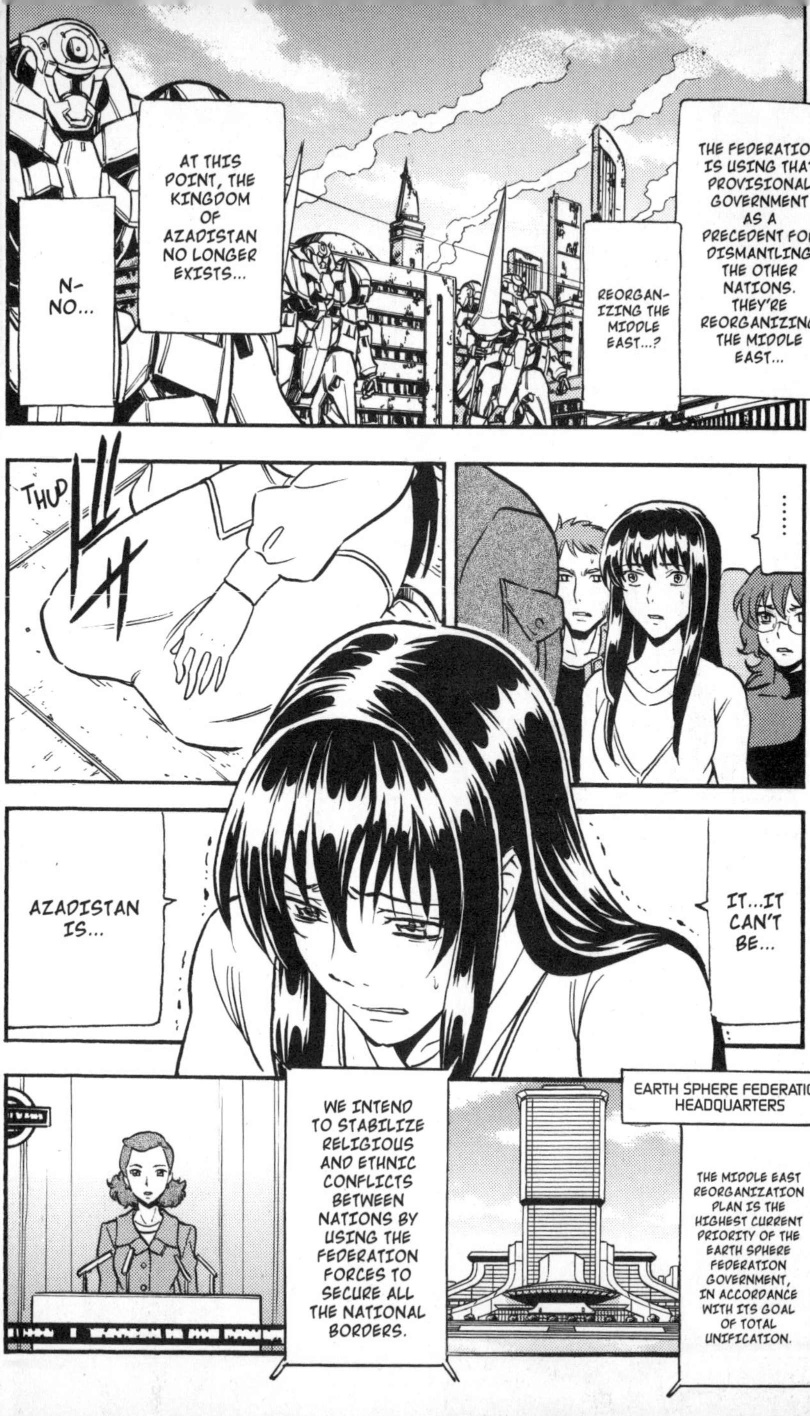
THE FEDERATION IS USING THAT PROVISIONAL GOVERNMENT AS A PRECEDENT FOR DISMANTLING THE OTHER NATIONS. THEY'RE REORGANIZING THE MIDDLE EAST...
REORGANIZING THE MIDDLE EAST...?
AT THIS POINT, THE KINGDOM OF AZADISTAN NO LONGER EXISTS...
N-NO...
......
THUD
IT...IT CAN'T BE...
AZADISTAN IS...
EARTH SPHERE FEDERATION HEADQUARTERS
THE MIDDLE EAST REORGANIZATION PLAN IS THE HIGHEST CURRENT PRIORITY OF THE EARTH SPHERE FEDERATION GOVERNMENT, IN ACCORDANCE WITH ITS GOAL OF TOTAL UNIFICATION.
WE INTEND TO STABILIZE RELIGIOUS AND ETHNIC CONFLICTS BETWEEN NATIONS BY USING THE FEDERATION FORCES TO SECURE ALL THE NATIONAL BORDERS.

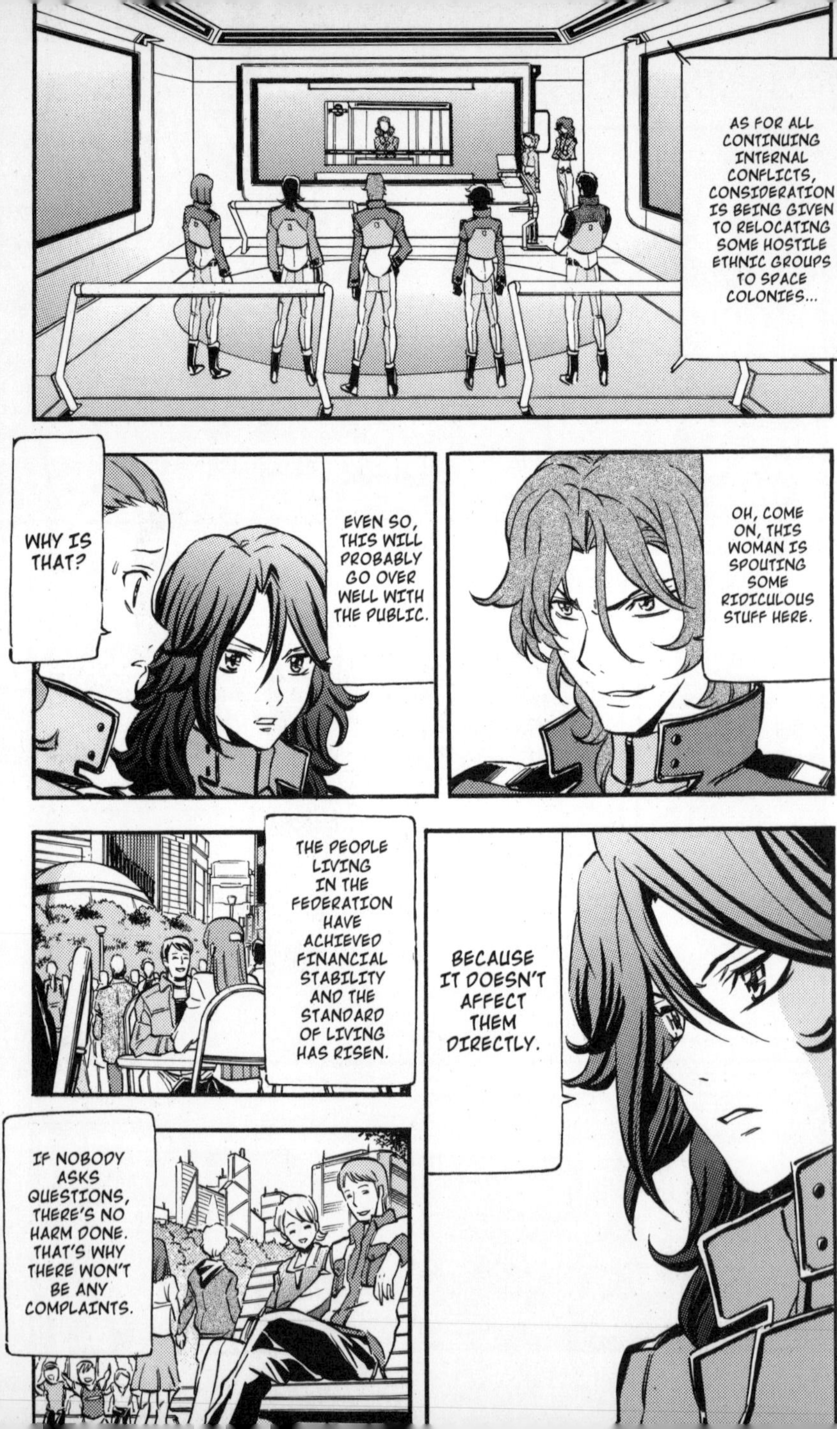
AS FOR ALL CONTINUING INTERNAL CONFLICTS, CONSIDERATION IS BEING GIVEN TO RELOCATING SOME HOSTILE ETHNIC GROUPS TO SPACE COLONIES...
OH, COME ON, THIS WOMAN IS SPOUTING SOME RIDICULOUS STUFF HERE.
EVEN SO, THIS WILL PROBABLY GO OVER WELL WITH THE PUBLIC.
WHY IS THAT?
BECAUSE IT DOESN'T AFFECT THEM DIRECTLY.
THE PEOPLE LIVING IN THE FEDERATION HAVE ACHIEVED FINANCIAL STABILITY AND THE STANDARD OF LIVING HAS RISEN.
IF NOBODY ASKS QUESTIONS, THERE'S NO HARM DONE. THAT'S WHY THERE WON'T BE ANY COMPLAINTS.

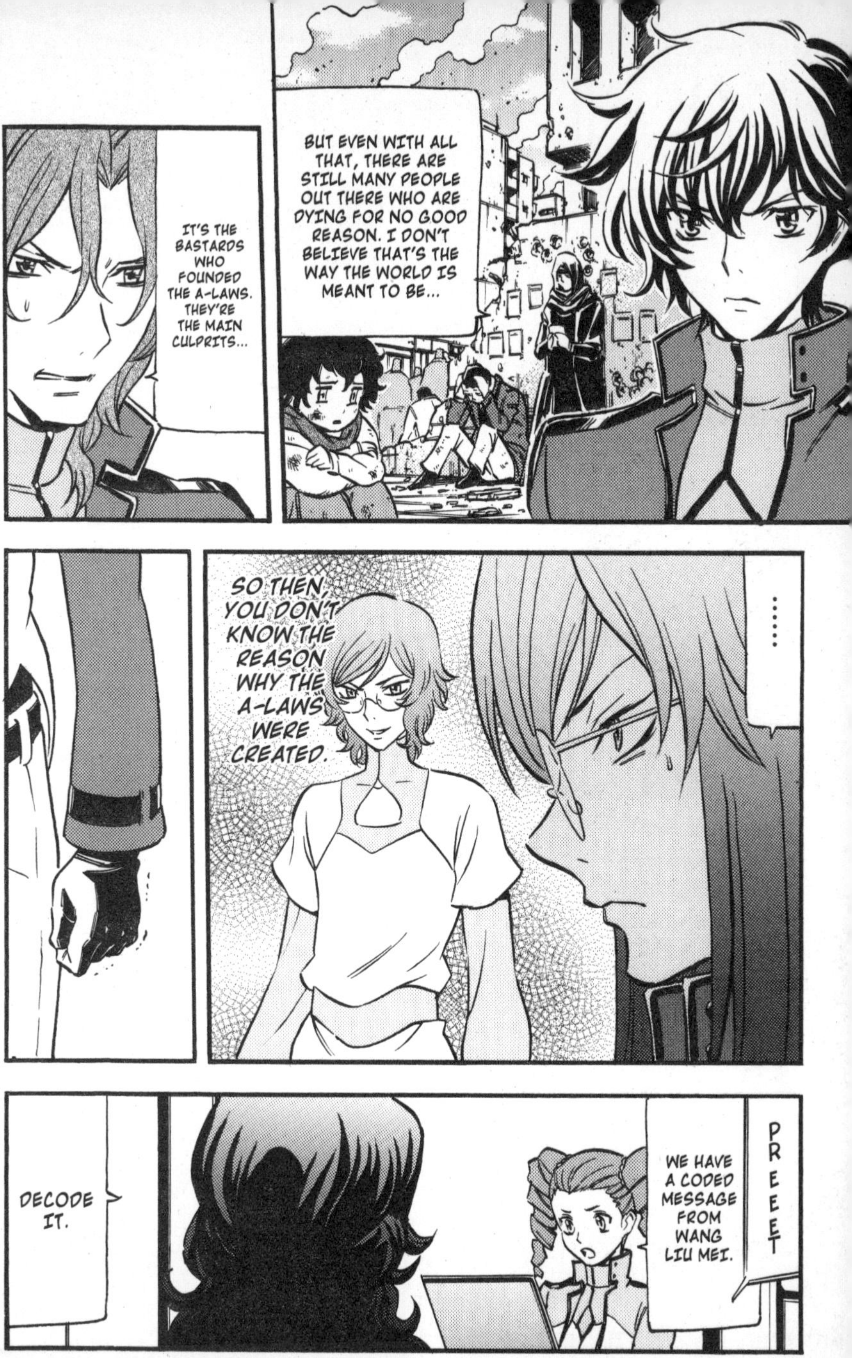
BUT EVEN WITH ALL THAT, THERE ARE STILL MANY PEOPLE OUT THERE WHO ARE DYING FOR NO GOOD REASON. I DON'T BELIEVE THAT'S THE WAY THE WORLD IS MEANT TO BE...
IT'S THE BASTARDS WHO FOUNDED THE A-LAWS. THEY'RE THE MAIN CULPRITS...
......
SO THEN, YOU DON'T KNOW THE REASON WHY THE A-LAWS WERE CREATED.
PREEET
WE HAVE A CODED MESSAGE FROM WANG LIU MEI.
DECODE IT.

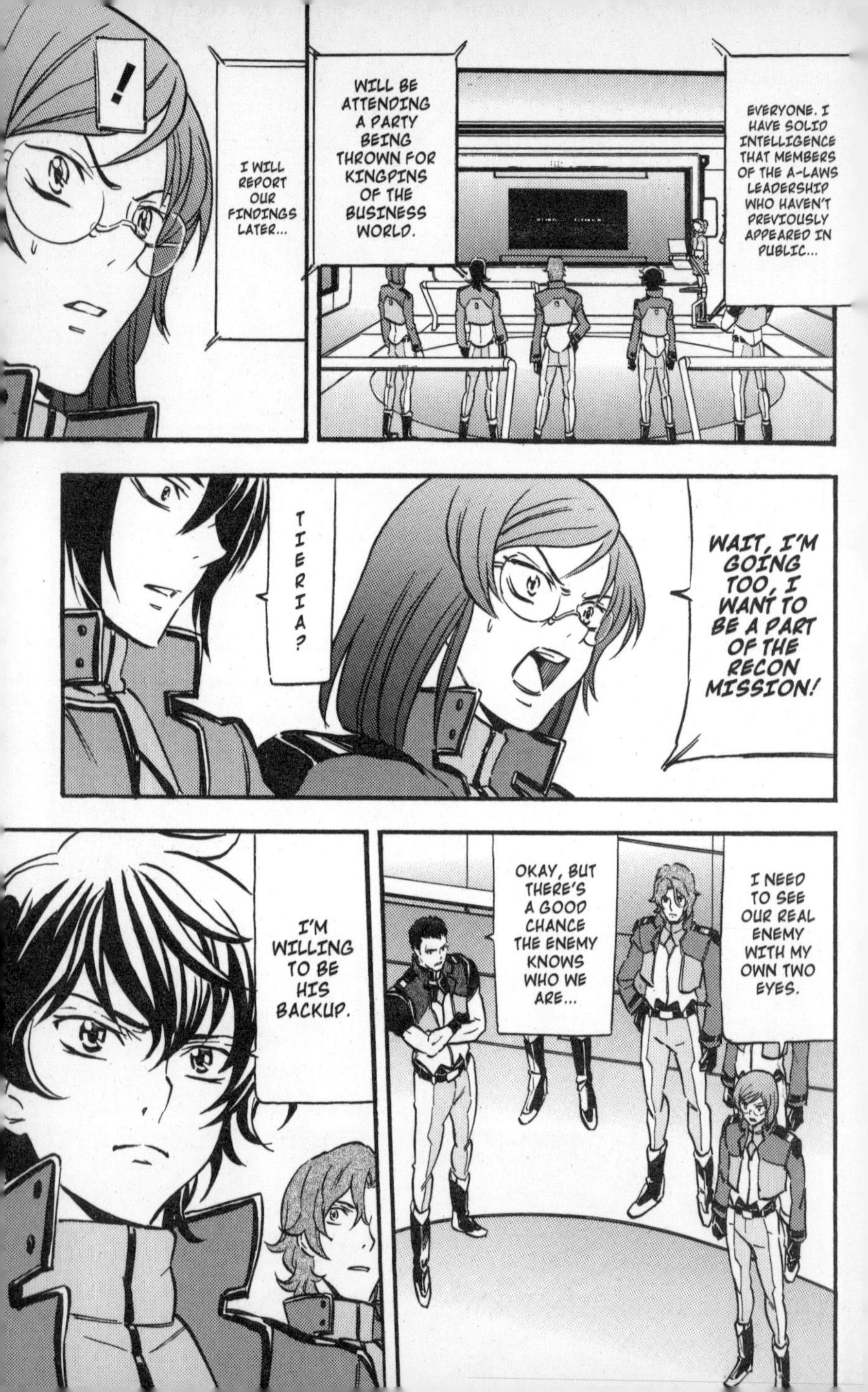
EVERYONE. I HAVE SOLID INTELLIGENCE THAT MEMBERS OF THE A-LAWS LEADERSHIP WHO HAVEN'T PREVIOUSLY APPEARED IN PUBLIC...
WILL BE ATTENDING A PARTY BEING THROWN FOR KINGPINS OF THE BUSINESS WORLD.
I WILL REPORT OUR FINDINGS LATER...
!
WAIT, I'M GOING TOO, I WANT TO BE A PART OF THE RECON MISSION!
TIERIA?
I NEED TO SEE OUR REAL ENEMY WITH MY OWN TWO EYES.
OKAY, BUT THERE'S A GOOD CHANCE THE ENEMY KNOWS WHO WE ARE...
I'M WILLING TO BE HIS BACKUP.

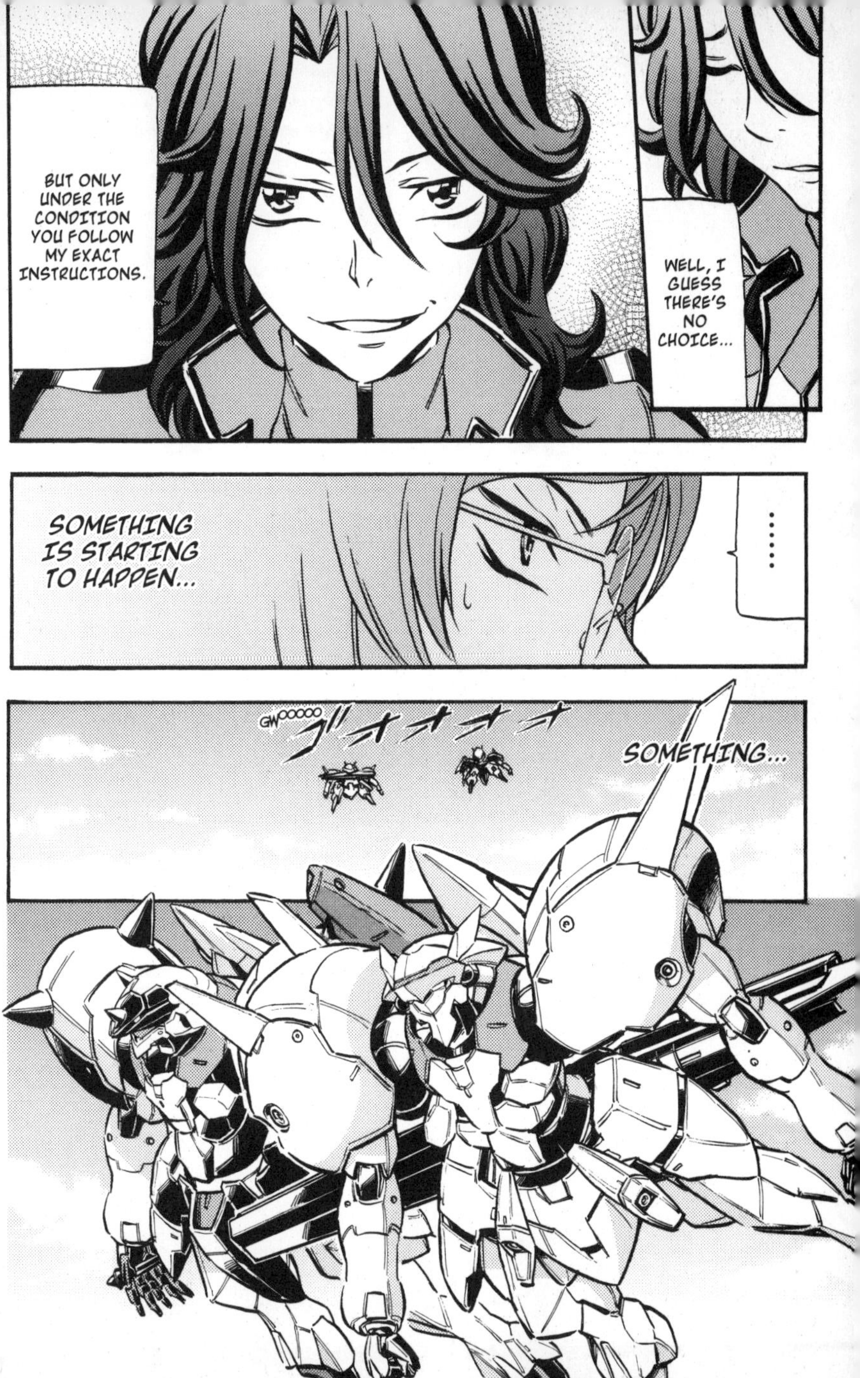
WELL, I GUESS THERE'S NO CHOICE...
BUT ONLY UNDER THE CONDITION YOU FOLLOW MY EXACT INSTRUCTIONS.
......
SOMETHING IS STARTING TO HAPPEN...
SOMETHING...
GWOOOOO
ゴオオオオ

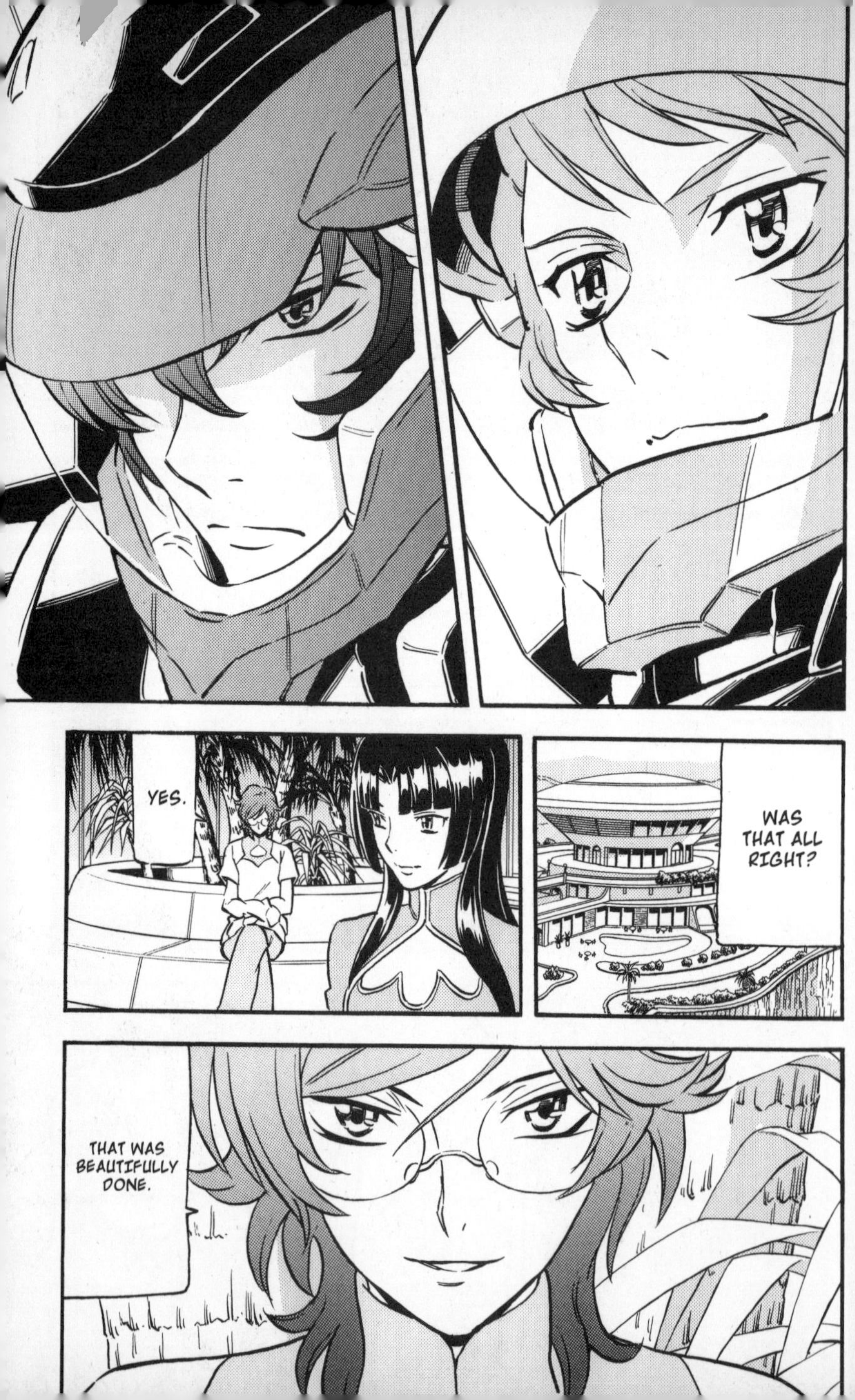
WAS THAT ALL RIGHT?
YES.
THAT WAS BEAUTIFULLY DONE.

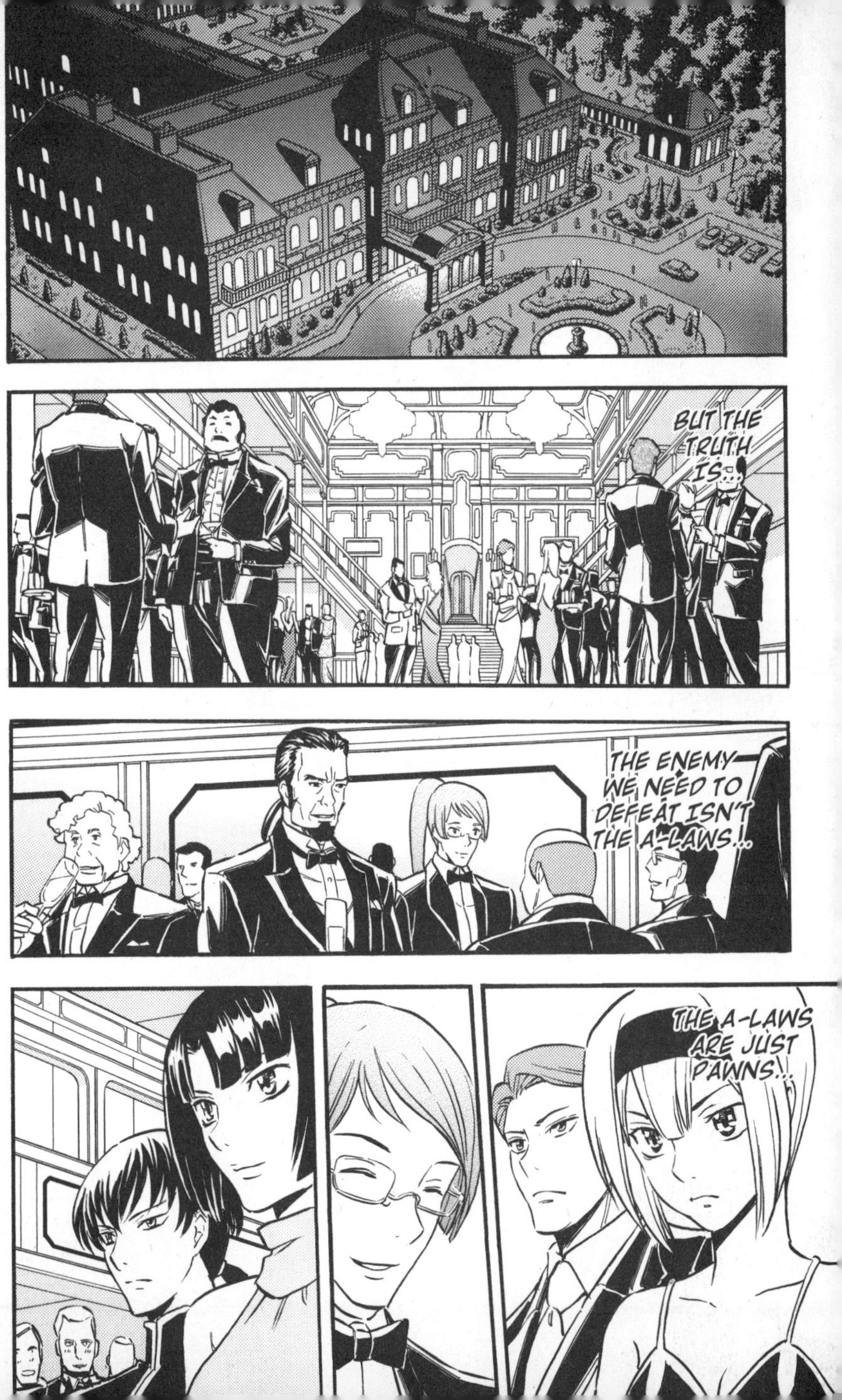
BUT THE TRUTH IS...
THE ENEMY WE NEED TO DEFEAT ISN'T THE A-LAWS...
THE A-LAWS ARE JUST PAWNS...

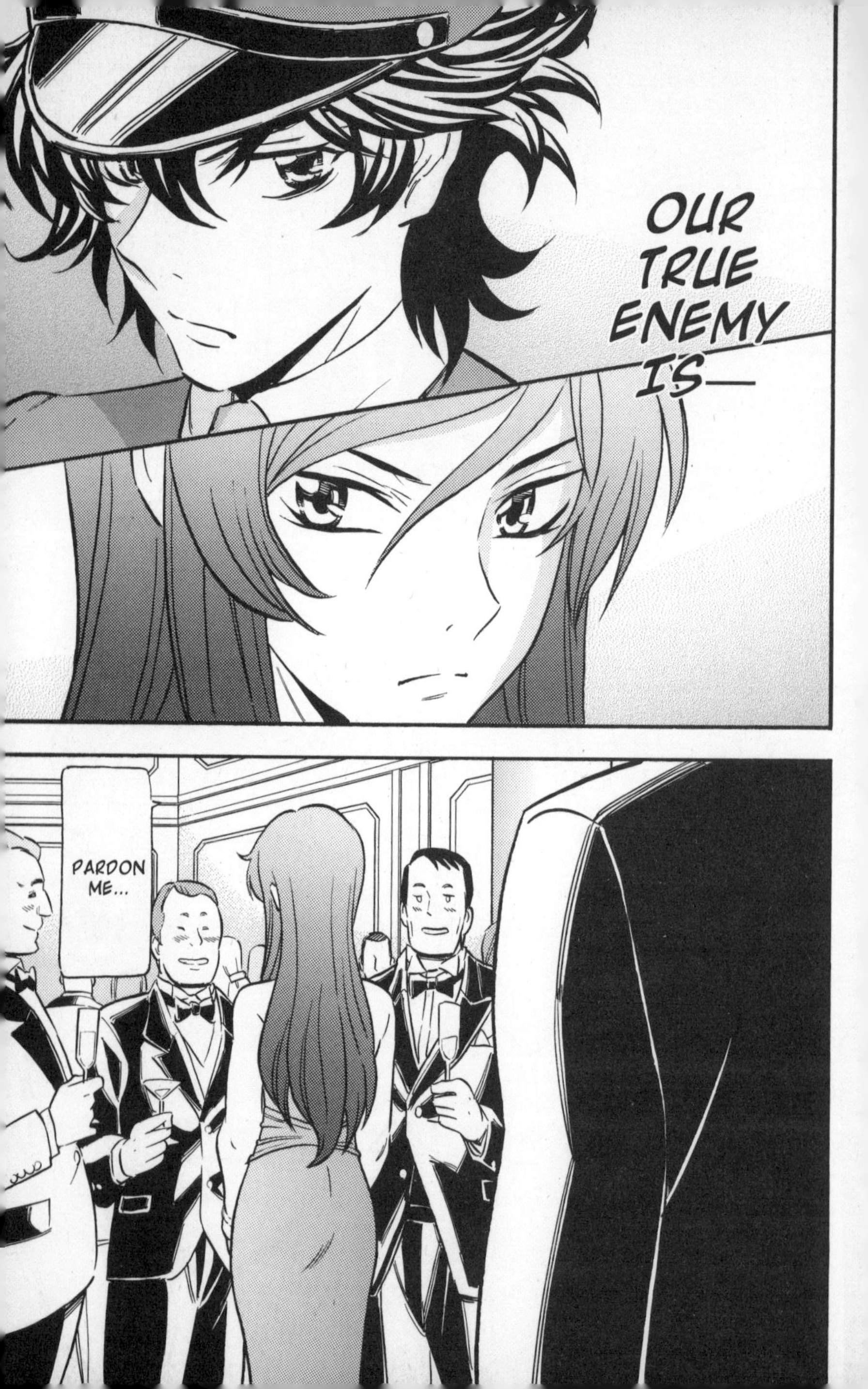
OUR TRUE ENEMY IS—
PARDON ME...

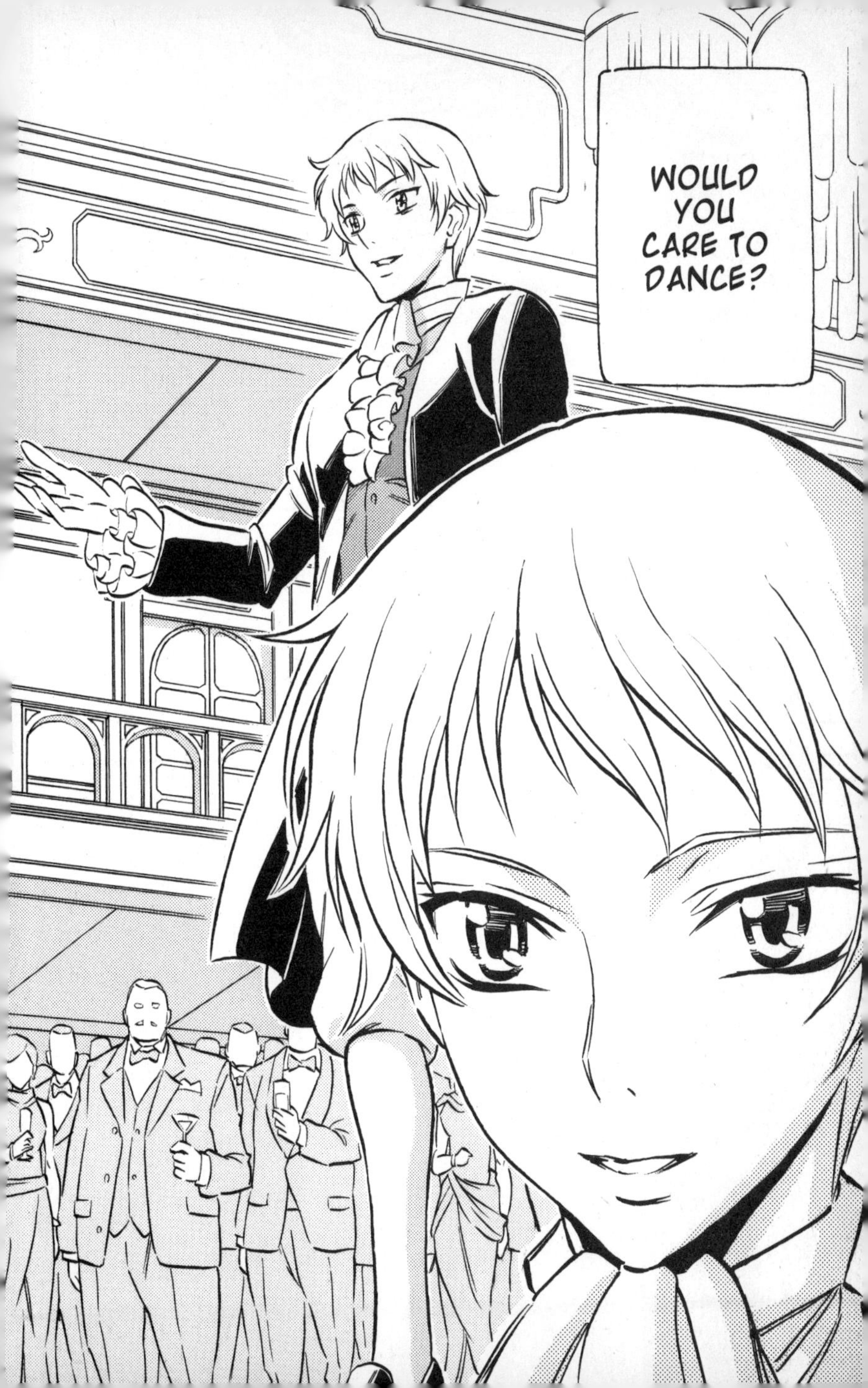
WOULD YOU CARE TO DANCE?

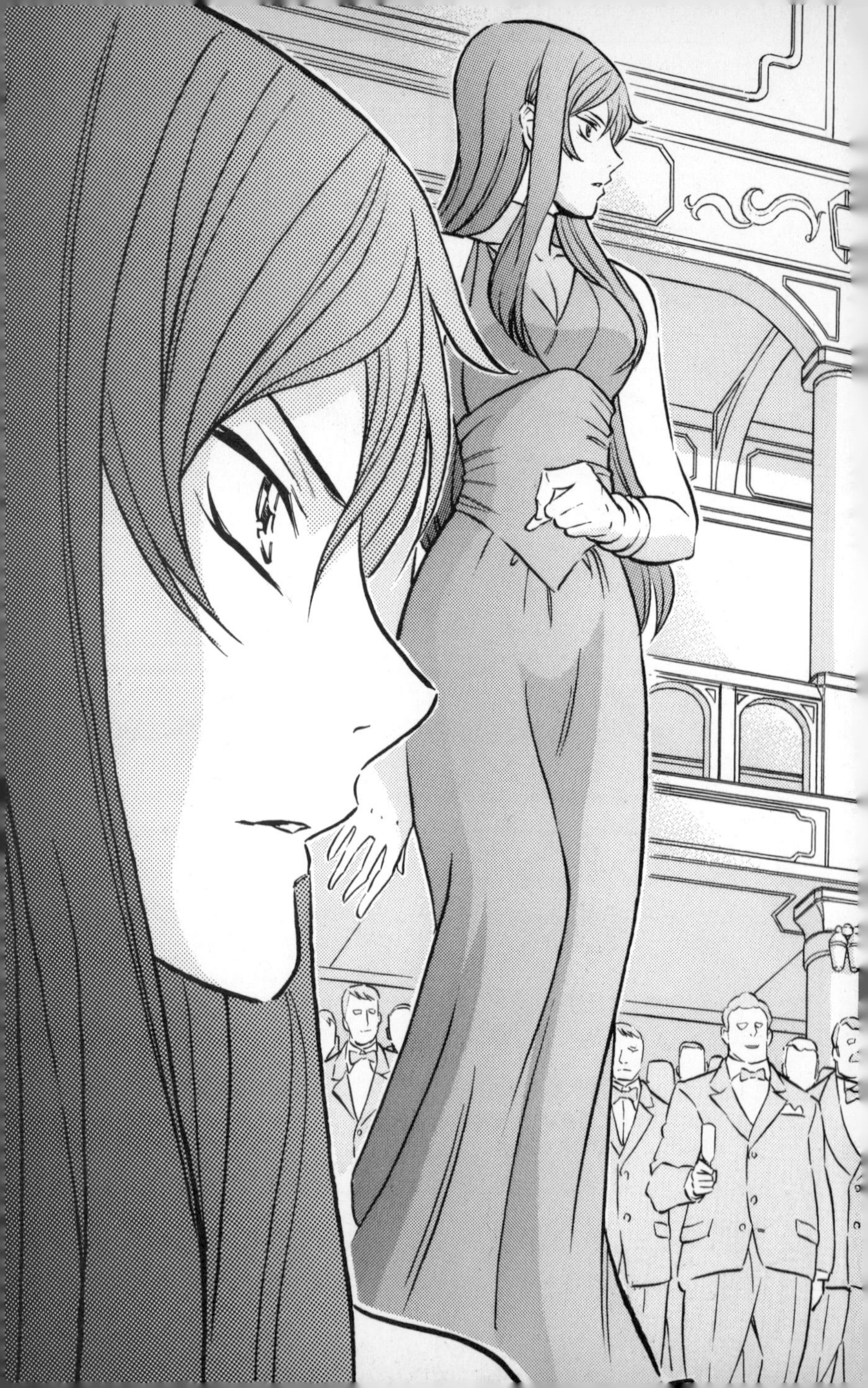

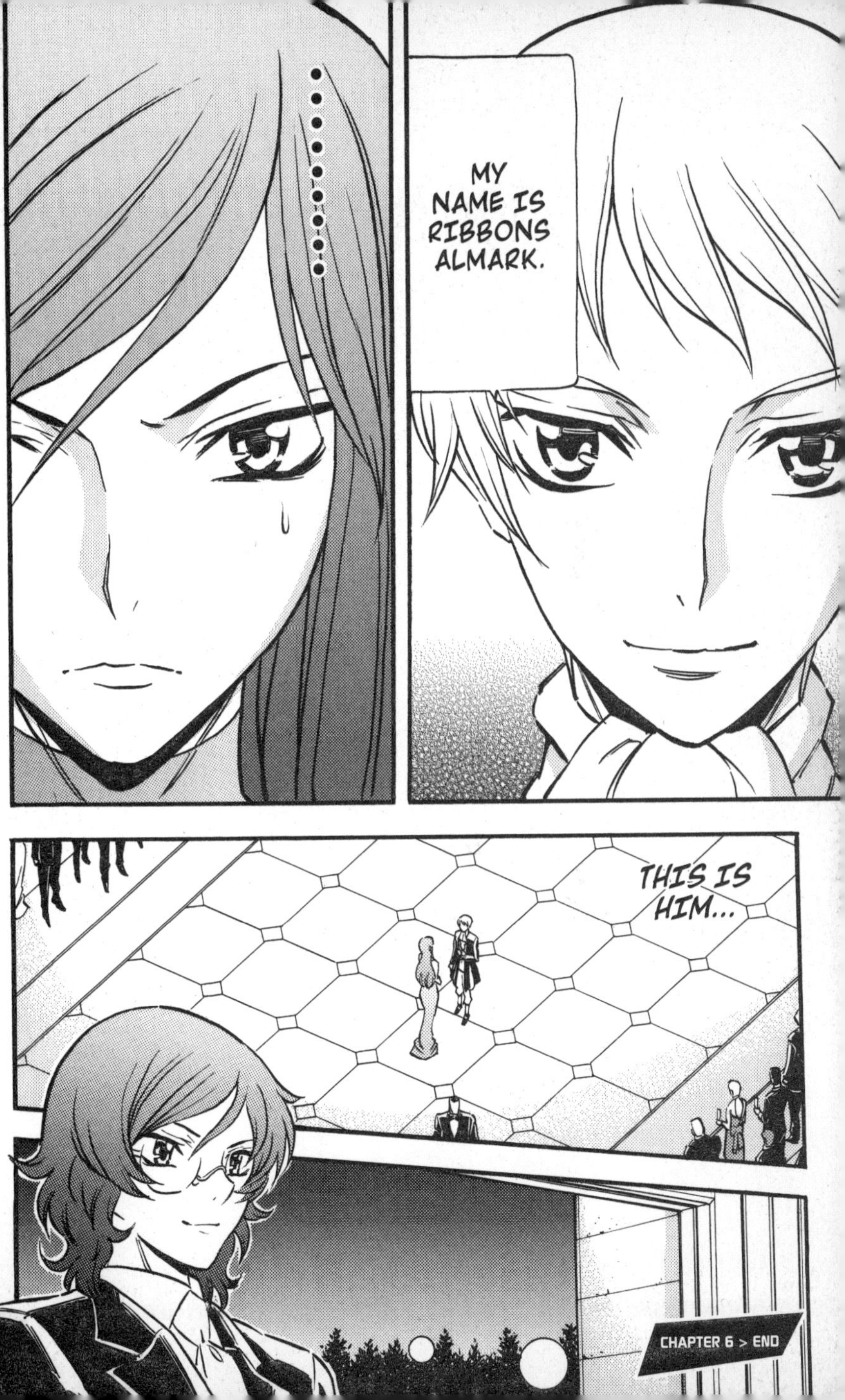
MY NAME IS RIBBONS ALMARK.
THIS IS HIM...
CHAPTER 6 > END

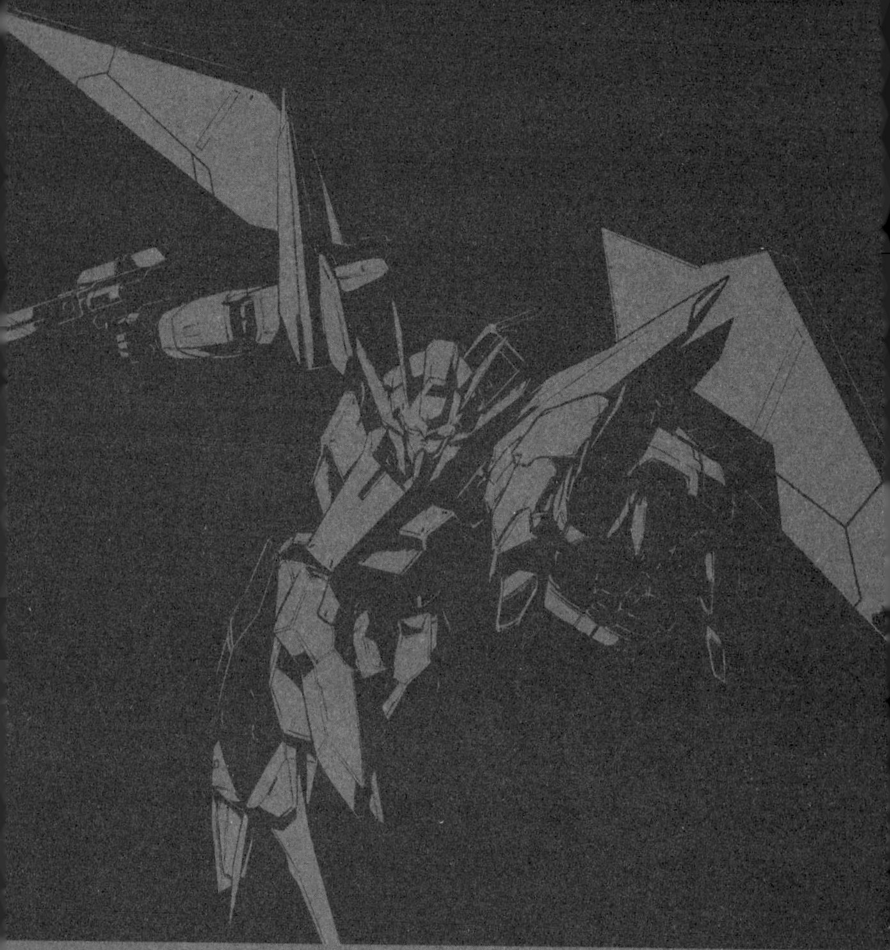

Continued on the
MOBILE SUIT GUNDAM 00
2nd.season Vol.03

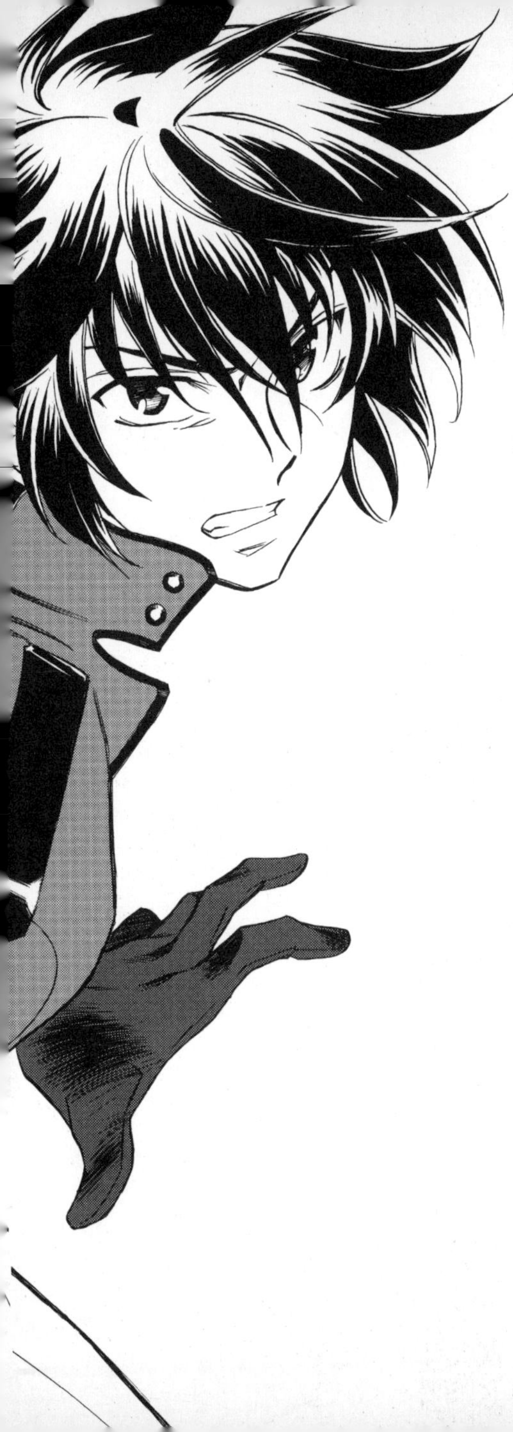

How do you do, dear readers! My name is Taro Siguma and I've been asked to write down a few words and pictures for Mr. Kouzoh Ohmori's latest installment of this manga.

☆

I have to say I look forward to and really enjoy reading every chapter of Mr. Ohmori's Gundam 00 manga.

The captivating mobile suit combat scenes are always so dramatic and exciting!

The page layouts, the details found in every Gundam unit--each page leaves me in awe of this work.

Also, I love the strength of the expressions on the character's faces Mr. Ohmori brings out in his art. I especially like Setsuna F. Seiei and Mister Bushido so I took this opportunity to draw them for this page!

☆

Mr. Ohmori, please keep up the fantastic work and continue to fire passions of Gundam 00 everywhere!

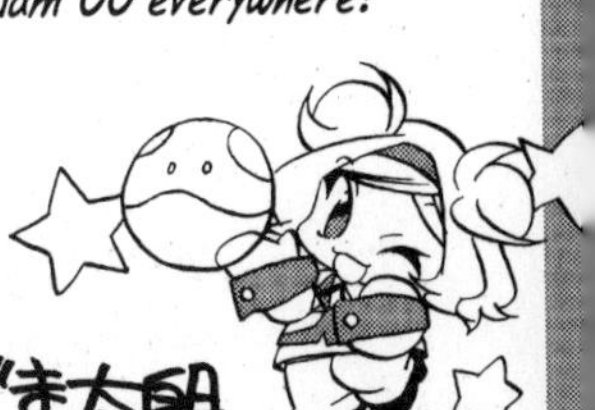

しぐま太朗.

Taro Siguma

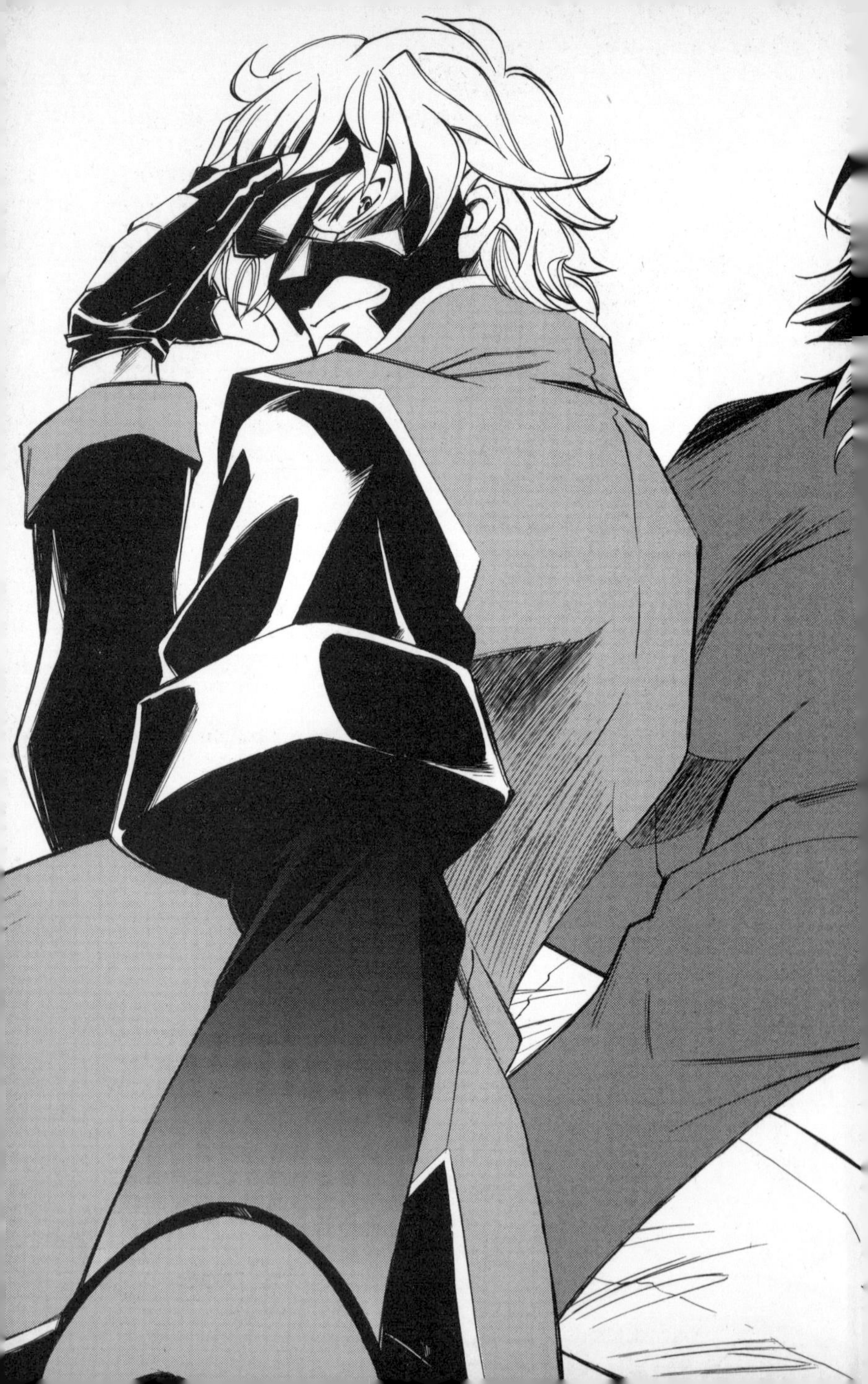

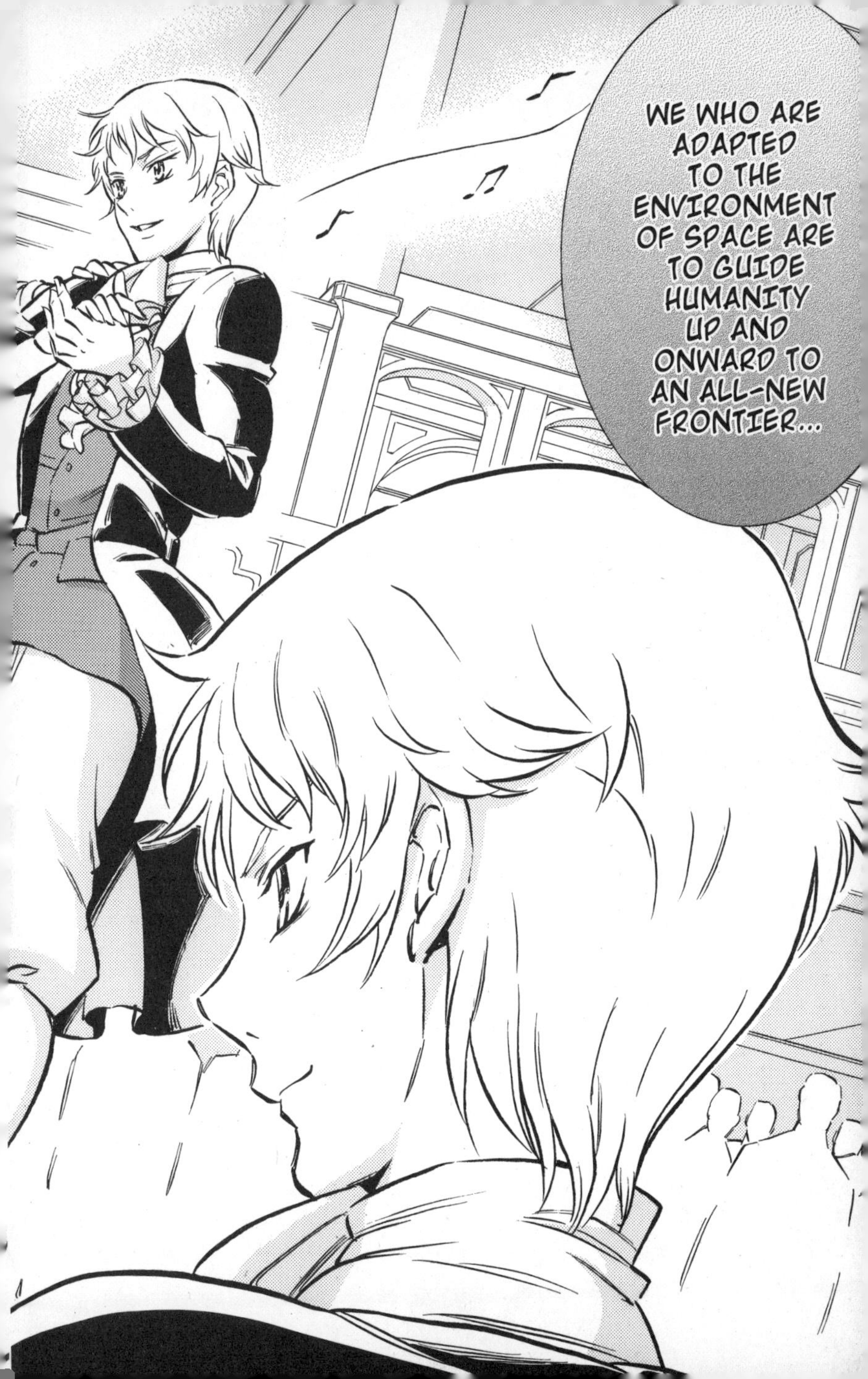
WE WHO ARE ADAPTED TO THE ENVIRONMENT OF SPACE ARE TO GUIDE HUMANITY UP AND ONWARD TO AN ALL-NEW FRONTIER...